Lecture Notes
in Economics and
Mathematical Systems

Managing Editors: M. Beckmann and W. Krelle

297

V. Fedorov H. Läuter (Eds.)

Model-Oriented Data Analysis

Proceedings of an IIASA (International
Institute for Applied Systems Analysis)
Workshop on Data Analysis
Held at Eisenach, GDR, March 9–13, 1987

Springer-Verlag
Berlin Heidelberg New York London Paris Tokyo

Managing Editors

Prof. Dr. M. Beckmann
Brown University
Providence, RI 02912, USA

Prof. Dr. W. Krelle
Institut für Gesellschafts- und Wirtschaftswissenschaften
der Universität Bonn
Adenauerallee 24–42, D-5300 Bonn, FRG

Editors

Prof. Dr. Valeri Fedorov
International Institute for Applied Systems Analysis (IIASA)
Schloßplatz 1, A-2361 Laxenburg, Austria

Prof. Dr. Henning Läuter
Academy of Sciences of the GDR
Karl-Weierstraß-Institute for Mathematics
Mohrenstr. 39, GDR-1086 Berlin

ISBN 3-540-18596-8 Springer-Verlag Berlin Heidelberg New York
ISBN 0-387-18596-8 Springer-Verlag New York Berlin Heidelberg

Printed in Germany

Printing and binding: Druckhaus Beltz, Hemsbach/Bergstr.
2142/3140-543210

PREFACE

The workshop on *Model-Oriented Data Analysis* was organized by the International Institute for Applied Systems Analysis and the Karl Weierstrass Institute for Mathematics of the Academy of Sciences of the GDR.

The main topics were

- Optimal experimental design
- Regression analysis
- Model testing and applications.

Under the topic *Optimal experimental design* new optimality criteria based on asymptotic properties of relevant statistics were discussed. The use of additional restrictions on the designs was also discussed, inadequate and nonlinear models were considered and Bayesian approaches to the design problem in the nonlinear case were a focal point of the special session. It was emphasized that experimental design is a field of much current interest.

During the sessions devoted to *Regression analysis* it became clear that there is an essential progress in statistics for nonlinear models. Here, besides the asymptotic behavior of several estimators the non-asymptotic properties of some interesting statistics were discussed. The distribution of the maximum-likelihood (ML) estimator in normal models and alternative estimators to the least-squares or ML estimators were discussed intensively.

Several approaches to *resampling* were considered in connection with linear, nonlinear and semiparametric models. Some new results were reported concerning simulated likelihoods which provide a powerful tool for statistics in several types of models. The advantages and problems of bootstrapping, jackknifing and related methods were considered in a number of papers.

Under the topic of *Model testing and applications* the papers covered a broad spectrum of problems. Methods for the detection of outliers and the consequences of transformations of data were discussed. Furthermore, robust regression methods, empirical Bayesian approaches and the stability of estimators were considered, together with numerical problems in data analysis and the use of computer packages.

From our point of view the topics in the workshop are of broad interest in statistical data analysis. Some of the papers have more a survey character, others are directed to original results on special problems. We believe that these proceedings will give stimulating hints for statisticians and data analysts both in theoretical and in practical aspects.

We would like to thank the members of the Program Committee: O. Bunke, GDR; J. Dupačová, Czechoslovakia; F. Pukelsheim, Federal Republic of Germany; and H.P. Wynn, UK, for their constructive cooperation in the time before and during the workshop. It is difficult to overestimate the contribution of the organizing committee, led by Ms. E. Herbst, IIASA, and Dr. F. Auert, GDR, to the success of the workshop.

July, 1987

V.V. Fedorov
H. Läuter

TABLE OF CONTENTS

Part III. Model Testing and Applications

PART I.

OPTIMAL EXPERIMENTAL DESIGN

AN APPROACH TO EXPERIMENTAL DESIGN FOR GENERALIZED LINEAR MODELS

Kathryn Chaloner
School of Statistics
University Of Minnesota
St. Paul MN 55108, U.S.A.

1. INTRODUCTION

A detailed discussion of a Bayesian approach to design for nonlinear problems is given in Chaloner and Larntz (1986). In that paper a theory of Bayesian design for concave criteria is discussed and then applied to a logistic regression model. This model is an example of a generalized linear model as defined by McCullagh and Nelder (1983). Generalized linear models are a large class of models which include many important special cases. In this paper we describe how this approach to design can be implemented in any generalized linear model and look at a logistic regression example.

In linear design problems the Bayesian approach is similar to the non-Bayesian approach (see e.g. Fedorov 1981, Pilz 1983, or Chaloner 1984). In problems other than linear problems, however, the Bayesian approach can yield very different designs.

2. GENERALIZED LINEAR MODELS

In a generalized linear model independent measurements, $y_1,\ldots,y_n$, are taken. The distribution of the y's depends on unknown parameters. The density of an observation y is of the following form:

$$p(y;\lambda,\tau) = \exp\{[\ a(y)\ \lambda\ -\ b(\lambda)\ ]/\ c(\tau)\ +\ d(y,\tau)\} \tag{1}$$

for some λ and τ and for some functions a, b, c and d. If τ is known the distribution is in the exponential family and has natural parameter λ. If τ is unknown this distribution is generally not a member of the exponential family.

The first two moments of a(y) are:

$$E(a(y)\,|\,\lambda,\tau)\ =\ \mu\ =\ b'(\lambda) \qquad \text{and} \qquad Var(a(y)\,|\,\lambda,\tau)\ =\ b''(\lambda)\ c(\tau)\ , \tag{2}$$

where primes denote differentiation with respect to λ.

In a generalized linear model the mean of a(y), μ, depends on k explanatory variables, possibly including a constant term. The values of the k explanatory variables, for the ith observation, are denoted by $\underline{x}_i = (x_{i1},x_{i2},\ldots,x_{ik})^T$. We suppose that the values of x can be chosen from a set X which is a compact subset of k-dimensional Euclidean space. The distribution of y is related to these explanatory variables through the link function g. This function is a monotone function of μ and is linear in $\underline{x}$. For an observation y at $\underline{x}$ we have $g(\mu) = \underline{x}^T \beta$.

This class of models, described in McCullagh and Nelder (1983), includes many frequently encountered models. Special cases include linear, logistic and probit regression models. Linear models are given when y has a normal distribution and the link function is the identity, that is $g(\mu) = \mu$. Logistic regression models are given when y has a Binomial distribution, a(y) is the proportion of "successes", μ is the probability of success and the link function is $g(\mu) = \log(\mu/(1-\mu))$.

3. BAYESIAN OPTIMAL DESIGN

Suppose our interest is in the estimation of the set of parameters $\beta^T=(\beta_1,\ldots,\beta_k)$, or functions of these parameters, and τ is a nuisance parameter. We can choose n values of the explanatory variable $\underline{x}$ at which to observe independent measurements $y_1,\ldots\ldots,y_n$. Suppose that the values of $\underline{x}_i$ must be chosen from some compact set X. To choose the values of the design points we treat the problem as a decision problem and choose the points to maximize our expected utility. Exact calculations are usually difficult to implement so we use an asymptotic approximation to our expected utility as our criterion to be optimized. The approximation is based on the approximate normality of the posterior distribution, as described, for example, in Berger (1985) page 224. We denote the full set of parameters as $\theta = (\beta,\tau)^T$. If the density for an observation y_i at $\underline{x}_i$ is $p(y_i;\theta,\underline{x}_i)$ then the (r,s) entry of the expected Fisher information matrix is:

$$I_{rs}(\theta,\underline{x}_1\ldots,\underline{x}_n) = -\ E \sum_{i=1}^{n} \frac{\delta^2}{\delta\theta_r\delta\theta_s} \log p(y_i;\theta,\underline{x}_i)\ . \tag{3}$$

The expectation is over the sampling distribution of y given θ.

In design problems a common approach is to solve the approximate design problem of choosing a probability measure on X rather than n particular points. Such an optimal design measure can be rounded systematically to give n design points. Under the approach of thinking of a design as a measure η on X, the expression (3) can be written as:

$$I_{rs}(\theta,\eta) = -\ E\ n \int \frac{\delta^2}{\delta\theta_r\delta\theta_s} \log p(y;\theta,\underline{x})\ \eta(d\underline{x})\ . \tag{4}$$

The posterior distribution of θ is approximately normal with variance covariance matrix $I(\theta,\eta)^{-1}$.

Note also that if the model is linear in the natural parameters λ, and the scale parameter τ is known, then the expected Fisher information matrix is also the actual value of the second derivative of the log likelihood. Both linear and logistic regression models correspond to this "canonical" link function.

3.1 The information matrix for a generalized linear model

The information matrix for a generalized linear model has a special form because of the form of the density (1). If the scale parameter τ is known then $\theta = \beta$ and the (r,s) entry of the k by k information matrix for a design taking observations at $\underline{x}_1,\ldots,\underline{x}_n$ is given by:

$$\sum_{i=1}^{n} \left(\mathrm{var}(a(y_i)\,|\,\underline{x}_i,\, \lambda,\, \tau\, \right)^{-1} \frac{d\mu}{d\omega}^{2}\, x_{ir}\, x_{is} \quad . \tag{5}$$

where $\omega = g(\mu)$. This expression is derived, for example, in McCullagh and Nelder 1983, page 33. The structure was also used in Zacks (1977) without the scale parameter τ. Note that the dependence on τ is only through a multiplicative factor from the variance of $a(y)$.

If the scale parameter τ is unknown then the information matrix $I(\theta,\eta)$ is (k+1) by (k+1) with entries corresponding to differentiation with respect to τ. The expected information matrix matrix is block diagonal, with the off diagonal entries for differentiation with respect to β_i and τ being zero. The inverse information matrix is therefore also block diagonal. The approximate posterior variance of β is given by the inverse of the k by k matrix with entries given by (5). This matrix just depends on τ through a multiplicative factor. We denote this matrix as $I_\beta(\theta,\eta)$, and its inverse as $I_\beta(\theta,\eta)^{-1}$, irrespective of whether τ is known or unknown.

We further simplify (5) by defining

$$w(\underline{x},\beta) \;=\; (b''(\,\lambda(\underline{x}^T\beta)\,))^{-1}\, \frac{d\mu}{d\omega}^{2}. \tag{6}$$

Then for a design measure, η, using expressions (2) and (6) we can write

$$I_\beta(\theta,\eta) = (c(\tau))^{-1} \int\; w(\underline{x},\beta)\; \underline{x}\underline{x}^T \;\; \eta(d\underline{x}) \;. \tag{7}$$

3.2 Criteria for design

We will use two criteria for design which correspond to two different utility functions. The first criterion is to choose a measure η on X that maximizes

$$\varphi_1(\eta) = E \log \det I_\beta(\theta,\eta). \tag{8}$$

The expectation is over the prior distribution on θ. The measure η is to be chosen from the set H, the set of all probability measures on X. This criterion corresponds to D-optimality in linear problems.

The second criterion is that of minimizing the approximate expected posterior variance of the specific parameters of interest and corresponds to A-optimality in linear problems. The design measure is chosen to maximize

$$\varphi_2(\eta) = - E \operatorname{tr} B(\beta)\, I_\beta(\theta,\eta)^{-1}. \tag{9}$$

The matrix $B(\beta)$ is a square symmetric matrix of weights representing what functions of β are to be estimated. If linear combinations of β are of interest $B(\beta)$ is a matrix of known weights. If nonlinear functions of β are of interest then $B(\beta)$ depends on β. We call this criterion φ_2-optimality and it corresponds to A-optimality in linear problems. This criterion requires that the quantities to be estimated or predicted are precisely specified and possibly weighted. We express this criterion as maximizing the negative of the variance so that both φ_1 and φ_2 are criteria to be maximized.

Other criteria could also be used. Tsutakawa (1972,1980), Läuter (1972,1974), Dubov (1977), Zacks (1977), Cook and Nachtsheim (1982) and Pronzato and Walter (1985) use these and related criteria.

3.3 The theory of Bayesian design

The theory used in Chaloner and Larntz (1986) is for criteria which are concave on H, the set of probability measures on X. In that paper we did not specifically consider nuisance parameters, such as τ, but their presence presents no additional difficulties.

If, for each θ, the function $\log \det I_\beta(\theta,\eta)$ and the function $-\operatorname{tr}B(\beta)I_\beta(\theta,\eta)^{-1}$ are concave functions on H, the set of probability measures on X, then the functions φ_1 and φ_2 are therefore also concave functions on H if the expectations exist and φ is well defined. As we assume that X is compact there must exist a probability measure in H that maximizes the criterion function.

The concavity of the criterion function over H enables the equivalence theorem of Whittle (1973) to be applied assuming certain regularity conditions are satisfied. Using this theorem a design is optimal if and only if its directional derivative in the direction of all single point designs is everywhere nonpositive. If a design is optimal then the roots of this derivative function are the support points of the optimal design measure.

One advantage of having a concave criterion is that to verify a particular design is optimal we need only examine the derivative function in the direction of one point designs and show that it is nonpositive over X.

3.4 Design for generalized linear models

For a generalized linear model the information matrix is given by (7). Thus, if the values of β were known the design problem would be equivalent to a linear problem. If the approach were taken of designing to be optimal for a best guess of the unknown parameters (as in Silvey, 1980, Chapter 6, or, Chernoff, 1953) we could apply the methods of linear design. If the parameters are unknown and have a prior distribution both $\varphi_1(\eta)$ and $\varphi_2(\eta)$ are concave over H.

We may note that if our prior distribution is such that β and τ are independent then we may replace the factor that depends on τ by its expected value. Thus if we have this prior independence we may ignore the fact that τ is unknown in considering optimal design. We may, therefore, take $c(\tau)$ as identically equal to one in the subsequent discussion.

Because the information matrix takes the particular structure in (7) the directional derivatives for a design η in the direction x take a similar form for any generalized linear model. For φ_1-optimality the directional derivative for a design η in the direction x is

$$d(\eta,\underline{x}) = E \; w(\underline{x},\beta) \; \underline{x}^T \, I(\beta,\eta)^{-1}\underline{x} \; - k. \tag{10}$$

Where the expectation is over the prior distribution on β and k is the dimension of x. For φ_2-optimality with a weight matrix $B(\beta)$ the directional derivative for a design η in the direction x is

$$d(\eta,\underline{x}) = E \; w(\underline{x},\beta) \; \mathrm{tr}\, B(\beta)\, I(\beta,\eta)^{-1}\underline{x}\underline{x}^T \, I(\beta,\eta)^{-1} + \varphi_2(\eta). \tag{11}$$

The expectation is again over the prior distribution on β.

4. AN EXAMPLE

A logistic regression model corresponds to a binomial sampling distribution for y and a logit link function. Specifically for n_i observations taken at x_i, the single explanatory variable, the response y_i is binomial with n_i trials and probability of success, $a(y_i) = y_i/n_i$, and $\mu = p(x_i,\theta)$. There is no unknown scale parameter and $\beta = (\beta_0,\beta_1)^T$. The mean of $a(y_i)$ is related to x by

$$g(\mu) = \log(\, p(x_i,\beta) \,/\, (\, 1-p(x_i,\beta)\,)\,) \; = \; \beta_0 + \beta_1 x_i \,.$$

For a design η the information matrix, $I(\beta,\eta)$, is

$$I(\beta,\eta) \; = \; \int p(x,\beta)\,(1-p(x,\beta))\,\underline{x}\underline{x}^T \; \eta(d\underline{x})$$

where $\underline{x}^T = (1, x_i)$.

In Chaloner and Larntz several examples of design for the logistic regression model are given for a variety of criteria and prior distributions. We take just one prior distribution here and describe the design in detail. We also compare the design to that using a design which is optimal for a best guess of the parameter values.

The prior distribution is specified in terms of the slope β_1 and the ratio $\gamma = \beta_0/\beta_1$. This ratio, γ, is the value of x at which the probability, $p(\gamma,\beta)$, is one half. We take β_1 and γ to be independent and both have a uniform distribution over an interval. Specifically, β_1 is uniform on [6,8] and γ is uniform on [-1,1]. Numerical methods of finding designs for particular criteria are given in Chaloner and Larntz. The criterion and derivatives must be evaluated using numerical integration and the designs found using numerical optimization methods.

4.1 φ_1-optimality

For φ_1-optimality a design on seven points was found in Chaloner and Larntz The design is displayed graphically as a probability measure in Figure 1.

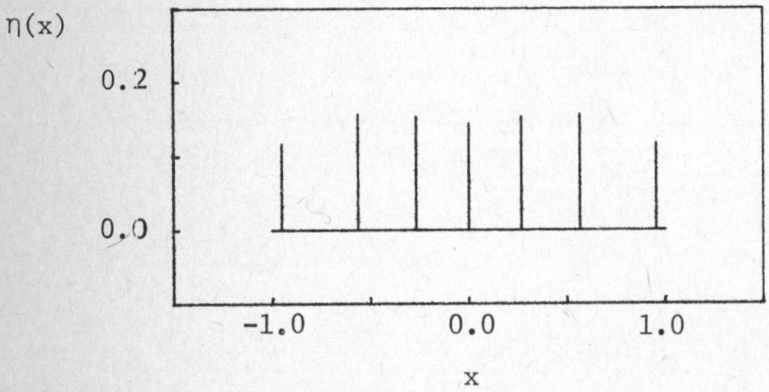

FIGURE 1 The φ_1-optimal design, η_1.

The design space was taken to be that where the explanatory variable x lay in the interval [-1.2,1.2]. To verify that the design above is indeed close to optimal the derivative function (11) can be examined. A plot of the derivative function is given in Figure 2 and the derivative does indeed appear to be nonpositive everywhere. As the derivative is nonpositive outside the interval [-1.2,1.2] the design cannot be improved upon by enlarging the design space.

We examine this design further by comparing it to the locally optimal design which maximizes the determinant of the information matrix at the best guess of the parameter values. A natural choice of best guess is the prior mean of γ and β_1, that is 0 and 7 respectively. The locally optimal design is a two point design with half the mass at .2205 and half at -.2205.

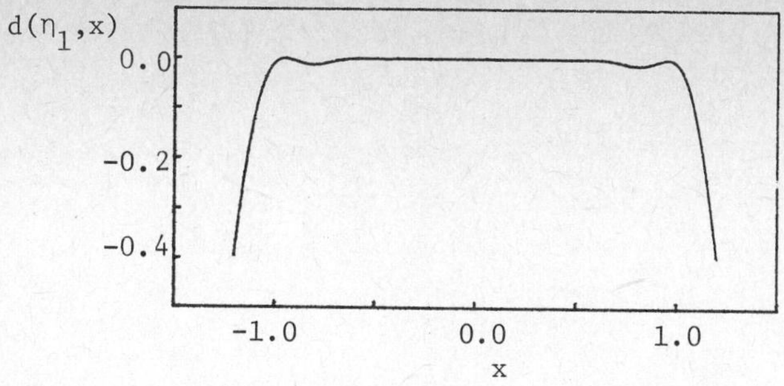

FIGURE 2 The derivative function for the design, η_1 shown in figure 1.

To compare the two designs we can look at a plot of the value of logdet$I(\beta,\eta)$ for the design measures. Figure 3 is a perspective plot of this surface for the φ_1-optimal design with seven support points and Figure 4 is the corresponding plot for the locally optimal two point design. The surface is plotted over the support of the prior distribution as a function of γ and β_1 and is on the same scale in the two figures.

We see, not surprisingly, that the locally optimal design is better than the φ_1-optimal design at the prior mean of the parameters in the center of the region. The locally optimal design is, however, extremely inefficient for values of γ far from the prior mean of zero. The value of the function in Figure 3 ranges from -6.36 to -3.81 and in Figure 4 from -14.9 to -2.99.

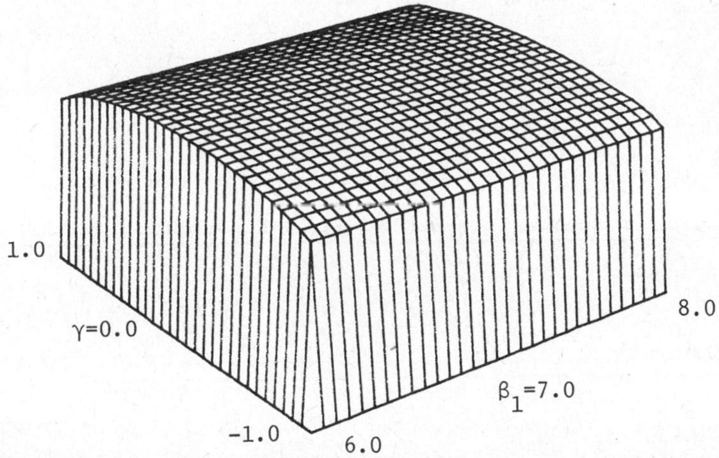

FIGURE 3 The value of logdet $I(\beta,\eta)$ for the φ_1-optimal design, η_1.

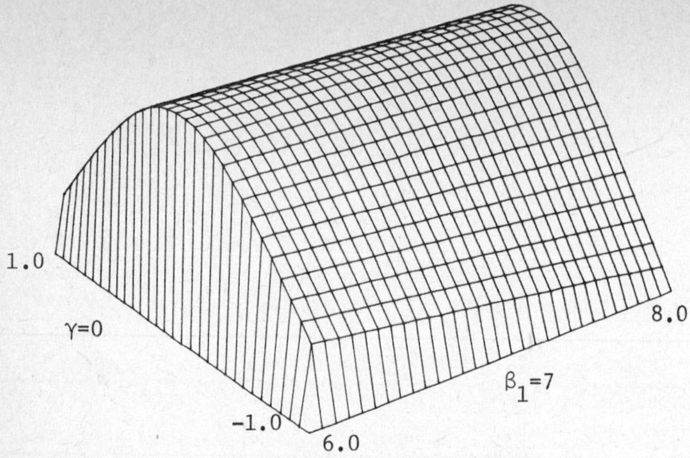

FIGURE 4 The value of logdet $I(\beta,\eta)$ for the locally optimal design, η_2.

To compare these designs numerically we can calculate the sample sizes required to give the same efficiency under the φ_1-optimality criterion and the locally optimal criterion. The locally optimal design, η_2, gives a criterion value $\varphi_1(\eta_2) = -6.951$ compared to an optimal value of $\varphi_1(\eta_1) = -4.578$. For the locally optimal design to be as efficient under the φ_1-optimal criterion approximately 3.3 times as many observations would be required. Conversely, at the prior mean for (γ,β_1) of (0,7) the value of logdet $I(\beta,\eta_1)$ is -4.036 and logdet $I(\beta,\eta_2)$ is -2.993. So only 1.7 times as many observations in the η_1 design are required for η_1 to be as efficient as η_2 in terms of local optimality.

Thus, the φ_1-optimal design, η_1, is quite efficient in terms of local optimality wheras the locally optimal design, η_2, is very inefficient in terms of φ_1-optimality.

4.2 φ_2-optimality

We now very briefly give an example of a φ_2-optimal design for the same prior distribution. For this criterion it is necessary to specify exactly what is to be estimated. The example chosen here is that of estimating γ. The φ_2-optimal design found by Chaloner and Larntz is displayed in Figure 5 and has 6 support points.

The locally optimal design that maximizes $-\text{tr } B(\beta)\, I(\beta,\eta)^{-1}$ for the prior mean of the unknown parameters puts all mass at the single design point $x=\gamma$ and is therefore not of much practical use. A comparison with the locally D-optimal design,

η_2, as described in the section 4.1, is made as this design is sometimes recommended as a useful all purpose design.

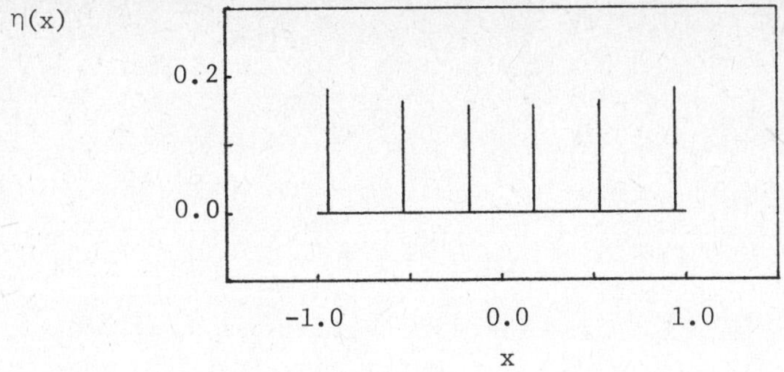

FIGURE 5 The φ_2-optimal design for estimating γ, η_3.

The locally D-optimal design, η_2, gives a criterion value $\varphi_2(\eta_2)$ = -83.035 compared to an optimal value of $\varphi_2(\eta_3) = -.356$. This striking contrast is due to the gross inefficiency of η_2 for γ close to -1 or +1 and β_1 close to 8. For the locally optimal design to be as efficient under the φ_2-optimal criterion approximately 255 times as many observations would be required. Conversely, at the prior mean for (γ,β_1) of (0,7) the value of tr $B(\beta)\ I(\beta,\eta_3)^{-1}$ is .326 and tr $B(\beta)\ I(\beta,\eta_2)^{-1}$ is .141. So only just over twice as many observations in the η_3 design are required for η_3 to be as efficient as η_2 in terms of local optimality.

ACKNOWLEDGEMENT

I would like to thank my colleagues R. D. Cook, K. Larntz and L. Tierney for their helpful suggestions and careful reading of this paper. I also thank V.V. Fedorov for bringing the work by Dubov (1977) and Fedorov (1981) to my attention.

REFERENCES

Berger, J.O. (1985). Statistical Decision Theory and Bayesian Analysis (second edition), Springer-Verlag, New York.

Chaloner, K. (1984). Optimal Bayesian experimental design for linear models. Ann. Statist. 12, 283-300.

Chaloner, K. and Larntz, K. (1986). Optimal Bayesian design applied to logistic regression experiments. University of Minnesota, School of Statistics, Technical report number 483.

Chernoff, H. (1953). Locally optimal designs for estimating parameters. Ann.Math. Statist., 24, 586- 602.

Cook, R.D. and Nachtsheim, C.J. (1982). Model robust, linear-optimal designs. Technometrics, 24, 49-54.

Dubov, E.L. (1977). D-optimal designs for nonlinear models under the Bayesian approach. In Regression Experiments. Moscow University Press, 103-111. (In Russian.)

Fedorov, V.V. (1972). The Theory of Optimum Experiments. Transl. and edited W.J. Studden and E.M. Klimko, Academic Press, New York.

Fedorov, V.V. (1981). Active regression experiments. In Mathematical methods of experimental design. Nauka Press, Siberian Section, 19-73. (In Russian.)

Läuter, E. (1974) Experimental design in a class of models. Math. Oper. u.Statist., 5, 379-396.

Läuter, E. (1976). Optimal multipurpose designs for regression models. Math.Oper. u. Statist., 7, 51-68.

McCullagh, P. and Nelder, J.A. (1983). Generalized Linear Models. Chapman and Hall, London.

Pilz, J. (1983). Bayesian estimation and experimental design in linear regression models. Teubner-Texte, Leibzig.

Pronzato, L. and Walter, E. (1985). Robust experiment design via stochastic approximation. Mathematical Biosciences, 75, 103-120.

Silvey, S.D. (1980). Optimal Design. Chapman and Hall, London and New York.

Tsutakawa, R.K. (1972). Design of an experiment for bioassay. Jour. Amer.Statist. Assoc., 67, 584-590.

Tsutakawa R.K. (1980). Selection of dose levels for estimating a percentage point of a logistic quantal response curve. Applied Statistics, 29, 25-33.

Whittle, P. (1973). Some general points in the theory of optimal experimental design. Jour. R. Statist. Soc., Ser. B, 35, 123-130.

Zacks, S. (1977) Problems and approaches in design of experiments for estimation and testing in nonlinear problems. In: Multivariate Analysis IV, ed. P.R. Krishnaiah, North-Holland, Amsterdam, 209-223.

MINIMUM BIAS ESTIMATION - DESIGNS AND DECISIONS

Norman R. Draper and Elizabeth R. Sanders
University of Wisconsin-Madison, U.S.A.

1. INTRODUCTION

Response surface analysis concerns the empirical investigation of an unknown functional relationship, $\eta = \eta(x_1, x_2, \ldots, x_k)$, between a response variable η and k coded predictor variables $\underset{\sim}{x}' = (x_1, x_2, \ldots, x_k)$.

The function η is, typically, approximated over some region of interest R by a low order polynomial

$$g(\underset{\sim}{x}) = \underset{\sim}{x}_1' \underset{\sim}{\theta}_1, \tag{1.1}$$

where the $p_1 \times 1$ vector $\underset{\sim}{x}_1$ contains terms needed to produce a polynomial of degree d_1; $\underset{\sim}{\theta}_1$ is the corresponding $p_1 \times 1$ vector of parameters to be estimated. R is contained in an operability region O, a region in the $\underset{\sim}{x}$-space in which experimental runs can be performed. (It could happen that R = O, as is typically assumed when the criterion of D-optimality is involved.) The standard approach is then to assume that $\underset{\sim}{y}_u = \underset{\sim}{x}_{1u}' \underset{\sim}{\theta}_1 + \varepsilon_u$, where $u = 1, 2, \ldots, N$ denotes the observations available, where y_u is the observed value of η at the conditions that give rise to the vector $\underset{\sim}{x}_{1u}$, and where $\underset{\sim}{\varepsilon} = (\varepsilon_1, \varepsilon_2, \ldots, \varepsilon_N)' \sim N(\underset{\sim}{0}, \underset{\sim}{I}\sigma^2)$, and then to estimate $\underset{\sim}{\theta}_1$ by least squares.

If we define $\underset{\sim}{X}_1$ as the $N \times p_1$ matrix whose uth row is $\underset{\sim}{x}_{1u}'$ and write $\underset{\sim}{y} = (y_1, y_2, \ldots, y_N)'$, then the least squares estimate of $\underset{\sim}{\theta}_1$ is $\hat{\underset{\sim}{\theta}}_1 = (\underset{\sim}{X}_1'\underset{\sim}{X}_1)^{-1}\underset{\sim}{X}_1'\underset{\sim}{y}$, and the vector of fitted values is $\hat{y}(\underset{\sim}{x}) = \underset{\sim}{x}'\hat{\underset{\sim}{\theta}}_1$.

There are two sources of error in such a procedure: sampling error ε in observing y and bias error due to the difference between the approximating polynomial and the true function. We shall assume that $\eta(\underset{\sim}{x})$ is a polynomial of degree d_2

$$\eta(\underset{\sim}{x}) = \underset{\sim}{x}_1'\underset{\sim}{\theta}_1 + \underset{\sim}{x}_2'\underset{\sim}{\theta}_2 \tag{1.2}$$

where the $p_2 \times 1$ vector $\underset{\sim}{x}_2$ contains the remaining terms needed for the full polynomial of degree d_2 and $\underset{\sim}{\theta}_2$ is the corresponding $p_2 \times 1$ vector of parameters.

Let $w(\underset{\sim}{x})$ be a weight function over O, and $\Omega^{-1} = \int_O w(\underset{\sim}{x})d\underset{\sim}{x}$. Define $\underset{\sim}{W}_{11}$, $\underset{\sim}{W}_{12}$, and $\underset{\sim}{W}_{22}$ via

$$\underset{\sim}{W}_{ij} = \Omega \int_O \underset{\sim}{x}_i \underset{\sim}{x}_j' w(\underset{\sim}{x})d\underset{\sim}{x} \tag{1.3}$$

where the integration is performed individually for each element of the matrix. The $\underset{\sim}{W}_{ij}$ are the moment matrices of the weight function $w(\underset{\sim}{x})$ over the operability region. The design criterion to be first considered is that of minimizing J, the integrated mean square error, defined as

$$J = N\Omega \int_O E[\hat{y}(\underset{\sim}{x}) - \eta(\underset{\sim}{x})]^2 w(\underset{\sim}{x})d\underset{\sim}{x}/\sigma^2. \tag{1.4}$$

This can be written as the sum of the integrated variance V, and the integrated squared bias B, the latter arising from terms of order greater than d_1 omitted from $\hat{y}(\underset{\sim}{x})$:

$$J = N\Omega \int_O V\{\hat{y}(\underset{\sim}{x})\} w(\underset{\sim}{x})d\underset{\sim}{x}/\sigma^2 + N\Omega \int_O \{E\hat{y}(\underset{\sim}{x}) - \eta(\underset{\sim}{x})\}^2 w(\underset{\sim}{x})d\underset{\sim}{x}/\sigma^2$$

$$= V + B. \tag{1.5}$$

For details, see Box and Draper (1959, 1963).

In various investigations seeking to minimize J in various experimental circumstances, one fact always emerged. Unless O was restricted and not much bigger than R, the bias contribution B played a much larger role (in J) than did V, and so it was prudent in general circumstances to choose a design slightly expanded from the all-bias design. The all-bias design was the one that minimized the contribution B alone and it tended to "crouch" somewhat within the region R and its points were not on the boundary.

This fact prompted Karson, Manson and Hader (1969) to suggest use of <u>minimum bias estimation</u>, that is, to estimate $\underset{\sim}{b}_1$, not by least squares, but by minimizing B. If the bias that arose from terms of orders $(d_1+1),\ldots,d_2$ were modest, running a full design of order d_2 could be a waste of resources. By fitting a minimum bias order d_1 model, one might be able to protect against bias while using fewer runs than required by a higher order design, and yet obtain a satisfactory fit. As shown by Karson, Manson and Hader (1969), the minimum bias estimator is given by

$$\underset{\sim}{\theta}_m = (\underset{\sim}{I} | \underset{\sim}{W}_{11}^{-1} \underset{\sim}{W}_{12}) \hat{\underset{\sim}{\theta}} = \underset{\sim}{W}\hat{\underset{\sim}{\theta}}, \tag{1.6}$$

say, where $\underset{\sim}{\theta} = (\underset{\sim}{X}'\underset{\sim}{X})^{-1}\underset{\sim}{X}'\underset{\sim}{y}$ is the vector of estimates obtained by fitting model (1.2) by least squares where $\underset{\sim}{X} = (\underset{\sim}{X}_1, \underset{\sim}{X}_2)$ and $\underset{\sim}{X}_2$ is the matrix whose uth row is $\underset{\sim}{x}_{2u}'$, the value of $\underset{\sim}{x}_2'$ with the uth observation values substituted.

The necessary and sufficient condition for obtaining a minimum bias estimator is that

$$E(\hat{\theta}_m) = (I|W_{11}^{-1}W_{12})\theta = W\theta. \tag{1.7}$$

The minimum value of B is then

$$\min B = N\{\beta_2'(W_{22}-W_{12}'W_{11}^{-1}W_{12})\beta_2\}/\sigma^2. \tag{1.8}$$

We see, from equation (1.6), that to get the minimum bias estimator of order d_1, we need to combine least squares estimators of order $\leq d_1$ with those of orders $(d_1+1),\ldots,d_2$. However, as pointed out by Karson, Manson and Hader (1969), we do not need to be able to estimate individually all the coefficients of order $> d_1$. Among questions we might ask are:

1. What designs, as far as seems possible, provide only those combinations of estimated coefficients that are needed, for the cases $(d_1,d_2) = (1,2)$ and $(2,3)$.
2. For a given set of data, which method of estimation should we use? (a) Least squares of order d_1; (b) minimum bias of order d_1; least squares of order d_2?

Aspects of minimum bias estimation that will not concern us here, will be found in Cote, Manson and Hader (1973), Ellerton and Tsai (1978), Karson (1970), Karson and Spruill (1975), Khuri and Cornell (1977), Liu and Karson (1980), Ott and Cornell (1974), and Thompson (1973). For related work see Evans and Manson (1978).

2. DESIGNS

The questions asked above can be tackled at various levels of generality. Here we discuss the case where R is spherical and of unit radius in the coded space, and where $W(x) = 1$ over R and is otherwise zero; this implies a uniform interest within R and none outside R. We summarize some of the results given by Draper and Sanders (1987).

2.1. Case $d_1 = 1$, $d_2 = 2$.

First order designs are used to fit a k-dimensional hyperplane $y = \theta_0 + \theta_1 x_1 + \ldots + \theta_k x_k + \varepsilon$ to the response variable. Use of the minimum bias hyperplane estimator minimizes the bias B arising from neglected second order terms $\theta_{11}x_1^2 + \ldots + \theta_{kk}x_k^2 + \theta_{12}x_1x_2 + \ldots + \theta_{k,k-1}x_kx_{k-1}$.

The only non-zero region moments of orders ≤ 4 are

$$\mu_2 = \Omega \int x_i^2 dx = (k+2)^{-1} \text{ and}$$

$$3\mu_4 = \Omega \int x_i^4 dx = 3\Omega \int x_i^2 x_j^2 dx = 3\{(k+2)(k+4)\}^{-1}. \tag{2.1}$$

Evaluation of (1.7) shows that $\hat{\theta}_{1m},\ldots,\hat{\theta}_{km}$ are all unbiased but that

$$E(\hat{\theta}_{om}) = \theta_o + \mu_2 \Sigma \theta_{ii} \tag{2.2}$$

where the summation is from $i = 1,\ldots,k$. Note that only the sum of the pure quadratic components occurs in (2.2) and not the individual θ_{ii}'s.

It is not necessary to fit the full second order model to the data to obtain (1.6).

Consider a 2^k factorial design ($\pm a, \pm a, \ldots, \pm a$) or a 2^{k-p} fractional factorial design of resolution ≥ 5, possibly replicated, with a total of n_f points, plus n_o center points. Let $\bar{y}(=\hat{\theta}_o)$ be the overall average response and let $\bar{y}_f$ and $\bar{y}_o$ denote the average responses at the factorial points and center points respectively. Then

$$E(\bar{y}) = \theta_o + (n_f a^2/N)\Sigma\theta_{ii} \tag{2.3}$$

$$E(\bar{y}_f - \bar{y}_o) = a^2 \Sigma\theta_{ii}. \tag{2.4}$$

Thus, if there are no center points, so that $\bar{y} = \bar{y}_f$ and $n_f = N$, (2.2) is satisfied by taking $a^2 = \mu_2$ and $\hat{\theta}_{om} = \hat{\theta}_o$, the least squares estimator. This is a special case of the general fact pointed out by Karson, Manson and Hader (1969, pp. 465, 466) that designs which satisfy the condition

$$(X_1'X_1)^{-1}X_1'X_2 = W_{11}^{-1}W_{12} \tag{2.5}$$

always achieve a minimum for B using the least squares estimator. However, we cannot estimate $\Sigma\beta_{ii}$ separately in this case.

With $n_o > 0$ center points, we use

$$\hat{\theta}_{om} = \bar{y} + \beta(\bar{y}_f - \bar{y}_o), \tag{2.6}$$

with

$$\beta = \mu_2/a^2 - n_f/N. \tag{2.7}$$

to achieve minimum bias. Note that we have spent our additional runs wisely, obtaining an estimate of $\Sigma\theta_{ii}$ via (2.4). Moreover we see that the minimum bias estimator sensibly combines $\bar{y}$, a biased estimator of θ_o with $\bar{y}_f - \bar{y}_o$, an estimator which provides information on how large that bias may be. This is a recurring feature of the minimum bias estimator. By choice of design we can, in general, decide how much detail in the bias we wish to estimate.

Having achieved minimum B we can now (if $n_o > 0$) choose the values of a and n_o/n to minimize V which, for the present case, reduces to

$$V_m = 1 + k\mu_2/\lambda_2 + (\lambda_2-\mu_2)^2/(\phi_4-\lambda_2^2) \tag{2.8}$$

where λ_2 amd ϕ_4 are the second and fourth order design moments given by $N\lambda_2 = \Sigma_u x_{iu}^2$, $N\phi_4 = \Sigma_u x_{iu}^4$. The conclusions are that, if we restrict the design to the unit sphere, and if we use one factorial replication, the best design values of a and n_o are as given below. All the non-central points lie on the unit sphere R.

k = 1	2	3	4	5	6	7	8
a = 1	0.70	0.57	0.50	0.44	0.40	0.37	0.35
n_o = 2	2	2	3	2	4	3	5

2.2 Case $d_1 = 2$, $d_2 = 3$.

Second order designs are used to fit a k-dimensional quadratic surface to the response variable. Use of the minimum bias estimator would reduce the bias B arising from neglected third order terms, $\Sigma_i\theta_{iii}x_i^3 + \Sigma_i\Sigma_j\theta_{ijj}x_ix_j^2 + \Sigma_i\Sigma_j\Sigma_\ell\theta_{ij\ell}x_ix_jx_\ell$. The only non-zero region moments of order ≤ 6 are those in (2.1) and

$$15\mu_6 = \Omega\int x_i^6 d\underset{\sim}{x} = 5\,\Omega\int x_i^2x_j^4 d\underset{\sim}{x} = 15\,\Omega\int x_i^2x_j^2x_\ell^2 d\underset{\sim}{x}$$

$$= 15\{(k+2)(k+4)(k+6)\}^{-1}. \tag{2.9}$$

Evaluation of (1.7) shows that $\hat{\theta}_{om}$, and all $\hat{\theta}_{ijm}$ are unbiased but that

$$E(\hat{\theta}_{im}) = \theta_i + (\mu_4/\mu_2)\{\theta_{iii} + \Sigma\theta_{ijj}\}, \quad i = 1,2,\ldots,k, \tag{2.10}$$

where the summation is from $j = 1,\ldots,k$. Note that it is not necessary to estimate individual third order θ's to get (1.6).

We assume use of a response surface design for which

$$\Sigma_u x_{iu}^q = N\phi_q, \quad \text{for} \quad q = 4, 6,$$
$$= N\lambda_2, \quad \text{for} \quad q = 2, \tag{2.11}$$

and we write

$$\Sigma_u x_{ju}^p x_{ju}^q = N\phi_{pq} \tag{2.12}$$

for p = q = 2 and for p = 4, q = 2. All odd design moments up to and including order six are assumed to be zero. It follows that, if the third order model is true, the least squares estimators for the coefficients of a second order model are unbiased except for $\hat{\theta}_i$ for which

$$E(\hat{\theta}_i) = \theta_i + (\phi_4/\lambda_2)\theta_{ii} + (\phi_{22}/\lambda_2)\Sigma\theta_{ijj}. \tag{2.13}$$

Now let c_{3i} be the contrast obtained by taking the $\{x_i^3\}$ column vector, orthogonalizing it with respect to $\{x_i\}$ to give a vector x_{iii} say, and then computing the normalized form

$$c_{3i} = \underset{\sim}{x}'_{iii}\underset{\sim}{y}/(\underset{\sim}{x}'_{iii}\underset{\sim}{x}_{iii}), \tag{2.14}$$

(e.g., see Box and Draper, 1987, pp. 454-458, 472-474). It can be shown that $\underset{\sim}{x}_{iii} = \{x_i^3\} - (\phi_4/\lambda_2)\{x_i\}$ and

$$E(c_{3i}) = \theta_{iii} + \frac{\phi_{42} - \phi_4\phi_{22}/\lambda_2}{\phi_6 - \phi_4^2/\lambda_2}\Sigma\theta_{ijj}. \tag{2.15}$$

For a standard composite design, this reduces to Eq. (13.8.14) of Box and Draper (1987, p. 458).

Note that, if the design is rotatable, $\phi_4 = 3\phi_{22} = 3\lambda_4$, say, and if we also choose $\mu_4/\mu_2 = \lambda_4/\lambda_2$, then (2.10) is satisfied by the least squares estimator (2.13). Once again, this is the special case of designs that satisfy (2.5). Otherwise, we set

$$\hat{\theta}_{im} = \hat{\theta}_i + \beta c_{3i} \tag{2.16}$$

where, to satisfy (2.10),

$$\beta = \frac{3\mu_4}{\mu_2} - \frac{\phi_4}{\lambda_2}$$

$$= \frac{\phi_4 - 3\phi_{22}}{\lambda_2}\,\frac{\lambda_2\phi_6 - \phi_4^2}{\phi_4(\phi_4-3\phi_{22}) - \lambda_2(\phi_6-3\phi_{42})}\,. \tag{2.17}$$

These equations provide a condition on the design moments and a value for β. For example, for a complete factorial design, n_c points at locations $(\pm a,\pm a,\ldots,\pm a)$ plus star $(\pm a\alpha,0,\ldots,0),\ldots,(0,0,\ldots,\pm a\alpha)$ plus n_0 center points, in k dimensions, (2.17) leads to the design condition (for a spherical region)

$$a^2 = \mu_4(\alpha^2+2)/(3\mu_2\alpha^2)$$

$$= (\alpha^2+2)/\{(k+4)\alpha^2\} \tag{2.18}$$

whereupon

$$\beta = \frac{3}{k+4} \{3 - \frac{\alpha^2+2}{3\alpha^2} \frac{n_c + 2\alpha^4}{n_c + 2\alpha^2}\} . \tag{2.19}$$

This result was obtained by Manson in unpublished lecture notes via the application of the condition $\underset{\sim}{W}(\underset{\sim}{X}'\underset{\sim}{X})^{-}\underset{\sim}{X}'\underset{\sim}{X} = \underset{\sim}{W}$. See Karson, Manson and Hader (1969, p. 465).

If we wish to estimate θ_{iii} and $\Sigma\theta_{ijj}$ in (2.15) separately, additional data points are needed. For example, we can add a second, non-replicated set of axial points, as detailed by Draper and Sanders (1987); see that paper also for other design suggestions.

3. DECISIONS ON MODELS

3.1. Lower order least squares versus lower order minimum bias

Whenever the integrated mean square error of the lower order (d_1) minimum bias estimator is less than that of the lower order (d_1) least squares estimator, the minimum bias estimator will be preferred to the least squares estimator. This was discussed by Karson, Manson, and Hader (1969, pp. 468-474) and generalized by Seheult (1978). We can write

$$J_L - J_m = \mathrm{tr}\{(\underset{\sim}{\alpha}_2\underset{\sim}{\alpha}_2' - \underset{\sim}{M})(\underset{\sim}{A}-\underset{\sim}{Q})'\underset{\sim}{W}_{11}(\underset{\sim}{A}-\underset{\sim}{Q})\}, \tag{3.1}$$

where $\underset{\sim}{Q} = \underset{\sim}{W}_{11}^{-1}\underset{\sim}{W}_{12}$, $\underset{\sim}{A} = (\underset{\sim}{X}_1\underset{\sim}{X}_1')^{-1}(\underset{\sim}{X}_1\underset{\sim}{X}_2')$, $\underset{\sim}{\alpha}_2 = \underset{\sim}{\beta}_2/(\sigma/\sqrt{N})$ is the vector of standardized coefficients, and $\underset{\sim}{M} = (\underset{\sim}{X}_2'\underset{\sim}{X}_2 - \underset{\sim}{X}_2'\underset{\sim}{X}_1(\underset{\sim}{X}_1'\underset{\sim}{X}_1)^{-1}\underset{\sim}{X}_1'\underset{\sim}{X}_2)^{-1}$. Thus if (3.1) is positive, minimum bias estimation is preferred, while if it is negative, least squares estimation is preferred.

3.2. Lower order minimum bias versus higher order least squares

For larger biases, fitting a lower order approximation of any kind to the response surface is inadequate. When is $\underset{\sim}{\alpha}_2$ large enough to require the fitting of a higher order polynomial? We can argue that there is too much bias present in either lower order fit when we would reject, at a specified level of significance, α, the null hypothesis

$$H_0: \underset{\sim}{\tau}'\underset{\sim}{\tau} = 0 \quad \text{versus} \quad H_1: \underset{\sim}{\tau}'\underset{\sim}{\tau} \neq 0. \tag{3.2}$$

where $\underset{\sim}{\tau}'\underset{\sim}{\tau} = \underset{\sim}{1}'\underset{\sim}{Q}\underset{\sim}{\alpha}_2\underset{\sim}{\alpha}_2'\underset{\sim}{Q}\underset{\sim}{1}$. The estimator $\underset{\sim}{\tau} = \underset{\sim}{1}'\underset{\sim}{Q}\hat{\underset{\sim}{\alpha}}_2$ follows the multivariate normal distribution with mean vector $\underset{\sim}{1}'\underset{\sim}{Q}\underset{\sim}{\alpha}_2$ and variance-covariance matrix $\underset{\sim}{1}'\underset{\sim}{Q}\underset{\sim}{M}\underset{\sim}{Q}'\underset{\sim}{1}\sigma^2/N$; see Searle (1982, p. 190). The variance σ^2 is estimated via the residual mean square error obtained from the analysis of variance table used in fitting the coefficients needed to estimate $\underset{\sim}{\theta}_m$. From this information, the null distribution of $\hat{\underset{\sim}{\tau}}'\hat{\underset{\sim}{\tau}}$ can be derived and used to test the hypothesis in equation (3.2). In general, the decision rule will be to reject the null hypothesis whenever

$$\hat{\underset{\sim}{\tau}}\,\hat{\underset{\sim}{\tau}} \geq \underset{\sim}{1}'\underset{\sim}{Q}\underset{\sim}{M}\underset{\sim}{Q}'\underset{\sim}{1}F(1,\nu,\alpha), \tag{3.3}$$

where ν is the degrees of freedom for the residual mean square error and $F(1,\nu,\alpha)$ is the upper α point of an F distribution with 1 and ν degrees of freedom. We would choose to graduate the response surface with the higher order least squares estimation whenever equation (3.3) is satisfied.

3.3 General procedure

Combining the two results above suggests use of:

(a) lower order least squares estimation if (3.1) $\leq$ 0,
(b) lower order minimum bias estimation if (3.1) $>$ 0 and (3.2) is not rejected
(c) higher order least squares estimation if (3.2) is rejected.

3.4 Application to rotatable designs, spherical R

For the special case of rotatable designs of order d_1 set in spherical regions of interest, it turns out that $\underset{\sim}{Q} = q_1\underset{\sim}{Z}$ and $\underset{\sim}{A} = q_2\underset{\sim}{Z}$, where q_1 is a function of the region moments, q_2 is a function of the design moments, and $\underset{\sim}{Z}$ is a matrix of constants specific to the order of the terms guarded against. In the present case, $\hat{\underset{\sim}{\tau}}'\hat{\underset{\sim}{\tau}} = \underset{\sim}{1}'\underset{\sim}{Z}\hat{\underset{\sim}{\alpha}}_2\hat{\underset{\sim}{\alpha}}_2'\underset{\sim}{Z}'\underset{\sim}{1}$ and $C^2 = \underset{\sim}{1}'\underset{\sim}{Z}\underset{\sim}{M}\underset{\sim}{Z}'\underset{\sim}{1}$. When $\underset{\sim}{Z}\underset{\sim}{M}\underset{\sim}{Z}'$ consists of diagonal blocks, with each block associated only with a set of correlated terms in $\hat{\underset{\sim}{\alpha}}_2$ (such as, for example, the set $\hat{\alpha}_{111}, \hat{\alpha}_{122}, \ldots, \hat{\alpha}_{1kk}$), our rule becomes: Use

(a) lower order least squares estimation when $\hat{\underset{\sim}{\tau}}'\hat{\underset{\sim}{\tau}} \leq C^2$.

(b) lower order minimum bias when $\hat{\underset{\sim}{\tau}}'\hat{\underset{\sim}{\tau}} > C^2$ and $\hat{\underset{\sim}{\tau}}'\hat{\underset{\sim}{\tau}} \leq C^2F(1,\nu,\alpha)$.

(c) higher order least squares estimation when $\hat{\underset{\sim}{\tau}}'\hat{\underset{\sim}{\tau}} > C^2F(1,\nu,\alpha)$.

Note that the assumption of rotatability does not imply that (2.5) is satisfied.

For some example data to which this method has been applied for $d_1 = 2$, $d_2 = 3$, see Derringer (1969, p. 8); the same data appear in an exercise in Box and Draper (1987, p. 266, 7.28).

3.5 Comments

When the above test is applied, for example as in Section 3.4, some practicalities become evident. For $d_1 = 1$, $d_2 = 2$, for instance, the test involves only one measure of curvature, Σb_{ii}. Any decision made is correct as far as that measure is concerned. However, it would be possible for, say, b_{11} to be large and positive, and b_{22} to be large and negative, and yet Σb_{ii} to be small. It would also be possible for one or more of the b_{ij}, $i \neq j$, to be large. Thus the test for model type needs to be intelligently supplemented by other information on curvature, if any is available. Usually, in first order designs, the interactions can be estimated, either individually or in small groups. Often, information on individual b_{ii} is not readily available. However, typically, the b_{ii} are of the same sign in practical cases; saddles tend to occur less frequently.

Similar difficulties could arise in a $d_1 = 2$, $d_2 = 3$ situation where the test involves combinations like $(3b_{iii}+\Sigma_j b_{ijj})$. Supplementary information on other combinations of third order coefficients might then be sought. See, for example, Box, Hunter and Hunter (1978, p. 523).

In summary, it must be remembered that the test recommended here examines only one facet of lack of fit, and must be used in conjunction with other available lack of fit measures. The virtue of our suggested test procedure, however, is that it enables consideration of minimum bias polynomial estimators together with, and as alternatives to, the least squares hierarchy of polynomial models.

4. REFERENCES

Box, G. E. P. and Draper, N. R. (1959). A basis for the selection of a response surface design. Journal of the American Statistical Association, 54, 622-654.

Box, G. E. P. and Draper, N. R. (1963). The choice of a second order rotatable design. Biometrika, 50, 335-352.

Box, G. E. P. and Draper, N. R. (1987). Empirical Model-Building and Response Surfaces. Wiley, New York.

Box, G. E. P., Hunter, W. G., and Hunter, J. S. (1978). Statistics for Experimenters: An Introduction to Design, Data Analysis, and Model Building. Wiley, New York.

Cote, R., Manson, A. R., and Hader, R. J. (1978). Minimum bias approximation of a general regression model. Journal of the American Statistical Association, 68, 633-638.

Derringer, G. C. (1969). Sequential method for estimating response surfaces. Industrial and Engineering Chemistry, 61, 6-13.

Draper, N. R. and Sanders, E. R. (1987). Designs for minimum bias estimation. Unpublished MS.

Ellerton, R. R. W. and Tsai, W. Y. (1979). Minimum bias estimation and the selection of polynomial terms for response surfaces. Biometrics, 35, 631-636.

Evans, J. W. and Manson, A. R. (1978). Optimal experimental designs in two dimensions using minimum bias estimation. Journal of the American Statistical Association, 73, 171-176.

Karson, M. J. (1970). Design criterion for minimum bias estimation of response surfaces. Journal of the American Statistical Association, 65, 1565-1572.

Karson, M. J., Manson, A. R. and Hader, R. J. (1969). Minimum bias estimation and experimental design for response surfaces. Technometrics, 11, 461-475.

Karson, M. J. and Spruill, M. L. (1975). Design criteria and minimum bias estimation. Communications in Statistics, 4(4), 339-355.

Khuri, A. I. and Cornell, J. A. (1977). Secondary design considerations for minimum bias estimation. Communications in Statistics - Theory and Methods, A6(7), 631-647.

Liu, W. C. and Karson, M. J. (1980). Minimum bias estimation and designs for the slope of a response surface. American Statistical Association Proceedings of the Business and Economic Statistics Section, 415-420.

Manson, A. R. (undated). Personal lecture notes on minimum bias estimation. North Carolina State University.

Ott, L. and Cornell, J. A. (1974). A comparison of methods which utilize the integrated mean square error criterion for constructing response surface designs. Communications in Statistics, 3(11), 1053-1068.

Searle, S. R. (1971). Linear Models. Wiley, New York.

Seheult, A. (1978). Minimum bias or least squares estimation? Communications in Statistics - Theory and Methods, A7(3), 277-283.

Thompson, W. O. (1973). Secondary criteria in the selection of minimum bias designs in two variables. Technometrics, 15, 319-328.

EXPERIMENTAL DESIGNS WITH RESTRICTED MEASURES

V. V. Fedorov
IIASA, A-2361 Laxenburg, Austria

1. INTRODUCTION

In this paper the numerical procedures of the "exchange" type for construction of continuous optimal designs with restricted measures (see definitions in Fedorov, 1986, Wynn, 1982) are mainly considered. The "exchange" type procedures are based on the simple heuristic idea: at every subsequent step to delete "bad" (less informative) points and to include "good" (most informative) ones.

Before giving the mathematical formulation of the problem and to illuminate the place of the results in experimental practice, let us start with two simple hypothetical examples.

Example 1. Let X be an area where N observational stations have to be located. An optimal (or at least, admissible) location depends upon models describing a system: "object under analysis – observational techniques".

The regression models:

$$y_i = \eta(x_i, \vartheta) + \varepsilon_i, i = \overline{1,N} \tag{1}$$

are commonly used in experimental practice. Here y_i is a result of an observation of the i-th station, $\eta(x,\vartheta)$ is an a priori given function, ϑ is a vector of parameters to be estimated and ε_i is an error which one believes to be random (more detailed specification will be given later). The optimal location of stations has to provide the minimum of some measure of deviation of estimates $\hat{\vartheta}$ from true values of ϑ.

For sufficiently large N the location of stations can be approximately described by some distribution function $\xi(dx)$ and one needs to find an optimal $\xi^*(dx)$. If X is not uniform, then one comes to the restriction that the share $N(\Delta X)/N$ of stations in any given part ΔX cannot exceed some prescribed level. In terms of distribution functions, it means that

$$\xi(dx) \le \Psi(dx), \tag{2}$$

where Ψ is defined by an experimenter. Here is the crucial feature of the problem considered in this paper.

Example 2. Let some characteristic y_i be observed for members of a sample of size N. Every i-th member of this sample can be chosen from a group labelled by variables x_i. If the sampling is randomized, then the observed characteristic y_i can be described by some distribution $f(y/x_i, \vartheta)$.

In many cases, after some manipulations, the initial model can be reduced to (1), where $\eta(x_i,\vartheta)$ is an average characteristic of an i-th group and ε_i reflects a variation within this group. The size of any group (or number of units available for sampling) is normally bounded. When applied to a continuous version of the design problem one can easily repeat the considerations of the previous example and come to model (1), (2).

In what follows, it will be assumed that in model (1), (2):

- a response function is a linear function of unknown parameters, i.e. $\eta(x,\vartheta)=\vartheta^T f(x)$, $\vartheta \in R^m$ and functions $f(x)$ are given;
- errors ε_i are uncorrelated and $E[\varepsilon_i^2]=1$ (or $E[\varepsilon_i^2]=\lambda(x_i)$, where $\lambda(x)$ is known, this case can be easily transformed to the previous one).

As usual, some objective function Φ defined on the space of $m \times m$ information matrices

$$M(\xi)=\int_X f(x)f^T(x)\ \xi(dx)$$

will describe the quality (or accuracy) of a design ξ ($M^{-1}(\xi)$ as a normalized variance-covariance matrix of the least square estimators of parameters ϑ.

The purpose of optimum design of experiments is to find

$$\xi^* = \inf_\xi \Phi[M(\xi)] \ , \quad \int_X \xi(dx)=1, \tag{3}$$

$$\xi(dx)\le\Psi(dx) \ , \quad \int_X \Psi(dx)=Q\ge 1 \tag{4}$$

Constraint (4) defines the peculiarity of the design problem with respect to standard approaches. Similar to the moment spaces theory (compare with Krein and Nudelman, 1973 Ch. VII), a solution of (3) and (4) will be called "(Φ, Ψ)-optimal design". In practice, $\Psi(dx)$ restricts the number of observations in a given space element dx (see the examples).

Optimization problem (1) and (2) were considered by Wynn, 1982 and Gaivoronsky, 1985. To some extent, they translated a number of classical results from moment spaces theory to experimental design language. Gaivoronsky also analyzed the convergence of the iterative procedure for optimal design construction based on the traditional idea of steepest descent (see, for instance, Ermakov (ed), 1983, Wu and Wynn, 1976)

$$\xi_{s+1}=(1-\alpha_s)\xi_s+d_s\bar{\xi}_s \ , \tag{5}$$

$$\bar{\xi}_s = \underset{\xi}{Arg\min}\, \Phi[(1-\alpha_s)M(\xi_s)+\alpha\ M(\xi)],$$

where ξ has to satisfy (4) and some additional linear constraints:

$$\int_X q(x)\xi(dx)\le C \ . \tag{6}$$

Wynn briefly discussed a number of heuristic numerical procedures based on some results from the moment spaces theory.

General properties of optimal designs are discussed in Section 2. Section 3 deals with the formulation and basic analysis of the iterative procedure and its modifications. In Section 4, the possibility of applying similar procedures to the standard design problem is considered, while in Section 5 a comparatively simple numerical example is presented.

2. CHARACTERIZATION OF (Φ , Ψ)–OPTIMAL DESIGNS

In this section, the properties of optimal designs will be discussed only to the extent sufficient for the analysis of the proposed iterative procedures. More details can be found in Wynn, 1982.

The set of assumptions used later is the following:

a) X is compact , $X \in R^l$;

b) $f(x) \in R^m$ are continuous functions in X ;

c) $\Psi(x)$ is atomless;

d) there exists $c<\infty$ such that

$$\Xi_c(\Psi) = \{\xi : \Phi[M(\xi)] \leq c < \infty , \xi \in \Xi(\Psi)\} \neq \phi ,$$

where $\Xi(\Psi)$ is the set of designs satisfying (4);

e) $\Phi(M)$ is a convex function of M ;

f) $\Phi[(1-\alpha)M(\xi_1) + \alpha M(\xi_2)] = \Phi[M(\xi_1)] + \alpha \int_X \varphi(x,\xi_1)\, \xi_2(dx) + o(\alpha)$,

$\xi_1 , \xi_2 \in \Xi_c(\Psi) , c<\infty$;

c′) $\Psi(x)$ has a continuous density $\psi(x)$;

f′) derivatives $\dfrac{\partial \Phi}{\partial M} = \dot{\Phi}$ exist and are bounded for all designs satisfying (d).

Let $\overline{\Xi}(\Psi)$ to be a set of measures ξ which either coincide with Ψ or equal to 0.

Theorem 1. If assumptions (a) – (e) hold, then there exists an optimal design $\xi^* \in \overline{\Xi}(\Psi)$.

Proof. The existence of an optimal design follows from (d)–(e) and the compactness of the set of information matrices. The compactness of the latter is provided by (a) and (b). The fact that at least one optimal design has to belong $\overline{\Xi}(\Psi)$ is the corollary of Liapounov's Theorem on the range of a vector measure (see, for instance, Karlin and Studden, 1966, Ch. VIII, Wynn, 1982).

Note 1. Liapounov's Theorem leads to another result which can be useful in applications: for any design ξ there is a design $\overline{\xi} \in \overline{\Xi}(\Psi)$ such that $M(\xi) = M(\overline{\xi})$.

A function $\varphi(x,\xi)$ is said to separate sets X_1 and X_2 if there is a constant C such that $\varphi(x,\xi) \leq C$ (a.e. Ψ) on X_1 and $\varphi(x,\xi) \geq C$ (a.e. Ψ) on X_2 , (a.e. Ψ) means "almost everywhere with respect to the measure Ψ".

Theorem 2. If assumptions (a)–(f) hold, then a necessary and sufficient condition that $\xi^* \in \Xi(\Psi)$ is (Φ,Ψ)–optimal is that $\varphi(x,\xi^*)$ separates two sets: $X^* = \text{supp}\,\xi^*$ and $X \setminus X^*$.

This theorem was first formulated by Wynn, 1982. In Fedorov, 1986, a more accurate proof was given which is more illuminative for the formulation and analysis of the numerical procedures.

If instead of (c), one uses (c'), then a necessary and sufficient condition can be formulated in the form of the following inequality:

$$\max_{x \in X^*} \varphi(x,\xi^*) \leq \min_{x \in X \setminus X^*} \varphi(x,\xi^*) \tag{7}$$

If (f) is complemented by (f'), then

$$\varphi\ (x,\xi) = \gamma\ (x,\xi) - tr\ \dot{\Phi}\ (\xi)\ M(\xi)\ ,$$

where $\delta(x,\xi) = f^T(x)\ \dot{\Phi}\ (\xi)\ f(x)$, and (7) can be converted to

$$\max_{x \in X^*} \gamma\ (x,\xi^*) \leq \min_{x \in X \setminus X^*} \gamma\ (x,\xi^*) \tag{8}$$

3. NUMERICAL PROCEDURE OF EXCHANGE TYPE

Theorem 2 gives a hint on how to construct optimal designs numerically: if for some given design ξ one can find a couple of sets:

$$D \subset supp\ \xi \text{ and } E \subset X \setminus supp\ \xi\ ,$$

$$\int_D \varphi(x,\xi)\ \Psi(dx) > \int_E \varphi(x,\xi)\ \Psi\ (dx)\ , \tag{9}$$

$$\int_D \Psi\ (dx) = \int_E \Psi\ (dx)$$

then it is hoped that the design $\bar{\xi}$ with

$$supp\ \bar{\xi} = supp\ \xi \setminus D \cup E$$

will be "better" than ξ. The repetitions of this procedure can lead to an optimal design.

A number of algorithms based on this idea can be easily invented. In this paper one of the simplest algorithms is considered in detail and it is evident that thorough consideration of others from this cluster is routine technique.

In what follows, the fulfillment of (c′) is assumed.

Algorithm. Let

$$\lim_{s \to \infty} \delta_s = 0\ ,\ \lim_{s \to \infty} \sum_{s=1}^{\infty} \delta_s = \infty \text{ and } \lim_{s \to \infty} \sum_s \delta_s^2 = k < \infty\ . \tag{10}$$

Step a. There is a design $\xi_s \in \Xi(\Psi)$. Two sets D_s and E_s with equal measures:

$$\int_{D_s} \psi\ (x)\ dx = \int_{E_s} \psi\ (x)\ dx = \delta_s$$

and including, correspondingly, points:

$$x_{1s} = Arg \max_{x \in X_{1s}} \delta\ (x,\xi_s) \text{ and } x_{2s} = Arg \min_{x \in X_{2s}} \delta\ (x,\xi_s)\ , \tag{11}$$

where $X_{1s} = supp\ \xi_s$ and $X_{2s} = X \setminus X_{1s}$, have to be found.

Step b. The design ξ_{s+1} with the supporting set

$$supp\ \xi_{s+1} = X_{1(s+1)} = X_{1s} \setminus D_s \cup E_s \tag{12}$$

is constructed.

Iterative procedure (10)–(12) is based on the approximation ($\delta \to 0$):

$$\int_Q \varphi\ (x,\xi)\ \psi\ (x)\ dx \approx \varphi\ (\bar{x},\xi)\ \delta\ ,\ \bar{x} \in Q\ ,\ \int_Q \psi\ (x)\ dx = \delta\ ,$$

The analysis of the iterative procedure becomes simpler if

(g) for any design $\xi \in \overline{\Xi}(\Psi)$:

$$|M(\xi)| \geq \zeta > 0 .$$

This assumption is not very restrictive. If, for instance, $\psi(x) \geq q > 0$ and the functions $f(x)$ are linearly independent on any open finite measure subset of X, then (g) is valid.

For most optimality criteria, (g) leads to the fulfillment of the following inequalities:

$$\Phi \leq K_1 < \infty , \frac{\partial \Phi}{\partial M_{\alpha\beta}} \leq K_2 < \infty , \frac{\partial^2 \Phi}{\partial M_{\alpha\beta}\, \partial M_{\alpha\delta}} \leq K_3 < \infty , \tag{13}$$

$$1 \leq \alpha , \beta , \delta , \delta \leq M ,$$

for any $\xi \in \overline{\Xi}(\Psi)$. Otherwise (17) is supposed to be included in (g).

Theorem 3. If assumptions (a), (b), (c'), (e)–(g) hold, then $\{\xi_3\}$ *converges weakly:*

$$\lim_{s \to \infty} \Phi [M(\xi_s)] = \inf_{\xi} \Phi [M(\xi)] = \Phi^* \tag{14}$$

Proof. The approach is standard for optimization theory (in the statistical literature see, for instance, Wu and Wynn, 1978). Therefore, some elementary considerations will be omitted.

Expanding (see (g) and (17)) by a Taylor series in δ_s gives:

$$\Phi[M(\xi_{s+1})] = \Phi[M(\xi_s)] + \delta_s [\gamma(x_{2s}, \xi_s) - \gamma(x_{1s}, \xi_s)] + \delta_s^2 K_s , \tag{15}$$

where $|K_s| \leq K_0 = K_0(K_1, K_2, K_3)$. Due to this inequality and (10) the sequence $S_{2s} = \{\sum_s K_s \delta_s^2\}$ converges. By definition:

$$\gamma(x_{2s}, \xi_s) - x_{1s}, \xi_s) \leq 0 ,$$

and therefore the sequence:

$$S_{1s} = \sum_s \delta_s [\gamma(x_{2s}, \xi_s) - \gamma(x_{1s}, \xi_s)]$$

monotonically decreases.

From (g) and (15):

$$K_1 \geq \Phi[M(\xi_{2+1})] = \Phi[M(\xi_0)] + S_{1s} + S_{2s} \geq \Phi^*$$

leads to the boundness of S_{1s}.

Subsequently, the monotonicity of $\{S_{1s}\}$ provides its convergence and the convergence of $\{\Phi[M(\xi_s)]\}$. Assume that

$$\lim_{s \to \infty} \Phi [M(\xi_s)] = \Phi^1 \geq \Phi^* + \alpha , \alpha > 0 . \tag{16}$$

Then, from Theorem 2 and assumptions (b), (c') it follows that

$$\gamma(x_{2s}, \xi_s) - \gamma(x_{1s}, \xi_s) \leq b < 0$$

and

$$\lim_{s \to \infty} S_{1s} \leq b \lim_{s \to \infty} \sum_s \delta_s = -\infty , \tag{17}$$

$$\lim_{s \to \infty} \Phi[M(\xi_s)] \leq -\infty .$$

The contradiction between (16) and (17) proves the theorem.

Note 1. In (10)-(12), there is some uncertainty in the choice of D_s and E_s. Somehow they have to be located around x_{1s} and x_{2s}. When $\psi(x)$ = const (and one arrives at this case by the transformation $dx = \psi(x)dx$), then x_{1s} and x_{2s} could be the "geometrical" centers of D_s and E_s.

Note 2. The iterative procedure can be more effective (especially in the first steps) if there is a possibility to easily find

$$D_s^* = \mathrm{Arg} \max_{D_s \in X_{1s}} \int_{D_s} \gamma(x,\xi_s)\psi(x)dx$$

and

$$E_s^* = \mathrm{Arg} \min_{E_s \in X_{2s}} \int_{E_s} \gamma(x,\xi_s)\psi(x)dx \tag{18}$$

subject to

$$\int_{D_s} \psi(x)dx = \int_{E_s} \psi(x)dx = \delta_s . \tag{19}$$

Note 3. When δ_s is sufficiently small and

$$\int_D f(x)f^T(x)\psi(x)dx \approx f(x_{1s})f^T(x_{1s})\delta_s ,$$

$$\int_E f(x)f(x)\psi(x)dx \approx f(x_{2s})f^T(x_{2s})\delta_s$$

then the calculations can be simplified if one uses the following recursion formula (see, for instance, Fedorov, 1972):

$$(M \pm \delta ff^T)^1 = (I \mp \frac{\delta M^{-1}ff^T}{1 \pm \delta f^T M^{-1} f}) M^{-1}$$

$$= (I \mp \delta M^{-1}ff^T)M^{-1} + 0(\delta^2) .$$

The modified version of the algorithms, presented in Note 2, gives a hint for the construction of

Algorithm 2.

Step a. The same as (18) but instead of (19)

$$\int_{D_s} \psi(x)dx = \int_{E_s} \psi(x)dx \tag{20}$$

(no constraints on the sizes of D_s and E_s!).

Step b. Coincides with step b of algorithm 1.

This algorithm seems to be rather promising for changing the structure of an initial design ξ_0 rapidly, but allows some oscillation regimes, at least principally. The author failed to prove its convergence. Probably some combination of both considered algorithms (for instance, the majorization of (20) by some vanishing sequence δ_s) could be useful.

It must be noted that the sequences $\{\delta_s\}$ defined by (10), for instance, $\{\delta_s = (s+m)^{-1}\}$ give the slow convergence of $\{\Phi_s\}$ where $\Phi_s = \Phi[M(\xi_s)]$ is close enough to $\Phi[M(\xi^*)]$. Empirically, it was found that if δ_s is reduced when $\Phi_{s+1} \geq \Phi_s$ then the iterative procedure converges faster than for other choices of $\{\delta_s\}$.

4. EXCHANGE ALGORITHM IN THE STANDARD DESIGN PROBLEM

The possibility of using the algorithms similar to (10)-(12) for design problem (3) (without constraint (4)) was somehow overlooked in the design theory.

The simplest analogue can be formulated as follows:

Step a. There is a design ξ_s. Two points

$$x_{1s} = \text{Arg} \max_{x \in X_s} \varphi(x, \xi_s) \text{ and } x_{2s} = \text{Arg} \min_{x \in X} \varphi(x, \xi_s) , \tag{21}$$

where $X_s = \text{supp}\, X$ have to be found.

Step b.

$$\xi_{s+1} = \xi_s - \delta_s \xi(x_{1s}) + \delta_s \xi(x_{2s}) , \tag{22}$$

where $\xi(x)$ is a design with one supporting point x.

The sequence $\{\delta_s\}$ can be chosen as in (10). The convergence of the algorithm can be proven similarly to Theorem 3.

It is worthwhile noting that the convergence of procedures (21), (22), in the discrete case (when $\delta_s = K/N$, where K is integer and N is the total number of observations) is questionable, because proof of Theorem 3 is essentially based on the fact that $\delta_s \to 0$.

5. EXAMPLE

Algorithm (14)-(16) becomes particularly simple when $\psi(x) \equiv$ const (using the appropriate transformation of X' axes, any problem with the continuous $\psi(x)$ can be transformed to this case and sets D_s and E_s are elements of some regular grid G_s. Further simplification is possible when the dimension of X is small (say not more than 3). Then the grid G_0 can be chosen rather dense at the very first step and one can execute computations with $\delta = \psi(x)\Delta$, $\delta_s \equiv \delta$, $G_s \equiv G_0$, where Δ is a volume of one element of G_0.

In Figures 1 and 2 and Tables 1 and 2, the results of the computation for D-criterion and for the two dimensional polynomial model are presented. The form of X is rather irregular and corresponds to some region where an observation network has to be chosen to analyze the concentration of pollutants.

REFERENCES

Ermakov, S. ed. (1983) Mathematical Theory of the Design of Experiments (in Russian), Moscow, Nauka, p.386.

Fedorov, V. (1986) Optimal Design of Experiments: Numerical Methods, WP-86-55, Laxenburg, Austria, International Institute for Applied Systems Analysis.

Gaivoronsky, A. (1985) Stochastic Optimization Techniques for Finding Optimal Submeasures, WP-85-28, Laxenburg, Austria, International Institute for Applied Systems Analysis.

Karlin, S. and W.J. Studden (1966) Tchebycheff Systems: With Applications in Analysis and Statistics. New York: Wiley & Sons, p.586.

Krein, M.G. and A.A. Nudelman (1973) Markov Moment Problem and Extremal Problems, Moscow, Nauka, p.552.

Wu, C.F. and Wynn, M. (1978) The Convergence of General Step-Length Algorithms for Regular Optimum Design Criteria, Ann.Statist., **6**, 1273-1285.

```
 1.00 !                  x
 0.92 !                x . x x
 0.83 !            x x . . . .
 0.75 !        x x . . 0 . . 0
 0.67 !        . 0 0 . . . . .
 0.58 !      x . . . . . . . .
 0.50 !    x . 0 0 . . . . . . x
 0.42 !  x . . . . . . . . . . . x
 0.33 !x . . . . . . . . . . . . x
 0.25 !. . . . . . . . . . . . .
 0.17 !x . . . . . . . . . . . . x x
 0.08 !  x x x . . . 0 . . . . . . . x
 0.00 !        0 . . . . . . 0 . 0 . .
-0.08 !        . . . . . . . . . . . x
-0.17 !        . . 0 . 0 . . . . . .
-0.25 !        . . . . . . . . . . 0
-0.33 !      x . . . . . . . 0 . . . x
-0.42 !      . 0 . . . . . . . . . . . x x x x
-0.50 !      . 0 x 0 . . . . . . x 0 x   x x x
-0.58 !      x x   x . . . . . .
-0.67 !              . . . . . .
-0.75 !            x x . . . 0 .
-0.83 !                x 0 . . . x
-0.92 !                  x . x . . x
-1.00 !                    x   x x
        --------------------I--------------------)
   Xmin = -1.000                    Xmax =  1.000
```

Figure 1. Initial design:
x - boundary points, 0 - design points

DETERMINANT OF INITIAL INFORMATION MATRIX
2.41918e-07

INITIAL COVARIANCE MATRIX

5.245					
-1.742	13.531				
-17.323	22.317	113.980			
0.278	3.593	5.047	6.236		
-7.853	3.824	18.292	0.235	24.288	
-0.822	10.042	19.410	9.864	7.370	53.942

Table 1. Initial design characteristics

```
 1.00 !                  0
 0.92 !                x . 0 0
 0.83 !            x x . . . .
 0.75 !        0 x . . . . . .
 0.67 !          . . . . . . .
 0.58 !      x . . . . . . . .
 0.50 !    x . . . . . . . . . x
 0.42 !  x . . . . . . . . . . . x
 0.33 !0 . . . . . . . . . . . . x
 0.25 !0 . . . . . . . . . . . .
 0.17 !0 . . . . . . . . . . . . x x
 0.08 !  x x x . . . . . . . . . . . x
 0.00 !        . . . . . 0 0 0 . . . .
-0.08 !        . . . . . . . . . . . x
-0.17 !        . . . . . . . . . . .
-0.25 !        . . . . . . . . . . .
-0.33 !      x . . . . . . . . . . . x
-0.42 !      . . . . . . . . . . . . . x x 0 0
-0.50 !      0 . x . . . . . . . x x x   x x 0
-0.58 !      0 0   x . . . . . .
-0.67 !              . . . . . .
-0.75 !            x x . . . . .
-0.83 !                x . . . . x
-0.92 !                  x . x . . 0
-1.00 !                    0   0 0
        --------------------I--------------------)
   Xmin = -1.000                    Xmax =  1.000
```

Figure 2. Final design:
x - boundary points, 0 - design points

FINAL COVARIANCE MATRIX

6.552					
-0.062	4.070				
-7.121	2.451	13.636			
-0.226	1.080	1.165	2.694		
-7.122	0.213	7.487	0.717	11.101	
-3.294	5.213	10.859	1.140	5.544	25.15

VALUE OF THE DETERMINANT
9.62639e-05

Table 2. Final design characteristics

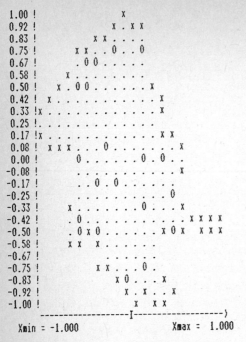

NUISANCE PARAMETER EFFECTS IN BALANCED DESIGNS

Johan Fellman
Swedish School of Economics and Business Administration, Helsinki, Finland

1. INTRODUCTION

In experimental design the linear model often contains extra parameters, in which the experimenters are not interested. Usually the elimination of these "nuisance" parameters reduces the precision of the estimators of the main parameters. *E.g.*, in block designs the parameters measuring the block effects are nuisance parameters. Ehrenfeld (1955) studied the effect of the nuisance parameters. He studied the design matrix and his main result was that in a non-singular model the nuisance parameters are without effect if and only if the columns corresponding to the nuisance parameters are orthogonal to the columns corresponding to the main parameters. Later the nuisance parameter problem has been studied in a more general framework and results have been obtained for the singular case (Fellman, 1976, 1978, 1985, Baksalary 1984).

2. NOTATIONS AND THEORETICAL RESULTS

In the 1940's Rao (1945 a, b) studied the estimability of parametric functions under singular linear models. His method was later developed by Fellman (1974). The core of this method is the following results.

Consider the linear model $(Y, X\alpha, \sigma^2 I)$. The parametric function $\theta = c'\alpha$ is estimable if and only if there exists a solution vector ρ of the equation

$$X'X\rho = c. \tag{2.1}$$

The corresponding estimator is $\hat{\theta} = \rho'X'Y$ and $\mathrm{Var}(\hat{\theta}) = \rho'X'X\rho$. These results are used in this study.

We consider the linear models

$$(Y, X_1\tau + X_2\beta, \sigma^2 I) \tag{2.2}$$

and

$$(Y, X_1\tau, \sigma^2 I) \tag{2.3}$$

where X_1 is an N x k matrix,
X_2 is an N x m matrix and their elements are assumed to be known and both matrices may be rank deficient,
τ is a k-dimensional vector of main parameters and
β is an m-dimensional vector of nuisance parameters.

The model (2.3) is obtained from the model (2.2) by the simplifying assumption that the nuisance parameters are lacking.

Using the partition $X = (X_1, X_2)$ the information matrix of model (2.2) can be written

$$M = X'X = \begin{bmatrix} X_1'X_1 & X_1'X_2 \\ X_2'X_1 & X_2'X_2 \end{bmatrix} = \begin{bmatrix} A & B \\ B' & D \end{bmatrix} \quad \text{(say)} \tag{2.4}$$

The matrix A is the information matrix of the model (2.3).

We shall also use the following notations. The column-space (range) of a matrix H and the orthogonal complement of this space are denoted C(H) and $C^{\perp}(H)$, respectively. If $a \in \mathbb{R}^{k+m}$ then we introduce the (k+m)-partition $a' = (\bar{a}', a^{o\prime})$.

If $\theta = \bar{c}'\tau$ is estimable with respect to (2.2) then the optimal estimator is $\hat{\theta} = \rho'X'Y$, where ρ is a solution of the equation

$$M\rho = c \tag{2.5}$$

and $c' = (\bar{c}', o)$. The variance of the estimator is $\mathrm{Var}(\hat{\theta}) = \sigma^2\rho'M\rho$.

We have the following theorem.

THEOREM 2.1. (Fellman 1976, 1978). Let M be a non-negative symmetric (k+m)x(k+m) matrix with the k+m partition (2.4), let $c = (\bar{c}', 0)'$ be a (k+m)-dimensional vector, which belongs to C(M) and let ρ be a solution of the equation $M\rho = c$. Then the equation

$$A\bar{r} = \bar{c} \tag{2.6}$$

has a solution $\bar{r}$ and

$$\rho'M\rho \geq \bar{r}'A\bar{r}, \tag{2.7}$$

with equality if and only if $r = (\bar{r}', 0)'$ is a solution of the equation $Mr = c$

It is easily seen that a necessary and sufficient condition for equality in (2.7) is that

$$B'\bar{r} = 0. \tag{2.8}$$

The inequality (2.7) indicates that the optimal estimator with respect to model (2.3) is never inferior to the optimal estimator with respect to model (2.2). If equality is obtained in (2.7) then the parametric function θ is said to be estimable with maximal accuracy with respect to model (2.2). Necessary and sufficient conditions that an estimable parametric function is estimable with maximal accuracy are given elsewhere (Fellman, 1976, 1978, 1985).

3. APPLICATIONS

Balanced 2-way design. Suppose that we have performed a balanced experiment with k treatments and m blocks. If additivity holds, we have the model

$$y_{ij} = \tau_i + \beta_j + \mu + \eta_{ij} \qquad \begin{matrix} (i = 1,\ldots,k) \\ (j = 1,\ldots,m) \end{matrix}$$

where i,j are the treatment and block subscripts, respectively, τ_i, β_j, and μ are fixed unknown parameters and η_{ij} have the mean zero and the variance σ^2. Using the matrix notation $Y = X\alpha + \eta$

$$Y = \begin{bmatrix} y_{11} \\ y_{12} \\ \vdots \\ \vdots \\ y_{km} \end{bmatrix} \quad X = \begin{bmatrix} 1 & 0 \ldots 0 & 1 & 0 \ldots 0 & 1 \\ 1 & 0 \ldots 0 & 0 & 1 \ldots 0 & 1 \\ \vdots & \vdots & \vdots & \vdots & \vdots \\ 1 & 0 \ldots 0 & 0 & 0 \ldots 1 & 1 \\ \vdots & \vdots & \vdots & \vdots & \vdots \\ 0 & 0 \ldots 1 & 1 & 0 \ldots 0 & 1 \\ 0 & 0 \ldots 1 & 0 & 1 \ldots 0 & 1 \\ \vdots & \vdots & \vdots & \vdots & \vdots \\ 0 & 0 \ldots 1 & 0 & 0 \ldots 1 & 1 \end{bmatrix}, \; \alpha = \begin{bmatrix} \tau_1 \\ \vdots \\ \tau_k \\ \beta_1 \\ \vdots \\ \beta_m \\ \mu \end{bmatrix}, \; \eta = \begin{bmatrix} \eta_{11} \\ \eta_{12} \\ \vdots \\ \eta_{km} \end{bmatrix} \tag{3.1}$$

Apart from the factor σ^2 the information matrix

$$M = X'X = \left[\begin{array}{ccc:ccc} m & 0 \ldots & 0 & 1 & 1 \ldots 1 & m \\ 0 & m \ldots & 0 & 1 & 1 \ldots 1 & m \\ \vdots & \vdots & \vdots & \vdots & \vdots & \vdots \\ 0 & 0 \ldots & m & 1 & 1 \ldots 1 & m \\ \hdashline 1 & 1 \ldots & 1 & k & 0 \ldots 0 & k \\ 1 & 1 \ldots & 1 & 0 & k \ldots 0 & k \\ \vdots & \vdots & \vdots & \vdots & \vdots & \vdots \\ 1 & 1 \ldots & 1 & 0 & 0 \ldots k & k \\ m & m \ldots & m & k & k \ldots k & km \end{array}\right] = \left[\begin{array}{c:c} A & B \\ \hdashline B' & D \end{array}\right] \tag{3.2}$$

We are interested only in the parameters $\tau_1,\ldots,\tau_k$ and consider $\beta_1,\ldots,\beta_m$ and μ as nuisance parameters. Only contrasts between the parameters $\tau_1,\ldots,\tau_k$ are estimable. On the other hand, every contrast between $\tau_1,\ldots,\tau_k$ is estimable.

Let $\bar{c}$ be an arbitrary contrast, then the equation $A\bar{r} = \bar{c}$ has the solution $\bar{r} = A^{-1}\bar{c} = \frac{1}{m}\bar{c}$. Now

$$B'\bar{r} = \frac{1}{m}B'\bar{c} = \begin{bmatrix} \Sigma\, c_i \\ \vdots \\ \Sigma\, c_i \\ m\Sigma\, c_i \end{bmatrix} = 0$$

and the presence of the nuisance parameters $\beta_1,\ldots,\beta_m$ and μ does not affect the precision of the estimate of any contrast of the τ's.

Balanced incomplete block design. In this case, not every treatment block combination is performed. The model (3.1) can be used if we only cancel some of the observations. The design is balanced if we require that every treatment occurs equally frequently and that every pair of treatments occurs equally frequently in the same block.

If the number of treatments is k,
the number of blocks is m,
the number of cells per block is b,
the number of replications of each treatment is u,
the number of times any two treatments occur in the same block is λ,
then the incomplete block design is balanced if $ku = mb$ and $\lambda(k-1) = u(b-1)$ (Kempthorne, 1952, p. 530).

The information matrix is

$$M = \left[\begin{array}{cccc:cccc} u & 0 & \dots & 0 & u_{11} & u_{12} & \dots & u_{1m}u \\ 0 & u & \dots & 0 & u_{21} & u_{22} & \dots & u_{2m}u \\ \vdots & \vdots & & \vdots & \vdots & \vdots & & \vdots \\ 0 & 0 & \dots & u & u_{k1} & u_{k2} & \dots & u_{km}u \\ \hdashline u_{11} & u_{21} & \dots & u_{k1} & b & 0 & \dots 0 & b \\ u_{12} & u_{22} & \dots & u_{k2} & 0 & b & \dots 0 & b \\ \vdots & \vdots & & \vdots & \vdots & \vdots & \vdots & \vdots \\ u_{1m} & u_{2m} & \dots & u_{km} & 0 & 0 & \dots b & b \\ u & u & \dots & u & b & b & b & bm \end{array}\right] = \left[\begin{array}{c:c} A & B \\ \hdashline B' & D \end{array}\right]$$

where $u_{ij} = 1$ if the treatment i is in the block j and $u_{ij} = 0$ if the treatment i is not in the block j. The distribution of zero's and one's in B depends on the chosen design but every block contains b cells and every treatment is replicated u times. From this it follows that

$$\sum_{i=1}^{k} u_{ij} = b \text{ and } \sum_{j=1}^{m} u_{ij} = u.$$

Only contrasts between the parameters $\tau_{1,\dots,}\tau_k$ are estimable. Analogously to the randomized block design it can be proved that every contrast is estimable.

Consider an arbitrary contrast $\theta = \bar{c}'\tau$. The equation $A\bar{r} = \bar{c}$ has the solution $\bar{r} = \frac{1}{u}\bar{c}$. The contrast is estimable with maximal accuracy if and only if

$$B'\bar{r} = 0. \qquad (3.3)$$

Such a contrast must satisfy the conditions

$$\sum_{i=1}^{k} u_{ij}\, c_i = 0 \qquad (j = 1,\dots,m). \qquad (3.4)$$

If the equation (3.3) is premultiplied by B we get the equation

$$BB'\bar{r} = 0 \qquad (3.5)$$

In the product

$$F = BB' = \begin{bmatrix} u_{11} & \dots & u_{1m} & u \\ \vdots & & \vdots & \vdots \\ u_{k1} & \dots & u_{km} & u \end{bmatrix} \begin{bmatrix} u_{11} & \dots & u_{k1} \\ \vdots & & \vdots \\ u_{1m} & \dots & u_{km} \\ u & \dots & u \end{bmatrix}$$

the element

$$f_{ij} = \sum_{t=1}^{m} u_{it}\, u_{jt} + u^2 = \begin{cases} \lambda + u^2 & \text{if } i \neq j \\ u + u^2 & \text{if } i = j \end{cases}$$

If we study a balanced incomplete block design $\lambda < u$ and

$$F = \begin{bmatrix} u + u^2 & \lambda + u^2 & \dots & \lambda + u^2 \\ \lambda + u^2 & u + u^2 & \dots & \lambda + u^2 \\ \vdots & \vdots & & \vdots \\ \lambda + u^2 & \lambda + u^2 & \dots & u + u \end{bmatrix}$$

is of full rank and the equation (3.5) has only the trivial solution $\bar{r} = 0$. Hence, no contrast satisfies the necessary condition and no contrast is estimable with maximal accuracy.

We observe quite contrary results for complete and incomplete designs. Therefore it may be of interest to study how much the nuisance parameters in BIBD reduce the efficiency of the estimates of the contrasts of the main (treatment) parameters.

Consider an arbitrary BIBD and an arbitrary contrast $\theta = \bar{c}'\tau$. The introduced method indicates that we have to solve the matrix equation

$$M\rho = c \tag{3.6}$$

where M is given in (3.2), $c' = (\bar{c}',0)$ and $\Sigma_{i=1}^{k} c_i = 0$. If we define $\rho' = (\bar{\rho}',\sigma',\delta)$ then the equation (3.6) is decomposable into the equations

$$u\rho_i + \sum_{j=1}^{m} u_{ij}\sigma_j + u\delta = c_i \qquad i = 1,\dots,k \tag{3.7)a}$$

$$\sum_{i=1}^{k} u_{ij}\rho_i + b\sigma_j + b\delta = 0 \qquad j = 1,\dots,m \tag{3.7)b}$$

$$u \sum_{i=1}^{k} \rho_i + b \sum_{j=1}^{m} \sigma_j + mb\delta = 0 \tag{3.7)c}$$

Following Kempthorne (1952 p. 80) we obtain

$$\sigma_j = -\delta - \frac{1}{b} \sum_{i=1}^{k} u_{ij}\rho_i \qquad j = 1,\dots,m$$

If this result is substituted in (3.7)a we get

$$u\rho_i + \sum_{j=1}^{m} u_{ij}\left[-\delta - \frac{1}{b} \sum_{s=1}^{k} u_{sj}\rho_s\right] + u\delta = c_i \qquad i = 1,\dots,k$$

If we observe that $\Sigma_j u_{ij} = u$, $\Sigma_i u_{ij} = b$, $\Sigma_j u_{ij}^2 = u$ and $\Sigma_j u_{ij} u_{sj} = \lambda$ for $s \neq i$ and if we introduce $R = \Sigma_{i=1}^{k} \rho_i$ and $H = u - (u - \lambda)/b$ we obtain $\rho_i = \lambda R/bH + c_i/H$. Furthermore, $Var(\hat{\theta}) = \rho'M\rho = \rho'c = \bar{\rho}'\bar{c} = \bar{c}'\bar{c}/H$. If we could estimate $\theta = \bar{c}'\tau$ without any nuisance parameters we should obtain the variance $\bar{c}'\bar{c}/u$. Hence the efficiency can be written (cf. Kempthorne, 1952, p. 533)

$$E = 1 - (u - \lambda)/bu. \tag{3.8}$$

We observe that for incomplete designs $\lambda < u$ and $E < 1$. This formula indicates that, in general, BIBD with great values of λ should be used.

TABLE 1 The efficiency of some designs given by Kempthorne (1952).

k	b	u	m	λ	E (%)	
3	2	2	3	1	75	Kempthorne p. 529
7	3	3	7	1	78	
7	4	4	7	2	88	
15	3	7	35	1	71	
15	7	7	15	3	92	
15	8	8	15	4	94	
31	3	15	155	1	69	
31	7	35	155	7	89	
40	4	13	130	1	77	Kempthorne p. 530
21	5	5	21	1	84	
31	6	6	31	1	86	
57	8	8	57	1	89	
6	3	5	10	2	80	Kempthorne p. 539
10	5	9	18	4	89	
28	7	9	36	2	89	
14	7	13	26	6	92	
8	4	7	14	3	86	

These efficiences can also be interpreted in another way. Consider that we have to estimate k treatments and our BIBD consists of m blocks with b cells each. Assuming that the experimental cost per cell is constant then we can compare our BIBD with a complete design with mb cells. Now each block has to contain k cells and the number of blocks is u = mb/k and the variance of the estimate is $\bar{c}'\bar{c}/u$. Hence the efficiency in (3.8) can also be interpreted as the efficiency when we compare a BIBD design with a complete design having the same number of cells.

4. REFERENCES

Baksalary, J.K. (1984).A study of the equivalence between a Gauss-Markoff model and its augmentation by nuisance parameters. Math. Operationsforsch. u. Statist., ser. statist., 15 (1984), 3-35.

Ehrenfeld, S. (1955).On the efficiency of experimental designs. Ann. Math. Statist., 26, 247-255.

Fellman, J. (1974). On the allocation of linear observations. Thesis. Comment. Phys.-Math. 44, 2-3, 27-78.

Fellman, J. (1976).On the effect of "nuisance" parameters in linear models, Sankhyā, 38 A, 197-200.

Fellman, J. (1978).On "nuisance" parameters in singular linear models. Swedish School of Economics and Business Administration, Helsingfors. Working papers 4, 11 pp.

Fellman, J. (1985).Estimation in linear models with nuisance parameters. Statistics & Decisions, Supplement Issue Nº 2. 161-164.

Kempthorne, O. (1952).The design and analysis of experiments, John Wiley and Sons, New York. XIX + 631 pp.

Rao, C.R. (1945a).Generalisation of Markoff's theorem and tests of linear hypotheses. Sankhyā, 7, 9-16.

Rao, C.R. (1945b).Markoff's theorem with linear restrictions on parameters. Sankhyā, 7, 16-19.

ADMISSIBILITY AND OPTIMALITY OF EXPERIMENTAL DESIGNS

Norbert Gaffke and **Friedrich Pukelsheim**
Institut für Mathematik der Universität Augsburg

1. INTRODUCTION

In this paper we study the relation between admissiblity and optimality of experimental designs. While it is standard decision theoretic reasoning that a statistical procedure which is uniquely optimal will necessarily be admissible, we here prove a converse to the effect that an admissible design is uniquely optimal with respect to the E-criterion and a specific choice of the parameter system of interest. The general equivalence theory may then be employed to obtain necessary conditions for admissibility.

As usual we choose the experimental conditions from a compact k-dimensional *experimental domain* $\mathcal{X} \subset \mathbb{R}^k$. We assume that under experimental conditions $x \in \mathcal{X}$ the real observation $Y(x)$ follows a linear model

$$Y(x) = x'\theta + \sigma e(x)$$

with uncorrelated errors $e(x)$ of unit variance. A *design* ξ is a probability distribution with finite support on the experimental domain $\mathcal{X}$, determining allocation and proportion of the experimental conditions.

The performance of a design ξ is determined through its $k \times k$ *moment matrix*

$$M(\xi) = \int_{\mathcal{X}} xx'\,d\xi.$$

Let $\mathcal{M}$ be the *feasible set* of moment matrices, assumed to be a convex and compact subset of nonnegative definite $k \times k$ matrices.

We shall study admissibility of a candidate matrix M in the set $\mathcal{M}$. It is illuminating to first discuss the case when the full parameter θ is of interest (Section 2). Before turning to the more general case of an s-dimensional parameter system $K'\theta$ (Section 4) we derive some intermediate results on information matrices (Section 3).

2. ADMISSIBILITY FOR THE FULL PARAMETER SET

Suppose $M \in \mathcal{M}$ is a moment matrix whose admissibility properties we wish to investigate. We call M *admissible for θ in $\mathcal{M}$* when no moment matrix $A \in \mathcal{M}$ satisfies $A \geq M$ and $A \neq M$, relative to the Löwner ordering $\geq$. To avoid trivialities we assume $M \neq 0$.

We shall show that every admissible moment matrix is E-optimal, i.e. it maximizes the minimum eigenvalue of an appropriate information matrix. However, the parameter system for which E-optimality is obtained is related to the candidate matrix M in an intrinsic manner: We choose the system $H'\theta$ from a full rank decomposition

$$M = HH',$$

where with $r = \operatorname{rank} M$ the $k \times r$ matrix H has full column rank r. An E-optimal moment matrix for $H'\theta$ in $\mathcal{M}$ is one which maximizes $\lambda_{\min}(C_H(A))$ over $A \in \mathcal{M} \cap \mathcal{A}(H)$, where $\mathcal{A}(H)$ is the convex cone of all nonnegative definite $k \times k$ matrices whose range contains the range of H, and

$$C_H(A) = (H'A^-H)^{-1} \quad \text{for } A \in \mathcal{A}(K).$$

We need an auxiliary lemma before turning to admissibility.

Lemma 1. *Let $A \in \mathcal{M}$ be a competing moment matrix. If A is E-optimal for $H'\theta$ in $\mathcal{M}$ then $A \geq M$.*

Proof. By construction the range of M contains (actually coincides with) the range of H, and we have

$$C_H(M) = (H'M^-H)^{-1} = (H'(HH')^-H)^{-1} = I_r.$$

Optimality of A yields $1 = \lambda_{\min}(C_H(M)) \leq \lambda_{\min}(C_H(A))$. Therefore $I_r \leq C_H(A)$, and pre- and postmultiplication with H and H' gives

$$M = HH' \leq HC_H(A)H' \leq A,$$

where the last inequality may be found for instance in Pukelsheim & Styan (1983, p. 147). □

We are now in a position to establish the relation between admissibility and unique E-optimality as announced above.

Theorem 1. *The moment matrix M is admissible for θ in $\mathcal{M}$ if and only if M is uniquely E-optimal for $H'\theta$ in $\mathcal{M}$.*

Proof. Suppose M is admissible. From Theorem 2 in Pukelsheim (1980, p. 344) we know that there exists an E-optimal moment matrix A for $H'\theta$ in $\mathcal{M}$. By Lemma 1 we have $A \geq M$, and admissibility of M forces $A = M$. This establishes unique E-optimality of M.

Conversely suppose M is uniquely E-optimal. Let A be a competing moment matrix satisfying $A \geq M$. Due to monotonicity A will also be E-optimal. But then uniqueness forces $A = M$, i.e. admissibility of M. □

Lemma 1 and Theorem 1 are closely related to Corollary 8.4 of Pukelsheim (1980, p. 359). Next we turn to the classical Theorem 7.1 on admissibility of Karlin & Studden (1966, p. 808), investigating the existence of a nonnegative definite matrix $N \neq 0$ or a positive definite matrix N satisfying the system of *normality inequalities*

$$\operatorname{trace}(AN) \leq \operatorname{trace}(MN) \quad \text{for all } A \in \mathcal{M}.$$

Employing customary notions of convex analysis we shall call a matrix N which satisfies this system of inequalities to be *normal to $\mathcal{M}$ at M*.

Theorem 2. *(i) If M is admissible for θ in $\mathcal{M}$ then there exists a nonnegative definite $k \times k$ matrix $N \neq 0$ which is normal to $\mathcal{M}$ at M.*
(ii) If there exists a positive definite $k \times k$ matrix N which is normal to $\mathcal{M}$ at M then M is admissible for θ in $\mathcal{M}$.

Proof. (i) From Theorem 1 we know that M is E-optimal for $H'\theta$ in $\mathcal{M}$. The general equivalence theory provides a necessary and sufficient condition of optimality in the following form, see Theorem 8 of Pukelsheim (1980, p. 356). Optimality holds if and only if for all $A \in \mathcal{M}$

$$\operatorname{trace}(H'GAG'HE) \leq \lambda_{\max}(H'M^{-}H) = 1/\lambda_{\min}(C_H(M)),$$

for some generalized inverse G of M and some matrix $E \in \operatorname{conv} S$. Here $\operatorname{conv} S$ denotes the convex hull of all $r \times r$ matrices of the form zz' such that z is a normalized eigenvector of $C_H(M)$ corresponding to $\lambda_{\min}(C_H(M))$. However, we have seen above that $C_H(M)) = I_r$, and so E actually is an arbitrary nonnegative definite $r \times r$ matrix with trace equal to 1.

Define the nonnegative definite matrix $N = G'HEH'G$. Then

$$\operatorname{trace} AN \leq 1 = \operatorname{trace} MN \quad \text{for all } A \in \mathcal{M}.$$

Hence N cannot be 0, and it satisfies the normality inequalities.
(ii) Let A be a competing moment matrix satisfying $A \geq M$. Then $0 \leq \operatorname{trace}\{(A-M)N\}$. On the other hand the normality inequalities yield $\operatorname{trace}\{(A-M)N\} \leq 0$. Therefore $\operatorname{trace}\{(A - M)N\} = 0$, and positive definiteness of N forces $A = M$. Thus admissibility is established. □

Our proof provides the additional information that in Theorem 2(i) we can choose N so as to satisfy $1 \leq \operatorname{rank} N \leq r = \operatorname{rank} M$.

Note that rank 1 matrices $M = cc'$ may well be admissible for the k-dimensional parameter θ. By Theorem 1 admissibility then holds if and only if M is uniquely optimal for $c'\theta$ in $\mathcal{M}$, and then Theorem 2(i) admits a rank 1 choice $N = dd'$.

Admissibility for a subset of the full parameter system admits a similar development, with slightly more technical input concerning information matrices.

3. INFORMATION MATRICES

Consider a fixed s-dimensional parameter system $K'\theta$ given by some $k \times s$ matrix K of full comlumn rank s. Admissibility for $K'\theta$ concentrates on the $s \times s$ information matrix for $K'\theta$ which, if $A \in \mathcal{A}(K)$ with $\mathcal{A}(K)$ defined as in the preceeding section, is given by

$$C_K(A) = (K'A^{-}K)^{-1}.$$

Recall that for the full parameter case a rank deficient moment matrix M may be admissible. Similarly a rank deficient information matrix $C_K(A)$ may prove admissible for $K'\theta$, provided we exercise some care when extending the matrix function C_K from $\mathcal{A}(K)$ to the convex cone $NND(k)$ of *all* nonnegative definite $k \times k$ matrices. The appropriate definition for an arbitrary matrix $A \in NND(k)$ is

$$C_K(A) = \lim_{\epsilon \downarrow 0}(K'(A + \epsilon I)^{-1}K)^{-1}.$$

Then $C_K(A)$ is nonsingular if and only if $A \in \mathcal{A}(K)$ and in this case

$$C_K(A) = (K'A^-K)^{-1},$$

see Lemma 2 in Müller-Funk, Pukelsheim & Witting (1985, p. 23). Another representation of the extended matrix function C_K was used in Gaffke (1987), namely

$$C_K(A) = \min_{L_K} L_K A L_K',$$

where the minimum is taken over all left inverses L_K of K (i.e. $L_K K = I_s$) and is carried out relative to the Löwner matrix ordering. That the minimum exists is a consequence of the Theorem in Krafft (1983). It can also be seen using the Gauss-Markov Theorem, as follows.

Consider a linear model with expectation $K\beta$ and dispersion matrix A, where $\beta \in \mathbb{R}^s$ is the unknown parameter vector. The set $\{L_K\}$ of left inverses of K defines the set of linear unbiased estimators for β, and the BLUE for β corresponds to a particular member L_K such that $L_K A L_K'$ is a minimum. We will call such a matrix L_K a left inverse of K *minimizing for A*, i.e.

$$L_K K = I_s \quad \text{and } C_K(A) = L_K A L_K'.$$

Equivalently one could say that L_K' is a minimum A-seminorm generalized inverse of K', see Rao & Mitra (1971, p. 46).

Both expressions for $C_K(A)$ coincide, as shown next.

Lemma 2. *For all nonnegative definite $k \times k$ matrices A we have*

$$\lim_{\epsilon \downarrow 0} (K'(A + \epsilon I)^{-1})^{-1} = \min_{L_K} L_K A L_K'.$$

Proof. Since for $\epsilon > 0$ the matrix $A + \epsilon I$ is positive definite, we know from the Gauss-Markov Theorem that

$$\min_{L_K} L_K(A + \epsilon I)L_K' = (K'(A + \epsilon I)^{-1}K)^{-1}.$$

Let L_K^* be a left inverse of K minimizing for A. Then

$$\min_{L_K} L_K A L_K' \le \min_{L_K} L_K(A + \epsilon I)L_K' \le L_K^*(A + \epsilon I)L_K^{*\prime},$$

and letting $\epsilon \to 0$ the assertion follows. □

With the extended definition of C_K a moment matrix $M \in \mathcal{M}$ is called admissible for $K'\theta$ in $\mathcal{M}$ when no moment matrix $A \in \mathcal{M}$ satisfies $C_K(A) \ge C_K(M)$ and $C_K(A) \ne C_K(M)$.

Again we wish to study a fixed moment matrix $M \in \mathcal{M}$. However, we now choose a full rank decomposition of its information matrix (which we assume to be nonzero)

$$C_K(M) = HH',$$

where with $t = \operatorname{rank} C_K(M)$ the $s \times t$ matrix H has full column rank t.

We shall have to investigate the parameter system $H'K'\theta$. The information matrices relative to the representations $(KH)'\theta$ and $H'(K'\theta)$ satisfy the following decomposition rule. The matrix functions C_{KH} and C_H are defined as above with KH and H instead of K and with domains $NND(k)$ and $NND(s)$, respectively.

Lemma 3. *For all nonnegative definite $k \times k$ matrices A we have*

$$C_{KH}(A) = C_H(C_K(A)).$$

Proof. When A is positive definite then

$$C_{KH}(A) = (H'K'A^{-1}KH)^{-1} = C_H((K'A^{-1}K)^{-1}) = C_H(C_K(A)).$$

Now take a nonnegative definite matrix A. For $\epsilon > 0$ then $C_K(A) \leq C_K(A+\epsilon I)$. Since $A+\epsilon I$ is positive definite we obtain $C_H(C_K(A)) \leq C_{KH}(A+\epsilon I)$. The right hand side becomes $C_{KH}(A)$ when $\epsilon \to 0$.

For the converse inequality let L_H be a left inverse of H minimizing for $C_K(A)$, and L_K be a left inverse of K minimizing for A. Obviously $L_H L_K$ is a left inverse of KH, and by Lemma 2

$$C_{KH}(A) \leq L_H L_K A L_K' L_H' = L_H C_K(A) L_H' = C_H(C_K(A)).$$

The two inequalities force equality, and the proof is complete. □

An analoguous decomposition rule holds for left inverses of KH minimizing for A.

Lemma 4. *A left inverse L_{KH} of KH is minimizing for A if and only if $L_{KH} = L_H L_K$ for some left inverse L_K of K minimizing for A and some left inverse L_H of H minimizing for $C_K(A)$.*

Proof. We first note that if L_K is a given left inverse of K, then the set of all left inverses of K is the linear manifold $L_K + B$ where B may be any $s \times k$ matrix with $BK = 0$. From this it is easy to see that L_K is minimizing for A if and only if $L_K A Q_K = 0$, where Q_K denotes the orthogonal projector onto the nullspace of K'. Similarly a left inverse L_{KH} of KH is minimizing for A if and only if $L_{KH} A Q_{KH} = 0$, where Q_{KH} is the orthogonal projector onto the nullspace of $(KH)'$.

To prove the direct part of the lemma let L_{KH} be a left inverse of KH minimizing for A. Consider the matrix equations

$$L_{KH} K X = L_{KH}, \quad \text{and} \quad X \cdot [K, AQ_K] = [I_s, 0].$$

Obvioulsy each of them separately has a solution. Moreover they have a common solution for X, by Theorem 2.3.3 in Rao & Mitra (1971, p. 25). In order to apply this theorem we must verify $L_{KH} K [I_s, 0] = L_{KH}[K, AQ_K]$, but this holds true in view of $L_{KH} A Q_{KH} = 0$ and $Q_K = Q_{KH} Q_K$. Setting $L_K = X$ and $L_H = L_{KH} K$, we have a left inverse L_K of K minimizing for A, a left inverse L_H of H, and $L_H L_K = L_{KH}$. In fact, L_H is minimizing for $C_K(A)$ since by Lemma 3

$$L_H C_K(A) L_H' = L_H L_K A L_K' L_H' = L_{KH} A L_{KH}' = C_{KH}(A) = C_H(C_K(A)).$$

The converse part is immediate: Evidently $L_H L_K$ is a left inverse of KH, and $L_H L_K A L_K' L_H' = L_H C_K(A) L_H' = C_H(C_K(A)) = C_{KH}(A)$. □

We shall now use these intermediate results for our discussion of admissibility and optimality.

4. ADMISSIBILITY FOR PARAMETER SUBSETS

Let $M \in \mathcal{M}$ be a fixed moment matrix. We resume the discussion of M being admissible for $K'\theta$ in $\mathcal{M}$. Assume that $C_K(M) \neq 0$ and choose a full rank decomposition $C_K(M) = HH'$ as in Section 3. We first present a result similar to Lemma 1.

Lemma 5. *Let $A \in \mathcal{M}$ be a competing moment matrix. If A is E-optimal for $H'K'\theta$ in $\mathcal{M}$ then $C_K(A) \geq C_K(M)$.*

Proof. By construction the range of $C_K(M)$ contains the range of H. Applying Lemma 3 we obtain

$$C_{KH}(M) = (H'C_K(M)^- H)^{-1} = (H'(HH')^- H)^{-1} = I_t.$$

Optimality of A yields $1 = \lambda_{\min}(C_{KH}(M)) \leq \lambda_{\min}(C_{KH}(A))$. Therefore $I_t \leq C_{KH}(A)$, and pre- and postmultiplication with H and H' yields

$$C_K(M) = HH' \leq HC_H(C_K(A))H' \leq C_K(A).$$

Note that $C_H(C_K(A)) = C_{KH}(A)$ is nonsingular and hence $C_K(A) \in \mathcal{A}(H)$. □

The following theorem on admissibility and E-optimality parallels Theorem 1.

Theorem 3. *The moment matrix M is admissible for $K'\theta$ in $\mathcal{M}$ if and only if M is E-optimal for $H'K'\theta$ in $\mathcal{M}$ and for any other E-optimal moment matrix $A \in \mathcal{M}$ for $H'K'\theta$ in $\mathcal{M}$ we have $C_K(A) = C_K(M)$.*

Proof. Follow the proof of Theorem 1, with Lemma 1 replaced by Lemma 5. Use Lemma 3 for the converse part. □

We are now in a position to present our main result: A proof based on E-optimality of Theorem 2 of Gaffke (1987).

Theorem 4. *(i) If M is admissible for $K'\theta$ in $\mathcal{M}$ then there exists a nonnegative definite $s \times s$ matrix $D \neq 0$ and there exists a left inverse L_K of K minimizing for M such that $L_K'DL_K$ is normal to $\mathcal{M}$ at M.*
(ii) If there exists a positive definite $s \times s$ matrix D and a left inverse L_K of K minimizing for M such that $L_K'DL_K$ is normal to $\mathcal{M}$ at M then M is admissible for $K'\theta$ in $\mathcal{M}$.

Proof. (i) By Theorem 3 the moment matrix M is E-optimal for $H'K'\theta$ in $\mathcal{M}$, and as shown above $C_{KH}(M) = I_t$. The general equivalence theory tells us that

$$\operatorname{trace}(H'K'GAG'KHE) \leq 1 \quad \text{for all } A \in \mathcal{M},$$

for some generalized inverse G of M and some nonnegative definite $t \times t$ matrix E with trace equal to 1. Define the matrix $N = G'KHEH'K'G$. Then

$$\operatorname{trace}(AN) \leq 1 = \operatorname{trace}(MN) \quad \text{for all } A \in \mathcal{M},$$

and $1 \leq \operatorname{rank} N \leq t$. The matrix $L_{KH} = H'K'G$ satisfies $L_{KH}KH = H'K'GKH = (C_{KH}(M))^{-1} = I_t$ and $L_{KH}ML_{KH}' = H'K'GMG'KH = I_t = C_{KH}(M)$, and thus is a left inverse of KH minimizing for M. Lemma 4 then ensures that $L_{KH} = L_H L_K$ where L_K is a left inverse of K minimizing for M. Setting $D = L_H'EL_H$ we obtain the desired representation

$$N = L_{KH}'EL_{KH} = L_K'L_H'EL_HL_K = L_K'DL_K.$$

(ii) Let A be a competing moment matrix satisfying $C_K(A) \geq C_K(M)$. Then

$$\begin{aligned} 0 &\leq \operatorname{trace}\{(C_K(A) - C_K(M))D\} \\ &\leq \operatorname{trace}\{(L_K A L_K' - L_K M L_K')D\} \\ &= \operatorname{trace}\{(A - M)L_K' D L_K\} \leq 0, \end{aligned}$$

and because of positive definiteness of D therefore $C_K(A) = C_K(M)$. □

The proof gives the aditional information that in Theorem 4(i) we can choose the $s \times s$ matrix D so as to satisfy $1 \leq \operatorname{rank} D \leq t = \operatorname{rank} C_K(M)$.

REFERENCES

Gaffke, N. (1987). Further characterizations of design optimality and admissibility for partial parameter estimation in linear regression. *Ann. Statist.*, **15**: to appear.

Karlin, S. and Studden, W.J. (1966). Optimal experimental designs. *Ann. Math. Statist.*, **37**: 783-815.

Krafft, O. (1983). A matrix optimization problem. *Linear Algebra Appl.*, **51**: 137-142.

Müller-Funk, U., Pukelsheim, F., and Witting, H. (1985). On the duality between locally optimal tests and optimal experimental designs. *Linear Algebra Appl.*, **67**: 19-34.

Pukelsheim, F. (1980). On linear regression designs which maximize information. *J. Statist. Plann. Inference*, **4**: 339-364.

Pukelsheim, F. and Styan, G.P.H. (1983). Convexity and monotonicity properties of dispersion matrices of estimators in linear models. *Scand. J. Statist.*, **10**: 145-149.

Rao, C.R. and Mitra, S.K. (1971). *Generalized Inverse of Matrices and Its Applications.* Wiley, New York.

OPTIMAL BLOCK DESIGNS FOR CORRELATED OBSERVATIONS

Joachim Kunert, Universität Trier,
FB IV - Abt. Mathematik/Statistik, Postfach 38 25, D-5500 Trier

1. INTRODUCTION

The paper considers a simple block model and assumes that the errors within the blocks are correlated according to a stationary first order autoregressive process with known lag one correlation coefficient λ. We restrict attention to the case $\lambda \geq 0$ and try to determine an optimal block design. The set of all block designs with v treatments and b blocks with k plots per block is denoted by $\Omega_{v,b,k}$. The position of the plots within the blocks is determined by the design. If design $d \in \Omega_{v,b,k}$ is applied then we assume that the vector of the measurements on the u-th block fulfills

$$y_{du} = T_{du}\tau + 1_k\beta_u + e_u \tag{1}$$

where β_u is the effect of the u-th block, T_{du} is the treatment design matrix in the u-th block, 1_k is the k-vector of ones and e_u is the vector of the errors in the u-th block. The covariance matrix of e_u is

$$S_\lambda = \sigma^2 \begin{bmatrix} 1 & \lambda & \lambda^2 & \cdots & & \lambda^{k-1} \\ \lambda & 1 & \lambda & & & \\ \lambda^2 & \lambda & 1 & & & \\ \cdot & & & \cdot & & \\ \cdot & & & & \cdot & \\ \cdot & & & \lambda & 1 & \lambda \\ \lambda^{k-1} & \cdots & & \lambda^2 & \lambda & 1 \end{bmatrix}$$

where $\sigma^2 > 0$ is unknown and $\lambda \geq 0$ is known. If we define $T_d=[T_{d1}',\dots,T_{db}']'$ and if $\times$ is the Kronecker product of matrices and I_b is the unit matrix of size b, then the vector of all measurements can be written as

$$Y_d = T_d\tau + I_b \times 1_k\beta + e\ . \tag{2}$$

Since we assume that the measurements on different blocks are uncorrelated, we have a covariance matrix of e which equals $I_b \times S_\lambda$. For a fixed design d the information matrix for the estimation of τ equals

$$\mathcal{C}_d = \sum_{u=1}^{b} T'_{du} S_\lambda^{-1} T_{du} - (1'_k S_\lambda^{-1} 1_k)^{-1} \sum_{u=1}^{b} T'_{du} S_\lambda^{-1} 1_k 1'_k S_\lambda^{-1} T_{du} . \tag{3}$$

The information matrix is the Moore-Penrose generalized inverse of the covariance matrix of the best linear unbiased estimate for the vector $\tau - (\tau' 1_v / v) 1_v$. It is the idea of optimal design therefore to search for designs which maximize some one-dimensional criteria of $\mathcal{C}_d$. We consider the class of φ_p criteria which are based on the eigenvalues $\mu_{d1} \geq \ldots \geq \mu_{dv-1} \geq 0$ of $\mathcal{C}_d$. For $p \in \mathbb{R}$, $p \neq 0$ we have

$$\varphi_p(\mathcal{C}_d) = \left(\frac{1}{v-1} \sum_{i=1}^{v-1} \mu_{di}^{-p}\right)^{-1/p} ,$$

$$\varphi_0(\mathcal{C}_d) = \left(\prod_{i=1}^{v-1} \mu_{di}\right)^{1/(v-1)} ,$$

and

$$\varphi_\infty(\mathcal{C}_d) = \mu_{dv-1} .$$

Then φ_0 is the well-known D-criterion, φ_1 the A-criterion and φ_∞ is the E-criterion. The criterion φ_{-1} is the trace of the information matrix. A design d* is φ_p-optimal if it maximizes $\varphi_p(\mathcal{C}_d)$ over a set of designs.

The $\mathcal{C}_d$-matrix for every $d \in \Omega_{v,b,k}$ has constant row and column sum zero. This implies that a design for which all off-diagonal elements of $\mathcal{C}_d$ are equal has $\mu_{d1} = \ldots = \mu_{dv-1}$. It is easy to see that a design d* for which $\mu_{d*1} = \ldots = \mu_{d*v-1}$ and which maximizes $\mathrm{tr}\,\mathcal{C}_d$ over a set of designs is φ_p-optimal over this set for all $p \geq 0$, that is for all φ_p-criteria which are of statistical relevance. To determine such a design it is necessary to make some definitions.

For a design $d \in \Omega_{v,b,k}$ define r_{di} as the number of appearances of treatment i in the design. For $1 \leq u \leq b$ let n_{diu} be the number of appearances of treatment i in block u. Further definc e_{diu} as the number of appearances of treatment i at an end plot of block u and $e_{di} = \sum_{u=1}^{b} e_{diu}$. Note that e_{diu} is either 0,1 or 2. The matrix with entries e_{diu} is the incidence matrix of a block design with b blocks of size 2. This design is called the end design of d. For treatment i and j the number m_{dij} counts how often the treatments appear adjacent to each other in the same block. The design d is called neighbor balanced if all m_{dij}, $i \neq j$, are equal and all $m_{dii} = 0$. The diagonal elements of $\mathcal{C}_d$ equal

$$c_{dii} = r_{di}(1+\lambda^2) - e_{di}\lambda^2 - 2m_{dii}\lambda - \frac{1-\lambda}{k-(k-2)\lambda} \sum_{u=1}^{b} \{n_{diu}(1-\lambda)+e_{diu}\lambda\}^2 \tag{4}$$

and the off-diagonal elements are

$$c_{dij} = -m_{dij}\lambda - \frac{1-\lambda}{k-(k-2)\lambda}\sum_{u=1}^{b}\{n_{diu}(1-\lambda)+e_{diu}\lambda\}\{n_{dju}(1-\lambda)+e_{dju}\lambda\} \qquad (5)$$

see Kunert (1987). In the following we want to determine optimality properties of certain block designs in the cases v = k and v < k.

2. E-OPTIMAL BLOCK DESIGNS IN THE CASE V = K

It was shown in Kunert (1987) that a design with

$$\sum_{u=1}^{b} n_{diu}n_{dju} = \frac{bk(k-1)}{v(v-1)} \quad \text{for all } i \neq j \qquad (6)$$

$$m_{dij} = \frac{2b(k-1)}{v(v-1)} \quad \text{for all } i \neq j \qquad (7)$$

$$\sum_{u=1}^{b} (n_{diu}e_{dju} + e_{diu}n_{dju}) = \frac{4b(k-1)}{v(v-1)} \quad \text{for all } i \neq j \qquad (8)$$

$$\sum_{u=1}^{b} e_{diu}e_{dju} = \frac{2b}{v(v-1)} \quad \text{for all } i \neq j \qquad (9)$$

in the case $k \leq v$ and $\lambda > 0$ has maximal $\mathrm{tr}\mathscr{C}_d$ and all off-diagonal elements of $\mathscr{C}_d$ equal. Consequently such a design is optimal. Since it takes a great number of blocks to achieve condition (9) we consider designs which fulfill conditions (6),(7) and (8) only. Kunert (1987) has shown that they are highly efficient under each φ_p-criterion. We want to determine exact E-optimality properties of some of them. Designs with properties (6),(7) and (8) were introduced by Kiefer and Wynn (1981).

In the case v = k condition (6) is fulfilled by every complete block design. Condition (7) means neighbor balance and condition (8) is fulfilled by every complete block design with neighbor balance.

We can construct complete block designs with neighbor balance whenever b is a multiple of v/2 and v is even, and whenever b is a multiple of v and v is odd, see, for instance, Gill and Shukla (1985). The cases b = v/2 and b = v are now considered in more detail. If v = 3 then the complete block design with neighbor balance $d \in \Omega_{3,3,3}$ also fulfills (9). However, for $v \geq 4$ it is impossible to fulfill (9) with only v or v/2 blocks. We therefore restrict attention to the case $v \geq 4$. We also restrict attention to the case $\lambda \geq 0$, since we know that for negative correlations there are nonbinary designs which perform even better that the designs fulfilling the whole set of conditions (6),(7),(8) and (9).

THEOREM 1 If $\lambda > 0$ and b = v/2 where v is even, then the neighbor balanced complete block design $d* \in \Omega_{v,v/2,v}$ is E-optimal over $\Omega_{v,v/2,v}$.

Proof: It was shown in Kunert (1987) that the smallest nonzero eigenvalue μ_{d*v-1} of $\mathscr{C}_{d*}$ fulfills

$$\mu_{d*v-1} \geq \xi = \{\frac{b(k-1)}{v(v-1)}\}\{\frac{k-(k-4)(\lambda-\lambda^2+\lambda^3)}{k-(k-2)\lambda}\} .$$

We now show that $\mu_{dv-1} \leq \xi$ for every $d \in \Omega_{v,v/2,v}$. If $\chi_{d,\xi} = \mathscr{C}_d - \xi I_v + (\xi/v)1_v1_v'$, then the eigenvalue μ_{dv-1} of $\mathscr{C}_d$ is less than ξ if $\ell'\chi_{d\xi}\ell < 0$ for a v-vector ℓ, and $\mu_{dv-1} \leq \xi$ if $\ell'\chi_{d\xi}\ell \leq 0$ for a v-vector ℓ with $\ell'1_v = 0$. Let x_{dij} denote the (i,j)-th entry of $\chi_{d,\xi}$.

(i) Assume the design d has one treatment i such that $r_{di} \leq v/2 - 1$. Then

$$x_{dii} \leq \frac{v-2}{2}(1+\lambda^2) - \frac{1-\lambda}{v-(v-2)\lambda}\frac{v-2}{2}(1-\lambda)^2 - \frac{v-1}{v}\xi < 0$$

and, consequently, $\mu_{dv-1} < \xi$.

(ii) Assume the design is equireplicate but one treatment appears at least twice at end plots. Then

$$x_{dii} \leq \frac{v}{2}(1+\lambda^2) - 2\lambda^2 - \frac{1-\lambda}{v-(v-2)\lambda}\{\frac{v-4}{2}(1-\lambda)^2 + 2\} - \xi(v-1)/v < 0$$

and, consequently, $\mu_{dv-1} < \xi$.

(iii) Assume the design is equireplicate and all $e_{di} = 1$ but there are treatments i and j which never appear adjacent to each other. Then

$$x_{dii} + x_{djj} - 2x_{dij} = c_{dii} + c_{djj} - 2c_{dij} - 2\xi$$

$$= v(1+\lambda)^2 - 2\lambda^2 - \frac{1-\lambda}{v-(v-2)\lambda}\sum_{u=1}^{b}\{n_{diu}(1-\lambda) + e_{diu}\lambda - n_{dju}(1-\lambda)$$

$$- e_{dju}\lambda\}^2 - 2\xi$$

$$\leq v(1+\lambda^2) - 2\lambda^2 - 2\xi < 0 .$$

(iv) Assume d is equireplicate, all $e_{di} = 1$ and all $m_{dij} = 1$, $i \neq j$. For each treatment i there is one treatment $j \neq i$, such that i and j appear at the opposite ends of the same block. Consider the vector ℓ with i-th and j-th entry $(v-2)/v$ and all other entries $-2/v$. Then $\ell'1_v=0$ and

$$\ell'\chi_{d\xi}\ell = x_{dii} + x_{djj} + 2x_{dij}$$

$$= v(1+\lambda^2) - 2\lambda^2 - 2\lambda - \frac{1-\lambda}{v-(v-2)\lambda}\sum_{u=1}^{b}\{(n_{diu} + n_{dju})(1-\lambda)$$

$$+ (e_{diu} + e_{dju})\lambda\}^2 - 2(v-2)\xi/v .$$

For the block u* with $e_{diu*} + e_{dju*} = 2$ we have

$$(n_{diu*} + n_{dju*})(1-\lambda) + (e_{diu*} + e_{dju*})\lambda \geq 2 .$$

Since $\sum\{(n_{diu} + n_{dju})(1-\lambda) + (e_{diu} + e_{dju})\lambda\} = (v-2)(1-\lambda) + 2$, we consequently have

$$c_{dii} + c_{djj} + 2c_{dij} \le v(1+\lambda^2) - 2\lambda^2 - 2\lambda - \frac{1-\lambda}{v-(v-2)\lambda}\{2(v-2)(1-\lambda)^2 + 4\}$$
$$= 2(v-2)\ \xi/v .$$

This completes the proof.

We now turn to the case $b = v$. Remember that there always is a neighbor balanced complete block design $d^* \in \Omega_{v,v,v}$, and that $\mu_{d^*v-1} \ge \xi$. However, not all neighbor balanced complete block designs in $\Omega_{v,v,v}$ perform equally well. What is more, there are designs which are not complete block designs and which perform better than some neighbor balanced complete block designs for some λ. As an example consider the designs in Table 1.

TABLE 1 Three designs in $\Omega_{4,4,4}$

$$h = \begin{matrix} 4 & 1 & 2 & 3^a \\ 1 & 2 & 3 & 4 \\ 3 & 4 & 1 & 2 \\ 2 & 3 & 4 & 1 \end{matrix} \qquad f = \begin{matrix} 1 & 4 & 3 & 2 \\ 4 & 3 & 2 & 1 \\ 1 & 2 & 4 & 3 \\ 3 & 1 & 2 & 4 \end{matrix} \qquad g = \begin{matrix} 1 & 2 & 4 & 1 \\ 2 & 4 & 1 & 2 \\ 3 & 1 & 3 & 4 \\ 4 & 3 & 2 & 3 \end{matrix}$$

[a] Take columns as blocks

It was shown in Kunert (1985) that f performs better than h if $\lambda \ge 0{\cdot}7$. Note that f is not a complete block design, but that it is neighbor balanced and that the end design of f is connected while that of h is not.

We now define a non empty set $\Delta_{v,v,v} \subset \Omega_{v,v,v}$, which contains the neighbor balanced complete block designs in $\Omega_{v,v,v}$, and which contains the E-optimal design. Let $\Delta_{v,v,v}$ be the set of all $d \in \Omega_{v,v,v}$ such that

d is equireplicate, (10)

d is neighbor balanced, (11)

no treatment appears at both end plots of the same block. (12)

Remember that (10) and (11) imply that every treatment appears at exactly two end plots. It was shown by Azzalini and Giovagnoli (1987) that (10) and (11) are necessary and sufficient for optimality in a simpler model without block effects. The designs in Table 1 are all in $\Delta_{4,4,4}$.

<u>THEOREM 2</u> Assume $b = k = v \ge 4$. If $0 \le \lambda < 1$ and if a design $d \in \Omega_{v,v,v}$ is E-optimal over $\Omega_{v,v,v}$, then $d \in \Delta_{v,v,v}$.

<u>Proof:</u> We know that there is a neighbor balanced complete block design d^* in $\Delta_{v,v,v}$ and $\mu_{d^*v-1} \ge \xi$. We now show that for every $d \in \Omega_{v,v,v}$ which is not in $\Delta_{v,v,v}$ we have $\mu_{d,v-1} < \xi$.

(i) Assume there is a treatment i such that $r_{di} \le v-1$. It was shown in case 1 of Theorem 3 of Kunert (1985) that then

$$x_{dii} \le [(v-1)\{-1+\lambda+\lambda^2(1-\lambda)\} - e_{di}\{2\lambda+(v-3)(\lambda^2-\lambda^3)\}]/\{v-(v-2)\lambda\} .$$

It can easily be seen that consequently

$$x_{dii} \leq (v-1)(\lambda^2-1)(1-\lambda)/\{v-(v-2)\lambda\} < 0$$

for all $\lambda < 1$, and not only for $\lambda \leq 4/5$ as stated in Kunert (1985).

(ii) Case 2 of Theorem 3 of Kunert (1985) solved the situation that $e_{di} \geq 3$ for an i.

(iii) Assume there is a treatment i and another treatment j such that $m_{dij} \leq 1$. Then

$$c_{dii} + c_{djj} - 2c_{dij} \leq 2v(1+\lambda^2) - 4\lambda^2 + 2\lambda .$$

Since $v(1+\lambda^2) - 2\lambda^2 + 2\lambda = \xi + 4\lambda^2(1-\lambda)/\{v-(v-2)\lambda\}$, we get that

$$\mu_{dt-1} \leq \xi + 4\lambda^2(1-\lambda)/\{v-(v-2)\lambda\} - \lambda < \xi .$$

(iv) Assume there is a block u such that treatment i appears at both ends of this block. It follows that

$$c_{dii} \leq r_{di}(1+\lambda^2) - 2\lambda^2 - \frac{1-\lambda}{v-(v-2)\lambda}\{(r_{di}-2)(1-\lambda)^2+4\} .$$

Since $r_{di} = v$ we have

$$\{v-(v-2)\lambda\}\, x_{dii} \leq 2(1-\lambda)\lambda^2 - 2(1-\lambda) < 0 .$$

This completes the proof.

If we exclude non-binary designs from the competition then Theorem 2 implies that the E-optimal design must be a neighbor balanced complete block design. For all neighbor balanced complete block designs d we have that $X_{d\xi}\{v-(v-2)\lambda\}/(\lambda^2-\lambda^3)$ is the information matrix of the end design of d in the block model with uncorrelated errors, see Kunert (1985). The end design of such a d is equireplicate and has v blocks of size 2. It is well-known that there is essentially only one connected block design in $\Omega_{v,v,2}$ and this design has second-smallest eigenvalue $2-2\cos(2\pi/v)$. This implies that for every complete block design $d \in \Omega_{v,v,v}$ we have

$$\mu_{dv1} \leq \xi + 2(\lambda^2-\lambda^3)\ \{1-\cos(2\pi/v)\}/\{v-(v-2)\lambda\}$$

and the bound is attained if the complete block design d* has neighbor balance and the end design of d* is connected. Such designs exist for all odd v, see Kunert (1985).

I have so far neither been able to show that these d* perform better than all nonbinary $d \in \Omega_{v,v,v}$ for all positive $\lambda < 1$, nor have I been able to find examples of nonbinary designs which actually perform better or equally well.

There is one exception. If v = 4 then the design g in Table 1 is a complete block design with neighbor balance and connected end design, and

$$\mu_{gv-1} = \xi + 2\{1-\cos(2\pi/v)\}(\lambda^2-\lambda^3)/\{v-(v-2)\lambda\}$$
$$= \xi + 2(\lambda^2-\lambda^3)/\{v-(v-2)\lambda\} .$$

Now take an arbitrary design $d \in \Omega_{4,4,4}$. It can only perform as well as g if $d \in \Lambda_{4,4,4}$. Then there are two treatments i and j which do not appear together at the opposite end plots of any block. It follows that

$$c_{dii} + c_{djj} - 2c_{dij} = 2v(1+\lambda^2)-4\lambda^2+4\lambda - \frac{1-\lambda}{v-(v-2)\lambda} \sum_{u=1}^{b} \{(n_{diu}-n_{dju})(1-\lambda) + (e_{diu} - e_{dju})\lambda\}^2 .$$

The fact that $k = 4$ and that no treatment appears adjacent to itself for all $d \in \Lambda_{v,v,v}$ implies that no treatment appears twice in a block unless it appears at an end plot. This implies that

$$c_{dii} + c_{djj} - 2c_{dij} \leq 2v(1+\lambda^2) - 4\lambda^2 + 4\lambda - \frac{1-\lambda}{v-(v-2)\lambda} 4\lambda^2 ,$$

since there are four blocks where either i or j appear at an end plot. Consequently,

$$\mu_{dv-1} \leq \xi + 2(\lambda^2-\lambda^3)/\{v-(v-2)\lambda\} = \mu_{gv-1} .$$

We thus have shown that g is E-optimal over $\Omega_{4,4,4}$. Note that the arguments in the proof do not hold for $v > 4$. However, Theorem 2 of Kunert (1987) shows that for $v \geq 5$ every complete block design with neighbor balance for every $0 < \lambda < 1$ and every φ_p-criterion has an efficiency of more than 99 %.

3. THE CASE V < K

Define $W_\lambda = S_\lambda^{-1} - (1_k' S_\lambda^{-1} 1_k)^{-1} S_\lambda^{-1} 1_k 1_k' S_\lambda^{-1}$. We get $\mathcal{C}_d = \sum_{u=1}^{b} T_{du}' W_\lambda T_{du}$. Let us consider one single block u. Then the i-th diagonal element of $T_{du}' W_\lambda T_{du}$ equals

$$n_{diu}(1+\lambda^2) - e_{diu}\lambda^2 - \frac{1-\lambda}{v-(v-2)\lambda} \{n_{diu}(1-\lambda) + e_{diu}\lambda\}^2 .$$

Restricting attention to the case $\lambda > 0$ we realize that, for fixed n_{diu} and e_{di}, then c_{dii} is maximal if treatment i appears only at end plots of such units where n_{diu} is small.

As an example consider the case $k = v + 1$. Then

$$\mathrm{tr}\mathcal{C}_d = b(v+1)(1+\lambda^2) - 2b\lambda^2 - \frac{1-\lambda}{v+1-(v-1)\lambda} \sum \sum \{n_{diu}(1-\lambda) + e_{diu}\lambda\}^2 .$$

Since $\sum\sum \{n_{diu}(1-\lambda) + e_{diu}\lambda\} = b(v+1)(1-\lambda) + 2b\lambda$, an upper bound for the trace is attained if $n_{diu} = 1 + 1/v$ and $e_{diu} = 2/v$ for all i and u. This clearly is impossible. The maximum attainable trace is reached if $n_{diu} \in \{1,2\}$ and $e_{diu} \in \{0,1\}$, e_{diu} being 1 only if $n_{diu} = 1$. The design f in Table 2 thus has maximal trace for $\lambda > 0$. Calculating c_{fij} with formula (5) we can see that f is φ_p-optimal over $\Omega_{4,12,5}$ for every $p \geq 0$.

TABLE 2 A design for k = v + 1

	1 1 1	2 3 4	3 4 2	4 2 3
	4 2 3	4 2 3	4 2 3	1 1 1
f =	2 3 4	1 1 1	2 3 4	2 3 4
	4 2 3	4 2 3	4 2 3	1 1 1
	3 4 2	3 4 2	1 1 1	3 4 2

If k is becoming larger the situation gets more difficult. Note that $T'_{du}W_\lambda T_{du}$ is the information matrix of a design consisting of a single block. Kunert and Martin (1987) show that for $\lambda > 1/2$, $trT'_{du}W_\lambda T_{du}$ is not maximal if every treatment appears equally often in block u. As an example consider the case v = 4 and k = 8. For b = 12 compare the two designs f and $g \in \Omega_{4,12,8}$ in Table 3. For small λ f performs universally better than g. Note that f is neighbor balanced and is a balanced block design. However, for $\lambda > 1/2$ the design g becomes better. The design g also is neighbor balanced but it is not a balanced block design. Note by comparing the traces that the gain in efficiency is not high. It seems logical therefore to restrict the competing designs to be balanced block designs.

TABLE 3 Two designs for k = 2v

	4 1 2 3	4 3 1 2	4 2 3 1		4 1 2 3	4 3 1 2	4 2 3 1
	1 2 3 4	3 1 2 4	2 3 1 4		1 2 3 4	3 1 2 4	2 3 1 4
	3 4 1 2	2 4 3 1	1 4 2 3		3 4 1 2	2 4 3 1	1 4 2 3
f =	2 3 4 1	1 2 4 3	3 1 4 2	g =	1 2 3 4	1 2 3 4	2 3 1 4
	4 1 2 3	4 3 1 2	4 2 3 1		3 4 1 2	2 4 3 1	1 4 2 3
	1 2 3 4	3 1 2 4	2 3 1 4		1 2 3 4	3 1 2 4	2 3 1 4
	3 4 1 2	2 4 3 1	1 4 2 3		3 4 1 2	2 4 3 1	1 4 2 3
	2 3 4 1	1 2 4 3	3 1 4 2		2 3 4 1	1 2 4 3	3 1 4 2

$$tr\mathscr{C}_f = 96\ (1 + \lambda^2) - 24\lambda^2 - \frac{4(1-\lambda)}{8-6\lambda}\{48 - 72\lambda + 30\lambda^2\}$$

$$tr\mathscr{C}_g = 96\ (1 + \lambda^2) - 24\lambda^2 - \frac{4(1-\lambda)}{8-6\lambda}\{60 - 108\lambda + 54\lambda^2\}$$

REFERENCES

Azzalini, A., and Giovagnoli, A. (1987). Some optimal designs for repeated measurements in the case of autoregressive errors. Biometrika, to appear.

Gill, P.S., and Shukla, G.K. (1985). Efficiency of nearest neighbor balanced block designs for correlated observations. Biometrika, 72: 539-544.

Kiefer, J., and Wynn, H.P. (1981). Optimum balanced block and Latin square designs for correlated observations. Ann. Statist., 9: 737-757.

Kunert, J. (1985). Optimal repeated measurements designs for correlated observations and analysis by weighted least squares. Biometrika, 72: 375-389.

Kunert, J. (1987). Neighbor balanced block designs for correlated observations. Biometrika, to appear.

Kunert, J., and Martin, R.J. (1987). Some results on optimal design under a first order autoregression and on finite Williams type II designs. Comm. Statist.-Theory and Methods, to appear.

CHARACTERIZATIONS AND EXAMPLES OF OPTIMAL EXPERIMENTS WITH QUALITATIVE AND QUANTITATIVE FACTORS

Viktor G. Kurotschka

1. CONDITIONAL REPRESENTATION OF EXPERIMENTS WITH QUALITATIVE AND QUANTITATIVE FACTORS

1.1 Conditioning and linearization of the model equations

We will denote by X the experimental region, i.e. the set of all experimental condition x under which an experiment can be alternatively performed. The experimental region of an experiment which is influenced by, say K_1 qualitative factors each being able to operate at, say I_k levels $(k = 1,\dots,K_1)$ can be represented by

$$X = X_1 := \times_{k=1}^{K_1} \{1,\dots,I_k\} \tag{1}$$

and a single experimental condition by

$$x_1 = (i_1,\dots,i_{K_1}) \quad , \quad i_k \in \{1,\dots,I_k\} \quad , \quad k = 1,\dots,K_1 \quad .$$

The experimental region of an experiment with K_2 quantitative factors of influence may be described by some convex set

$$X = X_2 \subset \mathbb{R}_{K_2} \quad \text{with some non empty } \times_{k=1}^{K_2} (a,b) \subset X_2 \quad . \tag{2}$$

The experiments considered in this paper are those with K_1 qualitative and K_2 quantitative factors and can be defined by having

$$X = X_1 \times X_2 = \times_{k=1}^{K_1} \{1,\dots,I_k\} \times X_2 \tag{3}$$

as their experimental region.

The true response of the experiment to the experimental condition

$$\eta: X \ni x \to \eta(x) \in \mathbb{R}$$

is usually modeled as a location parameter (expected value in the parametric and shift parameter in the nonparametric set up) of the observation $Y(x)$ which is asssumed to be a random variable.

Defining the error of the observation by

$$e(x) := Y(x) - \eta(x)$$

one obtains the following observation equations

$$Y(x) = \eta(x) + e(x) \quad , \quad x \in X \tag{4}$$

Restricting oneself to experiments with only finite many observations, say N , an experimental design can be described by

$$d = \begin{pmatrix} x_{(1)} & x_{(2)} & \ldots x_{(I)} \\ N(x_{(1)}) & N(x_{(2)}) & \ldots N(x_{(N)}) \end{pmatrix} \quad \begin{matrix} x_{(i)} \in X \ , \ i = 1,\ldots,I \\ \Sigma_{i=1}^{I} N(x_{(i)}) = N \end{matrix} \tag{5}$$

indicating that $N(x_{(i)})$ observations should be performed at experimental condition $x_{(i)}$, $i = 1,\ldots,I$.

If $X = X_1 = \times_{k=1}^{K_1}\{1,\ldots,I_k\}$, i.e. if X is in particular finite, then all experimental conditions $x_1 \in X_1$ can be listed in a design admitting $N(x_1)$ being zero for some $x_1 \in X_1$ getting the following representation (see also appendix):

$$d = N_{12\ldots K_1} := (N(i_1,\ldots,i_{K_1}); \begin{matrix} i_k=1,\ldots,I_k \\ k=1,\ldots,K_1 \end{matrix}) = (N(x_1); x_1 \in X_1) \tag{6}$$

where

$$N(x_1) = N(i_1,\ldots,i_K) \in \{0,1,\ldots,N\} \ , \ \Sigma_{x_1 \in X_1} N(x_1) = N$$

has the same meaning as before. The corresponding observation model (model of the experiment) in vector form

$$Y_d = \eta_d + \varepsilon_d$$

with components

$$Y_n(x_{(i)}) = \eta(x_{(i)}) + \varepsilon_n(x_{(i)}) \qquad \begin{matrix} n = 1,\ldots,N(x_{(i)}) \\ i = 1,\ldots,I \end{matrix}$$

will be considered under standard conditions, i.e. for each design d

$$X_d \text{ has a distribution } P^{X_d} \in \{P_{d,\theta};\theta \in \Theta\}$$

under which all single observations are (stochastically) independent and of equal precision, i.e.

$$\mathrm{Var}_\theta X_n(x_{(i)}) = \sigma^2(\theta) \quad , \quad \theta \in \Theta \ .$$

We further will only consider response functions η with a finite linear parametrization

$$\beta: \Theta \ni \theta \to (\beta_1(\theta),\ldots,\beta_r(\theta)) \in \mathbb{R}_r \quad ,$$

i.e. for which there exist a: $X \ni x \to a(x) \in \mathbb{R}_r$ so that for all $x \in X$ and all $\theta \in \Theta$

$$\eta(x) = \eta(x,\theta) = \Sigma_{\rho=1}^{r} a_\rho(x)\beta_\rho(\theta) = a^T(x)\beta(\theta)$$

If $X = X_1$ as in (1) then every response function η has a finite linear parametrization (see also appendix), the corresponding linear models are known as ANOVA experiments.
If $X = X_2$ as in (2) then finite linear parametrizations are motivated to some part by theoretical a priori knowledge about the experiment taking in consideration also some suitable transformation of the observation, to some part because the response function is a regression of a normal distributed variable on a normal distributed random vector and to another part that the linear parametrization comes from a formal approximation of the unknown response function by some system of (known) functions $a_1,\ldots,a_r$ on X_2 (Chebychev systems, systems of splines) with $\beta = (\beta_1,\ldots,\beta_r)$ representing the (unknown) expansion coefficients. The corresponding linear models for $X = X_2$ are often called general regression experiments.
If $X = X_1 \times X_2$ as in (3) a finite linear parametrization can be motivated by the following almost natural conditioning of the observation equations (4):

For each $x_1 \in X_1$ let

$$Y_{x_1}(x_2) := Y(x_1,x_2) \ , \ \eta_{x_1}(x_2) := \eta(x_1,x_2) \ , \ \varepsilon_{x_1}(x_2) := \varepsilon(x_1,x_2) \ ,$$

then for each $x_1 \in X_1$

$$Y_{x_1}(x_2) = \eta_{x_1}(x_2) + \varepsilon_{x_1}(x_2) \quad , \quad x_2 \in X_2$$

are experimental equations defined on X_2 so that for each of these conditional response functions η_{x_1}, $x_1 \in X_1$ a finite linear parametrization can be motivated as in the case $X = X_2$:

$$\eta_{X_1}(x_2) = a^T_{X_1}(x_2)\beta_{x_1} \quad , \quad x_2 \in X_2$$

with

$$\beta_{X_1} = (\beta_{x_1 1},\dots,\beta_{x_1 r(x_1)})^T$$

$$a_{X_1} = (a_{x_1 1},\dots,a_{x_1 r(x_1)})^T$$

By suitable arrangements and aggregation of the so defined partial regression model equations indexed by $x_1 \in X_1$

$$Y_{X_1}(x_2) = a^T_{X_1}(x_2)\beta_{X_1} + \varepsilon_{X_1}(x_2) \quad , \quad x_2 \in X_2 \tag{7}$$

on may obtain the linear model equations on the complete set $X = X_1 \times X_2$:

$$Y(x) = a^T(x)\beta + e(x) \;,\; x = (x_1,x_2) \in X_1 \times X_2 = X \quad ,$$

where of course the form of a and β highly depends on the kind of interaction which might exist between the qualitative and the quantitative factors.

The two extreme but also the two most important classes of models classified by interaction of the two kind of factors are treated in section 2 respectively in section 3.

1.2 Conditional representations of designs

The conditioning of the model equations almost naturally suggests also a conditioning of a design on $X = X_1 \times X_2$, namely the following representation:

$$d = (N_{12\dots K_1}, d(N_{12\dots K_1})) \tag{8}$$

where $N_{12\dots K_1} = (N(x_1), x_1 \in X_1)$ is defined as in (6) and assigns the number $N(x_1)$ of observations to each individual regression model (7) indexed by $x_1 \in X_1$.

$$d(N_{12\dots K_1}) := (d(x_1); x_1 \in X_1)$$

represents the system of the designs $d(x_1)$ for the individual regression models (7) indexed by $x_1 \in X_1$, namely

$$d(x_1) = ((t_{1n}(x_1),\dots,t_{K_2 n}(x_1)) \in X_2 \;;\; n = 1,\dots,N(x_1))$$

where obviously t_{kn} represents the level of the k'th factor present at the n'th replication of $x_1 \in X_1$.

This conditional representation of exact designs together with the conditioning of the model I have suggested to Dr. J. Köster, to Dr. J. Lopez-Troya and to Dr. W. Wierich who succeded to characterize optimal exact designs for some first basic models (see Köster (1976), Lopez-Troya (1982a) and (1982b), Kurotschka and Wierich (1984), Wierich (1984) and (1985)).

A more general approach introducing conditional generalized designs has been presented in Kurotschka (1981). The present paper deals with this more general approach taking into account more recent contributions in particular those of Dr. Wierich which will be explicitely cited.

In terms of generalized designs ξ defined as probability measures on $\mathcal{P}(X_1) \otimes (X_2 \cap \mathcal{B}_{K_2})$ the representation (8) corresponds to conditioning probability measures on product spaces (desintegration of measures):

$$\xi = \xi_1 \otimes \xi_{2|1} \tag{9}$$

where

$$\xi_1 = \nu = \Sigma_{x_1 \in X_1} \nu(\{x_1\}) \varepsilon_{x_1}$$

is a probability measure (a generalized design) on $(X_1, \mathcal{P}(X_1))$ assigning $N \cdot \nu(\{x_1\}) = N(x_1)$ observations to $x_1 \in X_1$ and generalizing $N_{12...K_1}$ and

$$\xi_{2|1} = \delta$$

is a Markov kernel from $(X_1, \mathcal{P}(X_1))$ to $(X_2, X_2 \cap \mathcal{B}_{K_2})$ representing for each $x_1 \in X_1$ a generalized design $\xi_{2|1}(x_1) = \delta(x_1)$ of the individual regression model indexed by $x_1 \in X$ assigning how the $N(x_1)$ observation should be distributed on X_2 and so generalizing $d(x_1)$.

With this conditional representation of ξ the information matrix for $\beta = (\beta_1, \beta_2)^T$ has the following form:

$$I_\beta(\xi) := \int a(x) a^T(x) \xi(dx) \tag{10}$$

$$= \Sigma_{x_1 \in X_1} \nu(\{x_1\}) \int_{X_2} a(x_1, x_2) a^T(x_1, x_2) \delta(dx_2, x_1)$$

which for different models, i.e. for differently aggregated a and ß simplifies the design problem substantially.

2. EXPERIMENTS WITH QUALITATIVE AND QUANTITATIVE FACTORS INTERACTING

2.1 General Intra Class Experiments

The extreme case of completely interacting factors can be described by the following definition:

Definition

An experiment with K_1 qualitative and K_2 quantitative factors will be called an experiment with completely interacting factors when the number of unknown, parameters of the finite linear parametrization of its response function

$$\eta: X_1 \times X_2 \ni (x_1,x_2) = \eta(x_1,x_2) = \Sigma_{\rho=1}^{r(x_1)} a_{x_1\rho}(x_2)\beta_{x_1\rho} \in \mathbb{R} \qquad (11)$$

precisely $r = \Sigma_{x_1 \in X_1} r(x_1)$, i.e. if $\beta_{x_1} = (\beta_{x_1 1},\ldots,\beta_{x_1\rho(x_1)})$ depends on $x_1 \in X_1$.

The statistical analysis of two simple examples of such experiments have been discussed in Searle (1979) and referred to as intra class regression experiments.

D- and A-optimum integer valued designs for such basic models had been characterized in Kurotschka and Wierich (1984)).

Here we follow the more general approach of Kurotschka (1981) which not only gives ready to apply solutions to the main design problems accociated with such experiment but also throughs some light on some specific difference betwenn A- and D-optimality criterion for a design.

According to the definition (2.1) the response function η of such an experiment with completely interacting factors which from now on will be called a general intra class regression experiment has the following aggregated finite linear parametrization:

$$\eta: X_1 \times X_2 \ni (x_1,x_2) \rightarrow \eta(x_1,x_2) = a^T(x_1,x_2)\beta \in \mathbb{R}$$

with

$$a = (1_{\{x_1\}}a_{x_1};x_1 \in X_1)^T \text{ and } \beta = (\beta_{x_1};x_1 \in X_1)^T$$

where $1_{\{x_1\}}$ is an indicator function on X_2 assiging a_{x_1} as regression vector to the response function when the level combination x_1 of the qualitative factors is present.

This aggregated form of the finite linear parametrization of η shows immidiately that

$$I_\beta(\xi) = I_\beta(\xi_1 \otimes \xi_{2|1}) = I(\nu \otimes \delta) =$$
$$= \mathrm{diag}(\nu(\{x_1\})I_{\beta_{x_1}}(\delta(x_1));\ x_1 \in X_1)$$

where

$$I_{\beta_{x_1}}(\delta(x_1)) = \int_{X_2} a_{x_1}(x_2) a_{x_2}^T(x_2)\,\delta(dx_2,x_1)$$

is the information matrix of the design $\delta(x_1)$ of the individual regression model indexed by $x_1 \in X_1$ for the parameter vector β_{x_1}.

The problem of finding D- and A-optimum designs ξ for β can know be solved conditionally by determining ν and δ: The maximization of

$$\det I_\beta(\xi) = \det I_\beta(\nu \otimes \delta) = \Pi_{x_1 \in X_1} \nu(\{x_1\})^{r(x_1)} \det I_{\beta_{x_1}}(\delta(x_1)) \qquad (12)$$

and the minimization of

$$\text{trace } I_\beta^{-1}(\xi) = \text{trace } I_\beta^{-1}(\nu \otimes \delta) = \Sigma_{x_1 \in X_1} (\text{trace } I_{\beta_{x_1}}^{-1}(\delta(x_1))/\nu(\{x_1\})$$

with respect to ν and δ has been solved in Kurotschka (1981) with the following results:

$\xi_D = \nu_D \otimes \delta_D$ is D-optimum for the whole parameter vector β in the class of all generalized designs iff for each $x_1 \in X_1$

1) $\delta_D(x_1)$ is a D-optimum design of the individual regression experiment indexed by $x_1 \in X_1$ for the parameter vector β_{x_1}.

2) $\nu_D(x_1) = r(x_1)/\Sigma_{x_1 \in X_1} r(x_1)$, where $r_1(x_1)$ is as before the number of components of β_{x_1}.

$\xi_A = \nu_A \otimes \delta_A$ is A-optimum for the whole parameter vector β in the class of all generalized designs iff for each $x_1 \in X_1$:

1) $\delta_A(x_1)$ is an A-optimum design of the individual regression experiment indexed by $x_1 \in X_1$ for the parameter vector β_{x_1}.

2) $\nu_A(x_1) = \sqrt{\text{trace } I_{\beta_{x_1}}^{-1}(\delta_A(x_1))} / \Sigma_{x_1' \in X_1} \sqrt{\text{trace } I_{\beta_{x_1'}}^{-1}(\delta_A(x_1'))}$

Besides the fact that these results for general intra class experiments reduce the design problems to pure regression type experiments (so that catalogues of existing literature on regression experiments can be used to provide examples) they also show how different the D- and the A-criterion judge the difficulty of a statistical analysis of a regression experiment, namely the D-criterion by the number of unknown parameters the A-criterion by the square root of the minimal achievable sum of variances of the Gauss Markov estimators for the unknown parameters.

Note that if one is only interested in a subset $\{\beta_{x_1}, x_1 \in X_1^0 \subset X_1\}$ of the parameters than the corresponding D- and A-optimal designs can be obtained by the above characterization of ξ_D respectively ξ_A replacing every X_1 by X_1^0 in the above characterization, because for $\beta^0 := (\beta_{x_1}; x_1 \in X_1^0)$ one obtains $\det I_{\beta^0}(\xi)$ and trace $I_{\beta^0}^{-1}(\xi)$ from (11) by substituting X_1^0 for X_1.

2.2 Experiments with partially interacting factors

Although the class of all intra class experiments is rather large and highly relevant for practical purposes (one has only to think of processes modeled by the individual regression setups indexed by $x_1 \in X_1$ indicating that they are highly depending on a combination x_1 of qualitative factors influencing the performance of the considered processes) it may quickly be left in particular if one statistically analyses such experiments discovering that not all components of β_{x_1} depend on x_1 so that for further investigations optimal designs are necessary which take into account that the factors are not completely interacting.

The case when qualitative and quantitative factors do not interact at all and which will be referred to as general analysis of covariance models will be treated in the next section in more detail. The case of partial interaction will here be only indicated by examples which I recently suggested for investigation:

Let $X_1 = \{1,\dots,I\}$, i.e. consider one quantitative factor with I different levels and let $X_2 = [-1,+1]$ a standard region for one qualitative factor and consider experiments with response function $(x_1 = i, x_2 = t)$

$$\eta_1(i,t) = \beta_{i1} + \beta_2 t + \beta_3 t^2$$

$$\eta_2(i,t) = \beta_{i1} + \beta_{i2} t + \beta_3 t^2$$

$$\eta_3(i,t) = \beta_{i1} + \beta_2 t + \beta_{i3} t^2$$

$$\eta_4(i,t) = \beta_{i1} + \beta_{i2} t + \beta_{i3} t^2$$

where η_2, η_3 define the intermediate models between the analysis of covariance type experiment with $\eta = \eta_1$ and the intra class regression experiment with $\eta = \eta_4$. (Further interesting models one gets for $\beta_{i1} = \beta_1$) .

Note that also the following practically highly relevant model is not an intra class regression with

$$\eta(i_1,i_2,t) = \beta_0 + \beta^{(1)}_{i_1} + \beta^{(2)}_{i_2} + \beta^{(1,2)}_{i_1 i_2 1} t + \dots + \beta^{(1,2)}_{i_1 i_2 r} t^r \quad .$$

Here the interaction between the two qualitative factors is described being dependent on the level t of some quantitative factor.

3. GENERAL ANOCA EXPERIMENTS

3.1 Analysis of the design problem and first optimality results

Traditionally one would say (in analogy to the notion in ANOVA) that the qualitative and quantitative factors do not interact with each other iff the response function η splits into two additive parts, one representing the effects of the qualitative the other those of the quantitative factors:

$$\eta: X_1 \times X_2 \ni (x_1,x_2) \rightarrow \eta(x_1,x_2) = \eta_1(x_1) + \eta_2(x_2) \in \mathbb{R}$$

In terms of the conditional representation and linearization of the model equation this can be expressed by the following conditions on

$$\eta(x_1,x_2) = a^T_{x_1}(x_2)\beta_{x_1} = \Sigma^{r(x_1)}_{\rho=1} a_{x_1\rho}(x_2)\beta_{x_1\rho} \quad ,$$

namely

$$a_{x_1 1} = 1$$

and

$$a_{x_1 2},\ldots,a_{x_1 r(x_1)} \text{ and } \beta_{x_1 2},\ldots,\beta_{x_1 r(x_1)} \text{ are independent of } x_1 \in X_1$$

so that

$$\eta(x_1,x_2) = \beta_{x_1,1} + \Sigma^{r}_{\rho=2} a_\rho(x_2)\beta_\rho = \eta_1(x_1) + \eta_2(x_2) \quad .$$

By the following renumbering

$$a_{2\rho} := a_{\rho-1} \;,\; \beta_{2\rho} := \beta_{\rho-1} \quad \text{and} \quad r_2 := r-1$$

and by taking into account that any $\eta_1(x_1) := \beta_{x_1 1}$ on X_1 has a finite (suitable, see appendix) linear parametrization, say $\beta_1 = (\beta_{11},\ldots,\beta_{1r_1})^T$ one obtains:

$$\eta(x_1,x_2) = \Sigma^{r_1}_{\rho=1} a_{1\rho}(x_1)\beta_{1\rho} + \Sigma^{r_2}_{\rho=1} a_{2\rho}(x_2)\beta_{2\rho} = a^T_1(x_1)\beta_1 + a^T_2(x_2)\beta_2 \qquad (13)$$

note that the representation $\eta = \eta_1 + \eta_2$ here is unique by the requirement that 1 and $a_{21},\ldots,a_{2r_2}$ are linearly independent on X_2 which follows iff one restricts oneself to "*relatively minimal linear parametrizations*" of the conditional model equations, that is to linearly independent systems of functions $a_{x_1 1},\ldots,a_{x_1 r}$.

This and the restriction to non degenerate designs has been made throughout the whole made paper without loss of too much generality but hopefully with sufficient win in basic understanding (although I am aware that generalized inverses have sometimes an unresistable attraction).

The conditional representation of a generalized (but also an integer valued concrete) design $\xi = \xi_1 \otimes \xi_{2|1}$ allows now the following representations of the relevant information matrices:

$$I_\beta(\xi) = I_{\begin{pmatrix}\beta_1\\ \beta_2\end{pmatrix}}(\xi_1 \otimes \xi_{2|1})$$

$$= \Sigma_{x_1 \in X_1} \int_{X_2} \begin{pmatrix} a_1(x_1) \\ a_2(x_2) \end{pmatrix} (a_1^T(x_1), a_2^T(x_2))\, \xi_{2|1}(dx_2, x_1)\, \nu(\{x_1\}) \tag{14}$$

$$= \begin{pmatrix} I_{\beta_1}(\xi_1) & I_{12}(\xi) \\ I_{12}^T(\xi) & I_{\beta_2}(\xi_2) \end{pmatrix}$$

where

$$I_{\beta_1}(\xi_1) = \int_{X_1} a_1 a_1^T d\xi_1 = \Sigma_{x_1 \in X_1} a_1(x_1) a_1^T(x_1)\, \nu(\{x_1\})$$

is the information matrix for β_1 of the design $\xi_1 = \nu$ (the marginal of ξ on X_1) of the ANOVA experiment with response function $\eta(x_1) = a_1^T(x_1)\beta_1$,

$$I_{\beta_2}(\xi_2) = \int_{X_2} a_2 a_2^T d\xi_2$$

is the information matrix for β_2 of the design $\xi_2 = \Sigma_{x_1 \in X_1} \xi_{2|1}(x_1)\, \nu(\{x_1\})$ (the marginal of ξ on X_2) of the regression experiment with response function $\eta(x_2) = a_2^T(x_2)\beta_2$ and

$$I_{12}(\xi) = \int_X a_1(x_1) a_2^T(x_2)\, \xi(d(x_1, x_2))$$

$$= \Sigma_{x_1 \in X_1} a_1(x_1) \int_{X_2} a_2^T(x_2)\, \xi_{2|1}(dx_2, x_1)\, \nu(\{x_1\}) \quad . \tag{15}$$

And from here one sees that

$$I_{\beta_1}(\xi) = I_{\beta_1}(\xi_1) - I_{12}(\xi) I_{\beta_2}^{-1}(\xi_2) I_{12}^T(\xi)$$

$$I_{\beta_2}(\xi) = I_{\beta_2}(\xi_2) - I_{12}^T(\xi) I_{\beta_1}^{-1}(\xi_1) I_{12}(\xi) \qquad \text{and} \tag{16}$$

$$\det I_\beta(\xi) = \det I_{\beta_1}(\xi_1) \det(I_{\beta_2}(\xi_2) - I_{12}^T(\xi) I_{\beta_1}^{-1}(\xi_1) I_{12}(\xi))$$

$$= \det I_{\beta_1}(\xi_1) \cdot \det I_{\beta_2}(\xi) = \det I_{\beta_1}(\xi) \cdot \det I_{\beta_2}(\xi_2)$$

$$\det I_{\beta_1}(\xi) = \det(I_{\beta_1}(\xi_1) - I_{12}(\xi) I_{\beta_2}^{-1}(\xi_2) I_{12}^T(\xi)) = \frac{\det I_\beta(\xi)}{\det I_{\beta_2}(\xi_2)}$$

$$\det I_{\beta_2}(\xi) = \det(I_{\beta_2}(\xi_2) - I_{12}^T(\xi) I_{\beta_1}^{-1}(\xi_1) I_{12}^T(\xi)) = \frac{\det I_\beta(\xi)}{\det I_{\beta_1}(\xi_1)}$$

and

$$\operatorname{trace} I_\beta^{-1}(\xi) = \operatorname{trace} I_{\beta_1}^{-1}(\xi) + \operatorname{trace} I_{\beta_2}^{-1}(\xi) \quad .$$

Because for any design ξ^* with

$$\int_{X_2} a_2 d\xi^*_{2|1} = 0$$

it follows that

$$I_\beta(\xi^*) = I_\beta(\xi_1^* \otimes \xi_2^*) \quad , \tag{17}$$

i.e. the design ξ^* has the same information matrix as the product of its marginals and

$$I_{\beta_i}(\xi^*) = I_{\beta_i}(\xi_i^*) \quad , \quad i = 1,2,... \tag{18}$$

i.e. the design ξ^* has the same information matrix for the parameter vectors β_1 and β_2 as its corresponding marginals ξ_1^* respectively ξ_2^* one obtains immediatly the following theoretically rather trivial but practically very useful characterization of optimum design (which has been used in Kurotschka (1981) to construct example, but not explicitly formulated because of its obvious validity):

Theorem

If a design ξ_2^* of the regression experiment with response function $\eta_2 = a_2^T \beta_2$ has the property

$$\int_{X_2} a_2(x_2)\xi_2^*(dx_2) = 0 \quad (\Leftrightarrow: \text{"Symmetry of } \xi_2^* \text{ w.r.t. } a_2\text{"})$$

then (the following three statements follow from (18)):

(1) Iff a design ξ_1^* of some ANOVA experiments with response function $\eta_1 = a_1^T \beta_1$ is Φ-optimal within some class Δ_1 of designs for some vector ψ_1 of linear independent functionals of β_1 then the product $\xi^* = \xi_1^* \otimes \xi_2^*$ is a Φ-optimum design of the ANOCA experiment characterized by the response function $\eta = a_1^T \beta_1 + a_2^T \beta_2$ for ψ_1 in the class of all designs ξ of the ANOCA experiment for which the marginal $\xi_1 \in \Delta_1$.

(ii) Iff ξ_2^* is in addition Φ optimal for some vector ψ_2 of linear independent functionals of β_2 in some class Δ_2 of designs of the above regression experiment then for any design ξ_1 of the ANOVA experiment the product $\xi^* = \xi_1 \otimes \xi_2^*$ is a Φ-optimum design of the corresponding ANOCA model in the class of all designs ξ of the ANOCA experiment for which the marginal $\xi_2 \in \Delta_2$.

(iii) The product design $\xi^* = \xi_1^* \otimes \xi_2^*$ is Φ-optimal for $\psi = (\psi_1, \psi_2)^T$ in the class of all designs ξ of the ANOCA experiment for which the marginals $\xi_1 \in \Delta_1$ and $\xi_2 \in \Delta_2$ iff ξ_1^* and ξ_2^* fullfill above condition (i), respectively (ii

Note

1) In the above statements $\emptyset$-optimal stands for any optimality criteria based on (the inverse of) the information matrix of a design.

2) I am aware that classically the name ANOCA (Analysis of Covariance) is referred to experiments where response functions η_2 are constituted by concomitant variables.

Nevertheless the use of this name for the more general experiments as regarded here is equally justified by the same formal arguments as in classical literature.

3) The above statements hold for generalized as well as for concrete design

4) The validity of the theorem is due to (18) and is obviously not entailed by the design ξ^* being a product design, i.e. (17). The role of product designs will be discussed in the next section.

Applications of the theorem (Examples)

1) If a_2 is the vector of one dimensional projections on X_2 and X_2 is sufficiently symmetric around 0 , such as a sphere, a cube, a simplex centred in zero then D- and A-optimum designs for β_2 are known which are symmetric w.r.t. a_2 (see multidimensional linear regression in Fedorov (1972) , note that the example in Kurotschka (1981) is of this type).

2) More generally a series of "higher order factorial regression" experiments with regression function $a_{2\rho}(x_2) = x_{21}^{p_1} \cdot \ldots \cdot x_{2K_2}^{p_{K_2}}$ of odd powers $p_1 + \ldots + p_K$ constitute a large class of examples where in particular D-optimal designs which are symmetric w.r.t. a_2 exist.

3) The system a_2 of trigonometric functions constitute popular models where the equidistant and equiweighted designs are D- and A-optimum and symmetric w.r.t. a_2 and therefore define classes of ANOCA models as examples for the above theorem.

3.2 The role of product design and further optimality results

To analyse the optimality of product designs, i.e. designs ξ for which $\xi_{2|1}$ is independent of $x_1 \in X_1$, i.e. $\xi = \xi_1 \otimes \xi_2$ it seems to me sufficiently essential to concentrate on experiments with

(A) 1 qualitative factor and

(B) K qualitative non interacting factors (see appendix for justification).

In my paper 1981 I expressed my conviction (argueing heuristically) that a restriction of optimality considerations to product designs is admissible. The first formal proof was published by Dr. Wierich (1986b) for the case (A). In the meantime there exist several rather general proofs justifying the restriction to product designs (including the case (B)) at least when optimality criteria are invariant with respect to linear reparametrizations of the ANOVA parameters β_1 (such as uniform optimality, D-optimality and several minimax-optimalities). Therefore it seems to be relevant to look closer at my results on product designs in (1981) and some of its obvious extensions: According to the general formulas (16) one obtains more or less immediately, after simplifying

$$I_\beta(\xi_1 \otimes \xi_2) = I_\beta(\nu \otimes \delta) = \begin{pmatrix} I_{\beta_1}(\nu) & \int a_1 d\nu \int a_2^T d\delta \\ \int a_2 d\delta \int a_1^T d\nu & I_{\beta_2}(\delta) \end{pmatrix}$$

for the

CASE (A): $\eta_1 : X_1 = \{1,\dots,I\} \ni x_1 = i \to \eta_1(i) = \beta_{1i} \in \mathbb{R}$.

$$I_{\beta_1}(\nu \otimes \delta) = \left(\left(\nu(i)\delta_{ii'} - c(\delta)\nu(i)\nu(i') \right)_{i'=1,\dots,I}^{i=1,\dots,I} \right)$$

with

$$\begin{aligned} c(\delta) &= \int a_2^T d\delta I_{\beta_2}^{-1}(\delta) \int a_2 d\delta \\ \det I_{\beta_1}(\nu \otimes \delta) &= (1-c(\delta))\Pi_{i=1}^I \nu(i) = (1-c(\delta))\det I_{\beta_1}(\nu) \\ \det I_\beta(\nu \otimes \delta) &= (1-c(\delta))\det I_{\beta_1}(\nu)\det I_{\beta_2}(\delta) \\ \det I_{\beta_2}(\nu \otimes \delta) &= (1-c(\delta))\det I_{\beta_2}(\delta) \end{aligned} \qquad (19)$$

Similarly simple one gets

$$\operatorname{trace} I_{\beta_1}^{-1}(\nu \otimes \delta) = I \cdot c(\delta)/(1 - c(\delta)) + \Sigma_{i=1}^I 1/\nu(i) \quad .$$

Observing that

$$\det\begin{pmatrix} 1 & \int a_2^T d\delta \\ \int a_2 d\delta & \int a_2 a_2^T d\delta \end{pmatrix} = (1 - c(\delta)) \det \int a_2 a_2^T d\delta$$

and that

$$I_{\binom{\beta_0}{\beta_2}}(\delta) := \begin{pmatrix} 1 & \int a_2^T d\delta \\ \int a_2 d\delta & \int a_2 a_2^T d\delta \end{pmatrix}$$

is the information matrix of a design δ of the regression experiment with response function

$$\eta_2^0 = \beta_0 + a_2^T \beta_2 \quad , \quad \beta_0 \in \mathbb{R} \quad ,$$

which Dr. Wierich called the pure regression part (and I preferably the "augmented regression experiment") one gets Dr. Wierich's alternative representation (see (Wierich (1986b) and (1987)):

$$\det I_{\beta_1}(\nu \otimes \delta) = I^0_{\beta_0}(\delta) \det I_{\beta_1}(\nu)$$

$$\det I_{\beta_2}(\nu \otimes \delta) = \det I^0_{(\beta_0,\beta_2^T)^T}(\delta) \tag{20}$$

$$\det I_{\beta}(\nu \otimes \delta) = \det I^0_{(\beta_0,\beta_2^T)^T}(\delta) \det I_{\beta_1}(\nu)$$

and

$$\operatorname{trace} I^{-1}_{\beta_1}(\nu \otimes \delta) = (1 - I^0_{\beta_0}(\delta))/I^0_{\beta_0}(\delta) + \operatorname{trace} I^{-1}_{\beta_1}(\nu) \quad .$$

Both representations show that product designs reduce the general design problems to problems of designing pure ANOVA and pure regression experiments but one has in addition to minimize $c(\delta) = 1 - I^0_{\beta_0}(\delta)$

also trace $I^{-1}_{\beta_2}(\nu \otimes \delta)$ is easy to determine as direct calculations show:

$$I_{\beta_2}(\nu \otimes \delta) = \int a_2 a_2^T d\delta - \int a_2 a_2^T d\delta = I^0_{\beta_2}(\delta) \quad .$$

Consequently one has

$$\operatorname{trace} I^{-1}_{\beta_2}(\nu \otimes \delta) = \operatorname{trace} I^{0^{-1}}_{\beta_2}(\delta) \tag{21}$$

$$\operatorname{trace} I^{-1}_{\beta}(\nu \otimes \delta) = \operatorname{trace} I^{0^{-1}}_{\beta_2}(\delta) + \frac{I_1 c(\delta)}{1 - c(\delta)} + \operatorname{trace} I^{-1}_{\beta_1}(\nu)$$

The validity of (21) is in general equivalent to

$$\int a_1^T d\nu \; I_{\beta_1}^{-1}(\nu) \int a_1 d\nu = 1 \tag{22}$$

which is true under general conditions on a_1, sufficient conditions which can be generalized are given in Wierich (1987). For experiments with K_1 non interacting qualitative factors, i.e.

CASE (B): $\eta_1 : X_1 = \times_{k=1}^{K_1}\{1,\dots,I_k\} \ni x_1 \to \eta_1(x_1) = \Sigma_{k=1}^{K_1}\alpha_{i_k}^{(k)} \in \mathbb{R}$

with control parametrization identified by $\alpha_{I_k}^{(k)} = 0$, $k = 1,\dots,K_1 - 1$

one can easily prove the validity of (20) directly and so obtain the same formulas (19), (20) and (21) for this case only $I_{\beta_1}(\nu)$ replaced by (23) from the appendix. Here the formulas (21) for the traces of product designs are less relevant because A-optimal product designs (in contrary to the D-optimum) need not to be A-optimum among all designs.

Examples and counter examples investigated by Kiefer's and Fedorov's equivalence theorem may be found in Wierich (1987).

4. APPENDIX: On optimum design of ANOVA experiments

The notions and results of this section represent (unless otherwise explicitely stated) a short summary of may papers (1967) and (1972) which have been republished by parts in (1971) respectively (1978) and are included here because of their restricted access and their relevance to the discussed problems.

To study design problems in terms of the information matrix the following two ANOVA models seem basic to me:

CASE (A): Experiments with one qualitative factor.

Because an experiment with K qualitative factors completely interacting has the same number of essentially unknown parameters (number of parameters of a relatively minimum parametrization) as the number of different experimental conditions $x_1 \in X_1 = \times_{k=1}^{K}\{1,\dots,I_k\}$ such an experiment can be looked upon (by renumbering the level combination using for instant lexicographical identification) as one factor experiment with $I_1 \cdot I_2 \cdot \ldots \cdot I_K$ different levels. The design problems remain essentially equally trivial.

By similar reasons and arguments one can justify the inportance of the less trivial

CASE (B): Experiments with K noninteracting qualitative factors.

If in an experiment with K factors one pair of factors (say the first two) interact then to the $I_1 \cdot I_2$ different level combinations there correspond $I_1 \cdot I_2$ unknown (essential) parameters which can be looked upon as effects of one factor having $I_1 \cdot I_2$ different levels, the merged model is then a (K - 1) factor experiment without interaction. The same merging of interacting factors can be done if two or more disjoint pairs (or tripels and so on) of interacting factors exist reducing the model to one with less but non interacting factors. The consequence for optimum design will be seen to be obvious.

It is convenient to use a nonsymmetric control parametrization not only because of their practical importance but also because it best discriminates between the two basic optimality notions: D- and A-optimality, also because of technical reasons, it is a relatively minimal parametrization:

$$\eta:\ \times_{i=1}^{K}\{1,\dots,I_k\} \ni x_1 \to \eta(i_1,i_2,\dots,i_K) = \Sigma_{k=1}^{K}\alpha_{i_k}^{(k)} \in \mathbb{R}$$

with the identification conditions: $\alpha_{I_k}^{(k)} = 0\ ,\ k \in \{1,\dots,K-1\}$.
Here we have

$$\beta^T = (\alpha_1^{(1)}\ ,\dots,\alpha_{I_1-1}^{(1)}\ ,\alpha_1^{(2)},\dots\ ,\alpha_1^{(K)}\ ,\dots,\alpha_{I_K}^{(K)}\ )$$

and

$$a^T = (1_{\{i_1=1\}},\dots,1_{\{i_1=I_1-1\}},1_{\{i_2=1\}},\dots,1_{\{i_K=1\}},\dots,1_{\{i_K=I_K\}})$$

which are coordinate functions (1-dimensional projections) on X_1 so that aa^T is a matrix of two dimentional projections so that it follows that

$$I_\beta(\nu) = \int aa^T d\nu \text{ depends on } \nu \text{ only through}$$

its two dimensional marginals $\nu_{k\ell}\ ,\ 1 \le k < \ell \le K$.
Identifying the number $N(i_1,\dots,i_K)$ of observations at the level combination $x_1 = (i_1,\dots,i_K)$ with $N \cdot \nu(\{i_1,\dots,i_K\})$ one obtains for $N \cdot \nu$ written as $N_{12\dots K} = (N(x);\ x \in X = \times_{k=1}^{K}\{1,\dots,K\}$

$$NI_\beta(\nu) = J_\beta(N_{12\dots k}) = \begin{pmatrix} D_1 & \overline{N}_{12} & \overline{N}_{1K} \\ \overline{N}_{12}^T & D_2 & \overline{N}_{2K} \\ \vdots & \vdots & \vdots \\ \overline{N}_{1K}^T & \overline{N}_{2K}^T & D_K \end{pmatrix}\ ,\quad N_{\ell k} = ((N\nu_{k\ell}(i,j))_{ij}) \tag{23}$$

where the $N_{\ell k}$ are matrices of the "second order totals" $N_{\ell k}(i_\ell,i_k)$, i.e. the total numbers of observation with the ℓ'th and k'th factor acting at level i_ℓ , respectively i_k , with bars on the $N_{\ell k}$ indicating the deletion of the last rows and columns subject to the control parametrization, and the D_k are diagonal matrices having the "first order totals" N_k , i.e. the total numbers $N_k(i_k)$ of observations with the k'th factor acting at level i_k . Here too, in all of the D_k except D_K , the last row and column is deleted subject to control parametrization.

By partial inversion formulae for matrices one obtains for $\psi(\beta) = \alpha_1 := (\alpha_1^{(1)},\dots,\alpha_{I-1}^{(1)})$:

$$J_\alpha(N_{12\ldots K}) = D_1 - (\overline{N}_{12},\ldots,\overline{N}_{1K}) \begin{pmatrix} D_2 \ldots \overline{N}_{2K} \\ \vdots \quad\quad \vdots \\ \overline{N}_{2K}^T \ldots D_K \end{pmatrix}^{-1} \begin{pmatrix} \overline{N}_{12}^T \\ \vdots \\ \overline{N}_{1K}^T \end{pmatrix} ,$$

and by Lagrange multiplier methods the main result:

A design $N^*_{12\ldots N}$ is an uniformly optimal design for α_1 in the class of all designs with fixed first order totals N_1, iff the second order totals N^*_{1k}, $k = 1,\ldots,K$ of $N^*_{12\ldots K}$ satisfy

$$N^*_{1k}(i_1,i_k) = \frac{N_1(i_1)N^*_k(i_k)}{N} , \; i_1 = 1,\ldots,I_1 , \; i_k = 1,\ldots,I_k , \; k = 2,\ldots,K ;$$

i.e. if $N^*_{12\ldots K}$ has *proportional second order totals* N_{1k}, $k = 2,\ldots,K$, i.e. if ν^* has proportional 2-dimensional marginals (to the 1-dimensional ν_1)

$$\nu_{1k} , \quad k = 1,\ldots,K ,$$

i.e. if the 2-dimensional marginals of ν^* of the first factor are product measures.

Note if the model results from merging 2 (or more) interacting factors to one then the corresponding uniform optimal design will have 3-dimensional marginals which are proportional to the two dimensional corresponding to the two merged factors (see Kurotschka (1972/78)).

For uniform optimal designs for a_1, i.e. those with proportional N^*_{1k}, $k = 2,\ldots,K$, one has an information matrix for α_1:

$$J_{\alpha_1}(N^*_{12\ldots K}) = ((N_1(i)\delta_{ii'} - N_1(i)N_1(i'))_{i'=1,\ldots,I}^{i=1,\ldots,I})$$

therefore D- and A-optimal designs in the class of all designs of total sample size N one gets if the second order totals N_{1k} are proportional to "D-optimal" first order totals defined by $N^*_1(i) = N/I$ respectively to "A-optimal" first order totals, defined by

$$N^*_1(i_1) = \begin{cases} N/(\sqrt{I_1 - 1} + I_1 - 1) , & i_1 = 1,\ldots,I_1 - 1 \\ N/\sqrt{I_1 - 1} + 1 , & i_1 = I_1 \end{cases} .$$

Observe that all these properties concerned with α_1 are compatible with the analogue properties for $\alpha_2,\ldots,\alpha_L$ so that one can speak of uniform optimal, D- and A-optimal designs for the first L factors. But such statements are obviously concerned with optimality properties of $I_{\alpha_1}(\nu),\ldots,I_{\alpha_L}(\nu)$ not with $I_{(\alpha_1^T,\alpha_2^T,\ldots,\alpha_L^T)^T}$, which has to be considered if one is dealing with statistical procedures based on joint information matrix rather then the partial. For the A-optimality this stronger result (minimizing the trace of the joint information matrix) follows immediatly from the partial results,

for all $L \leq K-1$. The main new contribution of Wierich (1986) is that the D-optimum design is one which is discribed above as a D-optimum for the first L factors, namely the design with proportional second order totals $N_{k\ell}$, $1 \leq k \leq L$, $k \leq \ell \leq K$ and balanced first order totals $N_1,\ldots,N_L$, $L = 1,\ldots,K$, or expressed in terms of ν:
ν has uniform 2-dimensional marginals $\nu_{k\ell}$, $1 \leq k < \ell \leq L$ and

$$\nu_{k\ell} = \nu_k \otimes \nu_\ell \ , \ 1 \leq k \leq L < \ell \leq K \ .$$

A last remark on critics and polemics against generalized designs in ANOVA experiments:
It is in contrary for ANOVA-experiments reasonable and informative to admit generalized designs, because $N(x_1)$, $x_1 \in X_1$ are seldom in practical problems interpreted as number of repetitions, but more often as size of the experimental unit (size of the field, amount of material of some given quality, extension of some region or space, and so on) and implicitely determines the unrestricted optimal allocation not disturbed by compromises of providing intervalued $N(\cdot)$, see for more details Kurotschka (1972b).

References

Bandemer, H. et al. (1977). Theorie und Anwendung der optimalen Versuchsplanung I. Akademie-Verlag, Berlin.

Bandemer, H. and Näther, W. (1980). Theorie und Anwendung der optimalen Versuchsplanung II. Akademie-Verlag, Berlin.

Fedorov, V.V. (1972). Theory of optimal experiments. Academic Press, New York.

Köster, J. (1976). Optimale Versuchsplanung bei Modellen der Kovarianzanalyse mit linearen Regressionsfaktoren. Dissertation, Universität Göttingen.

Kurotschka, V. (1967/71). Optimale Versuchspläne bei zweifach klassifizierten Beobachtungsmodellen. Dissertation, Universität Freiburg bzw. Metrika, 17, 215-232.

Kurotschka, V. and Dwyer, P.S. (1974). Optimum design of three way layouts without interactions. Math.Operat.forschung Statist. 5, 131-145.

Kurotschka, V. (1972a). Classes of optimal incomplete designs of ANOVA setting. Proc. Symp. Sym. Functions Statist. in Honor of Prof. P.S. Dwyer, Windsor, 183-195.

Kurotschka, V. (1972). Optimale Versuchsplanung bei Modellen der Varianzanalyse. Habilitationsschrift, Universität Göttingen.

Kurotschka, V. (1978). Optimal design of complex experiments with qualitative factors of influence. Commun. Statist. - Theor. Meth., A7, 1363-1378.

Kurotschka, V. (1981). A general approach to optimum design of experiments with qualitative and quantitative factors. In: Proc. of I.S.I. Golden Jubilee Intern. Conf. on Stat.: Appl. and New Directions, Calcutta, 353-368.

Kurotschka, V. and Wierich, W. (1984). Optimale Planung eines Kovarianzanalyse- und eines Intraclass Regressions-Experiments. Metrika 31, 361-378.

Lopes-Troya, J. (1982). Optimal designs for covariates models. J. Statist. Plann. Inference 6, 373-419.

Lopes-Troya, J. (1982a). Cyclic designs for a covariate model. J. Statist. Plann. Inference 7, 49-75.

Searle, S.R. (1979). Alternative covariance models for the two way crossed classification. Commun. Statist. A8, 799-818.

Wierich, W. (1984). Konkrete optimale Versuchspläne für ein lineares Modell mit einem qualitativen und zwei quantitativen Einflußfaktoren. Metrika 31, 285-301.

Wierich, W. (1985). Optimum designs under experimental constraints for a covariate model and an intra-class regression model. J. Statist. Plann. Inference 12, 27-40.

Wierich, W. (1986a). Optimality of k-proportional designs for simultaneous inference. Statistics 17, 179-187.

Wierich, W. (1986b). On optimal designs and complete class theorems for experiments with continuous and discrete factors of influence. J. Statist. Plann. Inference 15, 19-27.

Wierich, W. (1987). The D- and A-optimality of product design measures for linear models with discrete and continuous factors of influence. Habilitationsschrift, Freie Universität Berlin.

DESIGN AND ANALYSIS IN GENERALIZED REGRESSION MODEL F

M.B. Maljutov
Moscow State University, Moscow, USSR

Classical regression analysis has two appealing features from the point of view of applications:

1. Nonparametric nature: only two moments of measurements are supposed to be known instead of rarely known distributions.
2. Linear or iterative linear estimates are used which are easy to compute and analyze and which have some optimality properties.

Among numerous generalizations of classical regression methods (generalized linear models, minimal contrast estimates, etc.) we wish to point out one model which preserves both useful features of the classical model and at the same time is much more flexible in applications. I mean the following F-model which - as an intermediate step - appeared in estimating parameters of exponential family distributions (Barndorf-Nielsen, 1978), as an asymptotic principal part of errors in variable model (Fedorov, 1974), and was called "fitting expectations" in (Jennrich and Ralston, 1979).

It will at first be introduced in its simplest form without some technical conditions. Let measurements $y_1 \in R^1$ have distributions $P_\vartheta^{x_i}(\cdot)$, $x_i \in X$, $i = 1,\dots,N$, such that

$$E_\vartheta y_i = \eta(x_i,\vartheta) \tag{1}$$

$$Var\ y_i = v(x_i,\vartheta) \tag{2}$$

$$\vartheta \in \Theta \subset R^p$$

where $\eta(\cdot)$ and $v(\cdot)$ are smooth bounded functions of x,ϑ. The only available results are asymptotic when $N \to \infty$. Thus we need a condition of the weak convergence of the design measures:

$$\varepsilon_N := N^{-1}\Sigma_{i=1}^N 1_{x_i}(\cdot) \Longrightarrow \varepsilon \tag{3}$$

where ε is a probability measure on X.

The important asymptotic identifiability condition of ϑ via $\eta(\cdot,\vartheta)$ is crucial which excludes situations where a certain part of ϑ's components has influence only on $v(\cdot)$, e.g., in the variance components model. The global identifiability condition is as follows:

$$R(\vartheta,\vartheta') := \int (\eta(x,\vartheta) - \eta(x,\vartheta'))^2 \varepsilon(dx) > 0 \tag{4}$$

when $\vartheta \neq \vartheta'$, Θ is compact.

When investigating the local behavior of estimates with a good prior guess available it is sufficient to demand only the following condition

$$\int \varphi^T(x,\vartheta) v^{-1}(x,\vartheta)\varphi(x,\vartheta)\varepsilon(dx) := m(\vartheta) \tag{5}$$

is uniformly non-degenerate in Θ, $\varphi(\cdot) = \delta\eta(\cdot)/\delta\vartheta$.

In general "least squares" (LS) estimate $\arg\min_\vartheta \sum_{i=1}^{N} (y_i - \eta(x_i,\vartheta))^2 v^{-1}(x,\vartheta)$ is not even consistent for F-model, but the slight generalization of the iterative Newton-Gauss algorithm (NEGA) of evaluating LS estimate, namely the well-known iterative reweighted NEGA (IRNEGA) reaches the lower bound of the local asymptotically minimax (AM) quadratic risk which we will state below.

We also give the lower bound for the procedure's (i.e. design combined with estimate) performance and the procedures reaching this lower bound asymptotically are given.

Now we shall outline a general scheme for which our results are valid.

1. We consider multivariate measurements $y_i \in R^m$ fulfilling conditions analogous to those indicated previously. This MF-model includes the variance components (VC) model mentioned earlier (see Luanchi, 1983), estimation of grouped data (Luanchi and Maljutov, 1984), etc. Let us explain e.g. the connection between VC- and F-models. Let $y = X\beta + \Sigma_{i=1}^{r} U_i e_i$, e_i be mutually independent n_i-vectors of i.i.d. components, $Ee_i = 0, Ee_i^2 = \sigma^2$. Then $Ey = X\beta$, $Cov\, y = \Sigma_{i=1}^{r} U_i U_i^T \sigma_i^2$. Let the third and fourth moments of y be the functions of $\beta, \sigma_1^2, \cdots, \sigma_r^2$ (which is the case when the combined vector $(y^T, Vec\, yy^T)^T$ is described evidently by the MF-model.

2. Almost all the asymptotic results for the MF-model are available for sequential design (SD). The necessity of such a generalization was emphasized in Silvey (1980). An informal description of SD is as follows. After each measurement y_n we get a decision based on $y_1^n := (y_1,\ldots,y_n)$ whether to stop $(N = n)$ experiments. In this case a decision on the underlying distribution P_ϑ^x (in our case - an estimate of ϑ) is taken. Otherwise we choose a design point $x_{n+1}(y_1^n) \in X$ and make the following measurement y_{n+1}. We shall survey here only the case where the conditional distribution of y_{n+1} for given y_1^n is $P_\vartheta^{x_{n+1}}$ depending only on $x_{n+1}(y_1^n)$. It is clear that y_1^n is no more an independent sequence, but the martingale technique (Maljutov, 1983), using consecutive centerings provides us with sufficient information on the asymptotic behavior of estimates, including asymptotic confidence bands.

We omit here an accurate description of the measure P_ϑ^s on Y^N corresponding to SD-s (see Maljutov, 1983). Some notations are needed: $\bar{N}_\vartheta = E_\vartheta^s N$, $\bar{f}_\vartheta^x = \int f^x(y) P_\vartheta^x(dy)$.

The *static projection* $\pi_\vartheta^s(\cdot)$ of s is a measure on X such that for all $\beta \subset x$ (σ-field of X'_s subsets) $\pi_\vartheta^s(B) = \bar{N}_\vartheta^{-1} \Sigma_{k=1}^{\infty} P_\vartheta^s(x_k \in B, k \le N)$.

The *predictable projection* of s is a random measure on (X, x) such that for all $B \subset x$

$$\Pi_\vartheta^s(B) = \bar{N}_\vartheta^{-1} \Sigma_{k=1}^{N} 1(x_k \in B) \quad ,$$

$1(A)$ is an indicator of the event A. The sequence s_n of SD-s is called *asymptotically nonrandom* (ANR) if $\Pi_\vartheta^{s_n}$ converge weakly to the nonrandom measure π_ϑ (now we suppose X to be a complete separable metric space). The example of a sequence of SD-s not being ANR is the following.

Let $Y = (y^{(1)}, y^{(2)}), X = \{0\}$, $y_n^{(1)}$ be i.i.d. P_ϑ and $y_n^{(2)}$ be a probability of jumping from n to $n \pm 1$ is $1/2 \pm 1/3 sgn\, n$. Irrespectively of the initial position $y_n^{(2)} \to \pm\infty$ with probability $1/2$. Now let $N_{2m} = 2m + m sgn\, y_m^{(2)}$. Thus $N = 3m$ or m, $\Pi_\vartheta\{0\} = 3/2$ or $1/2$ with probabilities $1/2$. If both the stopping time and controls do not depend on noninformative chaotic variables and a sequence of SD-s is adaptive then usually we have an ANR sequence. Limit theorems' expressions for such cases usually depend only on π_{ϑ}^{s}. Asymptotic normality (AN) of common estimates is usually true. Otherwise limiting information matrices are random and the asymptotic distribution of common estimates is not normal.

The following two useful formulas generalizing the well-known Wald identities for SD are extensively used in proving our results.

Lemma 1. i) If $\sup \int |g^{x}(y)| P_{\vartheta}^{x}(dy) < \infty$ and $\sup \bar{N}_{\vartheta} < \infty$ then

$$E_{\vartheta}^{s} \Sigma_{n=1}^{N} g^{x_n}(yn) = \bar{N}_{\vartheta} \int \bar{g}_{\vartheta}^{x} \, \pi_{\vartheta}^{s}(sx) \tag{1}$$

ii) If $\sup \int (g_n^{x}(y))^2 P_{\vartheta}^{x}(dy) < \infty$, $\sup \bar{N}_{\vartheta} < \infty$ and

$$Var_{\vartheta}^{s} \Sigma_{n=1}^{N} g_{n,\vartheta}^{x_n} = 0$$

then

$$Var\, \Sigma_{n=1}^{N} g^{x_n}(y_n) = E_{\vartheta}^{s} \Sigma_{n=1}^{N} Var_{\vartheta}^{s} (g^{x_n}(y_n) / y_1^{n-1}) \, .$$

Letting ϑ to vary over Θ (e.g., being an initial guess, we denote by ϑ^* the true value of ϑ. SD for F-model is described by the equations

$$\left.\begin{aligned} E_{\vartheta^*}^{s}(y_n \mid y_1^{n-1}) &= \eta(x_n, \vartheta^*) \\ Cov_{\vartheta^*}^{s}(y_n \mid y_1^{n-1}) &= v(x_i, \vartheta^*) \end{aligned}\right\} \text{ a.e. when } N \geq n \, , \tag{2}$$

and regularity conditions from Maljutov, 1983. The lower bounds obtained there are accurate for ARD sequences and may be made higher otherwise. To derive such improved lower bounds we need the extra condition:

$$\Pi_{\vartheta}^{s_m} \text{ weakly converge random measure } \Pi_{\vartheta} \quad .$$

We normalize SD s_m by the condition $\bar{N}_{\vartheta^*}^{s_m} = m$ and consider two types of the lower bounds for the quadratic risk. The first one is valid for the certain class of iterative estimates and for any distribution P_{ϑ}^{x} satisfying (2). The second type is over any estimates but the additional supremum over certain class of distributions P_{ϑ}^{x} is introduced.

Let us formulate the first lower bound. For any $l_i \in R_p$, $\lambda_i > 0$, $i = 1,\dots,p$ let us introduce

$$R^{s}(\vartheta) = E_{\vartheta^*} \Sigma \lambda_i (l_i^T(\tau(y,\vartheta) - \vartheta^*))^2$$

where

$$\tau(y,\vartheta) = \vartheta + A_{\vartheta}(y) \Sigma_{i=1}^{N} B_{\vartheta}(x_i)(y_i - \eta(x_i,\vartheta))$$

is an arbitrary linear in residuals correlation for ϑ^*. Let

$$B(r) = \{\vartheta \in R^p : \|\vartheta - \vartheta^*\|^2 \leq r\}$$

and

$$R(\tau) = \lim_{c \to \infty} \lim_{m \to \infty} \sup_{\vartheta \in B(c/m)} m R^{s_m}(\vartheta) \, .$$

Theorem 1. Under regularity conditions outlined

$$R(\tau) \geq E \sum_{i=1}^{p} \lambda_i l_i^T m l_i \quad ,$$

where m is the random information matrix:

$$m = \int \varphi^T(x,\vartheta^*)v^{-1}(x,\vartheta^*)\varphi(x,\vartheta^*)\Pi_\vartheta^*(dx)$$

and the expectation is over distribution of Π_ϑ^*.

Let us consider any estimates T of ϑ^* such that

$$\sup E\|T\|^2 < \infty$$

over class $K(\eta,v)$ of distributions P_ϑ^x with the conditional means $\eta(\cdot)$ and covariances which are smaller in Loewner sense than $v(\cdot)$. Let

$$R^s(c) = \sup_{\vartheta \in B(c/m)} mE_\vartheta^{s_m} \sum_{i=1^p} \lambda_i(l_i^T(T-\vartheta))^2 \quad .$$

Theorem 2. Under regularity conditions outlined

$$\underline{\lim}_{c\to\infty} \lim_{m\to\infty} R^{s_m}(c) \geq E \sum_{i=1^p} \lambda_i l_i^T m l_i \quad .$$

Our last lower bound concerns procedures i.e., combined design and estimate. We fix differentiable function Φ of information matrices m, which is convex in m^{-1}, $\Phi \to +\infty$ when m approaches A degenerates matrix, $\Phi(m) \geq \varphi(m')$ if $m \leq m'$ in Loewner sense and $\Phi(\alpha m) = \alpha^{-1}\Phi(m)$, $\alpha > 0$.

As a consequence of theorem 1 we have

Theorem 3. Under regularity conditions outlined

$$\underline{\lim}_{c\to\infty} \underline{\lim}_{m\to\infty} m \sup_{\vartheta \in B(c/m)} \Phi(E_{\vartheta}^{s_m}[(\tau(\cdot,\vartheta)-\vartheta^*)(\tau(\cdot,\vartheta)-\vartheta^*)^T]^{-1} \geq \Phi(m_0) = \min \Phi(m) \quad .$$

This theorem justifies the intuitively obvious fact φ-optimal static design is also the best among SD-s. There is certainly a version of this theorem which corresponds to theorem 2.

The usual two-step procedure:

- The first εm experiments $(0 < \varepsilon < 1)$ are planned statically to provide (4) which is sufficient for $\sqrt{m}$-consistency of the LS-estimate $\hat{\vartheta}_0$ for ϑ^* Jennrich (1969).

- The remaining $(1-\varepsilon)m$ experiments are planned statically with normalized information matrix $m_0(\hat{\vartheta}_0)$. The first IRNEGA-estimate will provide us with $(1-\varepsilon)$-efficient estimate for ϑ^*.

I will not touch here asymptotic theory of IRNEGA-estimates for F-models which is developed in Maljutov (1983). The only remark is that this theory is the application of limit theorems for random fields, which is unavoidable when the estimates are interated.

The participation of R. Matos Marino is acknowledged in proving Theorems 1 and 2.

REFERENCES

[1] Barndorf-Nielsen , O. (1979). Information and exponential families. Wiley, New York.

[2] Fedorov, V.V. (1974). Regression problems with controllable variables subject to error. *Biometrika* 61 (1): 49-56.

[3] Jennrich, R. (1969). Asymptotic properties of nonlinear LS estimators. *Ann. Math. Stastist.*, 40: 633-643.

[4] Jennrich, R. and Ralston, M.L. (1979). Fitting nonlinear models to data. *Ann. Rev. of Biophys.*, Bioengineer.

[5] Luanchi, M. (1983). Thesis. Moscow Lomonosov University.

[6] Luanchi, M. and Maljutov, M.B. (1984). Estimation of regression parameters by grouped measurements in statistical methods. Perm. (In Russian).

[7] Maljutov, M.B. (1983). Lower bounds for the average duration of sequential design. Izv. vuzov. Matematik 11 (258): 19-41. (In Russian).

[8] Silvey, S.D. (1980). Optimal design. Chapman and Hall. London.

ROBUST EXPERIMENT DESIGNS FOR NONLINEAR REGRESSION MODELS

Luc Pronzato and Eric Walter
Laboratoire des Signaux et Systèmes
CNRS-Ecole Supérieure d'Electricité
Plateau du Moulon
91190 Gif-sur-Yvette France

1. INTRODUCTION

The design of experiments for parameter estimation gives rise to two different problems : first one has to define the criterion to be used to compare experiments, second one has to optimize it. The availability of algorithmic procedures intended to solve this optimization problem in a reasonably simple way thus appears as a preliminary requirement for the practical use of experiment design. Classically the definition of the optimality criterion is based upon the well-known asymptotic properties of maximum likelihood estimators. The most commonly used criterion is the determinant of the Fisher information matrix, and an experiment that maximizes this determinant is said to be *D-optimal* . This maximization can be carried out by using a specific algorithm when one is interested in a design measure (Fedorov 1972, Silvey 1980), or by resorting to classical nonlinear programming algorithms when one wants to optimize a discrete design.

When the model response is a nonlinear function of the parameters to be estimated, both approaches lead to an experiment that depends on the (unknown) value of the model parameters. The most traditional approach consists then in designing a D-optimal experiment for some reasonable nominal value of the parameters. An important consequence of such an approach is that the uncertainty on this nominal value is not taken into account. This has raised some doubts among experimenters about the practical interest of optimal experiment design. Several approaches have been proposed to overcome this difficulty. One of them consists in designing experiments in a *sequential* way by alternating estimation of the parameters and experiment design. Each estimation procedure improves the information available on the parameters, to be used during the next experiment design. Sequential design has been widely studied and applied in many situations (see e.g. Box and Hunter 1965, Fedorov 1972, D'Argenio 1981, DiStefano 1982), and when feasible it can be considered as an efficient answer to the problem raised by nonlinear models. However one is often faced with situations where a single experiment has to be performed. Moreover, any sequential design can be considered as consisting of a series of single experiment designs that have to be performed as best possible given the available information on the parameters. These two reasons give a particular importance to *nonsequential approaches*, that aim at designing single experiments while taking into account some characterization of the *parameter uncertainty*. For that purpose two methodologies seem particularly attractive.

The first one is *Bayesian* and assumes the knowledge of the prior distribution of the parameters. The criterion to be optimized is then the mathematical expectation of some classical non-robust criterion over the possible values of the parameters (Fedorov 1972, 1980, Goodwin and Payne 1977). Each evaluation of such a criterion requires the computation of a mathematical expectation, and this seems a tremendous obstacle to the practical use of this approach. To design discrete optimal experiments, we propose a *stochastic approximation algorithm* that enables Bayesian criteria to be optimized almost as simply as classical non-robust criteria would be. However such an approach may lead to very poor experiments for some particular values of the parameters associated with low values of the prior probability density function. When such a situation is unacceptable, one may prefer to optimize the worst possible performance of the experiment over the admissible domain for the parameters (Fedorov 1980, Silvey 1980, Landaw 1985). This *minimax* (or *maximin*) design only assumes that the parameters belong to some prior domain, without any hypothesis on their distribution. Here again the computational burden generally involved in minimax optimizations is an obstacle to the practical use of the approach. For that reason we describe some tools for designing discrete minimax optimal experiments at a reasonable cost.

Section 2 briefly states the problem and defines the notations to be used. Section 3 presents some criteria of optimality related to Bayesian design, some properties of the corresponding optimal experiments, and a stochastic approximation algorithm intended to optimize Bayesian criteria. Section 4 defines the minimax criterion to be used when Bayesian design is unacceptable. The particular case of exponential regression models, widely used in the biosciences, is considered. An algorithmic procedure for the optimization of minimax criteria is described.

2. PROBLEM STATEMENT

Denote by $\underline{y}$ the N-dimensional vector of all available measurements on the process, $\underline{\theta}$ the p-dimensional vector of the parameters to be estimated, and $\underline{e}$ the n-dimensional vector describing the experimental situation (e.g. sampling times, control variables...). Suppose that the measurement noise $\underline{\varepsilon}^*$ is additivewhite with zero mean and a distribution $f(\underline{\varepsilon}^*)$ independent from the value of $\underline{\theta}$. Denote by $\underline{y}_m(\underline{\theta},\underline{e})$ the output vector of the model with parameters $\underline{\theta}$, associated with the observations $\underline{y}$. If there is no error in the model structure, a "true value" $\underline{\theta}^*$ for the parameters exists, such that

$$\underline{y} = \underline{y}_m(\underline{\theta}^*,\underline{e}) + \underline{\varepsilon}^*. \quad (1)$$

Under some regularity conditions, the maximum likelihood estimator of $\underline{\theta}$ based on $\underline{y}$ is asymptotically normally distributed $N(\underline{\theta}^*, M_F^{-1}(\underline{\theta}^*,\underline{e}))$, where the Fisher information matrix $M_F(\underline{\theta},\underline{e})$ can be written as

$$M_F(\underline{\theta},\underline{e}) = X^t(\underline{\theta},\underline{e}).\Sigma^{-1}(\underline{e}).X(\underline{\theta},\underline{e}), \quad (2)$$

where

$$X(\underline{\theta},\underline{e}) = \partial\underline{y}_m(\underline{\theta},\underline{e})/\partial\underline{\theta}^t, \quad (3)$$

and

$$\Sigma^{-1}(\underline{e}) = \int_{\underline{\varepsilon}} \partial \ln f(\underline{\varepsilon})/\partial\underline{\varepsilon} \,.\, \partial \ln f(\underline{\varepsilon})/\partial\underline{\varepsilon}^t .\, f(\underline{\varepsilon})\, d\underline{\varepsilon}. \quad (4)$$

If the noise is also supposed to be white, then $\Sigma(\underline{e})$ is diagonal and one obtains the well-known expression

$$M_F(\underline{\theta},\underline{e}) = \sum_{i=1}^{N} (1/w_i).\partial y_{mi}(\underline{\theta},\underline{e})/\partial\underline{\theta}.\ \partial y_{mi}(\underline{\theta},\underline{e})/\partial\underline{\theta}^t, \quad (5)$$

where y_{mi} is the ith component of $\underline{y}_m$, and where w_i is the ith diagonal term of $\Sigma(\underline{e})$ (for an additive white noise $N(0,\sigma^2)$, $w_i=\sigma^2$). When $y_{mi}(\underline{\theta},\underline{e})$ is a nonlinear function of $\underline{\theta}$, the Fisher information matrix depends on $\underline{\theta}$, and the classical D-optimal design consists in maximizing the criterion

$$j_d(\underline{\theta},\underline{e}) = \det M_F(\underline{\theta},\underline{e}), \quad (6)$$

with respect to $\underline{e}$ for a given nominal value of $\underline{\theta}$. The uncertainty on this nominal value is not taken into account. The methodologies described in the following sections aim at removing the dependence on $\underline{\theta}$ by using some prior knowledge on the possible values of $\underline{\theta}$. Because of the large acceptance of D-optimality, we will focus our attention on criteria based upon the determinant of the Fisher information matrix.

3. BAYESIAN DESIGN

3.1. Criteria

In order to describe the prior parameter uncertainty, the parameter vector $\underline{\theta}$ is supposed to be distributed according to a known probability density function $p(\underline{\theta})$. The knowledge of $p(\underline{\theta})$ may result from previous experiments, or may simply express our uncertainty on the location of $\underline{\theta}^*$. Bayesian criteria of optimality then correspond to the mathematical expectation of some functional of the Fisher information matrix (Fedorov 1972, 1980, Goodwin and Payne 1977, Pronzato and Walter 1985, Walter and Pronzato 1985, 1987, Chaloner and Larntz 1986). Among the possible criteria that can be deduced from (6) consider the following ones.

Definition 3.1.

An experiment $\underline{e}_{ed}$ is said ED-optimal if it is associated with the maximum value over the admissible experimental domain $\mathbb{E}$ of the criterion

$$j_{ed}(\underline{\theta},\underline{e}) = E_{\underline{\theta}}\{j_d(\underline{\theta},\underline{e})\}, \tag{7}$$

where $j_d(\underline{\theta},\underline{e})$ is given by (6), and where $E_{\underline{\theta}}\{.\}$ denotes the mathematical expectation over the possible values of $\underline{\theta}$.

Definition 3.2.

An experiment $\underline{e}_{eid}$ is said EID-optimal if it is associated with the minimum value over $\mathbb{E}$ of the criterion

$$j_{eid}(\underline{\theta},\underline{e}) = E_{\underline{\theta}}\{1/j_d(\underline{\theta},\underline{e})\}. \tag{8}$$

In what follows the admissible experimental domain is supposed to be defined by

$$e_{imin} \leq e_i \leq e_{imax},\ i = 1,\dots, n. \tag{9}$$

It must be noted that, except when the Fisher information matrix does not depend on $\underline{\theta}$ or when $p(\underline{\theta})$ reduces to a discrete measure with one point of support, ED- and EID-optimality are not equivalent. An ED-optimal experiment maximizes the average value of a scalar measure of the information to be gained from the experiment, whereas an EID-optimal experiment minimizes the average value of a scalar measure of the asymptotic parameter uncertainty. As far as reducing parameter uncertainty is concerned, EID-optimality should be preferred to ED-optimality (see e.g. (Walter and Pronzato 1985, 1987, Pronzato 1986) for a comparison between these two criteria).

3.2. Properties

Linearity with respect to some parameters. Even if they are nonlinear in the parameters, model outputs often are linear in a subset of these parameters. The following theorem then extends to EID-optimal design a well-known property of D-optimal design.

Theorem 3.1.

If the following hypotheses are satisfied:

H1: the model output satisfies

$$y_{mi}(\underline{\theta},\underline{e}) = g^t(\underline{\theta}^{nl},\underline{e}).\,\underline{\theta}^l,\ i = 1,\dots, N, \tag{10}$$

with

$$\underline{\theta} = (\underline{\theta}^{lt}, \underline{\theta}^{nlt})^t, \tag{11}$$

H2: the noise is additive, white, and distributed independently from $\underline{\theta}$,

H3: the linear parameters $\underline{\theta}^l$ are distributed independently from the nonlinear parameters $\underline{\theta}^{nl}$,

then the EID-optimal experiment can be obtained with all components of $\underline{\theta}^l$ fixed at 1.

Proof.

From H1 and H2 the Fisher information matrix can be written (Pronzato 1986)

$$M_F(\underline{\theta}^l, \underline{\theta}^{nl}, \underline{e}) = \begin{bmatrix} I_p & O_p \\ O_p & D(\underline{\theta}^l) \end{bmatrix} . M_F(\underline{u}_p, \underline{\theta}^{nl}, \underline{e}) . \begin{bmatrix} I_p & O_p \\ O_p & D(\underline{\theta}^l) \end{bmatrix}, \qquad (12)$$

where I_p is the pxp identity matrix, O_p is the pxp null matrix, $\underline{u}_p$ is the p-dimentional vector with all entries equal to 1, $D(\underline{\theta}^l)$ is the diagonal matrix $\text{diag}\{\theta^l_j, j = 1,..., p\}$. Taking H3 into account, one has

$$j_{eid}(\underline{e}) = E_{\underline{\theta}l}\{ \prod_{j=1}^{p} (\theta^l_j)^{-2}\}. E_{\underline{\theta}nl}\{\det^{-1} M_F(\underline{u}_p, \underline{\theta}^{nl}, \underline{e})\}. \qquad (13)$$

The linear parameters $\underline{\theta}^l$ only appear in (13) as multiplicative terms that do not depend on $\underline{e}$. The EID-optimal experiment can therefore be obtained by minimizing $E_{\underline{\theta}nl}\{\det^{-1} M_F(\underline{u}_p, \underline{\theta}^{nl}, \underline{e})\}$ with respect to $\underline{e}$.

Reparameterization of the model. Among the attractive properties of D-optimal design is the fact that a D-optimal experiment is invariant with respect to any non-degenerated transformation applied to the model parameters. Unfortunately this property generally does not hold true for EID-optimal design. To prove it, consider a reparameterization of the model defined by $\underline{\lambda}(\underline{\theta})$. The EID-optimality criterion for the estimation of $\underline{\theta}$ can be written as

$$j_{eid}(\underline{e}) = E_{\underline{\theta}}\{\det^{-2}(\partial\underline{\lambda}^t/\partial\underline{\theta}). \det^{-1} M_F(\underline{\lambda}(\underline{\theta}), \underline{e})\}, \qquad (14)$$

which generally differs from $E_{\underline{\theta}}\{\det^{-2}(\partial\underline{\lambda}^t/\partial\underline{\theta})\}. E_{\underline{\theta}}\{\det^{-1} M_F(\underline{\lambda}(\underline{\theta}), \underline{e})\}$. Consequently the EID-optimal experiment for $\underline{\lambda}$ generally differs from the EID-optimal experiment for $\underline{\theta}$.

Remark. EID-optimal experiments are nevertheless invariant under any linear transformation (such as a change on the units in which the components of $\underline{\theta}$ are expressed), for then $\partial\underline{\lambda}^t/\partial\underline{\theta}$ is not a function of $\underline{\theta}$.

Replicated experiments. It is well known that D-optimal experiments often consist of replications of observations made under the same experimental conditions. This property has received a great deal of attention (see e.g. (Box 1968, Wynn 1972, Landaw 1980)). The following theorem indicates that EID-optimal experiments can also be expected to consist of replications of some minimal experiment (see (Pronzato 1986) for examples).

Theorem 3.2.

Subject to regularity conditions, any experiment $\underline{e}^*$ that corresponds to a stationary value of the criterion j_{eid} can be associated with a parameter value $\underline{\theta}_{eid}(\underline{e}^*)$ such that $\underline{e}^*$ also corresponds to a stationary value of the criterion $j_d(\underline{\theta}_{eid}(\underline{e}^*), \underline{e})$.

Proof.

Deriving (8) with respect to $\underline{e}$, one gets

$$\partial j_{eid}(\underline{e})/\partial\underline{e}\,|_{\underline{e}^*} = \int_{\underline{\theta}} \partial(1/j_d(\underline{\theta}, \underline{e}))/\partial\underline{e})\,|_{\underline{e}^*}. p(\underline{\theta}). d\underline{\theta}, \qquad (15)$$

which implies the existence of $\underline{\theta}_{eid}(\underline{e}^*)$ such that

$$\partial j_{eid}(\underline{e})/\partial\underline{e}\,|_{\underline{e}^*} = \partial(1/j_d(\underline{\theta}_{eid}(\underline{e}^*), \underline{e}))/\partial\underline{e})\,|_{\underline{e}^*}. \qquad (16)$$

The stationarity of $j_{eid}(\underline{e})$ at $\underline{e}^*$ therefore implies that of $j_d(\underline{\theta}_{eid}(\underline{e}^*), \underline{e})$. Consequently when the EID-optimal experiment is obtained for a stationary point of the criterion (8), this experiment is also a stationary point for the D-optimality criterion for some value $\underline{\theta}_{eid}$ of the parameters. Whenever this stationary point corresponds to the optimum of the criterion (6), the EID-optimal experiment will present the same properties of replications as a classical D-optimal experiment.

3.3. Algorithm

Stochastic approximation algorithms (Dvoretsky 1956, Poliak and Tsypkin 1973, Saridis 1974) are especially attractive for the optimization of criteria involving the computation of mathematical expectations. They permit to avoid any evaluation of such expectations and thus to save a considerable amount of computational time. The classical Robbins-Monro procedure, described here for the minimization of the criterion j_{eid}, can be written as

$$\underline{e}^{(k+1)} = \underline{e}^{(k)} - \lambda^{(k)} \frac{\partial}{\partial \underline{e}} (\det{}^{-1} M_F(\underline{\theta}^{(k)}, \underline{e}))|_{\underline{e} = \underline{e}^{(k)}}. \quad (17)$$

Whenever $\underline{e}^{(k+1)}$ does not belong to $\mathbb{E}$ as defined by (9), it is projected on its boundary. At each iteration k, $\underline{\theta}^{(k)}$ is randomly selected according to the prior probability density function $p(\underline{\theta})$ and $\lambda^{(k)}$ must satisfy some well known conditions that are fulfilled by the harmonic sequence $\lambda^{(k)}=\alpha/k$. Since it is well known (and easy to check experimentally) that the convenient choice for α is highly problem dependent, we have proposed a *scaled stochastic gradient algorithm*, where the scalar $\lambda^{(k)}$ is replaced by the diagonal matrix

$$\Lambda^{(k)} = \lambda^{(k)} \operatorname{diag} \{(e_{jmax} - e_{jmin}) / (\frac{1}{k} \sum_{i=1}^{k} [\frac{\partial}{\partial e_j} (\det{}^{-1} M_F(\underline{\theta}^{(i)}, \underline{e}))|_{\underline{e}=\underline{e}^{(i)}}]^2)^{1/2}, j=1,..., n\} \quad (18)$$

Note that $\Lambda^{(k)}$ can be computed iteratively. This scaling policy ensures a greater independence of the behavior of the algorithm from the problem considered. It implies that

$$\frac{e_i^{(2)} - e_i^{(1)}}{e_{imax} - e_{imin}} = \pm \alpha, \; i=1,..., n. \quad (19)$$

The convergence properties of the scaled stochastic gradient can be related (Pronzato 1986) to those of pseudogradient algorithms, which are studied in (Poliak and Tsypkin 1973). The convergence can be accelerated by changing the value of $\lambda^{(k)}$ only when the product of the gradients at iterations (k-1) and k has a negative value (Saridis, 1974). Examples illustrating the behavior of the algorithm can be found in (Pronzato and Walter 1985, Walter and Pronzato 1985, 1987). Note that this algorithm could also be used to optimize other criteria based upon the mathematical expectation of non-robust criteria over the possible values of the parameters. The choice of the prior distribution $p(\underline{\theta})$ can be made freely as long as one is able to generate parameter vectors $\underline{\theta}^{(k)}$ according to $p(\underline{\theta})$.

4. MINIMAX DESIGN

4.1. Criterion

The approach described in Section 3 designs experiments that are good on the average but can reveal very poor for some particular values of the parameter vector associated with very low values of $p(\underline{\theta})$. One might thus sometimes prefer to optimize the worst performance of the experiment over the admissible domain Θ for the parameters. This minimax (or maximin) policy has already been proposed (Fedorov 1980, Silvey 1980, Landaw 1985), but the complexity of minimax optimization appears as a tremendous obstacle to the practical use of such criteria. An algorithm intended to optimize these criteria in a reasonably simple way will be described in Section 4.4. The prior information on $\underline{\theta}$ is limited here to the knowledge of the admissible domain Θ. No hypothesis is made on $p(\underline{\theta})$. A possible criterion for optimality that can be deduced from (6) is given by

$$j_{mmd}(\underline{e}) = \min_{\underline{\theta} \in \Theta} [j_d(\underline{\theta}, \underline{e})]. \quad (20)$$

Definition 4. (Pronzato 1986, Walter and Pronzato 1987)
An experiment $\underline{e}_{mmd}$ is MMD-optimal if it maximizes the criterion $j_{mmd}(\underline{e})$ over $\mathbb{E}$. Equivalently, $\underline{e}_{mmd}$ satisfies

$$\underline{e}_{mmd} = \mathrm{Arg}\,[\max_{\underline{e} \in \mathbb{E}} [\, j_d(\underline{\theta}_{mmd}(\underline{e}),\underline{e})]], \tag{21}$$

with

$$\underline{\theta}_{mmd}(\underline{e}) = \mathrm{Arg}\,[\min_{\underline{\theta} \in \Theta} [\, j_d(\underline{\theta},\underline{e})]]. \tag{22}$$

4.2. Properties

As we shall see, MMD-optimal experiments can be shown to possess some properties that are similar to those obtained for EID-optimal experiments.

Linearity with respect to some parameters.

Theorem 4.1.

If Hypotheses H1 and H2 of Theorem 3.1 are satisfied, and if

H4: The admissible space for the parameters is such that the constraints on $\underline{\theta}^l$ are independent from those on $\underline{\theta}^{nl}$, then the MMD-optimal experiment can be obtained with all components of $\underline{\theta}^l$ fixed at 1.

Proof.

Taking H1 and H2 into account, the Fisher information matrix can be written as in (12). From H4, the MMD-optimal experiment can therefore be obtained by

$$\underline{e}_{mmd} = \mathrm{Arg}[\max_{\underline{e} \in \mathbb{E}} [\min_{\underline{\theta}^l} [\prod_{j=1}^{p} (\theta^l_j)^2].\min_{\underline{\theta}^{nl}} [\det \mathbf{M}_F(\underline{u}_p,\underline{\theta}^{nl},\underline{e})]]], \tag{23}$$

which implies

$$\underline{e}_{mmd} = \mathrm{Arg}\,[\max_{\underline{e} \in \mathbb{E}} [\min_{\underline{\theta}^{nl}} [\det \mathbf{M}_F(\underline{u}_p, \underline{\theta}^{nl}, \underline{e})]]]. \tag{24}$$

The search for a MMD-optimal experiment can thus be conducted in a parameter space reduced to $\underline{\theta}^{nl}$. This will result in appreciable savings of computational time when using a minimax optimization algorithm such as that described in Section 4.4.

Reparameterization of the model. Contrary to classical D-optimal experiments, MMD-optimal experiments are generally changed when a non-degenerated transformation is applied to the model parameters. To prove it, consider a reparameterization of the model defined by $\underline{\lambda}(\underline{\theta})$, and assume Θ transforms into Λ. When estimating $\underline{\theta}$, the MMD-optimality criterion (20) can be written as

$$j_{mmd}(\underline{e}) = \min_{\underline{\theta} \in \Theta} [\det^2(\partial\underline{\lambda}^t/\partial\underline{\theta}).\det \mathbf{M}_F(\underline{\lambda}(\underline{\theta}),\underline{e})] \tag{25}$$

and, unless the transformation $\underline{\lambda}(\underline{\theta})$ is linear, the experiment maximizing (25) generally differs from the MMD-optimal experiment for the estimation of $\underline{\lambda}$, that maximizes $\min_{\underline{\lambda} \in \Lambda} [\det \mathbf{M}_F(\underline{\lambda},\underline{e})]$.

Replicated experiments.

Theorem 4.2.

(i) If the following hypothesis is satisfied

H5: $\underline{\theta}_{mmd}(\underline{e})$ as given by (22) does not depend on $\underline{e}$,

then the MMD-optimal experiment is D-optimal for this value of $\underline{\theta}$.

(ii) If the following hypothesis is satisfied

H6: $\underline{e}_{mmd}$ is stationary and corresponds to a saddle point of the D-optimality criterion where j_d is stationary in $\underline{\theta}$,

then $\underline{e}_{mmd}$ corresponds to a stationary value of the criterion $j_d(\underline{\theta}_{mmd}(\underline{e}_{mmd}),\underline{e})$.

Proof.

(i) Trivial from (21)-(22).

(ii) Since $\underline{e}_{mmd}$ is supposed stationary,

$$\partial j_d(\underline{\theta}_{mmd}(\underline{e}),\underline{e}) / \partial \underline{e} \Big|_{\underline{e}_{mmd}} = \underline{0}, \tag{26}$$

with $\underline{\theta}_{mmd}(\underline{e})$ given by (22). Equation (26) can also be written

$$\partial \underline{\theta}_{mmd}{}^t(\underline{e}) / \partial \underline{e} \Big|_{\underline{e}_{mmd}} . \partial j_d(\underline{\theta},\underline{e}_{mmd}) / \partial \underline{\theta} \Big|_{\underline{\theta}_{mmd}(\underline{e}_{mmd})}$$

$$+ \partial j_d(\underline{\theta}_{mmd}(\underline{e}_{mmd}),\underline{e}) / \partial \underline{e} \Big|_{\underline{e}_{mmd}} = \underline{0}. \tag{27}$$

Since $\underline{e}_{mmd}$ is by hypothesis a saddle point solution where j_d is stationary in $\underline{\theta}$, one has

$$\partial j_d(\underline{\theta},\underline{e}_{mmd}) / \partial \underline{\theta} \Big|_{\underline{\theta}_{mmd}(\underline{e}_{mmd})} = \underline{0}, \tag{28}$$

and (27) reduces to

$$\partial j_d(\underline{\theta}_{mmd}(\underline{e}_{mmd}),\underline{e}) / \partial \underline{e} \Big|_{\underline{e}_{mmd}} = \underline{0}. \tag{29}$$

As a consequence of this theorem, MMD-optimal experiments will present the same property of replications as D-optimal experiments do when the condition of part (i) applies. When the conditions of part (ii) are satisfied, this will also be true whenever the stationary solution for $j_d(\underline{\theta}_{mmd}(\underline{e}_{mmd}),\underline{e})$ corresponds to the optimum.

The computational burden involved in minimax optimizations is a major obstacle to the practical use of minimax criteria for the design of experiments. However it is sometimes possible to take advantage of the model structure and the parameter constraints to transform the minimax design problem into a simple D-optimal design problem. Such a situation is met when theorem 4.2 part (i) applies, and the MMD-optimal experiment is then obtained by maximization of the D-optimality criterion $j_d(\underline{\theta}_{mmd},\underline{e})$. For a given model structure and a given admissible domain Θ, the first question to be answered therefore is whether or not H5 is satisfied. We shall see in the next section that this is true for a large class of exponential regression models.

4.3. Exponential regression models

Exponential regression models play an important role in physics and in the biosciences. For that reason the results that we recall now seem of special importance.

Theorem 4.3. (Melas 1981)

Suppose that hypothesis H2 of theorem 3.1 is satisfied as well as

H7: the ith model output is given by

$$\underline{y}_{mi}(\underline{\theta},\underline{e}) = \sum_{j=1}^{p} \theta^l{}_j \exp(-\theta^{nl}{}_j e_i), \tag{30}$$

where e_i is a scalar characterizing the experimental situation for the ith measurement (for instance the ith sampling time),

H8: the admissible domain for the nonlinear parameters $\underline{\theta}^{nl}$ is given by

$$\Theta^{nl} = \{ \underline{\theta}^{nl} \in \mathbb{R}^p \mid \theta^{nl}{}_1 \le \theta^{nl}{}_{max},\ \theta^{nl}{}_j - \theta^{nl}{}_{j+1} \ge \lambda_j,\ j=1,\dots, p\}, \tag{31}$$

where $\theta^{nl}{}_{max}$ and the λ_j are known,

then for any experiment $\underline{e}$ with at least 2p measurements $\underline{\theta}_{mmd}$ given by (22) is such that

$$\underline{\theta}^{nl}{}_{mmd} = (\theta^{nl}{}_{max}, \theta^{nl}{}_{max} - \lambda_1, \theta^{nl}{}_{max} - (\lambda_1 + \lambda_2), \dots, \theta^{nl}{}_{max} - \sum_{j=1}^{p-1} \lambda_j)^t. \tag{32}$$

If the conditions of theorem 4.3 and H4 are satisfied, then theorem 4.1 applies. Consequently theorem 4.2 part (i) applies too, and the MMD-optimal experiment is obtained by maximization of the classical D-optimality criterion for the parameter vector $(\underline{u}_p{}^t, \underline{\theta}^{nl}{}_{mmd}{}^t)^t$, where $\underline{\theta}^{nl}{}_{mmd}$ is given by (32). Note that this MMD-optimal experiment will present the same property of replications as those observed on D-optimal experiments.

If for some exponential regression models it is posssible to transform MMD-optimal design into a conventional problem of D-optimal design, the minimax optimization problem has generally to be handled as such. Next section presents an algorithm intended to optimize minimax criteria at a reasonable cost.

4.4. Optimization of minimax criteria

There are rather few general-purpose algorithms for solving minimax problems. Most of them are restricted to situations where one of the two vectors involved belongs to a finite set of values. They therefore do not apply here where both $\underline{\theta}$ and $\underline{e}$ belong to infinite sets. Shimizu and Aiyoshi (1980) have proposed a *relaxation procedure* involving the iterative construction of a set of representative values for one of the two vectors (here $\underline{\theta}$), and the solution of a series of minimax problems where $\underline{\theta}$ is restricted to this finite set of representative values. The initial minimax (here maximin) problem (21)-(22) can be viewed as the maximization, with respect to $\underline{e}$, of the scalar β subject to the constraint

$$\min_{\underline{\theta} \in \Theta} [\det M_F(\underline{\theta},\underline{e})] \geq \beta. \tag{33}$$

Inequality (33) is equivalent to

$$\det M_F(\underline{\theta},\underline{e}) \geq \beta,\ \forall\, \underline{\theta} \in \Theta, \tag{34}$$

and the maximin problem is an optimization problem with respect to $\underline{e}$, subject to an infinite number of constraints. The procedure relaxes the problem by taking into account a finite number of constraints only. The algorithm can be summarized as follows:

Step 1: Choose an initial parameter vector $\underline{\theta}^{(1)}$, and define a first set of representative values

$$\mathbb{S}^{(1)} = \{ \underline{\theta}^{(1)} \}, \tag{35}$$

set k=1.

Step 2: Solve the current relaxed problem

$$\underline{e}^{(k)} = \text{Arg} [\max_{\underline{e} \in \mathbb{E}} [\min_{\underline{\theta} \in \mathbb{S}^{(k)}} [\det M_F(\underline{\theta},\underline{e})]]]. \tag{36}$$

Step 3: Solve the minimization problem

$$\underline{\theta}^{(k+1)} = \text{Arg} [\min_{\underline{\theta} \in \Theta} [\det M_F(\underline{\theta},\underline{e}^{(k)})]]. \tag{37}$$

Step 4: if

$$\det M_F(\underline{\theta}^{(k+1)}, \underline{e}^{(k)}) \geq \min_{\underline{\theta} \in \mathbb{S}^{(k)}} [\det M_F(\underline{\theta},\underline{e}^{(k)})] - \delta, \tag{38}$$

where δ is a small predetermined constant, then stop and consider $(\underline{\theta}^{(k+1)}, \underline{e}^{(k)})$ as an approximate solution of the maximin problem. Else, include $\underline{\theta}^{(k+1)}$ into the set of representative values,

$$\mathbb{S}^{(k+1)} = \mathbb{S}^{(k)} \cup \{ \underline{\theta}^{(k+1)} \}, \tag{39}$$

increase k by one, and go to step 2.

Shimizu and Aiyoshi have shown (1980) that the procedure terminates in a finite number of iterations when the following assumptions (often satisfied for minimax design problems) hold:

H9: $\det M_F(\underline{\theta},\underline{e})$ is continuous in $\underline{\theta}$, differentiable with respect to $\underline{e}$, and with partial derivatives continuous in $\underline{e}$,

H10: the admissible experimental domain $\mathbb{E}$ is compact, and such that

$$\mathbb{E} = \{ \underline{e} \in \mathbb{R}^N \mid c_i(\underline{e}) \leq 0,\ i=1,\dots, q \}, \tag{40}$$

where the c_i are differentiable with respect to $\underline{e}$, with partial derivatives continuous in $\underline{e}$,

H11: the admissible domain for the parameters is nonempty and compact.

It must be noted that if one has to stop the procedure before the terminating condition (38) is satisfied, an approximate solution is nevertheless obtained, that satisfies a condition similar to (38) with a constant $\delta' \geq \delta$. Steps 2 and 3 require an optimization to be performed. Since the functions involved are not necessary unimodal (and it is possible to find very simple examples where they are not), their global optimum must be determined. The use of a global optimizer is therefore necessary. The implementation of such an algorithm, based upon an adaptive random search strategy, is described in (Pronzato et al. 1984).

5. CONCLUSIONS

EID- and MMD- optimal designs appear as two complementary answers to the problem of experiment design for estimating the parameters of a nonlinear model.

If it is acceptable to perform poorly for some unlikely values of the parameters, an EID-optimal experiment can be chosen, which will ensure good performances on the average. The representation of the prior uncertainty on the model parameters must then be probabilistic. If poor performances are unacceptable, MMD-optimality is to be preferred. This requires a deterministic representation of the prior uncertainty on the parameters.

A stochastic approximation algorithm has been described for the optimization of the EID-optimality criterion: it makes EID-optimal design almost as simple as classical D-optimal design. There are special cases of importance where MMD-optimal design transforms into D-optimal design. For other situations where the minimax optimization problem cannot be avoided a relaxation procedure has been described: an approximate minimax solution is obtained after a reasonable amount of calculations.

Both methodologies could be extended to the design of discriminating experiments, and to sequential design. For the later problem the method for updating the information after each estimation phasis would depend on the methodology chosen. When EID-optimality is used, each estimation phasis should provide a more accurate description of the distribution $p(\underline{\theta})$ of the model parameters (see e.g. (Steimer et al. 1984, Sheiner and Beal 1980) for a procedure for updating $p(\underline{\theta})$). On the other hand, when MMD-optimal design is used, each estimation phasis should provide a more accurate description of the admissible domain for the parameters. Methods recently developped for membership set estimation could be used for that purpose (Belforte and Milanese 1981, Walter and Lahanier 1986).

REFERENCES

Belforte, G. and Milanese, M. (1981). Uncertainty interval evaluation in presence of unknown but bounded errors: nonlinear families of models. Proc. IASTED Int. Symp. Modelling, Identification and Control, Davos, 75-79.

Box, G.E.P. and Hunter, W.G. (1965). The experimental study of physical mechanisms. Technometrics, 7(1), 23-42.

Box, M.J. (1968). The occurence of replications in optimal design of experiments to estimate parameters in nonlinear models. J. R. Stat. Soc., 30, 290-302.

Chaloner, K. and Larntz, K. (1986). Optimal Bayesian design applied to logistic regression experiments. Technical Report n°483, University of Minnesota, St. Paul.

D'Argenio, D.Z. (1981). Optimal sampling times for pharmaceutic experiments. J. of Pharmacokinetics and Biopharmaceutics, 9(6), 739-756.

DiStefano III, J.J. (1982). Algorithms, software and sequential optimal sampling schedule designs for pharmacokinetic and physiologic experiments. Math. and Comput. in Simul., 24, 531-534.

Dvoretsky, A. (1956). On stochastic approximation. Proc. 3rd Berkeley Symp. Math. Stat. and Probability. 39-55.

Fedorov, V.V. (1972). Theory of Optimal Experiments. Academic Press, New York.

Fedorov, V.V. (1980). Convex design theory. Math. Operationsforsch. Statist., Ser. Statistics, 11(3), 403-413.

Goodwin, G.C. and Payne, R.L. (1977). Dynamic system identification: experiment design and data analysis. Academic Press, New York.

Landaw, E.M. (1980). Optimal experiment design for biological compartmental systems with applications to pharmacokinetics. Ph.D. Dissertation, Univ. of California, Los Angeles.

Landaw, E.M. (1985). Robust sampling designs for compartmental models under large prior eigenvalue uncertainties. In J. Eisenfeld and C. DeLisi (Eds.), Mathematics and Computers in Biomedical Applications. North Holland Pub. Comp., Amsterdam.

Melas V.B. (1981). Optimal experiment design for exponential regressions (in Russian). In V.V. Penenko (Ed.), Mathematical Methods for Experiment Design. Nauka, Novosibirsk.

Poliak, B.T., and Tsypkin Ya. Z. (1973). Pseudogradient adaptation and training algorithms. Automation and Remote Control, 34(3), Part 1, 377-397.

Pronzato, L. (1986). Synthèse d'expériences robustes pour modèles à paramètres incertains. Thèse en Sciences. Université de Paris Sud. Orsay.

Pronzato, L., and Walter, E. (1985). Robust experiment design via stochastic approximation. Math. Biosci., 75, 103-120.

Pronzato, L., Walter, E., Venot, A., and Lebruchec, J.F. (1984). A general purpose global optimizer: implementation and applications. Math. and Comput. in Simul., 26, 412-422.

Saridis, G.N. (1974). Stochastic approximation methods for identification and control, a survey. IEEE Trans. on Autom. and Control, AC-19(6), 798-809.

Sheiner, L.B., and Beal, S.L. (1980). Evaluation of methods for estimating population pharmacokinetic parameters. I Michaelis Menten model. Routine clinical pharmacokinetic data. J. Pharmacokinetics and Biopharmaceutics, 8(6), 553-571.

Shimizu, K., and Aiyoshi, E. (1980). Necessary conditions for min-max problems and algorithm by a relaxation procedure. IEEE Trans. on Autom. Control, AC-25(1), 62-66.

Silvey, S.D. (1980). Optimal Design, Chapman & Hall, London.

Steimer, J.L., Mallet, A., Golmard, J.L., and Boisvieux, J.F. (1984). Alternative approaches to estimation of population pharmacokinetic parameters, comparison with NONMEM. Drug. Metab. Review, 15, 265-292.

Walter, E. and Piet-Lahanier, H. (1986). Robust nonlinear parameter estimation in the bounded noise case. Proc. 25th IEEE Conf. on Decision and Control, Athens, 1037-1042.

Walter, E., and Pronzato, L. (1985). How to design experiments that are robust to parameter uncertainty. Prep. 7th IFAC/IFORS Symp. on Identification and System Parameter Estimation, York, 921-926.

Walter, E., and Pronzato, L. (1987). Robust experiment design: between qualitative and quantitative identifiabilities. In E. Walter (Ed.), Identifiability of parametric models, 104-113. Pergamon. (to appear)

Wynn, H.P. (1972). Results in the theory and construction of D-optimum experimental designs. J.R. Stat. Soc., B 34, 133-147.

OPTIMAL DESIGN FOR NONLINEAR PROBLEMS

D.M. Titterington
Department of Statistics, University of Glasgow, Glasgow G12 8QQ, Scotland

1. INTRODUCTION

This paper provides a brief overview of some of the difficulties that arise in the implementation of optimal designs for nonlinear problems. The major source of difficulty is that the optimal design itself is a function of the true values of the unknown parameters, θ. As a result, the correct optimal design cannot be specified at the outset. In practice, a variety of strategies might be attempted, including the following:

(i) Choose a static design that is optimal for some prior guess at the values of the parameters.

(ii) Implement a sequential design, in which the allocation of later observations is modified on the basis of up-to-date estimates of the unknown parameters. Within this class of designs, it is convenient to distinguish between batch-sequential designs, in which the design strategy alters at comparatively infrequent intervals, and fully-sequential designs, where the parameter estimate and design strategy are updated after every observation.

One of the main points we shall make concerns the difficulty of validating interval estimation procedures within sequential design procedures.

The plan of the paper is as follows. Section 2 gives a taste of the scope of nonlinear problems, Section 3 outlines the optimal design theory that betrays the difficulties, and Section 4 comments on the problems of inference based on data from sequential design. A problem involving the estimation of a nonlinear function of the parameters in a linear model is discussed in Section 5 and Section 6 reports on part of a larger simulation study.

Although many references are cited later in the paper, it is appropriate to refer to Ford et al (1987) for a much more extensive review of the topic.

2. THE SCOPE OF NONLINEAR PROBLEMS

The starting point of our discussion is the regression model

$$Y = \eta(\theta;x) + \varepsilon \ , \tag{1}$$

in which Y is a response variable, η is the regression function, θ contains k unknown parameters, x is a set of design variables and the error ε has zero mean and variance σ^2. Errors on different observations are assumed uncorrelated and, in some circumstances, $\sigma^2 = \sigma^2(\theta;x)$.

A canonical form of the usual linear regression model has constant σ^2 and

$$Y = \theta^T x + \varepsilon \ . \tag{2}$$

So far as optimal design is concerned, the following all constitute nonlinear problems.

2.1. Nonlinear response function

This class of problems, in which $\eta(\theta;x)$ is a nonlinear function of θ, is exemplified by many of the models used for reaction rates in chemical kinetics. For example, with k=2, the formula

$$\eta(\theta;x) = \theta_1\{\exp(-\theta_2 x) - \exp(-\theta_1 x)\}/(\theta_1 - \theta_2)$$

is used by, among others, Box and Lucas (1959), to model a reaction of the form $A \to B \to C$. In the model, x represents time and η the concentration of substance B.

2.2. Linear regression with nonconstant variance

In this class, $\eta(\theta;x) = \theta^T x$, but σ^2 depends on θ and x.

2.3. Linear regression, but interest concentrated in a nonlinear function of the parameters

An example of this, studied by Ford and Silvey (1980), is provided by the quest for the stationary point in a "quadratic" regression model. To be specific, we have

$$Y = \theta_1 u + \theta_2 u^2 + \varepsilon , \quad -1 \leq u \leq 1, \tag{3}$$

with constant σ^2, and interest is concentrated in

$$g(\theta) = -\theta_1/2\theta_2 .$$

Another example is provided by the problem of inverse regression in simple linear regression.

2.4. Quantal response

In the simplest version of this, binary response, we have

$$\begin{aligned} Y &= 1 \quad \text{with probability } \eta(\theta;x) \\ &= 0 \quad \text{otherwise.} \end{aligned}$$

Specialising further, the case $\eta(\theta;x) = F(\theta^T x)$, in which F is the logistic distribution function, provides the linear logistic model. In its simplest version, $\theta^T x = \theta_1 + \theta_2 x$. For this case, interest may lie in estimating θ *per se*, or in, say, the pth quantile of $\eta(\theta;x)$, defined by

$$u_p = \theta_2^{-1}\{F^{-1}(p) - \theta_1\}.$$

Finally, in this Section, we comment that the broad areas of the identification of econometric models (Papakyriazis, 1978) and dynamic systems (Titterington, 1980) are also sources of nonlinear problems, in the context of this paper.

3. OPTIMAL DESIGN THEORY

We start by introducing some notation. We define $I(\theta;x)$ to be the

Fisher Information matrix associated with an observation Y at x, and we denote by $M(\theta;\xi)$ the per-observation information matrix associated with a design measure ξ on the design space $\mathcal{X}$. Thus

$$M(\theta;\xi) = \int_{\mathcal{X}} I(\theta;x)\xi(dx).$$

For exponential family problems with the structure given in (1),

$$I(\theta;x) = \{\sigma^2(\theta;x)\}^{-1}\nabla\eta\ \nabla\eta^T,$$

where $(\nabla\eta)^T = (\partial\eta/\partial\theta_1, \ldots, \partial\eta/\partial\theta_k)$. In the case of (2), of course,

$$I(\theta;x) = \sigma^{-2}xx^T. \qquad (4)$$

For the binary response problem,

$$I(\theta;x) = \{\eta(1-\eta)\}^{-1}\nabla\eta(\nabla\eta)^T.$$

We denote by Ξ the class of all design measures on $\mathcal{X}$.

The relative merits of different designs are typically judged on the basis of a scalar criterion, $\phi(\cdot)$, defined on the class, $\mathcal{M}(\theta)$, of information matrices. In what follows, we suppose that $\phi(\cdot)$ is a real-valued, concave, isotonic, positively homogeneous function, defined on NND(k), and that $\Phi(\cdot,\cdot)$ denotes the Fréchet derivative associated with ϕ. Specific choices for $\phi(\cdot)$ are associated with D-, A-, E- and c-optimality (Silvey, 1980, Pukelsheim and Titterington, 1983). The following general equivalence theorem provides alternative characterisations of a ϕ_θ-optimal design, which is a design, ξ^*, such that $M(\theta;\xi^*)$ maximises $\phi(M)$, for $M \in \mathcal{M}(\theta)$.

<u>Theorem</u> (Whittle, 1973, White, 1973)

The following are equivalent

(i) $\phi\{M(\theta,\xi)\}$ is maximised at $M(\theta,\xi^*)$.

(ii) $\Phi\{M(\theta,\xi^*), M(\theta,\xi)\} \leq 0$ for all $\xi \in \Xi$.

If, also, ϕ is differentiable at $M(\theta,\xi^*)$, (i) is equivalent to

(iii) $\Phi\{M(\theta,\xi^*), I(\theta,x)\} \leq 0$ for all $x \in \mathcal{X}$.

In principle, the theorem is useful for checking whether or not a proposed design is optimal, and for motivating sequential design procedures. In terms of the latter, two possible algorithms are as follows. In both of them $\{\hat\theta_n\}$ denotes a sequence of estimators of θ, where $\hat\theta_n$ is based on n observations, at $x_1, \ldots, x_n$, which constitute a design ξ_n.

<u>Algorithm A</u> : Choose x_{n+1} to maximise $\phi\{M(\hat\theta_n,\xi_{n+1})\}$.

<u>Algorithm B</u> : Choose x_{n+1} to maximise $\Phi\{M(\hat\theta_n,\xi_n); I(\hat\theta_n,x_{n+1})\}$. (Steepest ascent direction.)

The need to base sequential design on up-to-date estimates of θ betrays the fundamental difficulty created by nonlinear problems, namely, the dependence of the correct optimal design, and the applicability of the <u>Theorem</u>, on θ. Only in the linear case (c.f. (4)) does θ disappear. Of course, non-sequential designs can be used, by assuming a prior guess, $\hat\theta_o$, for θ, or by adopting a prior density, $\pi(\theta)$, for θ, and then basing all analysis on the averaged optimality criterion ϕ_π, where

$$\phi_\pi(\xi) = \int \phi\{M(\theta,\xi)\}\ \pi(\theta)\ d\theta;$$

see Laüter (1974).

4. <u>GENERAL QUESTIONS ABOUT SEQUENTIAL DESIGNS</u>

Given that we resign ourselves to the need to choose the sites of our observations sequentially, thereby creating a sequence of design measures, $\{\xi_n\}$, and an associated sequence of estimators $\{\hat{\theta}_n\}$, based on, say, maximum likelihood estimation, three crucial general questions arise.

Q1. As $n \to \infty$, does $\hat{\theta}_n \to \theta_T$, the true value of θ, in any sense?

Q2. As $n \to \infty$, does $M_n = M(\hat{\theta}_n, \xi_n) \to M(\theta_T, \xi^*)$, where ξ^* is a correct optimal design?

Q3. Suppose there is, in the case of prespecified (non-sequential) design, a procedure for generating exact or approximate interval estimates for θ, or functions thereof. Can the procedure be used safely with data generated by sequential design procedures, thereby effectively ignoring the fact that the design was generated sequentially in such a way that data $y_1, \ldots, y_n$ largely dictate the choice of x_{n+1}?

With regard to Q1 and Q2, the crucial question is Q1, in that, if $\hat{\theta}_n$ is consistent, then Q2 will generally follow by a continuity argument.

To illustrate the non-triviality of Q3 consider the very simple example of linear regression through the origin. (Although this is clearly not a nonlinear example, it adequately brings out the present difficulty.) Thus,

$$Y_i = \theta x_i + \varepsilon_i, \; i = 1, 2, \ldots \tag{5}$$

with $\varepsilon_i \sim N(0,1)$, independently for each i. Let $\hat{\theta}_n$ be the least squares (or maximum likelihood) estimator of θ, based on n observations. Thus

$$\hat{\theta}_n = \Sigma Y_i x_i / \Sigma x_i^2 \tag{6}$$

and, if the x_i are determined independently of the data, $\hat{\theta}_n \sim N(\theta, 1/\Sigma x_i^2)$. As a result, exact confidence intervals for θ are easily obtained.

Suppose, however, we generate the x_i by the sequential design algorithm: $x_1 = 1$, $x_i = Y_{i-1}$, $i = 2, \ldots$. Then (6) still provides the maximum likelihood estimator for θ, but the distributional result for $\hat{\theta}_n$ is no longer true exactly. Of course, the combination of model (5) along with the above design algorithm constitutes an AR(1) model: our problem can therefore be regarded as one of making inferences for stochastic processes; see Lai and Siegmund (1983), and Ford et al (1985) for a parallel discussion in the case of a more general Normal linear model.

For this example, we have remarked that the sequential nature of the design does not affect the identity of the maximum likelihood estimators, but it does, or might, affect interval estimation. Ford et al (1985) comment on another parallel to be drawn, in terms of this phenomenon, with the problems of making inferences from incomplete data (Rubin, 1976).

In these problems the distribution of $\hat{\theta}_n$, conditionally on the design achieved sequentially, is typically quite unlike its distribution were the design prespecified: see Ford and Silvey (1980) for empirical results and Ford et al (1985) for very simple examples. In many cases, however, the unconditional distribution of $\hat{\theta}_n$ does appear to allow the use of standard approximate interval estimation recipes. In fact, it does not seem appropriate, from a fundamental point of view, to make inferences conditionally on the sort of sequential design we envisage using. After all, we hope that the limiting design might be the correct optimal design. As such, the design itself should tell us something about θ and is therefore not ancillary.

The answers to questions Q1-3 have as yet not been obtained in any general sense. However, we now present some reassuring evidence for the cases of Sections 2.3 (for which theoretical and empirical results are available) and Section 2.4 (for which much of the work has been empirical). Other results, related to Section 2.4, appear in Wu (1985a).

5. LINEAR REGRESSION, WITH INTEREST IN A RATIO OF PARAMETERS

We recall Ford and Silvey's (1980) interest in estimating the turning point of the quadratic response curve subsumed in (3). The objective is to minimise the approximate variance (generated by the usual, Taylor-expansion argument of $g(\hat{\theta}_n)$, where $g(\theta) = -\theta_1/2\theta_2$. It turns out that this leads to a c-optimality criterion, in which the vector, c, is $\nabla g(\theta)$ and is proportional to $(1, 2g)^T$. Thus, the optimal design depends on the ratio θ_1/θ_2. Whatever value this ratio takes, the support points of both the optimal design and the sequential design generated by Algorithm B are concentrated at $u = \pm 1$. The nonlinear nature of the problem makes itself apparent in that the optimal weights depend on θ_1/θ_2. When $|\theta_1/\theta_2| = 1$, the optimal design turns out to be degenerate, concentrated on a single point ($u = +1$ or $u = -1$). Ford and Silvey (1980) provide confirmatory answers to questions Q1 and Q2. So far as Q3 is concerned, they provide encouraging empirical results in the form of coverage rates, for the obvious asymptotic 95% confidence interval for $g(\theta)$, in Monte Carlo experiments. However, theoretical backing was provided later, in Wu (1985b), to confirm that, asymptotically, at least, the answer to Q3 was indeed "Yes". It is important to remark that the key to the theoretical results in both papers was to concentrate on the pure error process $\{\varepsilon_i\}$ and to use standard limit theorems.

In an attempt to answer Q1-Q3 at a more general level, Wu (1985b) considered the estimation of a nonlinear function, $g(\theta)$, within the linear model defined by (2), but without the Normality assumption. The validity of standard, asymptotic interval estimates follows provided

$$n(\hat{\theta}_n - \theta)^T M_n (\hat{\theta}_n - \theta) \to \sigma^2\chi^2(k), \tag{7}$$

in distribution, as $n \to \infty$, where M_n is the per-observation information matrix from n observations. Wu (1985b) points out that, provided the errors $\{\varepsilon_i\}$ form a martingale difference sequence, conditions on $\{M_n\}$ laid out by Lai and Wei (1982) are sufficient to guarantee (7). Unfortunately, the nature of these conditions makes them difficult to verify in practice. That they are not necessary conditions is illustrated by the fact that they do not hold in the example of Ford and Silvey (1980)!

6. EMPIRICAL RESULTS FOR THE "DILUTION SERIES" MODEL

In this Section, we outline the main findings of a Monte Carlo study that was designed to compare the performances of various design strategies. More extensive discussion is provided in Ford et al (1987) and in the unpublished, University of Glasgow, Ph.D. Thesis of C.P. Kitsos.

The study is based on the "dilution series" model of Fisher (1922). We treat it simply as a binary response model, with

$$p(Y = 1|x) = \exp(-\theta x) = 1-p(Y = 0|x).$$

Estimation of θ is the objective of the experiment.

The optimal design is a degenerate measure at $x = 1.59/\theta$. We report results for a set of 1000 simulations, with sample size $N = 100$ in each run.

The following design procedures are compared in the present paper.

P1 : Static design, with all observations at $x = 1.59/\hat{\theta}_o$, where $\hat{\theta}_o$ is an initial guess for θ.

P2 : Batch-sequential design, with two batches of 50 observations, and $\hat{\theta}_n$ obtained by maximum likelihood.

P3 : Batch-sequential design, with four batches of 25 observations, and $\hat{\theta}_n$ obtained by maximum likelihood.

P4 : Fully sequential design, following an initial batch of 5 observations, and with $\hat{\theta}_n$ updated by the appropriate version of the following general stochastic approximation algorithm at each stage:

$$\hat{\theta}_{n+1} = \hat{\theta}_n + \{nM(\hat{\theta}_n;\xi_n)\}^{-1}U(y_{n+1}|x_{n+1},\hat{\theta}_n).$$

Here, $U(y|x,\theta)$ is the score function associated with a single observation.

When the level x is altered in methods P2, P3 and P4, the procedure adopted was to take $x_{n+1} = 1.58/\hat{\theta}_n$.

The true value for the parameter was $\theta_T = 3.18$ and comparison was made among three choices for the initial value $\hat{\theta}_o$, namely, 2.20, 3.18 and 7.15. To avoid divergence in P4, $\hat{\theta}_n$ was constrained within the interval (1.37, 199.70): for detailed explanation, see Ford et al (1987, Section 7).

The Table presents the sample average, $\overline{\theta}$, of the 1000 realisations of $\hat{\theta}_N$, the estimated mean squared error (EMSE) of $\hat{\theta}_N$, the "asymptotic" approximation to $\mathrm{var}(\hat{\theta}_N)$ and the empirical coverage rate (ECR) of the standard, approximate, 95% confidence interval for θ.

TABLE Results of simulation study (true θ = 3.18)

Procedure	$\hat{\theta}_o$	$\overline{\theta}$	EMSE	$\mathrm{var}(\hat{\theta}_N)$	ECR
P1	2.20	3.24	0.20	0.17	0.950
	3.18	3.20	0.17	0.16	0.952
	7.15	3.00	0.20	0.20	0.952
P2	2.20	3.25	0.22	0.17	0.945
	3.18	3.20	0.15	0.16	0.950
	7.15	3.24	0.20	0.20	0.955
P3	2.20	3.24	0.20	0.17	0.946
	3.18	3.19	0.16	0.16	0.950
	7.15	3.23	0.19	0.20	0.946
P4	2.20	3.21	0.16	0.17	0.955
	3.18	3.21	0.15	0.16	0.960
	7.15	3.24	0.17	0.20	0.953

In general, the results were reassuring, with acceptable coverage rates and EMSE's close to the values in the $\mathrm{var}(\hat{\theta}_N)$ column. It has to be said that two of the runs for P2 and $\hat{\theta}_o$ = 2.20 were discarded because of "divergence" and that, in this case, the sample skewness and kurtosis of $\hat{\theta}_N$ indicated clear non-Normality. The simulation study reported on in Ford et al (1987) is much more extensive, but reinforces these general remarks.

ACKNOWLEDGEMENT

The material in this paper owes much to the author's collaboration with Dr. I. Ford, Dr. C.P. Kitsos and Professor C.F.J. Wu.

REFERENCES

Box, G.E.P. and Lucas, H.L. (1959). Design of experiments in nonlinear situations. Biometrika, 46:77-90.

Fisher, R.A. (1922). On the mathematical foundation of theoretical statistics. Philosophical Transactions of the Royal Society of London, Series A, 22:309-368.

Ford, I., Kitsos, C.P. and Titterington, D.M. (1987). Recent advances in nonlinear experimental design. Submitted for publication.

Ford, I. and Silvey, S.D. (1980). A sequentially constructed design for estimating a nonlinear parametric function. Biometrika, 67:381-388.

Ford, I., Titterington, D.M. and Wu, C.F.J. (1985). Inference and sequential design. Biometrika, 72:545-551.

Lai, T.L. and Siegmund, D. (1983). Fixed accuracy estimation of an autoregressive parameter. Annals of Statistics, 11:478-485.

Lai, T.L. and Wei, C.Z. (1982). Least squares estimation in stochastic regression models, with applications to identification and control of dynamic systems. Annals of Statistics, 10:154-166.

Läuter, E. (1974). A method of designing experiments for nonlinear models. Mathematische Operationsforschung und Statistik, 5:697-708.

Papakyriazis, P.A. (1978). Optimal experimental design in econometrics. The time series problem. Journal of Econometrics, 7:351-372.

Pukelsheim, F. and Titterington, D.M. (1983). General differential and Lagrangian theory for optimal experimental design. Annals of Statistics, 11:1060-1068.

Rubin, D.B. (1976). Inference and missing data (with discussion). Biometrika, 63:581-592.

Silvey, S.D. (1980). Optimal Design. Chapman and Hall, London.

Titterington, D.M. (1980). Aspects of optimal design in dynamic systems. Technometrics, 22: 287-299.

White, L.V. (1973). An extension to the general equivalence theorem for nonlinear models. Biometrika, 60:345-348.

Whittle, P. (1973). Some general points in the theory of optimal experimental design. Journal of the Royal Statistical Society, Series B, 35:123-130.

Wu, C.F.J. (1985a). Efficient sequential designs with binary data. Journal of the American Statistical Association, 80:974-984.

Wu, C.F.J. (1985b). Asymptotic inference from sequential design in a nonlinear situation. Biometrika, 72:553-558.

PART II.

REGRESSION ANALYSIS

LEAST MEDIAN OF SQUARES FOR UNMASKING IN TRANSFORMATIONS AND MULTIPLE REGRESSION

A.C. ATKINSON, IMPERIAL COLLEGE, LONDON, U.K.

1. INTRODUCTION

The purpose of this paper is to summarize some recent work on the use of robust regression for detecting multiple outliers and groups of influential observations. The two situations studied are multiple regression and transformation of the response in a linear model.

Methods based on the deletion of single observations are effective if there is only one outlier. But sometimes when there are several outliers, single deletion methods fail to reveal all, or even any, of these. In such examples, the outliers are said to be masked. Of course, if the presence of several outliers is suspected, it is theoretically possible to consider deletion of all m-tuples of a given size. However the combinatorial explosion of possibilities rules out an exhaustive search. For example, if the number of observations n=30, deletion of all sets of 4 observations leads to evaluation of 27 405 combinations.

As a tractable alternative for a regression model without transformation, Atkinson (1986a) suggested a two-stage procedure. The first, exploratory, stage uses least median of squares regression, a robust method which resists nearly 50% of contamination in the data, to identify potential outliers and influential observations. As a result of the robust analyst the data are provisionally divided into n-m 'good' observations and m 'bad' ones. In the second, confirmatory, stage, standard single-deletion regression diagnostics are used to check the n-m good observations. To investigate the properties of the m deleted observations Atkinson (1986a) developed addition diagnostics which measure the effect on the analysis of the data of reintroducing deleted data points one at a time. These methods are described slightly more fully in Section 2.

The extension of this two-stage procedure to transformation of the response in a linear model is described in Section 3. The example studied is the parametic family of power transformations indexed by a scalar parameter λ. For the exploratory stage Atkinson (1986a) suggests the use of least median of square regression over a grid of λ values. Plots of the robust residuals as λ varies are informative about departures from the model. The confirmatory stage is concerned with the influence of individual observations on inferences about λ. The two measures used are the approximate score statistic for the transformation (Atkinson, 1973) and the quick estimate of the transformation parameter (Atkinson, 1982). Examples of addition and deletion versions of both statistics are given in Section 3.

2. LEAST MEDIAN OF SQUARES REGRESSION

In this section a brief description is given of the exploratory use of least median of squares regression for the detection of multiple outliers. A book length treatment is provided by Rousseeuw and Leroy (1987).

Suppose that the majority of the observations follow the standard linear regression model

$$E(Y) = X\beta, \tag{1}$$

where the n x p matrix X consists of the known values of the p carriers which are functions of the explanatory variables. The errors are assumed additive and independent with constant variance σ^2.

For the parameter value b let the residual $r_i = y_i - x_i^T b$. Then two criteria for the choice of b are:

Least Sum of Squares Regression: $\min_b \Sigma r_i^2$

Least Median of Squares Regression: $\min_b \text{median}\, r_i^2$.

The intention of least median of squares regression in the presence of outliers is to fit a line to the 'good' observations whilst revealing the 'bad' observations as such.

The numerical method used to find b is a form of random search. If the rank of the regression model is p, samples of p observations are taken, to each of which, except for singular samples which are abandoned, the regression model can be fitted exactly. Such samples are called 'elemental sets'. Sampling with calculation of the median of the non-zero residuals continues until either a stable pattern of residuals emerges, or until there is a specified probability, for a given level of contamination, of obtaining at least one elemental set which consists solely of 'good' observations.

For the Jth elemental set let the residuals be r_{iJ}, at least p of which will be zero. If the elemental set giving rise to the minimum median squared residual is denoted by T, then

$$\tilde{r}_T^2 = \underset{N_T}{\text{median}}\, r_{iT}^2 = \min_J \underset{N_J}{\text{median}}\, r_{iJ}^2 \tag{2}$$

where N_T and N_J are the number of non-zero residuals, usually n-p. As an estimate of σ^2 Atkinson (1986a) suggests $\tilde{s}^2 = \tilde{r}_T^2$. The estimate is used to provide standardized least median of squares residuals $\tilde{r}_i = r_{iT}/\tilde{s}$.

Fig. 1 is an index plot of the standardized residuals $\tilde{r}_i$ for the stack loss data introduced by Brownlee (1965, p.454). There are 21 observations and 3 exploratory variables, to which a first order model is fitted. To obtain Fig. 1, 1,000 elemental sets were sampled. The four observations

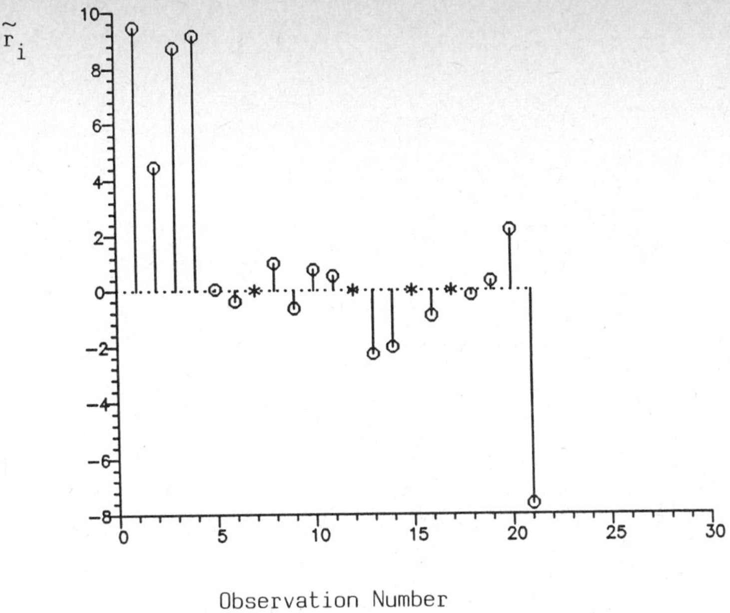

FIGURE 1 Brownlee's stack loss data: index plot of standardized least median of squares residuals $\tilde{r}_i$.

forming the resulting optimum elemental set are marked in the figure by crosses. The plot clearly indicates that observations 1, 3, 4 and 21 are outliers and raises doubts about observation 2. This analysis agrees with that of Andrews (1974) and with the least median of squares results of Hampel et al (1986, pp 330-2). Atkinson (1986a) illustrates, for this example, the evolution of the robust residuals with the number of elemental sets sampled. A very full analysis of the stack loss data is given by Daniel and Wood (1980, Chapter 5). Atkinson (1985, § 12.4) summarizes this and other analyses.

The result of Rousseeuw (1984) and of Atkinson (1986a) show that least median of squares is an excellent exploratory tool. However, the estimates of the parameters of the linear model have poor properties and a second, confirmatory, stage is required. Rousseeuw (1984) uses the least median of squares estimate as a starting point for robust regression using M estimators. To check the n-m 'good' observations Atkinson (1986a) uses half-normal plots of deletion residuals and of modified Cook statistics to which simulation envelopes are added. These least-squares regression diagnostics are described in the books of Belsley, Kuh and Welsch (1980), Cook and Weisberg (1982), Atkinson (1985) and of Weisberg (1985, Cap. 5 and 6). The addition diagnostics for the effect of adding back in each of the m deleted observations are described by Atkinson (1986a). Examples are qiven, for the stack loss data, of the analogues of residuals and of modified Cook statistics.

3. TRANSFORMATION OF THE RESPONSE

Quite different diagnostic methods are required when transformation of the response is investigated. Again the strategy is in two stages, exploratory and confirmatory. As an example we consider the parametric family of power transformations analysed by Box and Cox (1964). In normalized form this is

$$z(\lambda) = (y^{\lambda} - 1)/(\lambda \dot{y}^{\lambda-1}) \qquad (\lambda \neq 0) \tag{3}$$

$$= \dot{y}\log y \qquad (\lambda = 0)$$

where $\dot{y}$ is the geometric mean of the y_i. The hope is that there is some value of the parameter λ for which the transformed observations will satisfy the linear model (1) to an adequate degree.

For the normalized transformation (3), with the assumption of normal errors, the loglikelihood of the observations, maximized over the parameters of the linear model, is given by

$$L_{max}(\lambda) = -(n/2)[1 + \log\{2\pi R(\lambda)/n\}]. \tag{4}$$

In (4) $R(\lambda)$ is the residual sum of squares of the $z(\lambda)$ given by

$$R(\lambda) = z(\lambda)^T(I - H)z(\lambda), \tag{5}$$

where the hat matrix $H = X(X^TX)^{-1}X^T$. The maximum likelihood estimate of λ is the value $\hat{\lambda}$ for which the profile loglikelihood $L_{max}(\lambda)$ is maximized.

To unmask information about the dependence of the estimated transformation on several outliers. Atkinson (1986a) uses a plot of the least median of squares residuals of $z(\lambda)$, denoted $\tilde{r}_1(\lambda)$, calculated for 21 values of λ between -1 and 1. Changes in the pattern of the residuals as λ varies are indicative of potential outliers and leverage points. Fig. 2 is such a plot for an altered version of the poison data analysed by Box and Cox (1964). The original data consist of the results of a 3x4 factorial experiment with 4 replicates per cell, in which the response is survival time. There is strong evidence of the need for a transformation and the inverse transformation is indicated. To show the effect of a single outlier we fellow Andrews (1971) and alter y_{20} from 0.23 to 0.13. As a result, the likelihood analysis indicates the log, rather than the reciprocal, transformation.

Fig. 2 shows that the effect of the changed observation is not apparent from the robust analysis at λ=1. The largest least median of squares residuals belong to the largest observations. But, as λ approaches -1, the robust residuals all become small, with the exception of that for the altered observation 20 which increases in magnitute to -17.13. The next greatest residual in magnitute is -3.99 for observation 35. The plot clearly indicates the anomalous nature of observation 20.

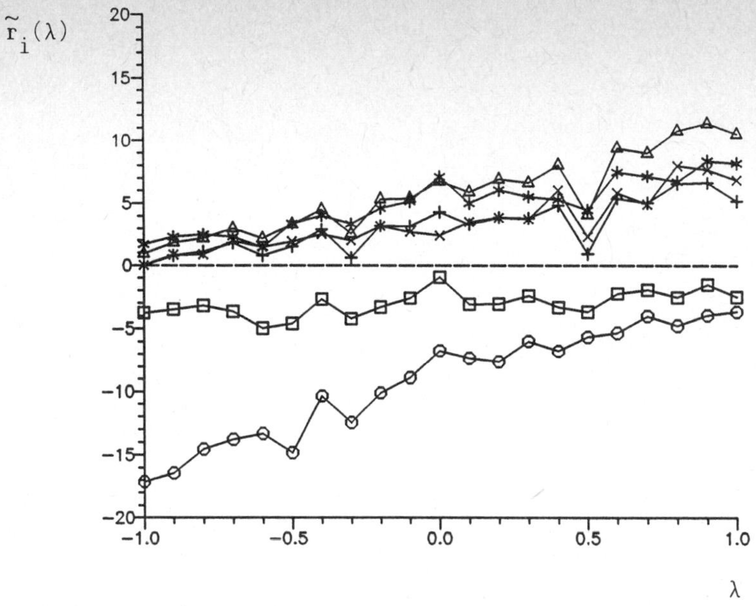

FIGURE 2 Altered Box and Cox poison data: plot of robust residuals $\tilde{r}_i(\lambda)$ against λ. ○ altered observation 20.

As a result of the exploratory plots of $\tilde{r}_i(\lambda)$, of which Fig. 2 is an example, up to m observations may be suspected of being outlying. The influence of these observations on inferences about λ is checked in the second, confirmatory stage of the analysis.

Hypotheses about the value of λ can be tested using the approximate score statistic $T_p(\lambda)$ introduced by Atkinson (1973). For confirmatory use, the statistic is evaluated from a fit of the model to the n-m 'good' observations. To check the effect of deletion of each of these observations, the statistic $\tilde{T}_{p(i)}(\lambda)$ can be used, in which the effect of deletion is estimated. Similarly, the effect of adding back into the analysis each of the m deleted observations can be estimated from the addition diagnostic $\tilde{T}_{P[i]}(\lambda)$ described by Atkinson (1986a). Related addition and deletion diagnostics for $\tilde{\lambda}$, the quick estimate of the transformation parameter, are described in the same paper.

As an example of the confirmatory stage of the analysis we use the record times for 35 Scottish hill races listed by Atkinson (1986b), together with the distance of the race, in miles, and the climb in feet. For the calculations in this paper, the time for race 18, which is 3 miles long, has been corrected from 1 hour 18 minutes to 18 minutes.

Analysis of the transformed data using least median of squares shows that observations 7, 11, 33 and 35 have large positive residuals. The plot of $\tilde{r}_i(\lambda)$ against λ given by Atkinson (1986a) shows that, initially, the residuals decrease as λ decreases. The score statistic for all 35 observations and the plot of the profile loglikelihood $L_{max}(\lambda)$ both suggest that the square root transformation, $\lambda=0.5$, is appropriate. However, the confirmatory analysis reveals the importance for this conclusion of some of the suggested outliers.

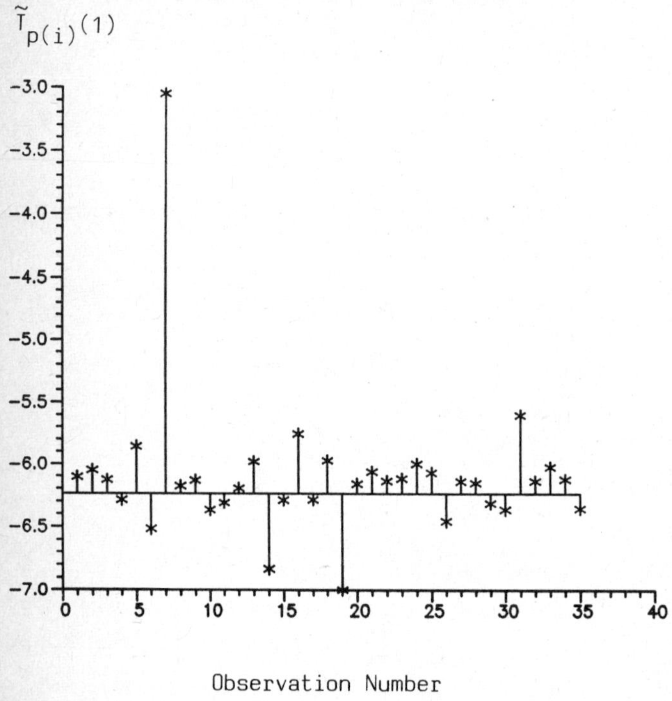

FIGURE 3 Corrected hill racing data: index plot of approximate score statistic $\tilde{T}_{P(i)}(1)$.

Fig. 3 is an index plot of the deletion estimate of the score statistic $\tilde{T}_{P(i)}(1)$ for the hypothesis of no transformation. For all observations $T_p(1) = -6.24$ and there is strong evidence of the need for a transformation. However, the plot shows how important observation 7 is to this conclusion. If observation 7 is deleted, $T_p(1) = -3.17$, close to the value of the estimate in Fig. 3. Fig. 4 shows the index plot of the quick estimates

$\tilde{\lambda}_{(i)}(1)$ and $\tilde{\lambda}_{[i]}(1)$, collectively called $\tilde{\lambda}_i(1)$, which is centred around 0.79. The plot reveals not only the importance of reintroducing the deleted observation 7, but also the importance of observation 33, which was previously masked. The implication is that if both observations 7 and 33 are deleted, there will be no further evidence for a transformation. Fig. 5, in which both observations have been deleted, does indeed show that all the evidence for the transformation, as measured by the approximate score statistic $T_p(1)$, depends on observations 7 and 33. The same conclusion

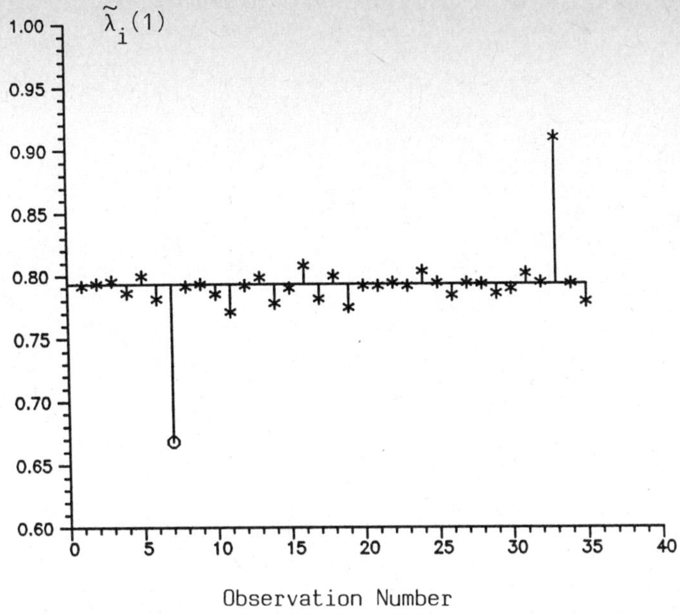

FIGURE 4 Corrected hill racing data: index plot of quick estimate $\tilde{\lambda}_i(1)$; observation 7 deleted.

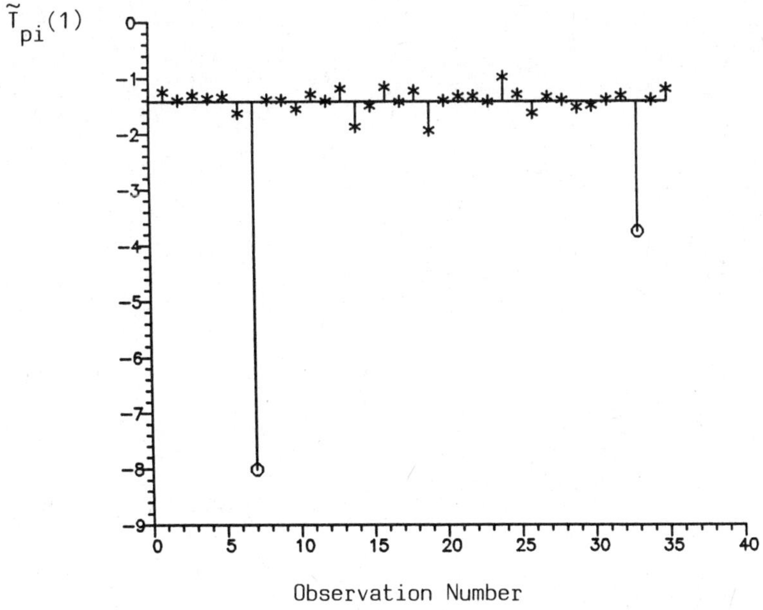

FIGURE 5 Corrected hill racing data: index plot of approximate score statistic $\tilde{T}_{pi}(1)$; observations 7 and 33 deleted.

follows from the plots of the profile loglikelihood as observations are deleted given in Atkinson (1986a).

These examples show the use of the two-stage procedure in which an exploratory analysis using robust regression is followed by a confirmatory analysis based on least squares diagnostic methods.

Further examples involving transformation of the response are given by Atkinson (1986a). Atkinson (1986b) gives plots of profile loglikelihoods for several examples, including those of the present paper. In these examples the plot of the robust residuals as λ varies is more informative than the plot of least squares residuals as a function of λ. But, when the observations come from a balanced design, established diagnostic methods based on least squares provide the required information with appreciably reduced computation. These methods, for transformations, include those based on added variable plots (Cook and Weisberg, 1982, § 2.4; Atkinson, 1985, Chapters 6-9) and on measures of the effect of deletion of single observations (Cook and Wang, 1983; Atkinson, 1985, § 12.3).

REFERENCES

Andrews, D.F. (1971). A note on the selection of data transformations. Biometrika 58: 249-54.

Andrews, D.F. (1974). A robust method for multiple linear regression. Technometrics 16: 523-31.

Atkinson, A.C. (1973). Testing transformations to normality. J. R. Statist. Soc. B 35: 473-9.

Atkinson, A.C. (1982). Regression diagnostics, transformations and constructed variables (with discussion). J.R. Statist. Soc. B 44: 1-36.

Atkinson, A.C. (1985). Plots, Transformations, and Regression. Oxford, U.K.: University Press.

Atkinson, A.C. (1986a). Masking unmasked. Biometrika 73: 533-41.

Atkinson, A.C. (1986b). Aspects of diagnostic regression analysis. (Discussion of paper by Chatterjee and Hadi). Statistical Science 1: 397-402.

Atkinson, A.C. (1988a). Transformations unmasked. Submitted for publication.

Atkinson, A.C. (1988b). Robust regression and unmasking transformations. Proc. Second Tampere Conf. Statistics. Tampere, Finland: University of Tampere, Department of Mathematical Sciences.

Belsley, D.A., Kuh, E. and Welsch, R.E. (1980). Regression Diagnostics. New York: Wiley.

Box, G.E.P. and Cox, D.R. (1964). An analysis of transformations (with discussion). J.R. Statist. Soc. B 26: 211-46.

Brownlee, K.A. (1965). Statistical Theory and Methodology in Science and Engineering (2nd edn.) New York: Wiley.

Cook, R.D. and Wang, P.C. (1983). Transformations and influential cases in regression. Technometrics 25: 337-43.

Cook, R.D. and Weisberg, S. (1982). Residuals and Influence in Regression. New York and London: Chapman and Hall.

Daniel, C. and Wood, F.S. (1980). Fitting Equations to Data (2nd edn.). New York: Wiley.

Hampel, F.R., Ronchetti, E.M. Rousseeuw, P.J. and Stahel, W.A. (1986). Robust Statistics. New York: Wiley.

Rousseeuw, P.J. (1984). Least median of squares regression. J. Amer. Statist. Assoc. 79: 871-80.

Rousseeuw, P.J. and Leroy, A. (1987). Robust regression and outlier detection. New York: Wiley.

Weisberg, S. (1985). Applied Linear Regression (2nd edn.). New York: Wiley.

CONDITIONED ESTIMATORS OF NONLINEAR PARAMETERS

Henning Läuter, Berlin (GDR)

1. INTRODUCTION

The estimation of nonlinear parameters is of special interest in different fields. Mostly in nonlinear estimation problems it is tried the statistical methods known for linear parameters to use in a direct way also for nonlinear problems. We point out that it is necessary to include the special form of the nonlinearities into the estimation procedure. We discuss the conditioned estimators derived by Läuter (1986) and give a computational procedure for these new estimators.

2. ESTIMATION OF NONLINEAR PARAMETERS

Let P be the distribution of a variable $y \in R^n$. On the basis of an observation of y we will estimate the parameter $\lambda(P)$.
As examples for λ we mention:

1. Let $P_1, \dots, P_k$ be distributions in R^p and $m_1, \dots, m_k$ be positive integers. For a function φ and for $P=(P_1, \dots, P_k)$ we define

$$\lambda(P)=\int\dots\int\varphi(x_{11}, \dots, x_{1m_1}, x_{21}, \dots, x_{km_k}) \prod_{i=1}^{k} \prod_{j=1}^{m} P_i(dx_{ij}). \quad (1)$$

For instance the error rate for misclassification in the discriminant analysis is of this type (Läuter (1985)).

2. For the variable $y \in R^n$ the representation

$$y=X(\beta)+\varepsilon, \quad \beta \in R^k$$

holds where X depends nonlinearily on β. Here $\lambda(P)=\beta$ is to be estimated. Especially growth curve models are of this type, e. g.

$$y_i = \beta_1 + \beta_2 \exp(\beta_3 t_i) + \varepsilon_i, \quad t_i \in R^1, \; i=1,\dots,n. \tag{2}$$

3. For the variable $y \in R^n$ the linear model

$$y = X\beta + \varepsilon, \quad \beta \in R^k$$

holds and $\lambda(P) = \mu(\beta)$ for a nonlinear function μ is to be estimated.

There are several **principles** for estimating $\lambda(P)$. One of the frequently used methods is the substitution procedure. Here one estimates P by $\hat{P}_n$ and $\lambda(\hat{P}_n)$ is the estimate for $\lambda(P)$. In some other cases one defines an estimator $\hat{\lambda}$ in an implicite form. Especially in nonlinear regression one computes the least squares estimator (l.s.e.) $\hat{\beta}$ for β by

$$|y - X(\hat{\beta})|^2 = \min_\beta |y - X(\beta)|^2$$

and one uses $\hat{\beta}$ or $\mu(\hat{\beta})$ as the estimator for $\lambda(P)$. In some other situations one takes the U-statistics as an estimator for $\lambda(P)$. For this we assume that in (1) φ is symmetric in each of the k tupels $x_{i1},\dots,x_{im_i}$, $i=1,\dots,k$. For samples $y_{i1},\dots,y_{in_i}$ of the distribution P_i, $n_i \geq m_i$ we define

$$\hat{\lambda} = \frac{1}{c} \sum \varphi(y_{1i_1},\dots,y_{1i_{m_1}}, y_{2j_1},\dots,y_{kl_{m_k}})$$

where the summation goes on all indices with

$$i_1 < i_2 < \dots < i_{m_1},$$

$$j_1 < j_2 < \dots < j_{m_2}, \dots, l_1 < l_2 < \dots < l_{m_k}.$$

The c denotes the number of such different sets of indices:

$$c = \binom{n_1}{m_1} \cdots \binom{n_k}{m_k}.$$

The asymptotic behaviour of these estimators is investigated extensively. Ibragimov & Khasminski (1981) and Läuter (1985) proved the asymptotic minimax property of the substitution estimator and the U-statistics for functionals (1). The l.s.e.

in nonlinear regression is strongly consistent under general conditions. Jennrich (1969) and Bunke & Schmidt (1980), Wu (1981) showed this for a compact space for the nonlinear parameter. Läuter (1987) gave results for unbounded nonlinear parameters. The nonasymptotic behaviour is of special interest. A simple example was given by Läuter (1986). We considered i.i.d. normally distributed variables $y_1, \ldots, y_n$ with $y_i \sim N(\beta, 1)$ and $\lambda(P) = e^{\beta}$ is to be estimated. The maximum likelihood estimator (m.l.e.) is

$\hat{\beta} = \frac{1}{n} \sum_{i=1}^{n} y_i = \bar{y}$. We have $E\, e^{\hat{\beta}} = e^{\beta}\, e^{\frac{1}{2n}}$. For $\bar{y}$ is a sufficient and complete statistics the $\tilde{\lambda} = e^{\hat{\beta} - \frac{1}{2n}}$ is the best unbiased estimator for $\lambda(P)$. Moreover $\bar{\lambda} = e^{\hat{\beta} - \frac{3}{2n}}$ has

the minimal mean squared error in the set $\{\rho\, e^{\hat{\beta}} : \rho \in R^1\}$. In this case we see that $\tilde{\lambda}$ has a smaller variance than $e^{\hat{\beta}}$ and additionally $\tilde{\lambda}$ is unbiased. Therefore in some situations the usually used m.l.e. or l.s.e. can be improved as in the variance as in the bias.

We mention as another example an exponential model. We assume the model (2) with $\varepsilon_i \sim N(0, \sigma^2)$. One finds by simulations that the m.l.e. $\hat{\beta}_1$, $\hat{\beta}_2$, $\hat{\beta}_3$ yield biased estimations for β_1, β_2, β_3. As an example we give the values for n=6, $t_6 = -t_1 = 5$, $t_5 = -t_2 = 3$, $t_4 = -t_3 = 1$,

$\sigma^2 = \frac{1}{4}$, $\beta_1 = 1.0$, $\beta_2 = 2.0$, $\beta_3 = -.3$. One gets $E\hat{\beta}_1 = .873$, $E\hat{\beta}_2 = 2.11$, $E\hat{\beta}_3 = -.301$, var $\hat{\beta}_1 = .35$, var $\hat{\beta}_2 = .52$, var $\hat{\beta}_3 = .004$. The quite large bias of the $\hat{\beta}_1$ and $\hat{\beta}_2$ is disturbing. But how one can improve these estimators ? The problem consists in the general definition of an appropriate estimator in nonlinear situations.

3. CONDITIONED ESTIMATORS

The concept of conditioned estimators gives a good approach for nonlinear parameter estimations. The idea to this method comes from some stability demands on the estimators.

Definition 1: The estimator $\tilde{\lambda}$ is called **conditioned unbiased** estimator w.r. to $\hat{\lambda} = \hat{\lambda}(y)$ and η if

- η is a random variable in R^n with $E(\eta \mid y) = 0$,

- for all $y_0 \in R^n$ there is a $\tilde{y}_0 \in R^n$ with

$$E\left\{ \hat{\lambda}(\tilde{y}_0 + \eta) \mid y=y_0 \right\} = \hat{\lambda}(y_0) \qquad (3)$$

- the estimator $\tilde{\lambda}$ is defined by $\tilde{\lambda}(y_0) = \hat{\lambda}(\tilde{y}_0)$.

Definition 2: The estimator $\tilde{\lambda}$ has a **conditioned minimal mean squared error** if all conditions in definition 1 are fulfilled, only (3) is replaced by

$$E\left\{ (\hat{\lambda}(\tilde{y}_0+\eta)-\lambda(P))(\hat{\lambda}(\tilde{y}_0+\eta)-\lambda(P))' \mid y=y_0 \right\} =$$

$$=\min_{z\in R^n} E\left\{ (\hat{\lambda}(z+\eta)-\lambda(P))(\hat{\lambda}(z+\eta)-\lambda(P))' \mid y=y_0 \right\}. \qquad (4)$$

Example: We consider as above $y_i = \beta + \varepsilon_i$, $\varepsilon_i \sim N(0,1)$, $i=1,\dots,n$ and $\lambda(P)=e^{\beta}$, $\hat{\lambda}=e^{\hat{\beta}}$. Let η be independent of y and $\eta \sim N(0,I)$ then $\tilde{\lambda}=\exp(\hat{\beta}-\frac{1}{2n})$ is a conditioned unbiased estimator w.r. to $\hat{\lambda}$ and $\bar{\lambda}=\exp(\hat{\beta}-\frac{3}{2n})$ has a conditioned minimal mean squared error. We remember that these estimators $\tilde{\lambda}$ and $\bar{\lambda}$ were best unbiased resp. optimal in the mean squared distance. Moreover it holds

$$E(\tilde{\lambda}-e^{\beta})^2 < E(\hat{\lambda}-e^{\beta})^2, \quad E(\bar{\lambda}-e^{\beta})^2 < E(\hat{\lambda}-e^{\beta})^2 .$$

In this example we see that these conditioned estimators are better than the m.l.e. We remark that for linear estimators in linear models the BLUE $\hat{\lambda}$ coincides with the conditioned estimators.

For the computation of the conditioned estimators it is convenient to approximate the conditions (3) and (4). For instance we approximate $E\{\hat{\lambda}(\tilde{y}_0+\eta) \mid y=y_0\}$ by

$$E\left\{ \hat{\lambda}(\tilde{y}_0+\eta) \mid y=y_0 \right\} \approx \frac{1}{l} \sum_{i=1}^{l} \hat{\lambda}(\tilde{y}_0 + \eta^{(i)})$$

when $\eta^{(1)},\dots,\eta^{(l)}$ are realizations of η. Sometimes one substitutes y_0+a instead of $\tilde{y}_0$ and then we have

$$E\left\{ \hat{\lambda}(\tilde{y}_0+\eta) \mid y=y_0 \right\} \approx \frac{1}{l} \sum_{i=1}^{l} \hat{\lambda}(y_0 + a + \eta^{(i)}). \qquad (5)$$

Up to now the distribution of η was known but not fixed. In general this distribution should be data dependent. For $y+\eta$ describes points around y the conditioned estimators include the behaviour of $\hat{\lambda}$ around $\hat{\lambda}(y)$.

4. DATA FITTED CONDITIONED ESTIMATORS

We pointed out that for estimating $\lambda(P)$ the substitution method gives the estimator $\hat{\lambda}=\lambda(\hat{P}_n)$. Now we generate l subsamples of the given sample and denote the corresponding estimations of P by $P^{*(1)},\ldots,P^{*(l)}$. If y+a is considered instead of y then the estimations of P_a (distribution of y+a) are $P^{*(1)}_a,\ldots,P^{*(l)}_a$.

Definition 3: A **data fitted conditioned unbiased** estimator w.r. to $\hat{\lambda}$ is $\lambda(\hat{P}_{\tilde{a}})$ where $\tilde{a}$ fulfils the condition

$$\frac{1}{l}\sum_{i=1}^{l}\lambda(P^{*(i)}_{\tilde{a}})=\lambda(\hat{P}). \tag{6}$$

Here we study the variation of λ in the neighbourhood of $\hat{P}$ without any additional conditions on random variables. By re-sampling we generated "new" distributions around $\hat{P}$ and insofar this $\lambda(\hat{P}_{\tilde{a}})$ is a data fitted conditioned estimator.

Example: We consider $y_i=\beta+\varepsilon_i$, $\varepsilon_i\sim N(0,\sigma^2)$, i=1,2 and $\lambda(P)=e^{\beta}$. If we use the subsamples y_1 ;y_2 ;y_1 ,y_2 then the data fitted estimator is defined by

$$\tilde{\lambda}=\frac{3\,e^{2\bar{y}}}{e^{y_1}+e^{y_2}+e^{\bar{y}}}.$$

One finds $0<E(e^{\bar{y}}-\lambda(P))^2-E(\tilde{\lambda}-\lambda(P))^2$ and this tends to ∞ for $|\beta|\to\infty$.

A general result was given by Läuter (1986). There was proved that the U-statistics is a data fitted conditioned estimator.

5. COMPUTATION OF A DATA FITTED CONDITIONED ESTIMATOR

Now we use the representation $\hat{\lambda}(y^{(i)})=\lambda(\hat{P}^{*(i)})$ where $y^{(i)}$ is the sample generated by our resampling method. Then (6) goes over in the condition

$$\frac{1}{l}\sum_{i=1}^{l} \hat{\lambda}(y^{(i)}+\tilde{a}) = \hat{\lambda}(y). \tag{7}$$

For the determination of $\tilde{a}$ we use a modified Gauss-Newton-procedure. We denote $\hat{\mu}(a) = \frac{d}{da}\hat{\lambda}(a)$ and follow the next steps:

1. Starting with an initial vector a_0, compute

$$\tilde{a}_1 = a_0 + l\left[\sum_{i=1}^{l} \hat{\mu}(y^{(i)}+a_0) \sum_{j=1}^{l} \hat{\mu}(y^{(j)}+a_0)\right]^{+} \cdot$$

$$\cdot \sum_{i=1}^{l} \hat{\mu}(y^{(i)}+a_0)\left[\hat{\lambda}(y) - \frac{1}{l}\sum_{j=1}^{l} \hat{\lambda}(y^{(j)}+a_0)\right]$$

2. Determine ρ_1 such that

$$\left(\frac{1}{l}\sum_{i=1}^{l} \hat{\lambda}(y^{(i)}+a_0+\rho(\tilde{a}_1-a_0)) - \hat{\lambda}(y)\right)^2 = \min_{\rho} .$$

3. $a_1 = a_0 + \rho_1(\tilde{a}_1 - a_0)$

4. Repeat the steps 1. to 3. with a_1 instead of a_0 and s. o.

Here A^+ denotes the Moore-Penrose-Inverse of the matrix A.

For this computational method it is possible to prove a convergence result (similar to Hartley (1961)). The so constructed sequence $a_0, a_1, \ldots$ converge and $a_i \to \tilde{a}$, $\tilde{a}$ fulfils (7). This procedure yields a data fitted conditioned estimator if $\hat{\lambda}$ is given explicitely.

Some modification is necessary if we will find a data fitted estimator in nonlinear regression. We assume that the regression model depends on the particular subsample:

$$y^{(i)} = X^{(i)}(\beta) + \varepsilon^{(i)} \tag{8}$$

$i=1,\ldots,l$. We denote the l.s.e. for β in (8) by $\hat{\beta}^{(i)}$ or $\hat{\beta}(y^{(i)})$. With $G^{(i)}(\beta)=\frac{d}{d\beta}X^{(i)}(\beta)$ we compute

$$\Gamma = \sum_{i=1}^{l} G^{(i)\prime}(\hat{\beta}^{(i)})G^{(i)}(\hat{\beta}^{(i)})$$

and let $\tilde{a}_1$ be the eigenvector of Γ to the largest eigenvalue. Then we determine such ρ_1 that

$$(\frac{1}{l}\sum_{i=1}^{l} \hat{\beta}(y^{(i)} + \rho\,\tilde{a}_1) - \hat{\beta}(y))^2 = \min_{\rho}$$

and put

$$a_1 = \rho_1\,\tilde{a}_1.$$

Now we denote by $\hat{\beta}_a^{(i)}$ such parameter which fulfils

$$G^{(i)}(\hat{\beta}_a^{(i)})(y^{(i)}+a-X^{(i)}(\hat{\beta}_a^{(i)}))=0$$

and define

$$\Gamma(a)=\sum_{i=1}^{l} G^{(i)\prime}(\hat{\beta}_a^{(i)})G^{(i)}(\hat{\beta}_a^{(i)}).$$

Then let $\tilde{a}_2$ be the eigenvector to the largest eigenvector of $\Gamma(a_1)$ and we determine such ρ_2 that

$$(\frac{1}{l}\sum_{i=1}^{l} \hat{\beta}(y^{(i)} + a_1 + \rho\,\tilde{a}_2) - \hat{\beta}(y))^2 = \min_{\rho}$$

holds. Now we put

$$a_2 = a_1 + \rho_2\,\tilde{a}_2$$

and repeat this procedure by replacing a_2 instead of a_1. Again the convergence of this procedure can be proved.

Example: We consider the exponential model (2) with the special values for $\beta_1, \beta_2, \beta_3$ and $t_1,\ldots,t_6$ given in section 2. Here one obtains

$$\tilde{a}=(.7329,\ .2532,\ .0505,\ -.0265,\ -.0486,\ -.0485)'$$

The mean squared error (MSE) of the l.s.e. computed with the corrected observations $y+\tilde{a}$ is about 15 % less than the MSE of the usual l.s.e. This shows the large statistical advantage in using the conditioned estimates in such exponential models.

REFERENCES

Bunke, H., W.H. Schmidt (1980). Asymptotic results on nonlinear approximation of regression functions and weighted least squares. Math. Operationsforsch. Statist., Ser. Statist. 11 3-22.

Hartley, H.O. (1961). The modified Gauss-Newton method for the fitting of non-linear regression functions by least squares. Technometrics 3 269-280.

Ibragimov, J.A., R. S. Khasminski (1981). Statistical Estimation: Asymptotic Theory. Springer-Verlag New York.

Jennrich, R.I. (1969).Asymptotic properties of non-linear least squares estimators. Ann. Math. Statist. 40 633-643.

Läuter, H. (1985). An efficient estimator for the error rate in discriminant analysis. Statistics 16 107-119.

Läuter, H. (1986). Estimation of nonlinear functionals with resampling methods. Invited paper on the summer school "Model choice", Holzhau, GDR.

Läuter, H. (1987). Note on the strong consistency of the least squares estimator in nonlinear regression. Manuscript.

Wu, Chien-Fu (1981). Asymptotic theory of nonlinear least squares estimation. Ann. Statist. 9 501-513.

Resampling Codes and Regenerated Likelihoods

S.-M.Ogbonmwan, University of Benin, Nigeria
R.J.Verrall, University of London, Goldsmiths' College, England
H.P.Wynn, City University, London, England

1 Introduction

This paper continues the work by Ogbonmwan and Wynn on the use of resampling and restricted reference sets to obtain simulated likelihoods for complex statistical models. These are particularly relevant when distributional properties are poorly specified but some parametric modelling is required. Comparisons are made with the normal theory likelihood for some simple autoregressive models.

In a previous paper Ogbonmwan and Wynn, 1987 (OW) sketched a theory of likelihood generation in semi-parameter models which showed itself applicable to two sample, regression and autoregressive models. We introduce here, along with the method in that paper, a further method in which whole alternative sample paths may be generated. We shall give some examples comparing the two methods. Relevant recent work is by Davison, Hinkley and Schechtman (1986).

2 The Likelihood

The technique in OW is as follows. Starting with a data set

$$\underline{x} = (x_1, \ldots, x_n)$$

we assume that there is some parameter dependent transformation

$$\underline{y}_\theta = g_\theta(\underline{x}) \text{ where } \underline{y}_\theta = (y_1, \ldots, y_m)_\theta.$$

If θ is a 'true' value of the parameter we assume a kind of exchangeability assumption. That is, we look at all $\underline{y}^*$ vectors in a 'reference set' $S(\theta)$ obtained from the original $\underline{y}_\theta$ by 'expansion'. Thus $S(\theta)$ may be all bootstrap samples or all versions of $\underline{y}_\theta$ obtained by sign change.

For each $\underline{y}^* \in S(\theta)$ we compute a statistic $T(\underline{y}^*)$ or alternatively resample from $S(\theta)$ to obtain a resampled set of $T(\underline{y}^*)$ values. This set will have an empirical distribution $\hat{F}_T(t)$, which may, if so required, be smoothed to obtain a density $\hat{f}_T(t)$. The hat in both cases denotes the fact that we have used empirically generated values. The likelihood, which we denote by L_1 (a second version will be given later) is

$$L_1(\theta) = \hat{f}_T(\tilde{t})$$

where $\tilde{t} = T(\underline{y}_\theta)$ is the statistic evaluated from the transformed raw data.

The rational for this is that if t is a rough sufficient statistic whose distribution given θ is reflected by $\hat{f}_T(t)$ then indeed L_1 will be roughly proportional to the true likelihood (by Neymann factorization). This method is reconstructive with the engine of reconstruction being the assumptions about $S(\theta)$. Special choices of $S(\theta)$ are referred to as resampling codes.

For certain models a more objective version of the process may be given by tracing backwards from $S(\theta)$ to reconstruct alternative samples for $\underline{x}$. Thus relabelling $S(\theta)$ as $S_y(\theta)$ alternatively construct an $S_x(\theta)$ by an inversion. If $\underline{y}^*$ is a typical member of $S_y(\theta)$ we reconstruct $\underline{x}^*$ by an inversion

$$\underline{x}^* = \tilde{g}^{-1}(\underline{y}^*)$$

The tilde over g denotes the fact that $\tilde{g}^{-1}$ may not be the precise inverse of g in all cases. The reversion may lose dimensions, or some entries in $\underline{x}^*$ may be fixed. This will become clearer in the examples. The $\underline{x}^*$ are to be considered as alternative samples that 'might have been produced' if θ were the true value of the parameter. For each $\underline{x}^*$ we then compute the value of a statistic, $T(\underline{x}^*)$, and procede as above to construct $\hat{f}_T(t)$ and the alternative likelihood

$$L_2(\theta) = \hat{f}_T(\tilde{t}),$$

where $\tilde{t}$ is now $T(\underline{x})$, the value for the raw data. We assume that $\tilde{g}^{-1}(g_\theta(\underline{x})) = \underline{x}$, so that the raw data can be reconstructed precisely and that therefore $\underline{x} \in S_x(\theta)$.

The ease with which one can reconstruct the sample $\underline{x}^*$ depends on computational efficiency and also any initial assumptions fed into the construction of $\tilde{g}^{-1}$.

The implementation of the procedures (to construct $L = L_1$ or L_2) has as its starting point <u>*storing* θ</u> on the computer and procedes to construct $L(\theta)$ for the stored value. The technique, in the construction of L_2 particularly, is thus similar to that of Diggle and Gratton (1984) for implicitly defined likelihood. It differs from more traditional bootstrap methods in that simulation takes place for a range of θ values rather than at an estimated value $\hat{\theta}$. Method 1 (L_1) is particularly powerful for large complex models which allow some degree of exhangeability after a parameter-dependent transformation and also a data reduction implied if the dimension of $\underline{y}$ is much less than the dimension of $\underline{x}$. We believe that a likelihood is a proper output for a large scale simulation in which different input parameter values for θ are used.

If the $\underline{y}^*$ are chosen uniformly from $S(\theta)$ then the reconstruction gives a distribution for the $\underline{x}^*$ which is uniform on $S_x(\theta) = \tilde{g}^{-1}(S_y(\theta))$. The construction of an exact low dimensional sufficient statistic is hampered by the discrete nature of this distribution and the finiteness of its support. The full randomisation likelihood is

$$\frac{1}{B} Prob(\underline{x}^* = \underline{x}|\alpha).$$

Usually this is equal to $\frac{1}{B}$ since $\tilde{g}^{-1}(\underline{y}) = \underline{x}$ and is therefore uninformative. We wish to replace this by

$$Prob(t(\underline{x}^*) = t(\underline{x})|\alpha)$$

with the probability now evaluated over $\hat{f}_T$. Thus the summary statistic t and the smoothing step become critical. In non-parametric theory the smoothing step is not used (see discussion in OW).

3 The Autoregressive Model

We revisit the autoregressive model considered in OW. The AR(1) is written

$$X_t - \alpha X_{t-1} = \varepsilon_t, \quad t = 1, \ldots, n.$$

Here the $\{\varepsilon_t\}$ are usually assumed to be an independent sequence with constant variance. Suppose now we have observations $x_0, \ldots, x_n$. We 'store' α and generate

$$y_t = x_t - \alpha x_{t-1}, \quad t = 1, \ldots, n.$$

If α is the true α then the $\{y_t\}$ are a set of true residuals. We perform resampling on the $\{y_t\}$ (for the stored value of α) to produce B vectors

$$\underline{y}^*_\alpha = (y^*_1, \ldots, y^*_n).$$

Notice that the dimension of $\underline{y}^*_\alpha$ is one less than the dimension of $\underline{x} = (x_0, \ldots, x_n)$

We may consider examples of the two methods described above. In OW we look at

$$T_1(\underline{y}^*) = \frac{\sum_{i=1}^{n} y^*_{i-1} y^*_i}{\sum_{i=1}^{n-1} (y^*_i)^2}$$

The alternative is to produce sample paths by constructing

$$x^*_0 = x_0, \qquad x^*_i = \alpha x^*_{i-1} + y^*_i \quad (i = 1, \ldots, n)$$

This is the $\tilde{g}^{-1}$ transformation mentioned above. We then calculate

$$T_2(\underline{y}^*) = \frac{\sum_{i=1}^{n} x^*_{i-1} x^*_i}{\sum_{i=1}^{n-1} (x^*_i)^2}.$$

In either case we can construct a likelihood by looking at a (smooth) distribution

$$\hat{f}_i(t_i|\alpha), \quad i = 1, 2$$

and setting

$$L_i(\alpha) = \hat{f}_i(\tilde{t}_i|\alpha), \quad i = 1, 2.$$

Notice that $\tilde{t}_2$ is merely

$$\hat{\alpha} = \frac{\sum_{i=1}^{n} x_{i-1} x_i}{\sum_{i=1}^{n-1} x_i^2},$$

the usual maximum likelihood statistic.

In the examples below we resample by simple bootstrap with sign changes giving $(2^n)!$ possible samples. We smooth by merely letting

$$\hat{f}_i(t) = \frac{1}{B}\#(t - d \leq t_i^* \leq t + d),$$

for the range of stationarity $-1 < t < 1$. Here d is a suitably chosen constant and data was generated by sampling the ε_t from a normal distribution with n=32.

We compare $L_1(\alpha)$ and $L_2(\alpha)$ with the exact Normal theory likelihood, $L(\alpha)$. The regenerated likelihood L_2 exhibits better behaviour. The likelihood L_1 behaves strangely outside the interval $[-1, 1]$ showing that T_1 may not be the appropriate statistic. Both T_1 and T_2 are approximately sufficient for α for large samples and show robustness for non-normal errors. It would be fairer to compare L_1 and L_2 with the likelihood based on the asmptotic distribution of $\hat{\alpha}$, which is normal or the more accurate saddlepoint approximation given in Phillips (1978) (see also Durbin (1980)). This will be the subject of a further paper.

The following figure compares the cumulative versions of the likelihoods L_1, L_2 and L for one data set:

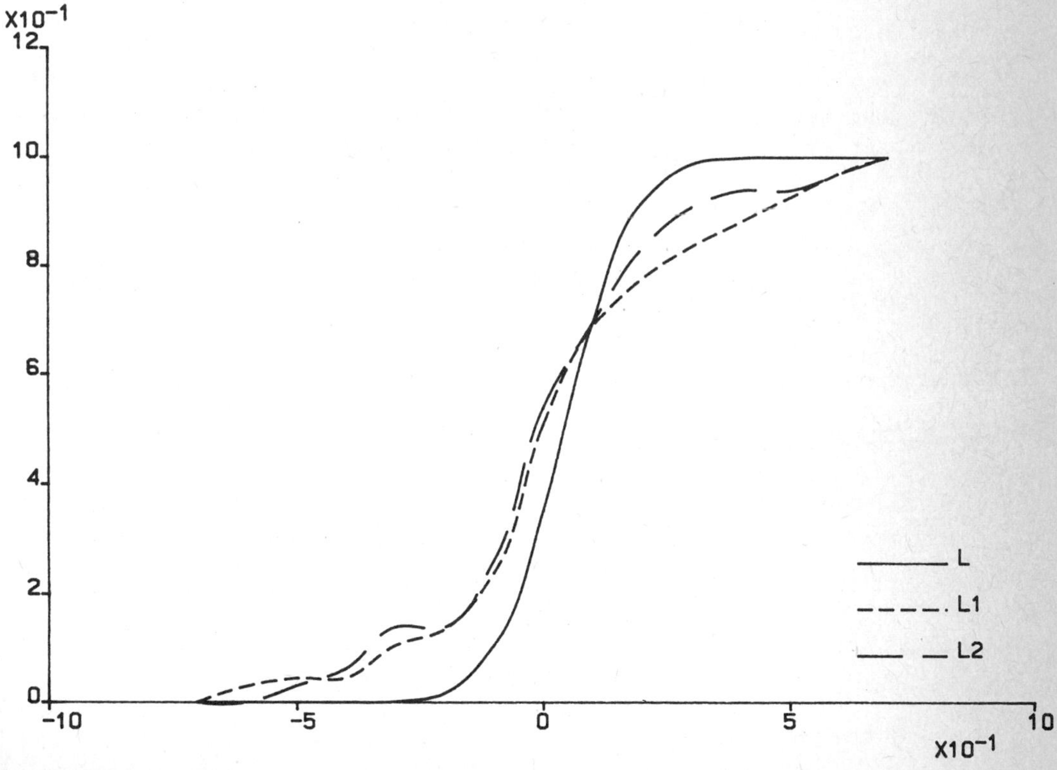

The following table compares the behaviour of L_1 and L_2 outside the [-1,1] range:

α	L_1	L_2
-2.0	0	0
-1.9	0	0
-1.8	0	0
-1.7	0	0
-1.6	1	0
-1.5	1	0
-1.4	0	0
-1.3	0	0
-1.2	0	0
-1.1	0	0
-1.0	0	0
-0.9	0	0
-0.8	1	0
-0.7	0	0
-0.6	1	0
-0.5	1	2
-0.4	0	1
-0.3	3	1
-0.2	5	2
-0.1	6	7
0.0	11	11
0.1	10	11
0.2	5	8
0.3	6	3
0.4	5	4

α	L_1	L_2
0.5	3	0
0.6	5	2
0.7	3	1
0.8	3	1
0.9	1	0
1.0	2	0
1.1	2	0
1.2	2	0
1.3	4	0
1.4	3	0
1.5	2	0
1.6	2	0
1.7	3	0
1.8	3	0
1.9	3	0
2.0	5	0
2.1	5	0
2.2	2	0
2.3	5	0
2.4	1	0
2.5	7	0
2.6	2	0
2.7	3	0
2.8	6	0
2.9	4	0

4 Conclusions

The likelihoods L_1 and L_2 in the general case are seen as alternatives to both the exact distribution theory likelihoods and likelihoods based on bootstrapping a single fit. For complex problems basing the statistic T on a transformed data set may be the most convenient. For simpler problems we advise reconstructions of alternative sample paths (method 2) and use of approximately sufficient statistics. The latter is an open problem as is the choice of statistic for method 1.

5 References

1.Davison,A.C., Hinkley,D.V. and Schechtman,E. (1986) Efficient Bootstrap Simulation. *Biometrika 73 555-566.*

2.Diggle,P.J. and Gratton,R.J. (1984) Monte Carlo methods of inference for implicit statistical models. *J. Roy. Statist. Soc. B 46 193-227*

3.Durbin,J. (1980) Approximations for densities of sufficient statistics. *Biometrika 67 311-333*

4.Ogbonmwan,S-M and Wynn,H.P. (1987) Resampling Generated Likelihoods. IV Purdue Symposium on Decision Theory and Related Topics, ed. S.S. Gupta *Academic Press, New York*

5.Phillips,P.C.B. (1978) Edgeworth and Saddlepoint approximations in the first-order noncircular autoregression. *Biometrika 65 91-98*

FLAT GAUSSIAN NONLINEAR REGRESSION MODELS

Andrej Pázman
Mathematical Institute SAS, CS-814 73 Bratislava, Czechoslovakia

1. INTRODUCTION

In the paper presented we consider gaussian nonlinear regression models, close to linear ones but still evidently nonlinear. Such models are called flat models. Every univariate nonlinear model becomes flat after a suitable reparametrization (Proposition 3); there are also many nontrivial examples of multivariate flat nonlinear models. The aim of the present paper is to show that nonlinear least squares estimates have in flat models very good nonasymptotic statistical properties.

1.1 The model

Let $Y_1, \ldots, Y_N$ be observed data and let us denote by $Y = (Y_1, \ldots, Y_n)^T$ the observed vector. The considered nonlinear regression model is of the form

$$\begin{aligned} &Y = \eta(\theta) + \varepsilon \\ &\varepsilon \sim N(0, \Sigma) \qquad (1) \\ &\theta \in \Theta \subset R^m \end{aligned}$$

where $\eta(\theta)$ is the systematic part of the model (= the mean of Y), ε is the gaussian error with the variance matrix Σ, θ is the vector of m unknown parameters $\theta_1, \ldots, \theta_m$.

<u>Regularity assumptions</u>:

i) The variance matrix Σ is nonsingular.

ii) The parameter space Θ is connected and it is open in R^m.

iii) The response function $\eta : \Theta \mapsto R^N$ has continuous second order derivatives $\partial^2\eta(\theta)/\partial\theta_i\partial\theta_j$ for every $\theta \in \Theta$.

iv) The vectors $\partial\eta(\theta)/\partial\theta_1, \ldots, \partial\eta(\theta)/\partial\theta_m$ are linearly independent for every $\theta\in\Theta$.

The (Fisher) information matrix $M(\theta)$ is equal to

$$M_{ij}(\theta) := \frac{\partial\eta^T(\theta)}{\partial\theta_i} \Sigma^{-1} \frac{\partial\eta(\theta)}{\partial\theta_j} \quad . \tag{2}$$

It is nonsingular because of the assumption iv).

The model is linear iff $\eta(\theta)$ is linear in the variables $\theta_1, \ldots \theta_m$. Evidently, $M(\theta)$ does not depend on θ in linear models. The last property motivates the following definition.

Definition 1: The model (1) is flat iff the information matrix $M(\theta)$ does not depend on θ.

Under a reparametrization of the model (1) we understand a twice continuously differentiable mapping $\beta(\theta)$ which is defined on Θ and which is regular (i.e. det $[\partial\beta/\partial\theta^T] \neq 0$;($\theta\in\Theta$)).

Definition 2: The model (1) is potentially flat iff it is flat after a suitable reparametrization.

2. PARAMETRIC PROPERTIES OF FLAT MODELS

Another equivalent definition of flat models is connected with the Čencov - Amari α-connections presented in Amari (1985). It can be easily shown that the coefficients of α-affine connections given in Amari (1985) Eq. (2.27) do not depend on α in the model (1), and they are given by the expression on the left-hand side of Eq. (3) given below.

Proposition 1. The model (1) is flat iff

$$\frac{\partial^2\eta^T(\theta)}{\partial\theta_i\partial\theta_j} \Sigma^{-1} \frac{\partial\eta(\theta)}{\partial\theta_k} = 0 \quad ; \quad (i, j, k\in\{1, \ldots, m\}) \tag{3}$$

for every $\theta\in\Theta$.

The proof can be obtained by differentiating the right-hand side of (2).

To measure the influence of the choice of the parameters on the nonlinearity of the model, Bates and Watts (1980) introduced a three-dimensional array measuring the parameter effect nonlinearity,

$[\partial^2\eta^T(\theta)/\partial\theta_i\partial\theta_j]\Sigma^{-1} e_k$; $(i, j, k\in\{1, \ldots, m\})$. Here e_k are orthonormal vectors in the tangent plane to the expectation manifold

$$\mathcal{E} := \{\eta(\theta) : \theta\in\Theta\},$$

(cf. also Ratkovsky (1984), chpt. 2.4).

Proposition 2. The model (1) is flat iff the array of the Bates and Watts measures of the parameter effect nonlinearity is zero.

Proposition 3. Every univariate model ($\dim \theta = 1$) is flat after a suitable reparametrization.

The proof is based on the simple differential equation for the new parameter β

$$d\beta/d\theta = \| d\eta(\theta)/d\theta \|_{\Sigma} .$$

Here $\|a\|_{\Sigma}^2 := a^T \Sigma^{-1} a$. Evidently, $M(\beta) = 1$ for every β.

Proposition 4. Let A be a nonsingular $m \times m$ matrix. If (1) is flat, then it is flat also after the reparametrization $\beta = A\theta$.

The proof follows from Definition 1.

Proposition 5. Model (1) is potentially flat iff for every $\theta \in \Theta$ and every i, j, h, k we have

$$\frac{\partial^2 \eta^T(\theta)}{\partial\theta_i \partial\theta_j} \Sigma^{-1} [I-P^{\theta}] \frac{\partial^2 \eta(\theta)}{\partial\theta_k \partial\theta_h} = \frac{\partial^2 \eta^T(\theta)}{\partial\theta_i \partial\theta_k} \Sigma^{-1} [I-P^{\theta}] \frac{\partial^2 \eta(\theta)}{\partial\theta_j \partial\theta_h} \tag{4}$$

where

$$P^{\theta} := \frac{\partial \eta(\theta)}{\partial \theta^T} M^{-1}(\theta) \frac{\partial \eta^T(\theta)}{\partial \theta} \Sigma^{-1} \tag{5}$$

(the projector onto the tangent plane to $\mathcal{E}$).

The proof follows from a statement from differential geometry, according to which every potentially flat model has a zero Riemannian - Christoffel curvature (cf. Eisenhart (1926) p. 25). We note that flat models in Amari (1985), p. 46 correspond to our potentially flat models. We chose our definition from classical differential geometry (Eisenhart (1926)) because it has a better statistical interpretation.

3. STATISTICAL PROPERTIES OF L. S. ESTIMATES

This section is based on the extension of results on the nonasymptotical probability density of nonlinear least squares estimates presented in Pázman (1984) and Pázman (1987).

By the L. S. estimate we understand the estimate

$$\hat{\theta} := \hat{\theta}(Y) := \arg\min_{\theta \in \Theta} \|Y - \eta(\theta)\|_{\Sigma}^2 . \tag{6}$$

Let $\bar{\theta}$ be the true (though unknown) value of θ. Take $r > 0$ and denote by

$$G(r) := \{ y \in R^N : \|y - \eta(\bar{\theta})\|_{\Sigma} < r \}$$

the sphere in the sample space which is centred at $\eta(\bar{\theta})$. We shall suppose that $\bar{\theta}, r$ are such that there is a solution of

(6) for every $Y \in G(r)$. Denote by

$$\Theta(r) := \{\hat{\theta}(Y) : Y \in G(r)\}$$

a subset of the parameter space Θ. The number r should be smaller than the radius of curvature of any geodesic curve on $\mathcal{E}$ or at least on the surface $\mathcal{E}(r) := \{\eta(\theta) : \theta \in \Theta(r)\}$ (cf. Pázman (1987) for details).

Proposition 6. The probability density of $\hat{\theta}$ is approximated on $\Theta(r)$ by the formula

$$q(\hat{\theta}|\bar{\theta}) := \frac{\det Q(\hat{\theta},\bar{\theta})}{(2\pi)^{m/2} \det^{1/2} M(\hat{\theta})} \exp\left\{-\frac{1}{2} \| P^{\hat{\theta}}[\eta(\hat{\theta}) - \eta(\bar{\theta})] \|_{\Sigma}^2\right\} \quad (7)$$

where $P^{\hat{\theta}}$ is given in Eq. (5) and where

$$Q_{ij}(\hat{\theta},\bar{\theta}) = M_{ij}(\hat{\theta}) + [\eta(\hat{\theta}) - \eta(\bar{\theta})]^T \Sigma^{-1} (I-P^{\hat{\theta}}) \frac{\partial^2 \eta(\hat{\theta})}{\partial \hat{\theta}_i \, \partial \hat{\theta}_j} .$$

If the model (1) is flat, then

$$Q_{ij}(\hat{\theta},\bar{\theta}) = \frac{\partial^2}{\partial \hat{\theta}_i \, \partial \hat{\theta}_j} \left\{\frac{1}{2} \| \eta(\hat{\theta}) - \eta(\bar{\theta}) \|_{\Sigma}^2\right\} .$$

If the model (1) is potentially flat, then $q(\hat{\theta}|\bar{\theta})$ is equal (up to a multiplicative norming constant) to the exact probability density of $\hat{\theta}$ obtained from a reduced sample space containing the set $G(r)$ as its inner part.

The proof follows from Pázman (1987). Especially the last statement follows from Eq. (21) there, after applying our definition of potentially flat models.

Proposition 7. If $\hat{\theta}$ is distributed according to $q(\hat{\theta}|\bar{\theta})$ on $\Theta(r)$ and if the model is flat, then the vector of random variables

$$v_i(\hat{\theta}) := [\eta(\hat{\theta}) - \eta(\bar{\theta})]^T \Sigma^{-1} \frac{\partial \eta(\hat{\theta})}{\partial \hat{\theta}_i} \; ; \quad (i = 1, \ldots, m)$$

is distributed according to a truncated normal distribution $N(0, M)$.

In case of $m = 1$ the proof is in Section 1 of Pázman (1984), in case of $m > 1$ it is included in the proof of Theorem 2 of the same paper.

Proposition 8. If the model is potentially flat, then the set

$$\{\theta : [\eta(\hat{\theta}) - \eta(\theta)]^T \Sigma^{-1} P^{\hat{\theta}} [\eta(\hat{\theta}) - \eta(\bar{\theta})] < c\} \quad (8)$$

is a confidence region, supposing that it is a subset of $\Theta(r)$. Here c is either a quantile of the χ^2-distribution (if Σ is known), or of the F-distribution (if $\Sigma = \sigma^2 I$ and σ is unknown, but estimated independently). The level of significance of the region is the level of the quantile plus the probability of the "lost part" of the sample space. This probability is bounded above by

$$1 - P\,[\chi^2_N < r^2].$$

The proof of the statement is an extension of Theorem 2 in Pázman (1984).

3.1 Possibility of numerical computations

The verification whether a regression model is flat or potentially flat, the computation of the probability density of $\hat{\theta}$ and the computation of the radius of curvature (cf. Pázman (1984), Appendix B) require the computation of first and second order derivatives of $\eta(\theta)$ in every point $\theta \in \Theta$ as well as some additional simple matrix computations. To obtain the confidence region (8) we need to compute these derivatives only at the point $\hat{\theta}$.

However, the necessity of computing first and second order derivatives of $\eta(\theta)$ is not new in nonlinear regression, because standard programs for computing L. S. estimates usually need such derivatives.

More details concerning the proofs and other details should be included in a subsequent paper prepared for the journal Statistics.

REFERENCES

Amari, S. (1985). Differential-Geometrical Methods in Statistics. Lecture Notes in Statistics N° 28. Springer-Verlag, Berlin.

Bates, D.M., Watts, D.G. (1980). Relative Curvature Measures of Nonlinearity. J. R. Statist. Soc. B, 42 (1): 1-25.

Eisenhart, L.P. (1962). Riemannian Geometry. Princeton Univ. Press, Princeton.

Pázman, A. (1984). Probability distribution of the multivariate nonlinear least squares estimates. Kybernetika (Prague) 20 (3): 209-230.

Pázman, A. (1987). On formulas for the distribution of nonlinear L. S. estimates. Statistics 18 (1): 3-15.

Ratkowsky, D.A. (1984): Nonlinear Regression Modeling. Marcel Dekker, New York.

ASYMPTOTICS FOR INADEQUATE NONLINEAR MODELS WITH HETEROSCEDASTIC VARIANCES

Wolfgang H. Schmidt
Humboldt-University, Berlin, GDR

1. INTRODUCTION

Several asymptotic results for the nonlinear regression model with heteroscedastic variances are presented. Special attention is paid to so-called inadequate models for both the vector of the unknown expectations as well as for the vector of the unknown variances. It is wellknown that fitting the data by inadequate models with only few parameters can lead to smaller mean squared errors than fitting by adequate models whereas the latter are known rather seldom only.

The construction of the estimators utilizes the Least-Squares approach following a method introduced by Jobson and Fuller (1980) for the linear regression model.

The proofs of all the results in this paper will be published elsewhere.

We consider observations

$$y_j = f_j + \sigma_j \varepsilon_j, \quad j=1,2,\ldots,n,\ldots$$

where f_j, $j\geq 1$ are real numbers and σ_j, $j\geq 1$ are positive numbers, both being unknown. The sequence $(\varepsilon_j)_{j\geq 1}$ constitutes a sequence of independent and identically distributed random variables with $E\,\varepsilon_1 = 0$ and $E\,\varepsilon_1^2 = 1$. The problem under consideration is the estimation of the vector of expectations $f = (f_j)_{j\geq 1} \in R^{\infty}$ or more presicely of a suitable chosen functional thereof. Given a parametric model for f

$$\mathcal{G} = \{g(\vartheta) = (g_j(\vartheta))_{j\geq 1}, \vartheta \in \bar{\Theta}\}, \quad \Theta \subset R^p, \quad \bar{\Theta} \text{ closure of } \Theta,$$

which may or may not be true ($f \in \mathcal{G}$, or $f \notin \mathcal{G}$) we introduce the projection parameter

$$\vartheta_f = \arg\min_{\bar{\Theta}} \sum_{j=1}^{n} u_j^{(n)} (f_j - g_j(\vartheta))^2$$

where $(u_j^{(n)})_{j=1,\ldots,n}$ is an array of weights.

Choosing the weights corresponds to fitting characteristics of the regression function well. E.g. it might be of interest to have an approximation of the regression function in a special interval with high precision not neglecting the information contained in the observations outside of the interval. For that purpose we introduce weighted Least-Squares estimators

$$\hat{\vartheta}_n = \arg\min_{\Theta} \frac{1}{n} \sum_{j=1}^{n} w_j^{(n)} (y_j - g_j(\vartheta))^2 + r_n(y,\vartheta)$$

where $w_j^{(n)} = w_j^{(n)}(y_1,\ldots,y_n)$ are random weights such that $w_j^{(n)} - u_j^{(n)}$ tends to zero in probability for n tending to infinity and $r_n(y,\vartheta)$ tends to zero in probability as well. Special cases are for $r_n(y,\vartheta) = 0$

(i) $w_j^{(n)} = u_j^{(n)} = 1$, ordinary LSE

(ii) $w_j^{(n)} = \hat{\sigma}_j^{-2}$, two-stage LSE where $\hat{\sigma}_j$ denotes a consistent estimator of σ_j. Such estimators can be easily derived if $\sigma_j = \sigma_j(\vartheta,\tau)$

depends besides on ϑ on a finite dimensional parameter $\tau \in \mathcal{T} \subset R^q$ only.

We use the following denotations:

For vectors $x,y,z \in R^{\infty}$

$$(x,y)_z = \frac{1}{n} \sum_{j=1}^{n} z_j x_j y_j$$

and

$$|x|_z^2 = (x,x)_z.$$

Further let P_{f_j,σ_j} be the distribution of y_j, $j=1,\ldots$

Then $P_{f,\sigma} = \bigtimes_{j=1}^{\infty} P_{f_j,\sigma_j}$ is the distribution of the sequence $(y_j)_{j\geq 1}$.

We use the symbol g_ϑ for the vector $(g_j(\vartheta))_{j\geq 1}$.

2. WEAK CONSISTENCY

We set up the following assumptions:

A1: $E|\varepsilon_1|^k < \infty$ for some $k \geq 2$

A2: The functions g_j are continuous on $\bar{\Theta}$ and for every compact $\mathcal{L} \subset \bar{\Theta}$ there is a $\delta > 0$, a constant $c < \infty$ and an integer n_0 such that for all $n \geq n_0$, $\vartheta \in \mathcal{L}$, $\vartheta' \in \bar{\Theta}$ with $\|\vartheta - \vartheta'\| < \delta$ it holds

$$|g(\vartheta') - g(\vartheta)|_u \leq c\,\|\vartheta - \vartheta'\|.$$

A3: $\sup_{j,\vartheta\in\mathcal{L}} |g_j(\vartheta)| < \infty$ for every compact $\mathcal{L} \subset \bar{\Theta}$.

A4: For every compact $\mathcal{L} \subset \bar{\Theta}$ there are a nondecreasing function $\psi_{\mathcal{L}} : [0,\infty) \longrightarrow [0,\infty)$ being positive on $(0,\infty)$ and an integer n_0 such that for all $\vartheta \in \mathcal{L}$, $\vartheta' \in \bar{\Theta}$ and $n \geq n_0$ it holds

$$|g(\vartheta') - g(\vartheta)|_u^2 \geq \psi_{\mathcal{L}}(\|\vartheta - \vartheta'\|).$$

In case Θ is unbounded $\psi_{\mathcal{L}}$ fulfils

$$\psi_{\mathcal{L}}(t) \underset{t \to \infty}{\longrightarrow} \infty$$

In what follows $\mathcal{H}$ and $\mathcal{E}$ are fixed compact subsets of R^{∞}.

A5: $\sup_{j, f \in \mathcal{H}} |f_j| < \infty$

A6: ϑ_f exists is uniquely determined and belongs to some compact $\mathcal{K} \subset \Theta$ for all sufficiently large n.

A7: For some integer $k \geq 2$ and every $\delta > 0$ it holds

$$\sup_{f \in \mathcal{H}, \sigma \in \mathcal{E}} P_{f,\sigma}\left(\sup_j |w_j^{(n)} - u_j^{(n)}| > \delta\right) = o(n^{-(k-2)/2}).$$

A8: For some integer $k \geq 2$ and every positive δ and $\varkappa$, all compact $\mathcal{L} \subset \bar{\Theta}$ it holds

$$\sup_{f \in \mathcal{H}, \sigma \in \mathcal{E}} P_{f,\sigma}\left(\sup_{\|\vartheta - \vartheta_f\| > \delta} |r_n(y,\vartheta)| > \varkappa\right) = o(n^{-(k-2)/2}).$$

Theorem 2.1 Under the assumptions A1,...A8 we have for every positive δ

$$\sup_{f \in \mathcal{H}, \sigma \in \mathcal{E}} P_{f,\sigma}(\|\hat{\vartheta}_n - \vartheta_f\| \geq \delta) = o(n^{-(k-2)/2})$$

in case that $\mathcal{E} = \{\sigma \in R^{\infty} \mid \underline{\sigma} \leq \sigma_j \leq \bar{\sigma},\ j=1,2,\dots\}$ for some $\underline{\sigma} > 0$ and $\bar{\sigma} < \infty$.

This theorem generalizes results by Malinvaud (1970) and Ivanov (1976).
(Remark: It was proved by Huet (1986) and Maljutov (1982) that the weights $w_j^{(n)} = \sigma_j^{-2}$ lead to inconsistency whenever $\sigma_j = h_j(\vartheta)$ depends on ϑ.)

Now it is our aim to estimate the unknown variances σ_j^2, $j=1,2,\dots$.
Suppose there is given a model for $\sigma^2 = (\sigma_j^2)_{j\geq 1}$, namely

$$\mathcal{D} = \{h(\vartheta,\tau) = (h_j(\vartheta,\tau))_{j\geq 1},\ \vartheta \in \bar{\Theta},\ \tau \in \bar{T}\}$$

Which may or may not be true ($\sigma^2 \in \mathcal{D}$ or $\sigma^2 \notin \mathcal{D}$). Again we use the Least-Squares approach to estimate τ, i.e.

$$\hat{\tau} = \arg\min_{\tau} \frac{1}{n} \sum_{j=1}^{n} s_j^{(n)} (\hat{e}_j^2 - h_j(\hat{\vartheta},\tau))^2$$

with $\hat{e}_j^2 = (y_j - g_j(\hat{\vartheta}))^2$

and $s_j^{(n)}$ are random weights approaching nonrandom weights $v_j^{(n)}$. Then it can be proved under some Lipschitz conditions on h that

$$|\hat{e}^2 - h(\hat{\vartheta},\tau)|_s^2 = |e^2 - h(\vartheta_f,\tau)|_s^2 + r_n(y,\tau)$$

where $r_n(y,\tau)$ fulfils A8 and $e_j^2 = (y_j - g_j(\vartheta_f))^2$.

Therefore the Theorem applies again and yields especially

$$\hat{\tau} - \tau_{f,\sigma} \xrightarrow{P_{f,\sigma}} 0 \text{ uniformly in } f \in \mathcal{H} \text{ and } \sigma \in \mathcal{E} \text{ with}$$

$$\tau_{f,\sigma} = \arg\min_{\tau} |\sigma^2 + \Delta^2 - h(\vartheta_f,\tau)|_v^2$$

and $\Delta_j^2 = (f_j - g_j(\vartheta_f))^2$, $j \geq 1$ denotes the model error for f.

Now it is natural to estimate σ_j^2 by $h_j(\hat{\vartheta},\hat{\tau})$, $j \geq 1$ and one gets

$$\sup_j |\hat{\sigma}_j^2 - \tilde{\sigma}_j^2| \xrightarrow{P_{f,\sigma}} 0$$

with

$$\tilde{\sigma}_j^2 = h_j(\vartheta_f, \tau_{f,\sigma}).$$

From this point of view it becomes clear that the model $\mathcal{D}$ is always a model for $\sigma^2 + \Delta^2$.

Now the procedure might be applied again to obtain two-stage estimators namely

$$\hat{\hat{\vartheta}} = \arg\min |y - g(\vartheta)|_{\hat{w}}^2$$

with $\hat{w}_j = h_j(\hat{\vartheta},\hat{\tau})^{-1}$

and

$$\hat{\hat{\tau}} = \arg\min_{\tau} |\hat{\hat{e}}^2 - h(\hat{\vartheta},\tau)|_{\hat{s}}^2$$

with $\hat{\hat{e}}_j^2 = (y_j - g_j(\hat{\hat{\vartheta}}))^2$

and $\hat{s}_j = (\hat{\sigma}_j^4(\mu_4 - 1) + 4\hat{\sigma}_j^2\hat{\Delta}_j^2 + 4\mu_3\hat{\Delta}_j)^{-1}$.

Here μ_3 and μ_4 are the third or the fourth moment of ε_1 respectively and $\hat{\Delta}_j = \hat{f}_j - g_j(\hat{\vartheta})$.

The consistency of $\hat{\hat{\tau}}$ can be proved in case of a repetition model

$$y_{ij} = f_i + \sigma_{ij}\varepsilon_{ij}, \quad i=1,\ldots,m, \quad j=1,\ldots,n_i$$

for $n_i \longrightarrow \infty$ for $i=1,\ldots,m$ and fixed or slowly increasing m.

3. STRONG CONSISTENCY

For simplicity let us assume from now on that we have adequate models for both f and σ, i.e. $\vartheta_f = \vartheta$ and $\tau_{f,\sigma} = \tau$ for some $\vartheta \in \Theta$ and $\tau \in \mathcal{T}$. Using the technique established by Jennrich (1969), which was extended by Jobson and Fuller (1980), the strong consistency for $\hat{\vartheta}_n$ and $\hat{\tau}_n$ can be proved. For this purpose we need the following assumptions:

A9: There are constants $\underline{\sigma} > 0$ and $\bar{\sigma} < \infty$ such that for all $j \geq 1$ $\underline{\sigma} \leq \sigma_j \leq \bar{\sigma}$.

A10: Θ is compact and the functions $g_j(\vartheta)$ are continuous in $\vartheta \in \bar{\Theta}$ for every $j \geq 1$.

A11: For all functions $l,k \in \mathcal{K} = \{(g_j(\vartheta))_{j\geq 1}, \vartheta \in \Theta\}$ there are real numbers (l,k) such that

$$\sup_{l,k \in \mathcal{K}} |(l,k)_n - (l,k)| \xrightarrow[n \to \infty]{} 0.$$

A12: $|g_\vartheta - g_{\vartheta'}| = 0$ implies $\vartheta = \vartheta'$.

Theorem 3.1 (Bunke,Schmidt (1980)). The assumptions A9,...,A12 together with A7 for k = 2 ensure

$$\hat{\vartheta}_n \xrightarrow{a.s.} \vartheta.$$

A suitable adaption of the same technique leads to the following result:

Theorem 3.2 The following assumptions together with A9 and A7 for k = 2, $w_j^{(n)} = s_j^{(n)}$, $u_j^{(n)} = v_j^{(n)}$ entail

$$\hat{\tau}_n \xrightarrow{a.s.} \tau :$$

A13: $E\varepsilon_1^4 < \infty$.

A14: Θ and $\mathcal{T}$ are compact and there is a constant $c < \infty$ such that

$$|g_j(\vartheta) - g_j(\vartheta')| \leq c\,\|\vartheta - \vartheta'\| \quad \text{for all } j \geq 1$$

and

$$|h_j(\vartheta,\tau) - h_j(\vartheta,\tau')| \leq c\,\|\tau - \tau'\| \quad \text{for all } j\geq 1 \text{ and all } \vartheta \in \Theta.$$

A15: For $\mathcal{K}_1 = \{(h_j(\vartheta,\tau))_{j\geq 1}, \tau \in \mathcal{T}\}$ it holds

$$\sup_{l,k \in \mathcal{K}_1} |(l,k)_v - (l,k)| \xrightarrow[n \to \infty]{} 0 \quad \text{for real numbers } (l,k).$$

A16: $|h_\tau - h_{\tau'}| = 0$ implies $\tau = \tau'$.

4. $\sqrt{n}$-CONSISTENCY

Now we give conditions under which

$$\sqrt{n}(\hat{\vartheta}_n - \vartheta) = O_P(1) \text{ and } \sqrt{n}(\hat{\tau}_n - \tau) = O_P(1)$$

are fulfilled.

Theorem 4.1 (Bunke,Schmidt (1980)). Besides of the assumptions A9,...,A12 let the following conditions be fulfilled:

A17: It holds A11 with $\mathcal{K}$ replaced by

$$\mathcal{H}_2 = \{(g_j(\vartheta))_{j\geq 1}, (\frac{\partial}{\partial\vartheta_i} g_j(\vartheta))_{j\geq 1}, (\frac{\partial^2}{\partial\vartheta_i\partial\vartheta_k} g_j(\vartheta))_{j\geq 1}, \vartheta\in\Theta;\ i,k = 1,\dots,p\}.$$

Here it is assumed that the function $g_j(\vartheta)$ are twice continuously partially differentiable with respect to ϑ.

A18: a) The limits

$$C = \lim_{n\to\infty} \frac{1}{n}\sum_{j=1}^{n} \sigma_j^2 u_j^2 \frac{\partial}{\partial\vartheta} g_j(\vartheta) \frac{\partial}{\partial\vartheta} g_j(\vartheta)^T$$

and

$$A = \lim_{n\to\infty} \frac{1}{n}\sum_{j=1}^{n} u_j \frac{\partial}{\partial\vartheta} g_j(\vartheta) \frac{\partial}{\partial\vartheta} g_j(\vartheta)^T$$

exist and are regular.

b) ϑ belongs to the interior of Θ.

c) It holds $n^{-1/2}\sum_{j=1}^{n} (w_j^{(n)}-u_j^{(n)})\,\sigma_j \frac{\partial}{\partial\vartheta} g_j(\vartheta)\,\varepsilon_j = o_P(1)$.

Then we have

$$\mathcal{L}(\sqrt{n}(\hat{\vartheta}_n-\vartheta)) \longrightarrow N(0,A^{-1}CA^{-1}).$$

In the next step $\sqrt{n}\,(\hat{\tau}_n-\tau) = O_P(1)$ is established. For this aim we introduce the following assumptions:

A19: Let the condition A11 with $\mathcal{H}$ replaced by

$$\mathcal{H}_3 = \mathcal{H}_1\cup\mathcal{H}_2\cup\{(\frac{\partial}{\partial\tau_k} h_j(\vartheta,\tau))_{j\geq 1}, (\frac{\partial^2}{\partial\tau_k\,\partial\tau_l} h_j(\vartheta,\tau))_{j\geq 1}, (\frac{\partial^2}{\partial\vartheta_i\,\partial\tau_k} h_j(\vartheta,\tau))_{j\geq 1}, \vartheta\in\Theta, \tau\in T, i=1,\dots,p, k,l=1,\dots,q\}$$

be fulfilled.

A20: There is a constant $c<\infty$ with

$$\left|\frac{\partial}{\partial\tau_k} h_j(\vartheta,\tau) - \frac{\partial}{\partial\tau_k} h_j(\vartheta',\tau)\right| \leq c\|\vartheta-\vartheta'\|$$

and

$$\left|(\frac{\partial}{\partial\tau_k} h_j(\vartheta,\tau))^2 - \left(\frac{\partial}{\partial\tau_k} h_j(\vartheta',\tau)\right)^2\right| \leq c\|\vartheta-\vartheta'\|$$

for all $j \geq 1, \tau\in T$, $k=1,\dots,q$.

A21: The limits

$$D = \lim_{n\to\infty} \frac{1}{n}\sum_{j=1}^{n} v_j^{(n)} \frac{\partial}{\partial\tau} h_j(\vartheta,\tau) \frac{\partial}{\partial\tau} h_j(\vartheta,\tau)^T$$

and

$$d_{kl} = \lim_{n\to\infty} \frac{1}{n}\sum_{j=1}^{n} v_j^{(n)} \frac{\partial^2}{\partial\tau_k\partial\tau_l} h_j(\vartheta,\tau),\ k,l=1,\dots,q$$

exist and D is regular.

Theorem 4.2 The conditions of Theorem 3.2 together with A19, A20 and A21 ensure $\sqrt{n}(\hat{\tau}_n-\tau) = O_P(1)$.

5. ASYMPTOTICALLY EFFICIENT ESTIMATORS

Here we use the estimators $\hat{\vartheta}_n$ and $\hat{\tau}_n$ as initial estimators for defining an one-step Gauss-Newton generalized iteration. We proceed according the lines in Jobson and Fuller (1980). Let us introduce the vector of the residuals and the centered squares of residuals

$$Z = \begin{pmatrix} y_1-g_1(\hat{\vartheta}_n) \\ \vdots \\ y_n-g_n(\hat{\vartheta}_n) \\ (y_1-g_1(\hat{\vartheta}_n))^2-h_1(\hat{\vartheta}_n,\hat{\tau}_n) \\ \vdots \\ (y_n-g_n(\hat{\vartheta}_n))^2-h_n(\hat{\vartheta}_n,\hat{\tau}_n) \end{pmatrix}$$

and the matrices

$$H(\vartheta,\tau) = \left(\begin{array}{c:c} 0 & X(\vartheta) \\ \hdashline H_1(\vartheta,\tau) & H_2(\vartheta,\tau) \end{array}\right)$$

and

$$\Psi(\vartheta,\tau) = \mathrm{Diag}\left[\sigma_1^2,\ldots,\sigma_n^2,\sigma_1^4\mathrm{Var}\,\varepsilon_1^2,\ldots,\sigma_n^4\mathrm{Var}\,\varepsilon_1^2\right]$$

with

$$X(\vartheta) = \left(\frac{\partial}{\partial\vartheta_i} g_j(\vartheta)\right)_{\substack{j=1,\ldots,n \\ i=1,\ldots,p}},$$

$$H_1(\vartheta,\tau) = \left(\frac{\partial}{\partial\tau_k} h_j(\vartheta,\tau)\right)_{\substack{j=1,\ldots,n \\ k=1,\ldots,q}},$$

$$H_2(\vartheta,\tau) = \left(\frac{\partial}{\partial\vartheta_i} h_j(\vartheta,\tau)\right)_{\substack{j=1,\ldots,n \\ i=1,\ldots,p}}.$$

Then the one-step version of the Gauss-Newton iteration procedure is defined to be

$$\begin{pmatrix} \hat{\hat{\tau}}_n \\ \hat{\hat{\vartheta}}_n \end{pmatrix} = \begin{pmatrix} \hat{\tau}_n \\ \hat{\vartheta}_n \end{pmatrix} + (H^T(\hat{\vartheta}_n,\hat{\tau}_n)\Psi^{-1}(\hat{\vartheta}_n,\hat{\tau}_n)H(\hat{\vartheta}_n,\hat{\tau}_n))^{-1}H^T(\hat{\vartheta}_n,\hat{\tau}_n)\Psi^{-1}(\hat{\vartheta}_n,\hat{\tau}_n)Z$$

Theorem 5.1 Let the assumptions of Theorem 4.1 and Theorem 4.2 be fulfilled. Moreover, assume that the matrices

$$I_n(\vartheta,\tau) = \frac{1}{n} H^T(\vartheta,\tau)\Psi^{-1}(\vartheta,\tau)H(\vartheta,\tau)$$

tend uniformly in $(\vartheta,\tau)\in\Theta\times\mathcal{T}$ to regular limits $I(\vartheta,\tau)$. Then we have

$$\mathcal{L}\left(\sqrt{n}\begin{pmatrix}\hat{\hat{\tau}}_n-\tau\\ \hat{\vartheta}_n-\vartheta\end{pmatrix}\right)\longrightarrow N(0,I^{-1}(\vartheta,\tau)).$$

Notice that $I(\vartheta,\tau)$ is the limit of the average Fisher-information matrix if the observations y_j are normally distributed. Therefore, using the local asymptotic normality of the family of probability distributions, it follows that the one-step version is asymptotically efficient. Similar results have been obtained by Maljutov (1982) for the special case $h_j(\vartheta,\tau)=h_j(\vartheta)$. Maljutov (1982) also proves the local asymptotic minimaxity for sequentially designed experiments.

The preceeding result can be utilized for the construction of an asymptotic $1-\alpha$ confidence region for the vector $\binom{\tau}{\vartheta}$, namely:

$$\left\{\binom{\tau}{\vartheta}\,\middle|\, n\begin{pmatrix}\hat{\hat{\tau}}_n-\tau\\ \hat{\hat{\vartheta}}_n-\vartheta\end{pmatrix}^T I_n(\hat{\vartheta}_n,\hat{\tau}_n)\begin{pmatrix}\hat{\hat{\tau}}_n-\tau\\ \hat{\hat{\vartheta}}_n-\vartheta\end{pmatrix}\le\chi^2_{p+q;1-\alpha}\right\}$$

Further it can be used for the construction of an asymptotic α-test for testing

$$H:\gamma(\vartheta,\tau)=\gamma_0 \quad \text{against} \quad K:\gamma(\vartheta,\tau)\neq\gamma_0$$

for a given parametric function

$$\gamma:\mathcal{T}\times\Theta\longrightarrow R^1.$$

The hypothesis is to be rejected if

$$n(\gamma(\hat{\hat{\vartheta}}_n,\hat{\hat{\tau}}_n)-\gamma_0)^T(C(\hat{\vartheta}_n,\hat{\tau}_n)I_n^{-1}(\hat{\vartheta}_n,\hat{\tau}_n)C^T(\hat{\vartheta}_n,\hat{\tau}_n))^{-1}(\gamma(\hat{\hat{\vartheta}}_n,\hat{\hat{\tau}}_n)-\gamma_0)$$
$$>\chi^2_{1,1-\alpha}.$$

Here $C(\vartheta,\tau)$ denotes the Jacobian of γ with respect to ϑ and τ.

6. REFERENCES

Bunke, H., Schmidt, W.H. (1980). Asymptotic results on non-linear approximation of regression functions and weighted least squares. Math. Operationsforsch. Statist. Ser. Statist. 11, 3-22.

Carroll, R.J., Ruppert, D. (1982). Robust estimation in heteroscedastic linear models, Ann. Statist., 10, 429-441.

Fuller, W.A., Rao, J.N.K. (1978). Estimation for a linear regression model with unknown diagonal covariance matrix, Ann. Statist., 6, 1149-1158.

Huet, S. (1986). Maximum likelihood and least-squares estimators for a non-linear model with heterogeneous variances. Statistics 17, 517-526.

Ivanov, A.W. (1976). An asymptotic expansion for the distribution of the nonlinear regression parameter. Theory of Prob. and Appl. 21, 557-570.

Jennrich, R.I. (1969). Asymptotic properties of nonlinear least squares estimators, Ann. Math. Stat., 40, 633-643.
Jobson, J.D., Fuller, W.A. (1980). Least Squares estimation when the covariance matrix and parameter vector are functionally related, JASA, 75, 176-181.
Maljutov, M.B. (1982). Lower bounds for an average number of sequentially designed experiments, Proceedings of USSR-Japan Symp. on Probability, Springer Lecture Notes.
Malinvaud, E. (1970). The consistency of nonlinear regressions. Ann. Math. Stat. 41, 956-969.
Schmidt, W.H., Zwanzig, S. (1986). Second order asymptotics in nonlinear regression, J. Multivariate Anal., 18, 187-215.

ERRORS IN THE FACTOR LEVELS: PARAMETER ESTIMATION OF HETEROSCEDASTIC MODEL AND ROBUSTNESS OF THE EXPERIMENTAL DESIGNS

I.N. Vuchkov and L.N. Boyadjieva
Department of Automation, Higher Institute of Chemical Technology, Sofia

1. INTRODUCTION

In the course of the planned experiment the selected factor levels are often established with errors. Then the correct model is

$$y = Z\beta + v \tag{1}$$

instead of the model

$$y = X\beta + v$$

where y is an $(n\times1)$ vector of observations, $Z=(1,f_2(z),f_3(z),\dots,f_p(z)$ and $X=(1,f_2(x),f_3(x),\dots,f_p(x))$, are the true and the selected $(n\times p)$ matrices respectively, β is a $(p\times1)$ vector of coefficients to be estimated and v is a $(n\times1)$ vector of the random response disturbance. At that $f_j(x)=(f_j(x_1), f_j(x_2),\dots,f_j(x_n))'$, where f_j, $j=2,3,\dots,p$ denotes given function of the factors and the $(q\times1)$ vectors of selected x_i and true z_i factor levels are connected with relation $z_i = x_i+e_i$, e_i being the $(q\times1)$ vector of factor errors in the ith trial, $i = 1,2,\dots,n$, $q \leqq p$.

Usually the following assumptions are accepted conserning the disturbance v and the matrix of factor errors $\varepsilon = (e_1,e_2,\dots,e_n)'$:

$$E(v) = 0,\ D(v) = \sigma_o^2 I,\ E(e) = 0,\ D(e) = \begin{cases}\mathrm{var}(e_i), & i=j,\\ \mathrm{cov}(e_i e_j), & i\neq j\end{cases} \tag{2}$$

where E and D indicate expectation and covariance matrix respectively. It is also assumed that all errors are independently distributed among the runs.

As the true design matrix Z is unknown, the model (1) has been transformed (Box, 1963) into a model having a design matrix X and modified responce disturbance, caused by the real response disturbance v and by the errors in the factor levels transmitted to the response. For linear in factors models it has been proved that the modified response disturbance has zero expectation and equal variances in all design points, thence the least squares estimate (LSE) $b=(X'X)^{-1}X'y$ is unbiased and efficient. For nonlinear in factors models the modified disturbance has nonzero expectation and different variances in all experimental points depending on selected factor levels, which result in biased and nonefficient LSE b.

That is why special methods must be used for estimation of nonlinear in factors models with errors. An iterative procedure (Fedorov, 1974) ensures consistent and asymptotically normal estimate of β for given second order moments of the factor errors and of the disturbance v. The procedure converges if initial estimate of β is close enough to the true vector β. But this condition may not be always be met if substantial errors occur in the factor level settings. In addition to this it is difficult to estimate the moments of disturbance v separately - for example the variance σ_o^2 in presence of factor errors.

Another possibility to estimate the nonlinear in factors models is the following transformation (Vuchkov and Boyadjieva, 1981) of the model (1)

$$y = F\beta + r \tag{3}$$

where $F=F+E_e(G)$, $r=v+(G-E_e(G))\beta$, $E_e(G)$ denotes the expectation of the matrix $G=Z-X$ with respect to the factor errors.

The design matrix F in the model (1) is nonrandom and known provided the moments of the factor errors are given. The disturbance r has a zero expectation and diagonal covariance matrix

$$D(r) = D(y) = \mathrm{diag}(\sigma_1^2,\sigma_2^2,\dots,\sigma_n^2) = \Sigma$$

with elements

$$\sigma_i^2 = \sigma_o^2 + \beta' A_i \beta + c_i, \quad i = 1,2,\dots,n \tag{4}$$

where $A_i = E_e((g_i-E_e(g_i))(g_i-E_e(g_i)'),$ (5)

$$c_i = 2E_{v,e}(v_i\beta'(g_i-E_e(g_i)),$$

and g_i' is the ith row of matrix G. If the disturbance v_i is independently distributed by e_i in a given run, then $c_i = 0$, $i = 1,2,\dots,n$.

The terms $\beta' A_i \beta$ and c_i in (4) are due to the factor errors and they increase the response variances from σ_o^2 to σ_i^2. In linear in factors models this increase is equal with all design points as A_i and c_i depend on error moments only. In addition F=X, as $E_e(G)=E(\varepsilon)=0$. For nonlinear with respect to factors models c_i and the elements of A_i-matrices depend on x_i as well, which causes variance heteroscedasticity.

Thence, for known factor error moments, the estimation of nonlinear models is reduced to estimation of model (3) with heteroscedastic variances. The best linear unbiased estimate (BLUE) for β is provided by the weighted least squares method:

$$b_\Sigma = (F'\Sigma^{-1}F)^{-1}F'\Sigma^{-1}y. \tag{6}$$

Since the elements of matrix Σ depend on the unknown parameter β, the estimate

$$b_s = (F'S^{-1}F)^{-1} F'S^{-1}y \tag{7}$$

can be applied instead of b_Σ if some estimates s_i^2 of σ_i^2 are available.

But as far as the true variances σ_i^2 differ from s_i^2 the estimate b_Σ doesn't coincide with b_s. While BLUE b_Σ allways results in more accurate model, in comparison to LSE $b=(F'F)^{-1}F'y$ the properties of b_s depend on variance estimation method. As compared to b, b_s is proved to be really more efficient if the variances are precisely estimated and their heteroscedasticity is substantial.

2. HETEROSCEDASTIC VARIANCE ESTIMATORS AND PROPERTES OF THE ESTIMATES b_s

The properties of the estimates b_s will be investigated when the following four methods discussed in (Horn, Horn, 1975) are used as variance estimators: MINQUE (Minimum Norm Quadratic Estimate), AUE (Almost Unbiased Estimate), ASR (Average of the Squared Residuals) and SV (Sample Variance). It as assumed that m replications are carried out in each of the n design points. The model for lth replication of the design is given by (3) with indices (l) added to denote the corresponding replication

$$y^{(l)} = F\beta + r^{(l)},\ l = 1,2,\dots,m. \tag{8}$$

The model for all m replications is expressed as follows:

$$\tilde{y} = \tilde{F}\beta + \tilde{r}, \tag{9}$$

with corresponding formulae to (6) and (7) of the form

$$b_{\Sigma} = (\tilde{F}'\tilde{\Sigma}^{-1}\tilde{F})^{-1}\tilde{F}'\tilde{\Sigma}^{-1}\tilde{y} = (F'\Sigma^{-1}F)^{-1}E'\Sigma^{-1}\bar{y}, \tag{10}$$

$$b_s = (\tilde{F}'\tilde{S}^{-1}\tilde{F})^{-1}\tilde{F}'\tilde{S}^{-1}\tilde{y} = (F'S^{-1}F)^{-1}F'S^{-1}\bar{y} \tag{11}$$

where $\tilde{y} = (y^{(1)'}, y^{(2)'}, \dots, y^{(m)'})'$ is an $(mn\times 1)$ vector, $\bar{y}=m^{-1}\Sigma_{l=1}^{m} y^{(l)}$ is an $(n\times 1)$ vector, $\tilde{F}=(F',F',\dots,F')'$ (m times) is an $(mn\times p)$ matrix, $\tilde{r}=(r^{(1)'}, r^{(2)'}, \dots, r^{(m)'})'$ is an $(mn\times 1)$ vector with $(mn\times mn)$ covariance matrix $D(\tilde{r}) = =\mathrm{diag}(\Sigma,\Sigma,\dots,\Sigma)$ (m times) and $\tilde{S}=\mathrm{diag}(S,S,\dots,S)$ (mtimes).

The unknown variances $\sigma^2 = (\sigma_1^2, \sigma_2^2, \dots, \sigma_n^2)$ are estimated through the vector $s^2 = (s_1^2, s_2^2, \dots, s_n^2)$ with one of the following forms depending on the methods mentioned above:

$$s^2_{MINQUE} = A_m^{-1}u,\ m \geqq 1, \tag{12}$$

$$s^2_{AUE} = B_m u,\ m \geqq 1, \tag{13}$$

$$s^2_{ASR} = u,\ m \geqq 1, \tag{14}$$

$$s^2_{SV} = (m-1)^{-1}(\Sigma_{l=1}^{m}(y^{(l)})^{*2} - m^{-1}(\Sigma_{l=1}^{m}y^{(l)})^{*2}),\ m \geqq 2, \tag{15}$$

where

$$A_m = I - 2m^{-1}\mathrm{diag}(k_{11}, k_{22}, \dots, k_{nn}) + m^{-1}K^{*2}, \tag{16}$$

$$K = F(F'F)^{-1}F',\ [K]_{ij} = k_{ij},\ i,j = 1,2,\dots,n \tag{17}$$

$$B_m = \mathrm{diag}(b_{11}, b_{22}, \dots, b_{nn}),\ b_{ii} = (1-m^{-1}k_{ii})^{-1},\ i = 1,2,\dots,n \tag{18}$$

$$u_m = m^{-1}\Sigma_{l=1}^{m}(\hat{r}^{(l)})^{*2},\ u_i = m^{-1}\Sigma_{l=1}^{m}\hat{r}_i^{(l)2}, \tag{19}$$

and $[(.)^{*2}]_{ij} = [(.)]_{ij}^2$.

The (n×1) vector u elements are the average values of the squared residuals from replicated trials in the design points. The (mm×1) residual vector is calculated by means of the LSE b for β:

$$(\hat{r}^{(1)'}, \hat{r}^{(2)'}, \dots, \hat{r}^{(m)'})' = \tilde{y} - \tilde{F}b = (I-\tilde{K})\tilde{r} = \tilde{Q}\tilde{r} \tag{20}$$

where $\tilde{Q} = (I-\tilde{K})$, $\tilde{K} = \tilde{F}(\tilde{F}'\tilde{F})^{-1}\tilde{F}'$ and

$$b = (\tilde{F}'\tilde{F})^{-1}\tilde{F}'\tilde{y}. \tag{21}$$

Two modifications are envisaged for the MINQUE method. A preliminary given positive number (in the first one) and the average of the squared residuals (in the second one) are substituted for the negative values of variance estimates which is possible to be obtained by MINQUE method in some of the design points.

The estimates of the b_s type: b_{MINQUE}, b_{AUE}, b_{ASR} and b_{SV}, the properties of which will be discussed are calculated with the aid of (11) where the weighted matrix S is determined through the elements of the vectors (12)-(15) respectively. The discussion is based on the investigation related to b_{MINQUE} and b_{SV} made in the appendix of (Rao, Subrahmaniam, 1971).

2.1. Unbiasedness of b_s

Theorem 1. The estimates of the b_s type b_{MINQUE}, b_{AUE}, b_{ASR} and b_{SV} are unbiased, i.e. $E(b_s) = \beta$ (if $E(b_s)$ exists), provided the disturbance $\tilde{r}$ is symmetrically distributed.

Proof. The following theorem of (Kakwani, 1967) will be used: Every estimate $\hat{\beta}$, the deviation of which from β has the form of $H(\tilde{r})\tilde{r}$ is unbiased i.e: $E(\hat{\beta}) = \beta$ (it is assumed that the mean $E(\hat{\beta})$ exists), provided $H(\tilde{r})=H(-\tilde{r})$) and $\tilde{r}$ is symmetrically distributed.

The deviation of b_s from β, obtained through (11) and (9), takes the following form:

$$b_s - \beta = (\tilde{F}'\tilde{S}^{-1}\tilde{F})^{-1}\tilde{F}'\tilde{S}^{-1}\tilde{r}.$$

Therefore in compliance with Kakwani's theorem, the estimates b_s are unbiased, provided the matrix $H(\tilde{r}) = (\tilde{F}'\tilde{S}^{-1}\tilde{F})^{-1}\tilde{F}'\tilde{S}^{-1}$ doesn't change as $\tilde{r}$ is replaced by $-\tilde{r}$. which in the event of nonrandom matrix $\tilde{F}$ is reduced to the establishment of the condition $S(\tilde{r}) = S(-\tilde{r})$, i.e. to

$$s^2(\tilde{r}) = s^2(-\tilde{r}) \tag{22}$$

where $s^2(\tilde{r})$ is determined by means of one of the relationships (12)-(15).

For the first three variance estimators it is clear that only vector u depends on $\tilde{r}$ as the matrices A_m and B_m are nonrandom according to (16)-(18). Consequently the test of (22) boils down to the verification of

$$u(\tilde{r}) = u(-\tilde{r}) \tag{23}$$

The formula for the element u_i of u can be obtained using (20) in order to present the vector $r^{(l)}$ and its ith element in the form

$$\hat{r}^{(l)} = \tilde{Q}^{(l)}\tilde{r}, \quad l = 1,2,\ldots,m$$

$$\hat{r}_i = q_i^{(l)'}\tilde{r}, \tag{24}$$

where $[Q^{(l)}]_{ij} = [\tilde{Q}]_{l+i,j}$, $i = 1,2,\ldots,n$, $j = 1,2,\ldots,mn$ and $q_i^{(l)'}$ stands for the i-th row of the matrix $Q^{(l)}$. The square of the residual in the lth replication at the ith design point from (24) is given with the following quadratic form:

$$\hat{r}_i^{(l)2} = \tilde{r}'q_i^{(l)}q_i^{(l)'}\tilde{r}$$

Thence

$$\hat{r}_i^{(l)2}(\tilde{r}) = \hat{r}_i^{(l)2}(-\tilde{r}). \tag{25}$$

Consequently from (25) and (19) it becomes clear that the condition (25) is fulfilled for the estimates b_{MINQUE}, b_{AUE} and b_{ASR}.

The fulfilment of (23) with the estimate b_{SV} can be established directly by rewriting (15) in the following form:

$$s_{SV}^2(r) = (m-1)^{-1}\Sigma_{l=1}^m(r^{(l)})^{*2} - m^{-1}(\Sigma_{l=1}^m(r^{(l)})^{*2},$$

where it is taken into account that from (8)

$$y^{(l)} - m^{-1}\Sigma_{l=1}^m y^{(l)} = X\beta + r^{(l)} - m^{-1}\Sigma_{l=1}^m(X\beta + r^{(l)}) = r^{(l)} - m^{-1}\Sigma_{l=1}^m r^{(l)}.$$

Consequently if the assumptions of Kakwani's theorem are met, the estimates b_{MINQUE}, b_{AUE}, b_{ASR} and b_{SV} are unbiased.

2.2. Consistency of b_s

This property will be discussed assuming that $m \to \infty$, with n and p being-fixed. Further on it is necessary to use the following:

(i) Theorem 2.3 from (Demidenko, 1981). The estimate b_Σ is consistent for β, provided $\lambda_{min}(F'F) \to \infty$, $m \to \infty$ and $\max_i \sigma_i^2 \leq d \leq \infty$ (λ_{min} stands for minimal matrix eigenvalue).

(ii) Theorem 2.4 from (Demidenko, 1981). The LSE b for heteroscedastic model (9) is consistent for β provided $\lambda_{min}(F'F) \to \infty$, $m \to \infty$ and $\max_i \sigma_i^2 \leq d \leq \infty$.

The consistency of b_s can be stated with the following

Theorem 2. Let s^2 can be determined by means of one of the vectors (12)-(15). Then b_s (see (11)) is consistent estimate for β provided

$\lambda_{min}(F'F) \to \infty$, $m \to \infty$ and $\max_i \sigma_i^2 \leqq d \leqq \infty$.

Proof. (Throughout the proof it is assumed that all probability limits plim (.) are taken for $m \to \infty$). The comparison of b_Σ and b_s from (10) and (11) shows that if

$$\text{plim } s^2 = \sigma^2 \tag{26}$$

then $b_s \approx b_\Sigma$, $m \to \infty$, and according to the theorem, mentioned in (i), b_s is a consistent estimator for β. Consequently, establishing the consistency of b_s means a verification of the relationship (26), i.e. verifying whether MINQUE, AUE, ASR and SV methods consistenly estimate the unknown variances. For the first three estimators it can be written using formulae (12)-(14)

$$\text{plim } s^2_{MINQUE} = \text{plim } A_m^{-1} \text{plim } u = (\text{plim } A_m)^{-1} \text{plim } u = \text{plim } u,$$

$$\text{plim } s^2_{AUE} = \text{plim } B_m \text{plim } u = \text{plim } u,$$

$$\text{plim } s^2_{ASR} = \text{plim } u,$$

since from (16)-(18) it follows that plim A_m and plim B_m are identity matrices:

$$\text{plim}[A_m]_{ij} = \begin{cases} \text{plim}(1-2m^{-1}k_{ii}+m^{-1}k_{ii}^2) = 1, \ i = j, \\ \text{plim}(m^{-1}k_{ij}^2) = 0, \ i \neq j, \end{cases}$$

$$\text{plim}[B_m]_{ij} = \begin{cases} \text{plim}(1-m^{-1}k_{ii})^{-1} = 1, \ i = j, \\ 0, \ i \neq j, \end{cases}$$

Therefore for MINQUE, AUE and ASR methods the condition (26) is reduced to a consistent estimation of variances by means of the vector u, i.e.

$$\text{plim } u = \sigma^2. \tag{27}$$

Seeking for the elements of plim u, we use the following ($m\times1$) vector of residuals from the replications at the ith design point:

$$\hat{r}_i = (\hat{r}_i^{(1)}, \hat{r}_i^{(2)}, \ldots, \hat{r}_i^{(m)\prime})' = y_i - \hat{y}_i = F_i\beta + r_i - F_i b = F_i(\beta - b) + r_i \tag{28}$$

where $r_i = (r_i^{(1)}, r_i^{(2)}, \ldots, r_i^{(m)})'$, $y_i = (y_i^{(1)}, y_i^{(2)}, \ldots, y_i^{(m)})'$, $\hat{y}_i = (\hat{y}_i, \hat{y}_i, \ldots, \hat{y}_i)'$ $r_i^{(1)}$, $y_i^{(1)}$ are the ith elements of ($n\times1$) vectors $r^{(1)}$ and $y^{(1)}$ from (8), b is LS estimate (21) and F_i is an ($m\times p$) matrix with equal rows of the form $(f_{i1}, f_{i2}, \ldots, f_{ip})'$, $f_{ij} = F_{ij}$, $i = 1,2,\ldots,n$, $j = 1,2,\ldots,p$.

Therefore u_i can be presented by (19) and (28) as

$$u_i = m^{-1}\Sigma_{l=1}^m \hat{r}_i^{(l)2} = m^{-1}\hat{r}_i'\hat{r}_i = m^{-1}((\beta-b)'F_i' + r_i')(F_i(\beta-b) + r_i)) =$$

$$(\beta-b)'(F_i'F_i/m)(\beta-b) + 2(r_i'F_i/m)(\beta-b) + (r_i'r_i/m)$$

Thence

$$\text{plim } u_i = (\beta\text{-plim } b)'\text{plim } (F_i'F_i/m)(\beta\text{-plim } b) +$$
$$+ 2\text{plim}(r_i'F_i/m)(\beta\text{-plim } b) + \text{plim}(r_i'r_i/m) \qquad (29)$$

The frist term in the right side of (29) is a quadratic form having vector (β-plim b) = 0 (as according to the theorem mentioned in (ii) plim b = β) and matrix with bounded elements, according to the determination of F_i

$$[\text{plim}(F_i'F_i/m)]_{rs} = (\Sigma_{l=1}^{m} f_{ir}f_{is}/m) = f_{ir}f_{is}, \; r,s = 1,2,\ldots,m.$$

Consequently, this term equals zero. The second term of (29) is zero too, since $\text{plim}(r_i'F_i/m)$ cam be regarded as a vector of probability limits of the covariances between the elements of r_i and F_i, which are zeros, F_i being a nonrandom matrix. Thence (29) reduces to

$$\text{plim } u_i = \text{plim}(r_i'r_i/m) = \text{plim}(\Sigma_{l=1}^{m} r_i^{(1)2}/m) = \sigma_i^2.$$

Regarding the estimation of σ^2 through SV it is well known (Gramer, 1946, § 27.4) that this method provides unbiased estimates for σ_i^2

$$E(s_{SVi}^2) = \sigma_i^2$$

whit variances of the form:

$$\text{var } (s_{SVi}^2) = m^{-1}\mu_4 - \sigma_i^2(m-3)/(m-1)m,$$

where $\mu_4 = E(y_i^{(1)} - E(y_i^{(1)}))^4$. Therefore $\text{var}(s_{SVi}^2) \to 0$, $m \to \infty$. Thence s_{SVi}^2 is consistent, i.e. $\text{plim} s_{SVi}^2 = \sigma_i^2$, i = 1,2,...,n, as an estimator who is unbiased and with variance tending asymptotically to zero (Johnston, 1972, § 9.1). This complets the proof.

2.3. Efficiency of b_s: Monte-Carlo simulations

The comparison of the efficiency of the b_s type estimates, b_Σ and b is usually based on sample covariance matrices, obtained by means of Monte-Carlo tests (Rao, Subrahmaniam, 1971) since attaining an approximation to the covariance matrix of b_s is still to be done. Summarized results from similar tests for estimates b_{MINQUE}, b_{AUE}, b_{ASR}, b_{SV} and b are given in Table 1.

The aim is to investigate these estimates in the case of small number of replications and without replications. The comparison is carried out through the value of the ratio between sample covariance matrix determinats for the estimates b_s and b, i.e. $|\hat{D}(b_s)|/|\hat{D}(b)|$. If the ratio is smaller than 1, the estimation by means of b_s is more efficien than the one, obtained through LSE b. The nearer this value is to the minimal one (determined by $|\hat{D}(b_\Sigma)|/|\hat{D}(b)|$, the closer in efficiency sence the estimates b_s are to the b_Σ. The heteroscedasticity is preset from $\max_i \sigma_i^2/\min_i \sigma_i^2 = 1.31$ to 19.46 vary-

TABLE 1 The values of $|\hat{D}(\hat{\beta})|/|D(\hat{b})|$ for estimates $\hat{\beta}$ of the type MINQUE, AUE, ASR, SV and BLUE.

n	$\max_i \sigma_i^2/\min_i \sigma_i^2$	m	MINQUE	AUE	ASR	SV	BLUE
	1,31	1	7.641	2.738	2.436	-	0.976
		3	2.485	2.077	2.039	5.668	1.007
		1	3.710	1.262	4.321	-	0.320
		2	1.374	1.052	1.118	4.423	0.293
9	13.30	3	1.092	0.933	0.939	1.835	0.341
		6	0.628	0.599	0.599	0.726	0.327
		10	0.445	0.439	0.439	0.452	0.298
		1	3.354	1.194	1.568	-	0.261
	19.46	3	0.944	0.801	0.811	1.324	0.273
		6	0.505	0.485	0.487	0.574	0.261
		1	2.593	1.132	3.396	-	0.633
8	6.41	2	2.075	1.595	1.532	32.173	0.673
		3	1.299	1.166	1.152	1.895	0.615
		6	0.947	0.920	0.920	1.032	0.706

ing error moments. The number of replications m is 1, 2, 3, 6 and 10, the sample size is 400. The models are two with coefficients $\beta = (5.8, 1.3, -8.5, 4.7, 5.5, -3.2)'$ and $\beta = (9.5, -6.5, 2.4, -2.4, -2.1, 1.8, 5.7)'$ whose elements correspond to the terms 1, x_1, x_2, x_1x_2, x_1^2 and x_2^2. They are estimated with two different design with n = 9 (-1,-1, 1,-1, -1,1, 1,1, 1,0, -1,0,0,1,0,-1, 0,0) and n = 8 (-1,-1, 1,-1, -1,1, 1,1, 1,0, 0,1, 0,0, 0,-1) points (for every point the values are given for x_1 and x_2 respectively. The two modifications of b_{MINQUE}, mentioned in 2 are calculated. The second modification prove to be more inefficientii in the case with m = 1 and more efficient than the first one with increasing number of replications. In Table 1 the values for MINQUE method in all cases with m = 1 are obtained by means of the first modification (a number 0.01 is substituted for negative variance estimates). All cases with $m \geqq 1$ correspond to the second one with the average of the squared residuals used in substitutions.

The results shown provide for the following conclusion. If replications are lacking, the estimates b_{MINQUE}, b_{AUE}, b_{ASR} and b_{SV} are less efficient than the LSE b. However with a moderate number of replications the estimates b_{MINQUE}, b_{AUE} and b_{ASR} grow more efficient than b with the heteroscedasticity increasing. The use of b_{SV} with moderate number of replication is risky because it can be less efficient than b. The b_{SV} efficiency becomes comparable with this of b_{MINQUE}, b_{AUE} and b_{ASR} for a large number of replication ($m \geqq 10$). Best results have been obtained by the use of b_{AUE}.

3. ROBUSTNESS OF EXPERIMENTAL DESIGNS TO ERRORS IN THE FACTOR LEVELS

Depending of the specific circumstances various requirements might be appropriate in the choice of experimental design. (Box, Draper, 1975). One of these requirments is the good behaviour of the design in presence of errors in the factor levels. It is assumed that β in the model (3) will be estimated by LSE $b = (F'F)^{-1}F'y$ rather than by BLUE b_Σ which leads to an efficiency loss depending on the variance heteroscedasticity.

This heteroscedasticity varies from design to design with a given model and factor error moments. Thence the criteria seeking for the robust design to factor errors can be formulated in a way that the design would ensure the least possible efficiency loss. Alternatively such criterion should select from several designs the one providing estimate b with improved covariance matrix caracteristic as compared to the others. Seeking such criteria one faces heteroscedasticity of variances and particularly their dependence on β which causes serious difficulties.

An attempt to alleviate these difficulties is made in (Vuchkov, Boyadjieva, 1983) where two criteria for robust design are proposed. In addition to (2) it is accepted that v_i is independently distributed by the factor errors e_i in each run. The first criterion use as a measure of heteroscedasticity the quantity

$$\alpha = \max_i \sigma_i^2 / \Sigma_{i=1}^n \sigma_i^2$$

where σ_i^2 is calculated using (4) with $c_i = 0$. The criterion is formulated as a difference between superior limit of α after β and the minimum value of $\alpha = \alpha_n = n^{-1}$, attainable when no errors occur:

$$\gamma_s = \sup_\beta \alpha - \alpha_n$$

It is shown that γ_s can be calculated by means of

$$\gamma_s = n^{-1}(\max_i \lambda_i - 1) \qquad (30)$$

if the following assumptions about diagonal elements of the matrix A_i from (5) and $\bar{A} = n^{-1}\Sigma_{i=1}^n A_i$ are fulfilled

$$[A_i]_{jj} \ll \sigma_o^2/\beta'\beta, [\bar{A}]_{jj} \ll \sigma_o^2/\beta'\beta, \; j = 1,2,\ldots,n. \qquad (31)$$

In (30) $\max_i \lambda_{ii}$ is the maximal root of the characteristic equation $|A_i - \bar{A}| = 0$

The fulfiment of (31) can be assertained in many practical cases with given factor error moments and some initial estimates of vector β norm $\beta'\beta$ and for σ_o^2. Consequantly if the conditions (31) are met then the maximum heteroscedasticity of variances after β with the design applied, can be estimated through $\sup_\beta \alpha$ while its deviation γ_s from α_n becomse a mesure of efficiency loss and thence a measure of robustness of the design to factor errors.

The second criterion chooses design that will provide for the smaller covariance matrix trace of estimate b. It implies a better design X_1 than X_2 provided the following inequality is fulfilled:

$$\tau = (tr(D(b)))_2 - (tr(D(b)))_1 < 0 \qquad (32)$$

where $(tr(D(b)))_i$ denotes the covariance matrix trace for the design X_i, $i = 1,2$. It is shown that (32) can be reduced to

$$\tau = \beta'\Delta R\beta + \sigma_o^2\Delta a < 0 \tag{33}$$

where $\Delta R = (\Sigma_{n=1}^{n} A_i k_{ii})_2 - (\Sigma_{i=1}^{n} A_i k_{ii})$, $\Delta a = (\Sigma_{i=1}^{n} k_{ii})_2 - (\Sigma_{i=1}^{n} k_{ii})_1$,

$k_{ii} = (F(F'F)^{-1}F')_{ii}$ and the indeces 1 and 2 correspond to the design X_1 and X_2. Criterion makes it possible to compare some designs regardless of β as the ellements of ΔR depend on the points of the design to be compared and on the factor error moments, while the quantity Δa depend on the design points. This possibility depend on ΔR matrix definitness and the sign of Δa.

Comparable design in sence of criterion τ are those one for which the matrix ΔR is positive definite and $\Delta a \geq 0$. Incomparable designs in the sense of τ are those ones, for which the matrix ΔR is not defined.

REFERENCES

Box, G.E.P. (1963). The effect of the errors in the factor levels and experimental designs. Technometrics, 5(2):247-262.

Box, G.E.P. and Draper, N.D. (1975). Robust designs. Biometrika, 62: 347-352.

Cramer, H. (1946). Mathematical methods of statistics. Princeton, Un.Pr.

Demidenko, E. Z. (1981). Linear and nonlinear regression, Finance and Statistics, Moscow (russia).

Fedorov, V.V. (1974). Regression problems with controlable variable subject to error. Biometrika, 61(1):49-56.

Horn, S.D. and Horn, R.A. (1975). Comparison of estimators of heteroscedastic variances in linear models. J. of the Amer. Statist. Assoc., 70(352):872-879.

Jacquez, J.A. and Norusis, M. (1973). Sampling experiments in the estimation of parameters in heteroscedastic linear regression. Biometrics, 29(4):771-779.

Johnston, N. (1972). Econometrics methods. McGraw-Hill, New York.

Rao, J.N.K. and Subrahmaniam, K. (1971). Combining independent estimators and estimation in linear regression with unequal variances. Biometrics, 27(4):971-990.

Vuchkov, I.N. and Boyadjieva, L.N. (1981). Errors in the factor levels and estimation of regression model parameters. J. Statist. Comput. Simul., 13:1-12.

Vuchkov, I.N. and Boyadjieva, L.N. (1983). The robustness of experimental designs against errors in the factor levels. J. Statist. Comp. Simul. 17:31-41.

DATA-SMOOTHING AND BOOTSTRAP RESAMPLING

G.A. Young
Statistical Laboratory, University of Cambridge,
16 Mill Lane, Cambridge CB2 1SB, U.K.

1. INTRODUCTION

This paper reviews aspects of the smoothed bootstrap approach to statistical estimation.

The basic problem underlying the bootstrap methodology is that of providing a simulation algorithm which produces realisations from an unknown distribution F, when all that is available is a sample from F. The bootstrap of Efron (1979) simulates, with replacement, from the observed sample. The smoothed bootstrap, discussed by Efron (1979, 1982) and Silverman and Young (1987), smooths the sample observations first and hence effectively simulates from a kernel estimate of the density f underlying F. This is achieved, without construction of the kernel estimate itself, by resampling from the original data and then perturbing each sampled point appropriately.

The bootstrap and smoothed bootstrap will be considered as competing methods of estimating properties of an unknown distribution F. Given a general functional α, which may relate to the sampling properties of a parameter estimate, it is required to estimate on the basis of a set of sample data the population value $\alpha(F)$ of this functional.

The standard bootstrap estimates $\alpha(F)$ by $\alpha(F_n)$, F_n denoting the empirical c.d.f. of the sample data. The smoothed bootstrap estimates $\alpha(F)$ by $\alpha(\hat{F})$, where $\hat{F}$ is a smoothed version of F_n. The simple idea underlying the bootstrap estimation, therefore, is that of using F_n or $\hat{F}$ as a surrogate or estimate for the unknown F. In many circumstances the bootstrap estimate will itself be estimated by resampling from F_n or $\hat{F}$, though as yet unpublished work by Davison and Hinkley points in the direction of 'bootstrap resampling without the resampling'.

Though conceived by Efron (1979) as a means of tackling complex estimation problems, for a discussion of smoothing there is some advantage in studying the very simplest case where the functional α is linear in F. Relevant questions to be considered are:

(i) When is it advantageous to use a smoothed bootstrap rather than the standard bootstrap?

(ii) How should the smoothing be performed? Is there any advantage in simulating from a 'shrunk' version of the kernel estimator, with the same variance structure as the sample data?

(iii) Is it possible to define data-driven procedures which will choose the degree of smoothing to be applied automatically?

2. SMOOTHED BOOTSTRAP PROCEDURE

Suppose $X_1,\ldots,X_n$ are independent realisations from an unknown r-variate F. Assuming F has a smooth underlying density f, a convenient smoothed bootstrap is obtained from the kernel estimator $\hat{f}_{h,s}$ of f defined by

$$\hat{f}_{h,s}(x) = (1+h^2)^{r/2}\, \hat{f}_h\{(1+h^2)^{\frac{1}{2}}x\} ,$$

$$\hat{f}_h(x) = |V|^{-\frac{1}{2}}\, n^{-1}\, h^{-r} \sum_{i=1}^{n} K\{h^{-1}\, V^{-\frac{1}{2}}\, (x-X_i)\} . \tag{2.1}$$

Here K is a symmetric probability density function of an r-variate distribution with unit variance matrix. Operationally V is taken as the variance matrix of the sample data and h is a parameter defining the degree of smoothing.

Realisations generated from $\hat{f}_h$ have expectation equal to $\bar{X}$, the mean of the observed sample, but smoothing inflates the marginal variances. Silverman and Young (1987) give a number of simple examples which show that smoothing of this type can have a deleterious effect on the bootstrap estimation: see also section 3. The kernel estimator $\hat{f}_h$ is therefore 'shrunk' to give an estimator $\hat{f}_{h,s}$ with second-order moment properties the same as those in the observed sample. Note that the mean of $\hat{f}_{h,s}$ is $\bar{X}/(1+h^2)^{\frac{1}{2}}$.

3. LINEAR FUNCTIONALS

For a linear functional $\alpha(F) = \int a(t)dF(t)$, the smoothed bootstrap estimator is $\hat{\alpha}_h(F) = \int a(t)\hat{f}_{h,s}(t)dt$. This estimator may be written

$$\hat{\alpha}_h(F) = \frac{1}{n} \sum_{i=1}^{n} w^*(X_i) \tag{3.1}$$

where

$$w^*(x) = \int a\{(1+h^2)^{-\frac{1}{2}}\, (x+hV^{\frac{1}{2}}\xi)\}\, K(\xi)d\xi \quad .$$

Using a Taylor expansion of a and the assumptions on the kernel function K, the mean squared error of $\hat{\alpha}_h(F)$ may, for h small, be expanded as

$$\text{MSE}\{\hat{\alpha}_h(F)\} = C_0 + C_1h^2 + C_2h^4 + O(h^6) \quad . \tag{3.2}$$

Here we have assumed that $V = [V_{ij}]$ is a fixed positive definite symmetric matrix and

$$C_0 = \frac{1}{n} \int \{a(t) - \mu\}^2\, dF(t) \quad ,$$

$$C_1 = \frac{1}{n} \int \{a(t) - \mu\}\, a^*(t)dF(t) \quad ,$$

$$C_2 = \frac{1}{n} [\ 2 \int \{a(t)-\mu\}\ a^{**}(t)dF(t) + \frac{1}{4} \int a^*(t)^2 dF(t)$$

$$+ \frac{1}{4}(n-1)\ \{ \int a^*(t)dF(t)\ \}^2\ ]$$

where $\mu = \int a(t)dF(t)$,

$$a^*(t) = D_V a(t) - t\cdot\nabla a(t) \ ,$$

$$a^{**}(t) = \frac{3}{8}\, t\cdot\nabla a(t) + \frac{1}{8}\, t^T H_a t - \frac{1}{2} D_V a(t) - \frac{1}{4}\, t\cdot\nabla(D_V a) + \frac{1}{8} D_V^{\,2} a(t) \ .$$

Here $D_V a(t) = \sum_i \sum_j V_{ij} \delta^2 a(t)/\delta t_i \delta t_j$,

$$(H_a)_{ij} = \delta^2 a(t)/\delta t_i \delta t_j \ .$$

See Silverman and Young (1987) for details of the manipulations.

The expansion (3.2) immediately gives the result:

<u>Lemma</u>

Provided $a(X)$ and $a^*(X)$ are negatively correlated, the mean squared error of the smoothed bootstrap estimator $\hat{\alpha}_h(F)$ of $\alpha(F)$ will be less than that of the unsmoothed estimate $\hat{\alpha}_0(F) = \int a(t)dF_n(t)$, for *some* $h > 0$. □

The corresponding result for the bootstrap estimator $\tilde{\alpha}_h(F) = \int a(t)\hat{f}_h(t)dt$, constructed from the unshrunk kernel estimator, requires $a(X)$ and $D_V a(X)$ to be negatively correlated.

As a simple example, suppose F is the univariate standard Gaussian distribution and let $a(t) = t^5$. With $V = 1$ we have,

$$\mathrm{cov}\{a(X), a^*(X)\} < 0$$

$$\mathrm{cov}\{a(X), D_V a(X)\} > 0 \ ,$$

so that smoothing, with shrinkage, is of potential value in bootstrap estimation of the fifth moment.

The lemma above states that if $C_1 < 0$ in (3.2) some small degree of smoothing at least is worthwhile. If also $C_2 < 0$ we might speculate that some larger degree of smoothing may be appropriate. If both $C_1 > 0$ and $C_2 > 0$ the appropriate bootstrap estimator is the unsmoothed estimator $\hat{\alpha}_0(F)$. Otherwise, the optimal smoothing parameter, in the sense of minimising the approximate MSE $C_0 + C_1 h^2 + C_2 h^4$ is given by $h = (2|C_1|/4C_2)^{\frac{1}{2}}$.

The quantities C_1 and C_2 depend on the unknown underlying distribution function F , and in general will be complicated functions of the moments of F. A possible strategy would be to choose h with reference to a standard distribution, such as the standard r-variate Gaussian. In circumstances where the sample data do not suggest any sensible statistical model, C_1 and C_2 can be estimated, for example by substitution of the sample moments.

Given estimates $\hat{C}_1, \hat{C}_2$ for C_1, C_2 an entirely data-driven strategy for choosing the degree of smoothing would be to take $h = 0$ if $\hat{C}_1 \geq 0$, $h = \infty$ if $\hat{C}_1 < 0$ and $\hat{C}_2 < 0$ and $h = (2|\hat{C}_1|/4\hat{C}_2)^{\frac{1}{2}}$ otherwise. The case $h = \infty$ corresponds to Efron's 'parametric bootstrap' (Efron, 1979).

Rather than choosing h by reference to (3.2), which gives an expansion for h in the neighbourhood of zero, the representation (3.1) of the estimator can be used in conjunction with computer algebraic manipulation to obtain an exact expression for $MSE\{\hat{\alpha}_h(F)\}$. This expression can then be minimised in h to obtain the optimal value of the smoothing parameter.

4. EXTENSION TO NON-LINEAR FUNCTIONALS

When an explicit bootstrap procedure is being used the functional α is unlikely to be linear. The ideas of Section 3 can be applied to bootstrap estimation for more general α, provided α admits a first-order von Mises expansion about F of the form

$$\alpha(\hat{F}) \simeq \alpha(F) + A(\hat{F} - F) , \tag{4.1}$$

for $\hat{F}$ 'near' F. The functional α is linear and hence representable as an integral, $A(F) = \int a(t)dF(t)$, and to first-order the sampling properties of the bootstrap estimator $\alpha(\hat{F})$ of $\alpha(F)$ are the same as those of the estimator $A(\hat{F})$ of $A(F)$. Provided $\sup|\hat{F}-F|$ is $O_p(n^{-\frac{1}{2}})$, the error in (4.1) will be $O_p(n^{-1})$.

5. EXAMPLE

Let F be an unknown univariate distribution and consider estimation of the skewness,

$$\alpha(F) = \frac{E_F(X - E_F X)^3}{\{E_F(X-E_F X)^2\}^{3/2}} .$$

Simple manipulations, easily performed by computer algebra, show that the linear approximation (4.1) is defined by

$$\begin{aligned} a(t) = (t(&-2\mu_1^4 t^2 + 3\mu_1^3\mu_2 t + 6\mu_1^3\mu_3 - 6\mu_1^2\mu_2^2 + 4\mu_1^2\mu_2 t^2 - 3\mu_1^2\mu_3 t \\ &- 3\mu_1\mu_2^2 t - 6\mu_1\mu_2\mu_3 + 6\mu_2^3 - 2\mu_2^2 t^2 + 3\mu_2\mu_3 t))/2(\mu_1^6 - 3\mu_1^4\mu_2 \\ &+ 3\mu_1^2\mu_2^2 - \mu_2^3)\sqrt{(\mu_2 - \mu_1^2)} , \end{aligned}$$

where $\mu_r = E_F X^r$.

The bootstrap estimator $\hat{\alpha}_h(F)$ is given by:

$$\hat{\alpha}_h(F) = \frac{\sum_{i=1}^n X_i^3}{nV^{3/2}(1+h^2)^{3/2}} + \frac{3\bar{X}h^2}{V^{\frac{1}{2}}(1+h^2)^{3/2}} - \frac{3\bar{X}}{V^{\frac{1}{2}}(1+h^2)^{\frac{1}{2}}} - \frac{\bar{X}^3}{V^{3/2}(1+h^2)^{3/2}} . \quad (5.1)$$

In the special case of F standard Gaussian, computer algebraic manipulation of the function a(t) gives a closed form approximation for the MSE of $\hat{\alpha}_h(F)$:

$$\text{MSE}\{\hat{\alpha}_h(F)\} \simeq \frac{6}{n(1+h^2)^3} , \quad (5.2)$$

and gives $C_1 = -18/n$, $C_2 = 36/n$. These values suggest, misleadingly, $h = \frac{1}{2}$.

In the general case, the formulae for C_1 and C_2 are complicated functions of the moments of F . With a manipulation package such as REDUCE it is straightforward to write FORTRAN subroutines to evaluate these coefficients: the moments of the observed sample are then substituted to yield estimates $\hat{C}_1, \hat{C}_2$. The formula for $\text{MSE}\{\hat{\alpha}_h(F)\}$, of which (5.2) is a special case, amounts to hundreds of lines of code. If $\mu_1 = 0$ it reduces to the simpler form:

$$\begin{aligned}\text{MSE}\{\hat{\alpha}_h(F)\} \simeq\ & (-8(h^2+1)^{\frac{1}{2}}h^4 n\mu_2^2\mu_3^2 - 16(h^2+1)^{\frac{1}{2}}h^2 n\mu_2^2\mu_3^2 \\ & + 48(h^2+1)^{\frac{1}{2}}h^2\mu_2^2\mu_3^2 - 12(h^2+1)^{\frac{1}{2}}h^2\mu_2\mu_3\mu_5 - 8(h^2+1)^{\frac{1}{2}}n\mu_2^2\mu_3^2 \\ & + 48(h^2+1)^{\frac{1}{2}}\mu_2^2\mu_3^2 - 12(h^2+1)^{\frac{1}{2}}\mu_2\mu_3\mu_5 + 4h^8 n\mu_2^2\mu_3^2 \\ & + 16h^6 n\mu_2^2\mu_3^2 + 24h^4 n\mu_2^2\mu_3^2 - 9h^4\mu_2^2\mu_3^2 + 9h^4\mu_3^2\mu_4 \\ & + 20h^2 n\mu_2^2\mu_3^2 + 36h^2\mu_2^5 - 24h^2\mu_2^3\mu_4 - 22h^2\mu_2^2\mu_3^2 \\ & + 4h^2\mu_2^2\mu_6 + 18h^2\mu_3^2\mu_4 + 8n\mu_2^2\mu_3^2 + 36\mu_2^5 - 24\mu_2^3\mu_4 \\ & - 13\mu_2^2\mu_3^2 + 4\mu_2^2\mu_6 + 9\mu_3^2\mu_4) \,/\, (4n\mu_2^5(h^2+1)^4)\ ) . \quad (5.3)\end{aligned}$$

Invariance of the estimator (5.1) under the transformation $X_i \to X_i+C$ $(i = 1,\dots,n)$ suggests the following procedure for choice of h . Centre the observations X_i by calculating $Y_i = X_i - \bar{X}$ $(i = 1,\dots,n)$. Then substitute $n^{-1}\sum_{i=1}^n Y_i^r$ for μ_r $(r = 2,\dots,6)$ in (5.3). This gives an estimate of the mean squared error of the bootstrap estimator as a function of h . Use a numerical routine to minimise this and use the minimising value of h for the bootstrap estimation itself.

For each of four underlying distributions - standard Gaussian, uniform on $[-1,1]$, Beta (5,3) and standard exponential - and two sample sizes, $n = 5$ and $n = 50$, 1000 datasets were generated. Table 1 shows, for each combination, the mean squared error over the 1000 replications of the bootstrap estimators $\hat{\alpha}_h(F)$, when h is chosen by various strategies. Strategy A takes $h = 0.0$ always, Strategy B takes $h = 0.5$ always, Strategy C estimates C_1, C_2 and chooses h according to the estimated values, as described in Section 3, while Strategy D is the procedure described above, based on (5.3).

Table 1 : MSE of bootstrap estimators, skewness example.

Distribution		N(0,1)	U[-1,1]	Beta(5,3)	Exp(1)
	$\alpha(F)$	0.0	0.0	-0.310	2.0
n	Smoothing Strategy				
5	A	0.3607	0.3566	0.3889	2.4497
	B	0.1847	0.1826	0.2341	2.7557
	C	0.2977	0.2950	0.3629	2.5674
	D	0.0912	0.0869	0.1554	3.0748
50	A	0.1092	0.0450	0.0650	0.4930
	B	0.0559	0.0230	0.0435	0.8661
	C	0.1066	0.0446	0.0649	0.5331
	D	0.0596	0.0218	0.0589	0.5490

The results of the simulation disappoint in that they do not provide concrete evidence in favour of any particular smoothing procedure. Automatic application of a small amount of smoothing can lead to substantially less accurate estimation: see the figure for the exponential simulation, $n = 50$. Strategy C is unlikely to make the estimation dramatically worse and generally leads to some improvement over the standard bootstrap. Strategy D can lead to considerably greater accuracy in the bootstrap estimation but, as the exponential simulation makes clear, may also lead to quite inappropriate choice of h . Errors in the linear expansion (4.1), which is the basis of strategies C and D, may, even for moderate sample size, be quite appreciable.

Automatic procedures for choosing the degree of smoothing should be used with caution. It is probably advisable to examine the sample data, using an estimator of the form (2.1) say, and then to choose h with reference to some suggested parametric family of distributions.

Acknowledgement

I am grateful to Bernard Silverman for permission to include details of our joint work.

REFERENCES

Efron, B. (1979). Bootstrap methods: another look at the jackknife. Ann. Statist., 7:1-26.
Efron, B. (1982). The Jackknife, the Bootstrap and Other Resampling Plans. Philadelphia: SIAM.
Silverman, B.W. and Young, G.A. (1987). The bootstrap: to smooth or not to smooth? Biometrika, 74. (To appear)

PART III.

MODEL TESTING AND APPLICATIONS

Model- and Method-Oriented Intelligent Software for Statistical Data Analysis

S.A. Aivazyan
Central Economics-Mathematical Institute of
the USSR Academy of Sciences
Moscow, USSR

1. Introduction

This paper deals with intelligent applied statistics software developed at CEMI (Central Economics-Mathematical Institute of the USSR Academy of Sciences). Every component of the software system under consideration represents a branch of applied statistics implemented as a comparatively small expert system (SES, 400-500 rules in the knowledge base). This is why the system is called a series of Method-Oriented Statistical Expert Systems, version 1 ("MOSES 1" is the abbreviation used officially, but in this paper "M1" will be used).

Every SES of the series:

(1) guides the user through the available literature, and methodological and software information related to specific features of the problem at hand;

(2) informs you which initial assumptions on the nature of the data to be processed and also the form of the model which should be used;

(3) assists in constructing a chain of statistical procedures and algorithms which have to make up the basic program and its automatic implementation;

(4) helps in interpreting intermediate and final results of statistical analysis and (if necessary) in generating additional control statements for continuing the process of statistical analysis;

(5) assists in choosing the form in which the results should be presented.

Basically, it is assumed that system M1 will be used mainly by statisticians. However, for comparatively simple statistical problems M1 can also be useful to economists, sociologists, physicists, engineers, etc, who are familiar with probability theory and statistics at the level of the graduate student of an economics or engineering department.

2. Method-Oriented Statistical Expert Systems: brief description of their structures

The series of Method-Oriented Statistical Expert Systems consist of a number of SES which can be used for solving problems arising in different areas (economics, sociology, health-care, technology, etc). Each specific expert system realizes statistical techniques of a branch of statistical analysis: a regression analysis SES, a classification SES, an exploratory statistical analysis SES, etc, and thus can be viewed as a model-oriented system.

The components of the series are compatible in the following sense:

(a) they are oriented toward the same user intelligence level (perhaps it would be more accurate here to use "intelligence interval").

(b) they are based on the same methodological principles of computer-aided assistance;

(c) there is a possibility of cross-references (when interacting with the computer, the user of the regression analysis SES can be advised that he should be consulted, say, by the classification SES, to solve his problem).

We now describe in brief the functional structure of the series of Method-Oriented Statistical Expert Systems M1:

(1) TSA is an expert system for *time series analysis*. The numerous planning and management bodies at the different levels of an economy constantly face the necessity of real-time analysis of changing indices, characterizing the state and dynamics of a system (economic, technological, etc). Similar problems arise in a number of research activities. There are the problems of smoothing of time series, their decomposition into a trend, periodic and random components, their extrapolation (prediction), locating the time and character of structural changes, etc.

(2) EDA is an expert system for *exploratory data analysis*. Unfortunately, there exists an unpleasant tradition in statistical studies: no attention is paid to the key stage of formulation and justification of the initial assumptions underlying the basic models of statistical data generation. Usually a statistical investigation begins as follows: "We assume that (or it is reasonable to assume that) the regression under consideration is linear and characterized by independent normally distributed random parameters. Then...". In reality, statistical data to be processed may be non-normal, dependent, heteroscedastic and so on. Statisticians have had to put up with such unjustifiable initial assumptions. Exploratory analysis has developed extensively in the past 10-15 years and, in

particular, projection pursuit methods aimed at investigating initial data to formulate adequate assumptions concerning their probabilistic and geometric nature and the mechanism of data generation. Only a few software systems exist which use these techniques (for example PS-ISP 1986), but no expert system is referenced anywhere. This is one of the reasons for EDA to become a component of M1.

(3) REGRAN is an expert system for *regression analysis*. The corresponding statistical techniques enable us to reveal and describe the dependence of a resulting response upon a set of explanatory variables. Regression analysis is probably the most widely used statistical approach. When using these techniques, the man-machine interaction is of paramount importance since there are various weakly formalized stages such as the choice of the general form of the model, the study of the collinearity phenomenon, the analysis of outliers, etc. The interaction with the SES and its advice are most valuable for a user at this stage. In fact this area of applied statistics can be considered basic for a number of other statistical approaches, and a large number of references from other components of M1 are related to REGRAN.

(4) CLASS is an expert system for *classification of objects and patterns*. Along with regression analysis, the corresponding statistical classification methods (pattern recognition, discriminant analysis, automatic classification, cluster analysis, etc) are the techniques widely used in applications and, first of all, in economics and social sciences. The problems of studying typology and type-generating features, diagnostics in technology and health care, preliminary data array processing to single out homogeneous portions of information, and many other problems are handled by this cluster of the statistical software. The advances of Soviet scientists in this field ensure the possibility of the creation of market competitive programs (at least in their functional contents).

(5) SEE is an expert system for solution and analysis of *simultaneous econometric equations*. The simultaneous econometric equations arising in the theory and practice of economic-statistical modeling are interrelated regression equations and identities in which the same variables in different equations can be both responses and explanatory variables. The interrelations under consideration can involve variables corresponding to lagged moments as well as the current one. SEE is intended to help a user to choose the model structure, to make it identifiable, estimate the coefficients of equations involved, etc.

(6) PROF is an expert system for construction and analysis of *production functions.* The production functions give a compact mathematical description of the relations between the final product outputs and resources. In particular, these functions are very helpful in the analytical study of resource efficiency and the involvement of a resource in production, in the prediction of the output level, etc. The functions are constructed and analyzed by using regression analysis and time series analysis.

3. Who is the User of M1 and how intelligent is M1?

M1 is intended for both the statistician and the user who, on the one hand, has his problem posed and knows his ultimate goal, and, on the other hand, is trained in applied statistics (i.e., knows basic concepts and definitions of regression models, regression analysis, time series and trend, classification with and without learning samples, multivariate observations and their projection on a plane, etc). Thus, among the users of M1 there are both statisticians (with different levels of knowledge) and non-statisticians (economists, sociologists, engineers, etc) having elementary knowledge in statistics.

To explain how M1 works, we decompose the possible statistical study into elements as follows:

Element 1: (formulation): refinement of the formulation of the problem and final objectives of the study.

Element 2: (methodology): the choice of appropriate statistical techniques, including the set of statistical procedures and the order of their performance for data processing.

Element 3: (computation): realization of the chosen set of statistical data processing techniques.

Element 4: (interpretation): discussion of intermediate and final results of statistical data processing, and derivation of conclusions, including recommendations for further investigation.

Among these four major elements of practically any statistical study only the last three can be partly automated and provided with computer-aided assistance in the frame of M1. Primarily, we consider how to help the user to choose adequate preliminary assumptions (hypotheses) concerning the geometric and probabilistic nature of data to be processed and to describe the model which generates these data (EDA is entirely intended for solving these problems, while in other components of the series these problems are thoroughly analyzed). The general idea of 'user-computer' interaction in M1's components follows the traditional principle "from general description to more and more method-oriented notions".

Thus, if one applies the three-level classification of intelligent software (see Hahn, 1985), M1 has to be placed at the second (middle) level.

As mentioned before, every component of M1 interacts with a knowledge base containing at most 400-500 rules and assertions. It is thus possible to realize the project on the IBM-XT or IBM-AT PC (or any compatible 16-digit PC).

The basic algorithmic languages are C-language, FORTRAN-77, and some other (ad hoc) languages.

4. References

PC-ISP: PC-Interactive Scientific Processor. User's Guide and Command Descriptions. Chapman and Hill Software. New York-London, 1986.

Hahn, G.J. More Intelligent Statistical Software and Statistical Expert Systems: Future Direction. In: The American Statistician, vol. 39 No. 1 (1985) pp. 1-19.

ASSESSING THE PERFORMANCE OF ESTIMATES WITHOUT KNOWLEDGE ON THE REGRESSION FUNCTION, THE VARIANCES AND THE DISTRIBUTIONS

Olaf Bunke
Humboldt University, Berlin, GDR

1. INTRODUCTION

In this paper we want to show, how the performance of estimates and models may be assessed without knowing the regression and variance functions and the distributions of the observations. It is only assumed, that there are independent observations y_{ij} $(i=1,\dots,m;\ j=1,\dots,n_i)$ with means and variances

$$E\,y_{ij} = f(x_i) = f_i,\quad D\,y_{ij} = v(x_i) = \sigma_i^2, \tag{1}$$

which are determined by the values of unknown regression and variance functions f and v for fixed "design points" x_i. Many different parametric or nonparametric estimates of these functions and estimates of parameters in approximative models for them have been proposed in the literature and are widely applied. Their bias, variance or more generally a risk

$$r(f,v,P_1,\dots,P_m) = E\,L\,[\delta(y),f,v] \tag{2}$$

for such estimators δ w.r.t. a loss function L give a description of their performance. The risk depends on the unknown distributions P_i of the observations y_{ij}, assumed to be the same for $j=1,\dots,n_i$. The MSE in estimating by a parametric model, say, by $g_{\hat{\beta}}$, is a special case of (2) and is a description of the performance of the model g_β.
The performance of the estimator may be assessed with an estimate of the risk (2). For this we need estimates of f,v and P_i leading to a "plug-in" risk estimate

$$\hat{r} = r(\hat{f},\hat{v},\hat{P}_1,\dots,\hat{P}_m). \tag{3}$$

Thus we are confronted with the semiparametric estimation problem of estimating the vectors

$$\underline{f} = (f_1,\dots,f_m),\quad \underline{v} = (\sigma_1,\dots,\sigma_m) \tag{4}$$

and the distributions P_i. As the calculation of maximum likelihood estimates turns out to be too complicated, we propose to derive Bayes estimates with respect to standard prior distributions, which in their noninformative limit case are identical to MLE's in some simple special cases. In this way we obtain some sensible structures of estimators, possibly being admissible by their Bayes property, and we could adapt the parameters of the priors trying to get accurate estimates of $\underline{f}$, $\underline{v}$ or P_i or of the risk (2).

In general it will be impossible to calculate explicitely the risk estimate (3) and it will be approximated by a smoothed "bootstrap estimate" (see Efron (1982))

$$\hat{r} = \sum_{k=1}^{B} L[\delta(y^{(k)}), \hat{f}, \hat{v}] / B, \tag{5}$$

where for each k $y^{(k)}$ is a sample of observations $y_{ij}^{(k)}$ simulated under the distributions $\hat{P}_i$.

A survey of methods derived under this approach is given in Bunke (1987).

2. BIVARIATE REGRESSION WITH KNOWN HOMOGENEOUS VARIANCE

For an illustration of the basic ideas we will discuss the special case of univariate real explanatory and dependent variables x_i and y_{ij}, that is, of bivariate regression, assuming that all variances are known and identical: $\sigma^2 = Dy_{ij}$.

We want to include in the prior a possible smoothness of the regression function, which may be described by a small value of its second order difference ratios, that is (see Silvermann (1986) or Titterington (1985)) of

$$T(f) = \sum_i |(f_{i+1}-f_i)(x_{i+1}-x_i)-(f_i-f_{i-1})(x_i-x_{i-1})|^2 / \\ / (x_{i+1}-x_i)(x_i-x_{i-1}). \tag{6}$$

Additionally to a probable smoothness of f we will assume, that its "mean" $\bar{f} = \sum_i f_i/m$ and "global slope"

$$b(f) = \sum_i (f_i-\bar{f})(x_i-\bar{x}) / \sum_h (x_h-\bar{x})^2 = c'\underline{f} \tag{7}$$

are "probably bounded" in the sense of a prior density

$$p(\underline{f}) \propto \exp[-(\xi \bar{f}^2 + \gamma b(f)^2 + \lambda T(f))/2] \tag{8}$$

with some (possibly small) constants ξ, γ and a constant λ, which characterizes the "degree of smoothness". These constants will be adapted later.

We assume that the "errors" $\varepsilon_{ij} = y_{ij}-f_i$ are i.i.d. with distribution P. The prior distribution of f,P is then assumed to give independent $\underline{f}$ and P, the density of $\underline{f}$ being (8) and the distribution of P being the Dirichlet distribution D_α with index measure α = a $N(o,\sigma^2)$ (see Hartigan (1983)). The prior mean of P will be the normal distribution $N(o,\sigma^2)$, while a characterizes the "dispersion" of the random distribution P around its mean.

The posterior means of f and P_i are Bayes estimates w.r.t. a square loss function. The results in Bunke (1985,1987) give the estimates

$$\hat{\underline{f}} = E(\underline{f}|y) = Q\,\bar{y} \tag{9}$$

$$\hat{P}_i = E(P_i|y) = k\,N(\hat{f}_i,\sigma^2+q_{ii}) + (1-k)\sum_{h,j} N(\hat{f}_i+e_{hj},q_{ii}+q_{hh})/n, \tag{10}$$

where $\bar{y}$ is the vector of means $\bar{y}_h = \sum_j y_{hj}/n_h$,

$$\tilde{Q} = ((q_{ih})) = [\xi m^{-2}\mathbb{1}\mathbb{1}'+\gamma cc'+\lambda H+\sigma^{-2}N]^{-1}, \tag{11}$$

$$N = \mathrm{Diag}\,[n_1,\ldots,n_m],\quad Q = \sigma^{-2}\tilde{Q}N \tag{12}$$

$\mathbb{1}$ is the vector of one's, H is the symmetric matrix of the quadratic form (6) ($T(f) = \underline{f}'H\,\underline{f}$), e_{hj} denote the "Bayes residuals" $y_{hj}-\hat{f}_h$ ($h=1,\ldots,m;\,j=1,\ldots,n_h$), $k=a/(a+n)$ and $n = \sum_h n_h$.

The density of the distribution (10) is a mixture of a normal density with mean $\hat{f}_i$ and a kernel density estimate based on the "pseudoobservations" $y_{ihj} = \hat{f}_i + e_{hj}$ with normal kernel and local bandwidths $\lambda_{ihj} = \sqrt{q_{ii}+q_{hh}}$.

A simulation of i.i.d. r.v.'s $y_{ij}^{(k)}$ under $\hat{P}_i$, as required in (5), is easily performed in a sequential manner. At first, a o-1-variable with k=P(0) and 1-k=P(1) is simulated. If the result is 0, then a value $y_{ij}^{(k)}$ is simulated under $N(\hat{f}_i,\sigma^2+q_{ii})$. If the result is 1, then an index h is generated under the uniform distribution P(h) = 1/m and afterwards an index j under $P(j) = 1/n_h$. Then a value $y_{ij}^{(k)}$ is simulated under $N(y_{ihj},q_{ii}+q_{hh})$.

If the main interest is in estimating f, the constants ξ,γ,λ may be adapted by minimizing an estimate $\hat{R}$ of the weighted MSE

$$R(\xi,\gamma,\lambda) = E\,\|\hat{\underline{f}}-\underline{f}\|_W^2 \quad (z_W^2 = z'W\,z). \tag{13}$$

Such an (unbiased) estimate is

$$\hat{R}(\xi,\gamma,\lambda) = \|\bar{y}\|^2_{B(Q)} - \sigma^2\,\mathrm{tr}\,V(Q), \tag{14}$$

$$B(Q)=(I-Q)'W(I-Q),\; V(Q)=W\,Q'N^{-1}Q-B(Q). \tag{15}$$

A numerical simplification is reached, if the matrix inversion in (11), which would be needed for all admitted combinations ξ, γ, λ, is calculated using the spectral decomposition of H:

$$H = \sum_i \varrho_i u_i u_i' \quad (\varrho_1 \leq \varrho_2 = 0 \leq \varrho_3 \leq \ldots \leq \varrho_m), \tag{16}$$

where u_i are orthonormal eigenvectors corresponding to the eigenvalues ϱ_i. We assume identical $n_i \equiv n$.
We may use $u_1 = m^{-1/2}\mathbb{1}$ and

$$u_2 = tc, \quad t^2 = \sum_i (x_i - \bar{x})^2 \tag{17}$$

and therefore we have:

$$\tilde{Q} = (\xi m^{-1} + n\sigma^{-2})^{-1} u_1 u_1' + (\gamma t^{-2} + n\sigma^{-2})^{-1} u_2 u_2' + \sum_{i=3}^{m} (\lambda\varrho_i + n\sigma^{-2})^{-1} u_i u_i'. \tag{18}$$

If the main interest is in estimating the risk (2), then the constants may be adapted by minimizing a bootstrap estimate $\hat{M}$ of the mean error $M = E|\hat{r} - r|$

$$\hat{M} = \sum_{k=1}^{B} |\hat{r}^{(k)} - \hat{r}| / B. \tag{19}$$

For (19) we need preliminary estimates $\hat{\underline{f}}$ and $\hat{P}_i$, e.g. (9) and (10) with $\xi = \gamma = 0$ and λ chosen by minimization of (14). Then $\hat{r}$ would be the risk estimate (3) calculated with the preliminary estimates, while $\hat{r}^{(k)}$ would be calculated in the same way, but replacing the original sample y by a sample $y^{(k)}$ simulated under the distributions $\hat{P}_i$.
The "semi-noninformative" choice $\xi = \gamma = 0$, which simplifies the calculation of risk estimates, will be sufficient in many cases. But if we try to derive a Bayes estimate of the risk (2) in place of the plug-in estimate (3), then one should allow positive constants ξ, γ, as it can be learned from the disadvantages of a Bayes estimate of the square of a normal mean w.r.t. an improper prior. Intuitively, the Bayes estimate $\tilde{r} = E(r|y)$ will be more accurate than the plug-in estimate (3) in the region of interesting regression functions and distributions described by the prior, because it minimizes the prior mean of $E|\hat{r} - r|^2$. But it requires a high computational effort in general, although for moderate n the sequential simulation proposed in Bunke (1987) may be realizable.

Bayes, best linear unbiased (with a linear model) and nonparametric spline, kernel and nearest neighbor estimators of $\underline{f}$ are linear or affine: $\hat{\underline{f}} = A\bar{y} + b$.

The unbiased estimator of the quadratic risk (12), which under a normal distribution P is best unbiased (see Bunke and Droge (1984)), is then

$$\hat{R} = \|\bar{y}\|^2_{B(A)} - 2b'W(I-A)\bar{y} + \sigma^2 \operatorname{tr} V(A) + \|b\|^2_W, \tag{20}$$

while the Bayes estimate would be

$$\tilde{R} = E(R|y) = \|Q\ \bar{y}\|^2_{B(A)} + \text{tr}\ Q\ B(A) - \\ - 2\ b'\ (I-A)\ Q\ \bar{y} + \|b\|^2_W + \sigma^2\ \text{tr}\ W\ A\ N^{-1}\ A'. \qquad (21)$$

<u>Example.</u> To give an impression of the form of the Bayes estimate $\hat{\underline{f}} = Q\ \bar{y}$ we have calculated Q in the case

$$x_i = i,\ m = 10,\ n_i = 1,\ x = o.1,\ \xi = \gamma = 0,\ \sigma^2 = 1. \qquad (22)$$

While H is a band matrix with elements

$$\begin{aligned} h_{ii} &= 1\ (i=1,m),\ 5\ (i=2,m-1),\ 6\ (3 \leq i \leq m-2) \\ h_{i\ i+1} &= -2\ (i=1,m-1),\ \ -4\ (2 \leq i \leq m-2) \\ h_{i\ i+2} &= 1\ (i=1,\dots,m),\ \ h_{ij} = 0 \text{ otherwise,} \end{aligned} \qquad (23)$$

the inverse (11) is approximately (we give only the lower triangular part):

.77									
.29	.41								
.04	.24	.40							
- .04	.09	.25	.40						
- .04	.01	.09	.24	.39					
- .02	-.01	.01	.09	.24	.39				
- .01	-.01	-.01	.01	..09	.24	.40			
.00	-.01	-.01	-.01	.01	.09	.25	.40		
.00	.00	-.01	-.01	-.01	.01	.09	.24	.41	
.00	.00	.00	-.01	-.02	-.04	-.04	.04	.29	.77

We see, that the estimates $\hat{f}_i$ are smoothing the observations nearly like moving averages with varying weights.

3. <u>THE GENERAL CASE</u>

The general case (1) with unknown heteroscedastic variances may be treated in an analogous way as the special case considered in section 2. The prior density for $\underline{f},\underline{v}$ would now include a term T(v) describing the smoothness of the variance function v, so that recalling the standard noninformative prior for variances (see Hartigan (1983)) one may assume a prior density

$$p(\underline{f},\underline{v}) \propto p(\underline{f}) \prod_i \sigma_i^{-1} \exp[-\varrho T(v)/2], \qquad (24)$$

where we use the density (8).

From Bunke (1987) we have a normal $N(\tilde{Q}\ \bar{y}, Q)$ as the conditional posterior distribution of $\underline{f}$ under a fixed $\underline{v}$, where $\tilde{Q} = Q(\underline{v})$ is given by (12), but $\sigma^{-2}N$ being replaced by

$$L(\underline{v}) = \mathrm{Diag}\,[n_1 \sigma_1^{-2}, \ldots, n_m \sigma_m^{-2}]. \tag{25}$$

The marginal posterior density of $\underline{v}$ is of the form

$$p(\underline{v}|y) = q(\underline{v}|y) \quad s(\underline{v}|y), \tag{26}$$

with the product of inverse Gamma densities

$$q(\underline{v}|y) \propto \prod_i \sigma_i^{-1-n_i} \exp[- \sum_j |y_{ij}-\bar{y}_i|^2/2\sigma_i^2] \tag{27}$$

and a residual factor s of relatively complicated structure (see Bunke (1987)). The Bayes estimates of $\underline{f}$ and $\underline{v}$ may be calculated approximatively, simulating independent values $\underline{v}^{(k)}$ under the distribution (26) and taking

$$\hat{\underline{f}} \approx \sum_k Q(\underline{v}^{(k)})\bar{y} s(\underline{v}^{(k)}| y) / \sum_h s(\underline{v}^{(h)}| y), \tag{28}$$

$$\hat{\sigma}_i^2 \approx \sum_k \sigma_i^{(k)} s(\underline{v}^{(k)}| y) / \sum_h s(\underline{v}^{(h)}| y). \tag{29}$$

The Bayes estimate of P_i is the posterior mean (w.r.t. the density (27)) of the distribution

$$k\ N\ (\hat{f}_i, \sigma_i^2 + e_i' Q(\underline{v})\ e_i) + (1-k) \sum_{h,j} W_{ihj}, \tag{30}$$

where

$$W_{ihj} = N\ (\hat{f}_i + (y_{hj} - \hat{f}_h)\ \sigma_i/\sigma_h,\ a_{ih}' Q(\underline{v})\ a_{ih}), \tag{31}$$

$$e_{ik} = \delta_{ik},\ a_{ih} = e_i - (\sigma_i/\sigma_h) e_h. \tag{32}$$

An approximation may be calculated by simulation as described in (28), (29). Another more crude approximation may be obtained replacing $\underline{v}$ by some nonparametric estimate $\hat{\underline{v}}$, e.g. one of those proposed in Bunke (1987):

$$\underline{f} \approx Q(\hat{\underline{v}})\ \bar{y} \quad , \ \hat{P}_i \approx (30) \text{ with } \underline{v} = \hat{\underline{v}}. \tag{33}$$

Such estimates would be "empirical Bayes estimates" calculated as Bayes estimates assuming $\underline{v}$ to be known and then replacing $\underline{v}$ by an estimate.

4. REFERENCES

Bunke,O. (1985). Bayesian estimators in semiparametric models. Preprint Nr. 102, Humboldt-Universität zu Berlin, Sektion Mathematik.

Bunke,O. (1987). Assessing the performance of regression estimators and models under nonstandard conditions. In: Seminarbericht Nr. 89 , Humboldt-Universität zu Berlin, Sektion Mathematik.

Bunke, O. and Droge, B. (1984). Bootstrap and cross-validation estimates of the prediction error for linear regression models. Ann. Statist. 12, 1400-1424.
Efron, B. (1982). The jackknife, the bootstrap and other resampling plans. SIAM CBMS-NSF Monograph 38.
Hartigan, J.A. (1983). Bayes theory. Springer Verlag, New York.

Experimental Design Technique in the Optimization of a Monitoring Network

V. Fedorov, S. Leonov, S. Pitovranov
International Institute for Applied Systems Analysis
Laxenburg, Austria

I. Introduction

The following main assumptions are crucial to the approach.

- The optimal design of an observational network is ***model oriented***. It is assumed that the observed values can be (at least approximately) described by a regression model containing unknown parameters.
- All uncertainties (observational errors, fluctuations of processes under investigation, small irregularities, deviations of the model from the "true" behavior, etc.) are absorbed by additive errors, which are assumed to be random.
- All objective functions (both in analysis and design) are formulated as expectations of some deviations of estimators from the "true" values. Most frequently it is the variance of an estimator or the variance-covariance matrix and some functions of it in multidimension cases.

The algorithms presented in this paper are oriented to the case where errors of observations are uncorrelated: $E[\varepsilon_i \varepsilon_j] = \sigma^2 \lambda^{-1}(x_i)\delta_{ij}$, where $\lambda(x)$ is the so-called "effectiveness function" reflecting the accuracy of observations at the given point x. It is assumed throughout this paper that the observed value y_i is a scalar. The generalization for more complicated situations, for instance y_i either a vector or a function of time, is straightforward (compare with Fedorov, 1972, Ch.5; Mehra and Lainiotis, 1976).

One can apply the method to a vector case when the concentration of several pollutants have to be observed. If the dynamics of some environmental characteristics are of interest then it becomes necessary to consider responses belonging to some functional space.

II. Optimality Criteria

This paper comprises two main types of optimality criteria: the first is related to the variance-covariance matrix of estimated parameters, while the second is based on variance characteristics of the response function estimators. Details can be found in Fedorov, 1972; Silvey, 1980; Atkinson & Fedorov (to be published).

Table 1 contains optimality criteria which can be handled with the help of the software described later. Formal definitions of optimality criteria are in the second column of the table and the corresponding dual optimization criteria are formulated in the third column.

Theoretically all of the algorithms discussed are valid for the case of linear parametrization: $\eta(x,\vartheta) = \vartheta^T f(x)$, where $f(x)$ is a vector of given functions. How to handle nonlinear models will be considered in Example 3.

Table 1.

Optimality criteria	$\Phi(D)$	$\lambda(x)f^T(x)D\dot{\Phi}Df(x)-tr\,\dot{\Phi}D=-\varphi(x,\xi)$
D-criterion	$\ln\|D\|$	$\lambda(x)d(x,\xi)-m$,
generalized D-criterion	$\ln\|A^TDA\|$	$\lambda(x)f^T(x)DA[A^TDA]^{-1}A^TDf(x)-s$, $s=\text{rank}A$
A-criterion	$tr\ D$	$\lambda(x)f^T(x)D^2f(x)-tr\ D$,
linear criterion	$tr\ AD,\ A\geq 0$	$\lambda(x)f^T(x)DADf(x)-tr\ AD$,
a-criterion	$\int_Z d(x,\xi)\omega(x)dx$	$A=\int_Z f(x)f^T(x)\omega(x)dx$,
extrapolation	$d(x_0,\xi)$	$\lambda(x)\{f^T(x)Df(x_0)\}^2-d(x_0,\xi)$, $A=f(x_0)f^T(x_0)$.

The following notations are used in Table 1:

- $D=D(\xi)=ND(\hat{\vartheta})$, where $D=D(\xi)$ is a normalized variance-covariance matrix, $D(\hat{\vartheta})$ is a variance-covariance matrix of the least square estimator $\hat{\vartheta}$, $D^{-1}(\xi)=M(\xi)\ =\ \sum_{i=1}^{n} p_i\ \lambda(x_i)f(x_i)f^T(x_i)$.
- ξ is a design, i.e.,$\xi=\{p_i,x_i\}_{i=1}^{n}$, where p_i is a fraction of observations which has to be located at a point x_i; p_i could be the duration, frequency or the precision of observation;
- m is a number of unknown parameters (dimension of ϑ) ;
- $\dot{\Phi}=\partial\Phi/\partial D=\{\partial\Phi/\partial D_{\alpha\beta}\}_{\alpha,\beta=1}^{m}$;
- $d(x,\xi)=f^T(x)Df(x)$ is a normalized variance of the estimator $\eta(x,\hat{\vartheta})$ at a given point x ;
- X is a controllable region, $x_i\in X$;
- A is a utility matrix, usually reflecting the significance of some parameters or their linear combinations;
- $\omega(x)$ is a utility function, usually reflecting the interest of a practitioner in the value of the response function at a point x.

The existence of a nonsingular optimal design is assumed for all optimality criteria in Table 1. Singular optimal designs (i.e. an information matrix $M(\xi^*)$ is singular, $|M(\xi^*)|=0$, in the regular case $D(\xi)=M^{-1}(\xi)$) can occur when rank $A<m$. In practice one can easily avoid singular designs applying to the regularized version of the initial problem (see Fedorov, 1986, section 2):

$$\Phi_\rho[D(\xi)]=\Phi[\{(1-\rho)M(\xi)+\rho M(\xi_0)\}^{-1}], \qquad (1)$$

where $|M(\xi_0)|\neq 0$.

Objective function (1) can also be used in cases where it is necessary to complement existing networks defined by ξ_0 by some new observational stations. D- and A-criteria are usually used when all unknown parameters are equally of interest. The first one is preferable, being invariant to linear transformation of unknown parameters (for instance when one needs to rescale some of them). usually chosen diagonal with elements $A_{\alpha\alpha}(\alpha=\overline{1,m})$ reflecting the significance of the corresponding parameters $\vartheta_\alpha (\alpha = \overline{1,m})$.

The last two criteria can be used when an experimenter is interested in the explicit estimation of a response function $\eta(x, \vartheta)$. For instance, if there are points $x_1, x_2, \ldots, x_j$ of special interest, then $\omega(x) = \sum_{k=1}^{j} \delta(x - x_k)$, where $\delta(x - x')$ is δ–function, and $\Phi(D) = \sum_{k=1}^{j} d(x_k, \xi)$.

III. First-Order Iterative Algorithm

III-1. *The algorithm*

We start with the iterative algorithm of the following form (for details see Fedorov 1986):

$$\xi_{s+1} = (1-\alpha_s)\xi_s + \alpha_s \xi(x_s), \tag{2}$$

where

ξ_s is a current design on a step s, $\xi_s = \{x_{is}, p_{is}, i = \overline{1,n_s}\}$, $\sum_{i=1}^{n_s} p_{is} = 1$,

$X_s = \{x_{is};\ i = \overline{1,n_s}\}$ is a supporting set of the design;

$\xi(x_s)$ is a design with the measure totally located at a point x_s.

The algorithm provides so-called forward and backward procedures. In the backward procedure, the "least informative" points are deleted from the current design, while conversely the forward procedure includes the new, "most informative" ones.

III-2. *Selection of* $\{x_s\}$ *and* $\{\alpha_s\}$.

For the forward procedure: $x_s = x_s^+ = \underset{x \in X}{\mathrm{Arg\,min}}\ \varphi(x, \xi_s)$, $\alpha_s = \gamma_s$.

For the backward procedure: $x_s = x_s^- = \underset{x \in X_s}{\mathrm{Arg\,max}}\ \varphi(x, \xi_s)$,

$$\alpha_s = \begin{cases} -\gamma_s, & p_j^{\cdot} \geq \gamma_s \\ -p_s^{\cdot}/(1-p_s^{\cdot}), & p_s^{\cdot} < \gamma_s \end{cases}, \quad p_s^{\cdot} = p(x_s^-) \text{ is a weight for a point } x_s^-.$$

The algorithm provides three choices of gain sequence $\{\gamma_s\}$:

(a) $\gamma_s = \dfrac{1}{n_0 + s}$, $s = 1,2,\ldots$; n_0 is a number of supporting points in an initial design. With this choice of γ_s, one can simulate the subsequent inclusion (deletion) of the most (least) informative stations.

(b) γ_s is defined by the steepest descent method, which provides the largest decrease of the objective functions in the chosen direction $\xi(x)$.

(c) $\gamma_s \equiv C_0$, where C_0 is a small constant ($0.01 \div 0.1$) which is defined by a user. This sequence does not satisfy traditional conditions $\lim_{s \to \infty} \gamma_s = 0$, $\sum_s \gamma_s = \infty$, $\sum_s \gamma_s^2 < \infty$, which are usually implied to prove the convergence of the iterative algorithms, but may be useful for the construction of the discrete designs.

Numbers of steps (length of excursion) for the forward and backward procedures are defined by the user.

III-3. *D-criterion.*

The algorithm "DOPT" is oriented for the construction of D-optimal designs providing the minimum of the determinant $|D(\vartheta)|$, $D(\vartheta)$ is a covariance matrix of the parameters' estimators. Simultaneously the algorithm minimizes $\sup_{x \in X} \lambda(x) d(x,\xi)$ (see Table 1) securing an effective estimation of the response function over set X. Moreover, in the case of normally distributed errors ε_i D-optimal design ensures the best value of the noncentrality parameter when the hypothesis $\sup_{x \in X} \eta^2(x, \vartheta_t) \geq \delta$, $\delta > 0$, is tested (see Fedorov, 1986).

The formulae for iterative recomputation of the covariance matrix and the determinant are

$$D(\xi_{s+1}) = (1-\alpha_s)^{-1} \left[D(\xi_s) - \frac{\alpha_s \lambda(x) D(\xi_s) f(x) f^T(x) D(\xi_s)}{1-\alpha_s + \alpha_s \lambda(x) d(x,\xi_s)} \right],$$

$$|D(\xi_{s+1})| = (1-\alpha_s)^{1-m} [1 - \alpha_s + \alpha_s d(x,\xi_s)]^{-1} \cdot |D(\xi_s)| .$$

The structure of a vector of basic functions $f(x)$ must be set in the corresponding subroutine. If the effectiveness function $\lambda(x)$ is not constant, then instead of $f(x)$ the functions $\lambda^{1/2}(x) f(x)$ have to be programmed.

III-4. *Some notes on the algorithm.*

Stopping rule. The calculations are terminated if:

(a) the convergence criterion is attained for the forward procedure: $m^{-1} \cdot |\varphi(x_s^+)| < \delta$, where δ is defined by a user (this means that the value of the directional derivative is small enough and, subsequently, ξ_s is close enough to the optimal design).

(b) a given number of iterations is attained.

Merging of supporting points in the forward procedure. Let h_k be a size of the k-th grid element defined during the mapping of X, $k = \overline{1,L}$; L is a dimension of controllable region X. If

$$|x_{i,k} - x^+_{s,k}| < C_{mer} h_k ; \; x_i \in X_s , \quad k = \overline{1,L} ,$$

then a point x_i is merged with a point x_s^+, constant C_{mer} being defined by a user.

Deleting of points with small weights in the forward procedure. If for some i, $p_{i,s} < \delta$, then a point $x_{i,s}$ is deleted from the design and $p_{j,s+1} = p_{j,s} / (1-p_{i,s})$, $j \neq i$. Both latter procedures help to avoid designs with a large number of supporting points.

IV. Optimization Algorithm of the Exchange Type

The algorithm has the form $\xi_{s+1} = \xi_s + \alpha_s \xi(x_s)$ where α_s can be either positive or negative.

From a computational point of view, the main difference in this algorithm from the one described in Section 3 is that the whole design is not recomputed at each step; all modifications concern only newly included ($\alpha_s > 0$) or deleted ($\alpha_s < 0$) points, which explains the origin of the term "exchange" in the title of the algorithm (see also Fedorov, 1986). The various modifications of the "exchange type" algorithm are particularly useful when some subset of an initial design has to be included in the final design (some prescribed observational stations have to be included in the final observational network). The algorithm can be easily adapted to solve the regularized versions of the originally singular design problems conserving some "regular" fractions of an initial design.

The presented software contains three modifications of the exchange procedure.

Deleting the least informative points from the initial design. The backward procedure is executed (some points are deleted) with $\alpha_s = -1/n_0$ and $x_s = \text{Arg}\max_{x \in X_s} \varphi(x, \xi_s)$, n_0 is the number of points in the initial design

A number of steps for deleting is chosen by a user. All points in the final design have equal weights. This procedure can be used, for instance, when it is necessary to find and remove a given number of the least informative stations

Inclusion of the most informative points. The forward procedure is executed with $\alpha_s = 1/n_0$, and $x_s = \text{Arg}\min_{x \in X} \varphi(x, \xi_s)$.

A number of steps for inclusion is chosen by a user.

For both of the above procedures, the normalization of the covariance matrix is carried out during the last step.

Normalization is not executed during the intermediate steps in order to make tangible either the decrease of the determinant $|D(\xi_s)|$ due to the deletion of the observational stations or its increase due to the inclusion of stations.

Standard exchange procedure. Forward and backward procedures are executed subsequentially, the initial procedure being chosen by a user. The number of steps for the forward and backward procedures are equal.

The choice of $\{x_s\}$ is as described above,

$$\alpha_s = \begin{cases} \gamma_s, & \text{forward procedure} \\ -min(\gamma_s, p_s^*), & \text{backward procedure} \end{cases}$$

There are two variants for the choice of gain sequence $\{\gamma_s\}$:

(a) $\gamma_s = \dfrac{1}{n_0 + 1 + l}$, $s = 1, 2, \ldots$; $[l]$ is an integer part of $(s-1)/2nn$;

γ_s changes after executing both forward and backward procedures, i.e., it is a "large iteration";

(b) $\gamma_s = C_0$, C_0 is a constant defined by the user. The popular Mitchell algorithm (Mitchell, 1974) can be considered as a particular case of this version. The Mitchell algorithm does not generally converge to an optimal solution.

VI. Linear Optimality Criteria

Algorithms LINOPT and LINEX are intended for the construction of linear optimal designs providing minima of the value $tr\ AD(\xi_s)$, where A is a utility matrix chosen by the user according to his needs.

The major difference in the algorithms LINOPT (first-order iterative algorithm) and LINEX (optimization algorithm of the exchange type) from DOPT and DOPTEX respectively, is that the function $\varphi(x, \xi_s)$ has the following presentation:

$$-\varphi(x, \xi_s) = \lambda(x) f^T(x) D(\xi_s) AD(\xi_s) f(x) - tr\ AD(\xi_s) .$$

More detailed information on software can be obtained from IIASA's Computer Service, see also Fedorov et al, 1987.

VII. Examples

Example 1. Linear parametrization, D-criterion.

To illustrate the possibilities of the proposed software, let us consider a comparatively simple example based on air pollution data from Modak and Lohani, 1985. The particular example we shall use is shown in Figure 1a, which gives isopleths of monthly mean values of SO_2 concentration for 9am in Taipei City, Taiwan. The original network contains eleven observing stations (see Figure 1b). The underlying model was chosen as a polynomial of the second degree with uncorrelated random additive errors:

$$y_i = \vartheta_1 + \vartheta_2 x_{1i} + \vartheta_3 x_{1i}^2 + \vartheta_4 x_{2i} + \vartheta_5 x_{2i}^2 + \vartheta_6 x_{1i} x_{2i} + \varepsilon_i ,$$

where (x_{1i}, x_{2i}) are coordinates of the i-th station. Of course, this model is too simple for a good approximation of the pattern presented in Figure 1a, but because of its simplicity one can easily understand the main features of the software.

The optimality criterion was taken equal to the normalized determinant of variance-covariance matrix (D-criterion).

(a) *Completely new network*. The purpose of this algorithm is to find the "best observation" network under the assumption that there are no constraints on the number of stations and their locations except that the stations have to be within the city's area.

The ratio of determinants for the original and optimal locations is greater than 10^4 (see Table 2). One can observe (Figure 1b) a typical (for the conventional optimal design) location of observation stations: most of them have to be on the boundary of the area and only a few (in our case only one) inside it. This should be compared with the result by Modak and Lohani, 1985, p.14, based on the so-called "minimum spanning tree" algorithm, where observing stations are mainly located inside the area. However, a comparison of results is conditional since the authors did not report the model used for the monthly averaged concentration of SO_2.

For illustrative reasons both DOPT and DOPTEX programs were used to construct the optimal allocation of observation stations and naturally they led to the same (up to computational accuracy) results. The optimal network consists of seven stations (the model contains six unknown parameters). Usually the number of observing stations is equal to the number of unknown parameters. The seventh point appears here due to some peculiarities in the controllable region. The variances of all parameters (except the intercept whose variance does not depend upon the allocation of stations) are reduced 10-20 times, see Table 1.

Theoretically the optimal design assumes that the accuracy of observations at the various points is different. Sometimes this demand is not realistic in practice but it is easy to verify theoretically that the design characteristics are quite stable under variation of weights (see Fedorov and Uspensky, 1975, p.56). The calculations confirm this fact for our example. For instance, from the optimal design, point 1 with small weight ($\sim$0.054) was removed from the design and for all others the weights were chosen equal 1/6 (so called saturated design: number of observation = number of unknown parameters). The ratio of the determinants of the variance-covariance matrices for the newly constructed design and D-optimal designs was found to be equal to $\sim$1,2. In terms of variances, the discrepancy ($\sim \sqrt[6]{1,2}$) is negligible.

(b) *Optimal observation network containing some stations with fixed positions*. When creating a new observation network, one can face the necessity of including in it some N_0 (for instance, well equipped) existing stations. If the total number N of stations is given, then one has to consider the following design problem

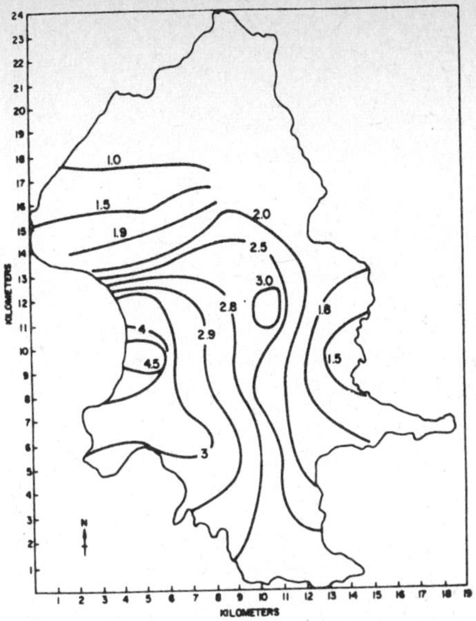

Figure 1a: Monthly average (January, 1981) concentration of SO_2 (in 0.1 ppm) for Taipei City and the existing observation network.

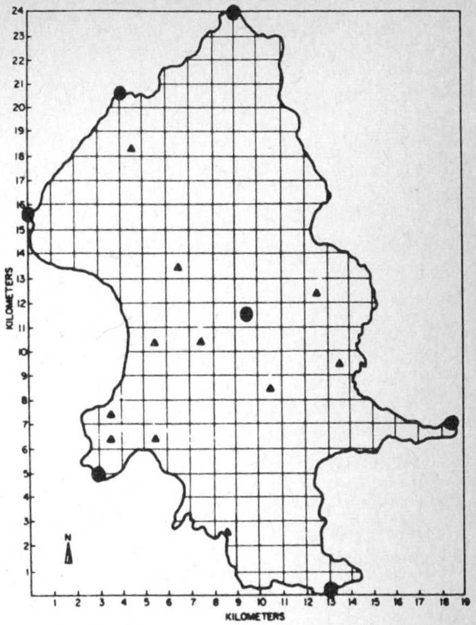

Figure 1b: ▲ - existing stations, • - new network, *D*-criterion.

Table 2: New Network, *D*-Criterion

****

INITIAL DESIGN

INITIAL COVARIANCE MATRIX

6.145					
5.487	30.835				
-21.406	-7.068	123.469			
13.228	39.169	-39.831	83.318		
5.754	38.872	-23.188	74.240	96.087	
29.515	89.311	-98.286	167.743	144.397	401.929

DETERMINANT OF INITIAL INFORMATION MATRIX

8.08280e-09

********** FINAL DESIGN ************

point	weight	coordinates	
1.	0.054	-0.5789	0.7500
2.	0.172	-0.6842	-0.5833
3.	0.130	-1.0000	0.3333
4.	0.162	1.0000	-0.4167
5.	0.157	0.3684	-1.0000
6.	0.165	-0.0526	1.0000
7.	0.159	0.0526	0.

FINAL COVARIANCE MATRIX

6.006					
0.176	3.492				
-6.221	1.419	11.718			
-0.155	0.922	0.982	2.664		
-6.452	-0.314	5.953	0.193	10.418	
-2.738	3.628	8.524	0.632	4.113	19.606

VALUE OF THE DETERMINANT

1.13645e-04

$$\xi_0^* = \operatorname*{Arg\,min}_{\xi} \Phi[(1-N_0/N)\xi + (N_0/N)\xi_0] ,$$

where ξ_0 describes the location and accuracy of an existing station required to be in the planned network. The results of the calculations for *D*-criterion are presented in Table 3.

Table 3: D-Optimal observation network with fixed stations.

********** FINAL DESIGN ************

point	weight	coordinates	
1.	0.091	-0.5789	-0.5000
2.	0.091	-0.4737	0.5000
3.	0.091	-0.0526	-0.8333
4.	0.091	0.1579	-0.3333
5.	0.091	0.3684	0.
6.	0.143	1.0000	-0.4167
7.	0.106	-0.0526	1.0000
8.	0.110	-0.6842	-0.5833
9.	0.094	-1.0000	0.3333
10.	0.093	0.3684	-1.0000

FINAL COVARIANCE MATRIX

5.579					
0.298	3.941				
-6.583	1.466	14.476			
0.335	0.960	0.565	3.148		
-6.736	-0.286	7.137	0.413	12.716	
-3.877	5.138	13.120	1.043	5.575	29.529

VALUE OF THE DETERMINANT
5.26021e-05

Example 2. Linear parametrization, A-criterion. Theoretically the optimal location of observational stations depends upon the chosen criterion of optimality. In practice the dependence is usually negligible. To confirm this fact, let us consider the A-criterion when the quality of a location is characterized by the average variance of the parameter estimators: $\Phi = m^{-1} \sum_{\alpha=1}^{n} D_{\alpha\alpha} = m^{-1} tr\, D$. The results of the calculation (program LINOPT) are presented in Table 4. The allocation of all observation stations coincides. The major traceable difference is in the "weights": the points which are closer to the origin have the greater weights (i.e. the accuracy (or number of repetitions) of observations has to be greater for the "central points").

Table 4: A-Optimal network.

********** FINAL DESIGN ************

point	weight	coordinates	
1.	0.240	-0.6842	-0.5833
2.	0.104	-0.5789	0.7500
3.	0.128	0.1579	0.9167
4.	0.123	0.3684	-1.0000
5.	0.051	-1.0000	0.3333
6.	0.117	1.0000	-0.4167
7.	0.237	-0.0526	0.

FINAL COVARIANCE MATRIX

4.112					
0.777	4.710				
-4.269	1.014	12.164			
0.211	1.132	1.493	3.169		
-4.730	-0.857	2.951	-0.519	10.331	
-1.661	4.375	6.991	1.302	3.228	18.299

VALUE OF THE DETERMINANT 0.00006880

VALUE OF THE CRITERION - trace (UTIL * D)
52.7850

Example 3. Nonlinear parametrization, D-criterion.

Let us assume we have a single source of pollutant and geographically homogenous region with spatial scale approximately 100 × 100km. A widely used model for the study of dispersion of various pollutants on this scale are Gaussian type models.

The concentration distribution from a single release is given by the Gaussian Puff Model as

$$\eta(x,\vartheta,t) = \frac{\vartheta_1}{(2\pi)^{3/2}\sigma_1\sigma_2\sigma_3} \exp\left[-\frac{(x_1-\bar{u}t)^2}{2\sigma_1^2} - \frac{x_2^2}{2\sigma_2^2}\right] \times$$

$$\times \left\{\exp\left[-\frac{(x_3-\vartheta_2)^2}{2\sigma_2^2}\right] + \exp\left[-\frac{(x_3+\vartheta_2)^2}{2\sigma_3^2}\right]\right\}$$

where η is the concentration, x_1 - axis is in downwind direction, x_2 axis in the horizontal crosswind direction, x_3 - axis in the vertical, t is the travel time, ϑ_1 is the total amount of material released at time t=0 σ_1, σ_2, σ_3 are the standard deviations of the Gaussian distributions in the x_1, x_2 and x_3 direction, $\bar{u}$ is the mean wind speed directed along x_1 - axis and ϑ_2 is the effective release height.

The time integrated surface concentration is given by the Gaussian Plume model as

$$\eta(x,\vartheta) = \frac{\vartheta_1}{\pi\bar{u}\,\sigma_2\sigma_3} \exp\left[-1/2\left(\frac{x_2^2}{\sigma_2^2} + \frac{\vartheta_2^2}{\sigma_3^2}\right)\right] \tag{3}$$

There are different parametrizations of standard deviation σ_2, σ_3 (Berliand, 1985). We use one of the simplest

$$\sigma_2 = (C_2\, x_1/\bar{u})^{1/2}, \ \sigma_3 = (C_3\, x_1/\bar{u})^{1/2}.$$

For obtaining some averaged (monthly, seasonal and annual) field of concentration it is necessary to formulae (3) averaged over climatological data for wind direction and wind speeds.

The physical problem can be formulated as the network design for monitoring of total amount of released material and effective release height.

In this example, unlike the linear case, we have to be concerned with the values of the parameters' estimates. The reason that in the linear case the variance-covariance matrix does not depend upon estimated parameters while in the nonlinear case (see Fedorov and Uspensky, 1975) this matrix (or more accurately its asymptotic value) depends upon the true values of the unknown parameters ϑ_t: $\lim_{N\to\infty} ND(\hat{\vartheta}_N) = M^{-1}(\vartheta_t,\xi)$, where $M(\vartheta,\xi) = f(\vartheta,x)f^T(\vartheta,x)\xi(dx)$, $f(\vartheta,x) = \frac{\partial\eta(x,\vartheta)}{\partial\vartheta}$, N is the number of observations and ξ is a limit design. Optimal designs formally defined as in linear case also depends upon ϑ_t , and is sometimes called locally optimal.

In this situation the following procedure is recommended: a user has to choose some probable (reasonable, admissible, etc.) values of ϑ and define intervals which will almost certainly contain true values of unknown parameters; for boundary points of these intervals, optimal designs have to be computed with the help of one of the above described programs; if the corresponding designs differ greatly from each other, an "average" design has to be constructed. Fortunately optimal designs are rather stable to the variation of parameters and therefore the latter procedure can be avoided.

The square area with the 50 × 50 mesh scale was used for computations, the source of pollutant was located in the origin. It was assumed that the wind's speed and frequency are equal for each direction of wind rise. The optimal design for this symmetric case are two consecutive circles if the operability region is sufficiently large. Otherwise the location of supporting points will depend upon the boundary shape. The dependence of the circles' radiuses on the value of assessed parameter of effective height can be seen in Figure 2. The dependence of optimal design on wind speed can be seen in Figure 3.

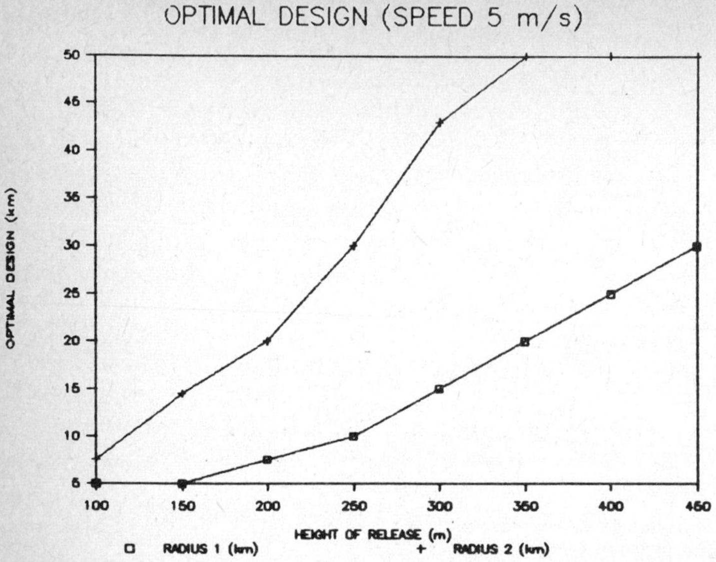

Figure 2: Dependence of the allocation of the optimal design stations on the height of pollutant release (wind speed is assumed constant in all directions and equal to 5m/sec).

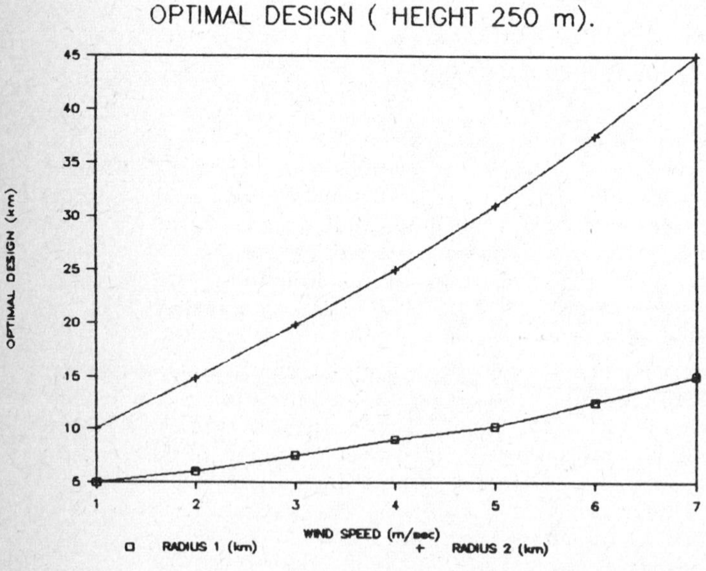

Figure 3: Dependence of the allocation of the optimal design stations on wind speed which is assumed uniform in all directions. (The weight of pollutant release is assumed constant and equal to 250m).

REFERENCES

Atkinson, A.C., V.V. Fedorov (1987) Optimum Design and Experiments. Encyclopedia of Statistical Sciences, New York: Wiley & Sons (to be published).

Berliand, M.E. (1985) Prediction and Regulation of Air Pollution. Leningrad: Gidrometeoizdat, p.272 (in Russian).

Fedorov, V.V. (1972) Theory of Optimum Experiments. New York: Academic Press, pp.292.

Fedorov, V.V., A.B. Uspensky (1975) Numerical Aspects of Design and Analysis of Experiments. Moscow, Moscow State University, p.167.

Fedorov, V.V. (1986) Optimal Design of Experiments: Numerical Methods. WP-86-55. Laxenburg, Austria, International Institute for Applied System Analysis

Fedorov, V.V., S. Leonov, M. Antonovsky, S. Pitovranov (1987) The Experimental Design of an Observation Network: Software and Examples, WP-87-05. Laxenburg, Austria, International Institute for Applied Systems Analysis.

Mitchell, T.J. (1974) An Algorithm for Construction of D-Optimal Experimental Designs. *Technometrics*, 16:203-210.

Mehra, R.K., D.G. Lainiotis (1976) Systems Identification: Advances and Case Studies. New York: Academic Press, p.593.

Modak, P.M., B.N. Lohani (1985) Optimization of Ambient Air Quality Monitoring Networks. *Environmental Monitoring and Assessment*, Part I-II, 5:1-53.

Silvey, S.D. (1980) Optimal Design. London: Chapman and Hall, p.86.

TESTING FOR OUTLIERS IN LINEAR MODELS AND BONFERRONI SIGNIFICANCE LEVELS

Stratis Kounias
University of Thessaloniki, Greece

1. INTRODUCTION

Consider the linear model $Y=X\beta+\varepsilon$ with uncorrelated observations and common variance σ^2. Then the vector of residuals is $e = Y-X\hat{\beta}$ where $X'X\hat{\beta} = X'Y$. An observation which differs "very much" form the fitted value has a large residual and is considered to be an outlier. Removing or adjusting residuals simplifies the description of the rest of the data because in the null case of no outliers, the residuals do behave much like a normal sample.

One approach is practical and subjective by plotting the residuals or the observed and the fitted values and examining the plot.

A suggestion (J. John and N. Draper 1978, J. Gentleman and M. Wilk 1975) is to replace the observation with the largest residual with its missing value, which is estimated from the remaining observations and continue similarly for the remaining outliers. They proceed to replace the k largest residuals and provide a statistic Q_k which is the difference between the sum of squares of residuals for the original data and the sum of squares of revised residuals resulting from fitting the basic model to the data remaining after omission of k data points.

When one outlier is present, the direct statistical treatment of residuals provides a complete basis for data-analytic judgments. When two or more outliers are present; the resulting residuals will often not have any noticeable statistical peculiarities.

The statistic commonly used to detect an outlier is the maximum normed residual $z_i = e_i/\sqrt{e'e}$ $i=1,\dots,n$ (C. Daniel 1960, W. Stefansky 1969). The joint distribution of a set of k normed residuals has the form of an inverted t distribution with n-p-k degrees of freedom. (C. Quesenberry and H. David 1961, H. Raifa and R. Schlaifer 1961, W. Stefansky 1972). Since the associated distribution is very complex, exact p values are difficult to obtain. These are evaluated either by using simulation or applying Bonferroni upper and lower bounds. The aim of the present paper is to demonstrate improvements of the Bonferroni bounds.

Let $P_i = P(|z_i| > d)$, $P_{ij} = P(|z_i| > d,\ |z_j| > d)$ $i \neq j$ etc, then use the notation:

$$S_1 = \sum_{i=1}^{n} P_i,\quad S_2 = \sum_{i<j}\sum P_{ij},\quad S_3 = \sum\sum\sum_{i<j<k} P_{ijk},\quad \text{etc}$$

where S_k is the sum of all k-fold intersections.

Our problem is to evaluate the critical value d i.e. $P(\max|z_i|>d)=\alpha$ and the distribution of $\max|z_i|$ is very complicated.

The first order upper Bonferroni bound is

$$R(\max|z_i|>d) \leqq S_1 \qquad (1)$$

and for a given d, $P(|z_i|>d)=P_i$ is easily computed. With more effort we can compute P_{ij} and P_{ijk} and use the lower and upper bound to approximate d.

Setting $S_1=\alpha$ we solve for d and this gives a conservative estimate (overestimate) of the actual critical value . In the case where all $|z_i|$ have the same distribution we find d from

$$P(z_i^2 > d^2) = \alpha/n \qquad (2)$$

for a given significance level α.

Actually we evaluate the left hand side for different values of d and find the one with the given probability α/n.

The second order lower bound is

$$S_1 - S_2 \leqq P(\max|z_i|>d) \qquad (3)$$

and equating S_1-S_2 with α we find a non-conservative estimate (underestimate) of the critical value d.

These values have been tabulated for the two and three-way layouts by using the first and second Bonferroni bounds (W. Stefansky 1972, R.Cook and P. Prescott 1981, J.Gaplin and D. Hawkins 1981). The last paper uses third order bounds.

2. IMPROVED BOUNDS

The accuracy of the Bonferroni significance level can be improved either by taking higher order bounds or by sharpening the bounds of a given order.

It is known (W. Feller, vol I, p 110) that if

$$A = \bigcup_{i=1}^{n} A_i \ , \quad S_i = \sum P(A_i) \ , \quad S_2 = \sum_{i<j} P(A_iA_j) \quad \text{etc, then}$$

$$\begin{aligned} P(A) &\leqq S_1-S_2+\ldots+S_m \quad \text{when } m \text{ is odd} \\ P(A) &\geqq S_1-S_2+\ldots+S_m \quad \text{when } m \text{ is even} \end{aligned} \qquad (4)$$

are called Bonferroni inequalities of order m.

In the outlier problem we have $A_i=\{|z_i|>d\}$, $A=\{\max|z_i|>d\}$

We present here two improvements

i) When the events are exchangeable i.e., when the residuals are equally correlated. This happens in orthogonal two level factorial designs, in balanced designs etc.

ii) When the events do not follow a specific pattern.

For the first case (i) the improved upper and lower bounds up to the third order are:

Upper bounds

$$P(A) \leqq S_1$$

$$P(A) \leqq S_1 - 2S_2/n \qquad (5)$$

$$P(A) \leq S_1-(2(2k-1)/k(k+1)S_2+(4/k(k+1))\, S_3$$

where $k=[3\, S_3/\, S_2]+2$

Lower bounds

$$P(A) \geq S_1/n$$

$$P(A) \geq (2/k(k+1)(k\, S_1-S_2) \quad \text{where} \quad k=[2S_2/S_1]+1 \tag{6}$$

$$P(A) \geq ((2n+k-1)/n(k+1))S_1-(2(n+2k-2)/nk(k+1))S_2+(6(nk(k+1))S_3$$

where $k=[2((n-2)S_2-3S_3)/((n-1)S_1-2S_2)]+1$

with $[x]$ denoting the integer part of x.

The proof is done through the indicator random variables.These are improvements of the Bonferroni bounds (4) which are derived from (5) and (6) by setting k=1.

Although the bounds (5) and (6) are quite satisfactory for practical problems, they can be improved in the case (ii) where the events are not exchangeable. This is the case of two and three-way layouts and in most regression problems.

D.Hunter (1976) gave the following second order bound:

$$P(A) \leq \sum_{i=1}^{n} P_i - \sum_{T} P_{ij} \tag{7}$$

the last summation is for all edges of the tree T.

The best bound is given by the maximum spanning tree using for example Kruskal's algorithm. In practice neighboring points have higher probabilities and then (7) becomes:

$$P(A) \leq \sum_{i=1}^{n} P_i - \sum_{i=1}^{n-1} P_{i,i+1} \tag{8}$$

In a two-way layout factorial design, let ρ_{ij} denote the correlation between e_i and e_j, then $P_{ij} = P(|z_i|>d)$ is an increasing function of ρ_{ij}.

If the design has R rows and C columns, then

$\rho_{ij} = -1/(C-1)$ between residuals in the same row

$\rho_{ij} = -1/(R-1)$ between residuals in the same column

$\rho_{ij} = -1/(R-1)(C-1)$ between residuals otherwise

If $R \geq C$ the maximum spanning tree is formed by linking all residuals in each row and then linking columns (K.Worsley 1982)

Inequalities (8) can still be improved

$$P(A) \leq \sum_{i=1}^{n} P_i - \sum_{i=1}^{n-1} P_{i,i+1} + \sum_{i=1}^{n-2} P_{i,i+1,i+2} \tag{9}$$

and also the lower bound of order two i.e.

$$P(A) \geq (2/k(k+1)(kS_1-S_2+\sum\sum_{j \geq i+2} P_{i,i+1,j}) \tag{10}$$

this improves the bound of D. Dawson and D. Sankoff (1967) and S. Kwerel (1975).

3. APPLICATION

If we have Bernoulli trials with probability of succes p and we are interested in testing for randomness, a statistic is the longest run of successes in n trials (Schwager 1984).

Let the events be:

A_i = { There is a run of k successes starting at trial i=1,...,N, N=n-k+1}

A = {There is a run of k successes in n trials}

TABLE 1. Comparison of bounds

n	k	p	L_1	L_2	L_3	EXACT	U_1	U_2
300	10	.5	.08884	.12382	.12382	.13351	.14232	.14258
1500	10	.5	.33264	.20593	.36361	.51918	.72711	.72852
300	15	.5	.00292	.00436	.00437	.00437	.00438	.00438
1500	15	.5	.56336	-5.19094	.57095	.88559	2.08708	2.11978
100	10	.7	.34910	.01535	.39393	.58008	.73580	.79093
300	10	.7	.62667	-6.93128	.63397	.93526	2.27401	2.48578

where:

L_1 : The second order improved Bonferroni bound

L_2 : The lower bound of Worsley (1985) using hypertrees

L_3 : The lower bound (improved) given in (10)

U_1 : The uppewr bound given in (9)

U_2 : The upper bound of Hunter given in (7)

Observe that in all cases the bounds L_3, U_1 perform better and are quite accurate in probabilities just above zero.

4. REFERENCES

Cook, R.D. and Prescott, P. (1981). On the accuracy of Bonferroni significance levels for detecting outliers in linear models. Technometrics, Vol 23, No. 1, 59-63.

Daniel, C. (1960). Locating outliers in factorial experiments. Technometrics, Vol 2, No. 2, 149-156.

Dawson, D.A. and Sankoff, D. (1967). An inequality for probabilities. Proc. Amer. Math. Soc. 18, 504-507.

Feller, W. (1968). An introduction to probability theory and its applications. Vol I (3rd ed.), New York, John Wiley.

Galpin, J.S. and Hawskins, D.M. (1981). Rejection of a single outlier in two- or three-way layouts. Technometrics, Vol 23, No. 1, 65-70.

Gentleman, J.F. and Wilk, M.B. (1975). Detecting outliers in a two-way table. I. Statistical behavior of residuals. Technometrics, Vol 17, 1-14.

Hunter, D. (1976). An upper bound for the probability of a union. Journal of Applied Probability, 13, 597-603.

John, J.A. and Draper, N.R. (1978). On testing for two outliers or one outlier in two-way tables. Technometrics, Vol 20, No 1, 69-78.

Kwerel,S.M. (1975). Most stringent bounds on aggregated probabilities of partially specified dependent probability systems. J. Amer.Statist. Assoc., 70, 472-479.

Quesenberry, C.P. and David, H.A. (1961). Some tests for outliers. Biometrika 48, 379-390.

Raiffa, H. and Schlaifer, R. (1961). Applied Statistical Decision Theory, Boston: Harvard University.

Schwager, S.J. (1984). Bonferroni sometimes loses. The American Statistician, 38, 192-197.

Worsley, K.J. (1982). An improved Bonferroni inequality and applications. Biometrika, 69, 297-302.

Worsley, K.J. (1985). Bonferroni (improved) wins again.The American Statistician, Vol 39, No 3, 235.

STABLE DECISIONS IN DISCRIMINANT, REGRESSION AND FACTOR ANALYSIS

J. Läuter, Academy of Sciences of the G.D.R.,
Karl Weierstraß Institute of Mathematics

1. INTRODUCTION

Two concepts will be treated to stabilize the multivariate analysis in high-dimensional applications:

(i) A method fitted to one-factor covariance structures. For the one-factor structure and for certain prior distributions of the parameters, the corresponding Bayes decision rules will be determined. According to their construction, these rules are admissible decisions.

(ii) If special multiple-factor structures are considered, the inverse matrix G^{-1} of the matrix of sums of products, G, can be replaced by a suitable diagonal matrix T. To improve this approximation in certain cases, an expansion by an infinite series

$$G^{-1} = T + (T - TGT) + (T - 2TGT + TGTGT) + \dots$$

will be proposed. By stepwise adding of terms of this series, a hierarchy of models is formed which can be applied for the optimization of solutions in practice.

The classical multivariate methods are usually constructed under the assumption that the parameters are known. Afterwards the parameters are replaced by their maximum likelihood estimates. For prognostic decisions, this two-step approach is often unstable and unreliable. High correlations of the variables, multicollinearity, and "overfitting" result in erroneous estimates. It will be seen that equalizing and smoothing methods lead to improved decisions. The known procedures of selection of variables, the partial annihilation of information, represent also an aid for stabilizing the results, but they are not the best and not the adequate way to overcome the difficulties.

2. THE ONE-FACTOR COVARIANCE STRUCTURE

2.1. Discriminant Analysis

Let us start from two normally distributed learning samples,

$$y_k^{(j)} \sim N_p(\mu^{(j)}, \Sigma) \qquad (1)$$

$$(j=1,2;\ k=1,\dots,n^{(j)};\ n^{(j)} \geq 1;\ n=n^{(1)}+n^{(2)} \geq p+2),$$

and an observation which has to be assigned to one of both populations,

$$y^{(0)} \sim N_p(\mu^{(l)}, \frac{1}{t}\Sigma) \qquad (l=1,2;\ t>0). \qquad (2)$$

The unknown parameters of the decision problem are $\mu^{(1)}$, $\mu^{(2)}$, Σ and l, where l denotes the unknown population. Variable t describes the precision of vector $y^{(0)}$ which is to be assigned. By introducing t we shall recognize a close connection between the different forms of discrimination rules (substitution rule, maximum likelihood rule).

The considered one-factor structure is defined by

$$\Sigma = K + w(\mu^{(1)} - \mu^{(2)})(\mu^{(1)} - \mu^{(2)})', \qquad (3)$$

where K is a positive definite diagonal matrix and w is a nonnegative number. This structure includes an algebraical relation between the mean values and the covariances which was also investigated by Sörbom (1974) and in program LISREL (Jöreskog and Sörbom (1984)). In practice observations $y^{(j)}$ of this kind result from an only non-observable primary variable $y_0^{(j)}$ by adding independent disturbances $v^{(j)}$:

$$y^{(j)} = y_0^{(j)} \beta + v^{(j)} + \alpha \qquad (j=1,2), \qquad (3a)$$

$$y_0^{(j)} \sim N_1(\mu_0^{(j)}, \sigma_0^2), \quad v^{(j)} \sim N_p(0, K). \qquad (3b)$$

α and β are vectors of scale constants.

In the following we want to construct discrimination rules which depend only on the statistics

$$x^{(1)} = y^{(0)} - y_{.}^{(1)}, \quad x^{(2)} = y^{(0)} - y_{.}^{(2)}, \quad G. \qquad (4)$$

$y_{.}^{(j)}$ are the sample means, and G is the matrix of sums of products,

$$G = (g_{hi}) = \sum_{j=1}^{2} \sum_{k=1}^{n^{(j)}} (y_k^{(j)} - y_{.}^{(j)})(y_k^{(j)} - y_{.}^{(j)})'. \qquad (5)$$

These rules are even those which are invariant under translations.
For a fixed $t=t_0$ we define according to S. DasGupta (1965)

$$t^{(l)}=((n^{(l)}+t_0)/n^{(l)})^{1/2} \qquad (l=1,2), \tag{6}$$

$$y=-t^{(2)}x^{(1)}+t^{(1)}x^{(2)}, \qquad z=t^{(2)}x^{(1)}+t^{(1)}x^{(2)}. \tag{7}$$

Let

$$L(l,j)=\begin{cases}0 & \text{if } j=l \quad \text{(right)}\\ 1 & \text{if } j\neq l \quad \text{(false)}\end{cases} \tag{8}$$

be the given loss function where l is the actual population ($l=1,2$) and j is the result of the decision ($j=1,2$). By the following theorem the admissibility of a special discrimination rule is obtained.

<u>Theorem 1:</u> For fixed positive $t=t_0$, c_i, ε_i ($i=1,\ldots,p$) with $c_1^{-1}+\ldots+c_p^{-1}<1$ and the 0-1 loss function (8), the rule which decides for the population j with the minimal value

$$\frac{n^{(j)}}{n^{(j)}+t_0}(y^{(0)}-y_.^{(j)})'(C-G)^{-1}(y^{(0)}-y_.^{(j)}) \qquad (j=1,2) \tag{9}$$

is admissible in the class of rules that are invariant under translations (cf. (4)). Here C is the pxp diagonal matrix

$$C=\mathrm{Diag}(c_i(ay_i^2+bz_i^2+g_{ii}+\varepsilon_i)) \qquad (i=1,\ldots,p), \tag{10}$$

$$a=a(t_0)=t_0/(2t^{(1)}t^{(2)}(t^{(1)}t^{(2)}-1)), \tag{11}$$

$$b=b(t_0)=t_0/(2t^{(1)}t^{(2)}(t^{(1)}t^{(2)}+1)). \tag{12}$$

y_i and z_i are the components of y and z.

The proof was submitted on conference DIANA2 (J. Läuter (1986a)). There a special prior distribution of the parameters is precribed, and the corresponding Bayes rule is constructed. The admissibility results from the fact that the Bayes rule is essentially unique. In practice the following limit rule can be applied:

$$j=\begin{cases}1 & \text{if } (y_.^{(1)}-y_.^{(2)})'(C-G)^{-1}(y^{(0)}-\frac{1}{2}(y_.^{(1)}+y_.^{(2)}))>0\\ 2 & \text{otherwise,}\end{cases} \tag{13}$$

where $C=\mathrm{Diag}(p((n^{(1)}n^{(2)}/(n^{(1)}+n^{(2)}))(y_{i.}^{(1)}-y_{i.}^{(2)})^2+g_{ii}))$ and

$y_{i.}^{(1)}$, $y_{i.}^{(2)}$ are the components of $y_{.}^{(1)}$, $y_{.}^{(2)}$.
In the customary discriminant analysis, G appears instead of matrix C−G. In the rules (9) and (13), C−G has very large diagonal elements which is a typical sign of the high stability.

In the next theorem a rule is provided which is especially designed for independent variables. In this rule only the inversion of a diagonal matrix appears.

<u>Theorem 2</u>: For fixed positive $t=t_0$, c_i, ε_i $(i=1,\dots,p)$ the rule which decides for the population j with the minimal value

$$\frac{n^{(j)}}{n^{(j)}+t_0}\,(y^{(0)}-y_{.}^{(j)})'\,C^{-1}\,(y^{(0)}-y_{.}^{(j)}) \qquad (j=1,2) \tag{14}$$

is admissible in the class of rules that are invariant under translations. Here C is defined by (10), (11), (12).

For practical applications the limit rule

$$j=\begin{cases} 1 \text{ if } (y_{.}^{(1)}-y_{.}^{(2)})'C^{-1}(y^{(0)}-\frac{1}{2}(y_{.}^{(1)}+y_{.}^{(2)}))>0 \\ 2 \text{ otherwise} \end{cases} \tag{15}$$

is offered where $C=\mathrm{Diag}((n^{(1)}n^{(2)}/(n^{(1)}+n^{(2)}))(y_{i.}^{(1)}-y_{i.}^{(2)})^2+g_{ii})$.

Examples of application and simulation experiments are contained in J. Läuter (1986a,b,c).

<u>2.2. Prediction in Regression Analysis with Stochastic Regressors</u>

We start from a learning sample

$$Y_k=\begin{pmatrix} y_{0k} \\ y_k \end{pmatrix} \sim N_{1+p}\left(\begin{pmatrix} \mu_0 \\ \mu \end{pmatrix}, \begin{pmatrix} \sigma_{00} & \sigma_0' \\ \sigma_0 & \Sigma \end{pmatrix}\right) \tag{16}$$

$(k=1,\dots,n;\ \ n\geq p+2)$ and a further observation $Y=(y_0\ \ y')$ of the same population. We want to predict y_0 by means of the other p components of Y under the information of the learning sample.

The special covariance structure used here is $\Sigma=K+w\,\sigma_0\sigma_0'$ (K positive definite diagonal matrix, $w\geq 0$). We shall consider only prediction rules which are invariant under translations. These are rules that predict $x_0=y_0-y_{0.}$ by means of $x=y-y_.$, g_{00}, g_0, G, where

$$Y_.=\begin{pmatrix} y_{0.} \\ y_. \end{pmatrix} \text{ and } \begin{pmatrix} g_{00} & g_0' \\ g_0 & G \end{pmatrix}=(g_{hi})=\sum_{k=1}^{n}(Y_k-Y_.)(Y_k-Y_.)' \tag{17}$$

are the mean vector and the matrix of sums of products of the learning sample. Let $L(y_0, \hat{y}_0) = (\hat{y}_0 - y_0)^2 = (\hat{x}_0 - x_0)^2$ be the quadratic loss of a prediction $\hat{x}_0 = \hat{y}_0 - y_0$.

Theorem 3: For fixed c_i ($c_i > 0$; $i=0,\dots,p$; $c_0^{-1}+\dots+c_p^{-1} < 1$) and ε_i ($\varepsilon_i > 0$; $i=1,\dots,p$), for $n \geq p+2$, the predictor

$$\hat{x}_0 = (c_0 - 1 - c_0 (n/(n+1)) x'(C-G)^{-1} x)^{-1} g_0' (C-G)^{-1} x \qquad (18)$$

is admissible in the class of all predictors that are invariant under translations. Here

$$C = \mathrm{Diag}(c_i((n/(n+1)) x_i^2 + g_{ii} + \varepsilon_i)) \qquad (i=1,\dots,p). \qquad (19)$$

x_i are the components of x.

In the special case of one regressor variable ($p=1$) we obtain

$$\hat{x}_0 = g_0 (b(n/(n+1)) x_1^2 + (b+1) g_{11} + c_1 (c_0 - 1) \varepsilon_1)^{-1} x_1 , \qquad (20)$$

where $b = c_0 c_1 - c_0 - c_1$. Under the conditions of theorem 3, the inequalities $b>0$ and $c_1(c_0-1)>0$ hold. Therefore this predictor implies a shrinkage compared with the classical predictor $\hat{x}_0 = g_0 g_{11}^{-1} x_1$.

In the next theorem a prediction rule is offered in which only the inversion of a diagonal matrix appears.

Theorem 4: For fixed positive c_i, ε_i ($i=1,\dots,p$) with $c_1^{-1}+\dots+c_p^{-1} < 1$, for $n \geq p+2$, the predictor

$$\hat{x}_0 = (1 - (n/(n+1)) x' C^{-1} x)^{-1} g_0' C^{-1} x \qquad (21)$$

is admissible in the class of all predictors that are invariant under translations. C is defined by (19).

In the case of one regressor variable ($p=1$), predictor

$$\hat{x}_0 = g_0 ((c_1 - 1)(n/(n+1)) x_1^2 + c_1 g_{11} + c_1 \varepsilon_1)^{-1} x_1 \qquad (22)$$

results. For varying values of c_1 und ε_1, the same predictors arise as in (20).

In practice all predictors of this section are also designed for stable smoothing of data and for stable replacing of missing values.

2.3. Stable Factor Analysis

The factor analysis serves the recognition of the structure of covariance matrices of p-dimensional variables y. We start from the Wishart distributed matrix of sums of products generated by n p-dimensional observations,

$$G \sim W_p(\Sigma, n-1), \tag{23}$$

and we use the one-factor structure defined by $\Sigma^{-1} = \Lambda - \nu\nu'$ where $\Lambda = \text{Diag}(\lambda_i)$ is a positive definite diagonal matrix, $\nu = (\nu_i)$ is a vector.

In the following ν is to be estimated. Vector ν is needed for forming a linear function of the observation y which has maximum correlation with the supposed factor variable y_0 (cf. (3a), (3b)): $\hat{y}_0 = \nu' y$. Let $L = \|\hat{\nu}\hat{\nu}' - \nu\nu'\|^2$ be the loss function where $\|X\| = (\sum_i \sum_j x_{ij}^2)^{1/2}$ is the Euclidean matrix norm.

Theorem 5: For fixed positive c_i, ε_i (i=1,...,p) with $c_1^{-1} + \ldots + c_p^{-1} < 1$, for $n \geq p+1$, an admissible estimator of ν is obtained as the eigenvector $\hat{\nu}$ of matrix $(C-G)^{-1}$ corresponding to the largest eigenvalue α which fulfils the additional normalization $\hat{\nu}'\hat{\nu} = \alpha$:

$$(C-G)^{-1}\hat{\nu} = \hat{\nu}\,(\hat{\nu}'\hat{\nu}). \tag{24}$$

Here C is defined by $C = \text{Diag}(c_i(g_{ii} + \varepsilon_i))$, i=1,...,p.

A disadvantage of this result is the missing invariance under linear scale transformations of the single variables. Therefore a further estimator assigned to the loss function

$$L = \|(\text{Diag}(\lambda_i - c_i\nu_i^2))^{-1/2}(\hat{\nu}\hat{\nu}' - \nu\nu')(\text{Diag}(\lambda_i - c_i\nu_i^2))^{-1/2}\|^2 \tag{25}$$

is to be constructed.

Theorem 6: For fixed positive c_i, ε_i (i=1,...,p) with $c_1^{-1} + \ldots + c_p^{-1} < 1$, for $n \geq \min(p+1, 5)$, and for the loss function (25), an admissible estimator of ν is obtained in the following way: Compute

$$D = (\text{Diag}(g_{ii} + \varepsilon_i))^{-1}, \quad B = (C-G)^{-1}, \quad t = (n-3)/2,$$

$$A = D^{-1/2}(B + \frac{1}{t}\,\text{Diag}(B))D^{-1/2}; \tag{26}$$

determine vector x which maximizes

$$2x'Ax - (x'x)^2 - \frac{1}{t}x'\,\text{Diag}(xx')x; \tag{27}$$

compute $\hat{\nu} = D^{1/2}x$. Matrix C is defined as in theorem 5.

This result has a close connection with the known principal component analysis. If the terms associated with t are neglected, that is, n is considered to be very large, and if $\varepsilon_i=0$, $c_i=c$ $(i=1,\dots,p)$, then $\hat{v}$ is the solution of $G\hat{v}=\mathrm{Diag}(G)\,\hat{v}\,\alpha$ corresponding to the largest eigenvalue α which fulfils the additional normalization

$$(c\hat{v}'(\mathrm{Diag}(G))^{-1}\hat{v}-1)/\hat{v}'(\mathrm{Diag}(G))^{-1}\hat{v}=\alpha. \tag{28}$$

Hence under the mentioned neglects, the principal component method appears as the solution of the factor problem with minimal Bayes risiko. Thus the essential difficulty in estimating the specific variances of the variables vanishes in factor analysis.

3. APPROXIMATION OF THE INVERSE COVARIANCE MATRIX

In former papers (J. Läuter (1986b,c)) we have shown that the diagonal matrix

$$T_0=(\mathrm{Diag}(G(\mathrm{Diag}(G))^{-1}G))^{-1} \tag{29}$$

can be considered as a stable substitute for G^{-1} if certain multiple-factor structures are assumed. To improve this approximation in applications with relatively large samples, an expansion of G^{-1} can be used the first term of which is even T_0 or a multiple $T=cT_0$. If we put

$$A_0=T_0^{1/2}GT_0^{1/2},\quad A=cA_0,\quad B=I-A, \tag{30}$$

it follows that (cf. Faddejev and Faddejeva (1963))

$$A^{-1}=(I-B)^{-1}=I+B+B^2+B^3+\dots,$$

$$G^{-1}=T+T^{1/2}(I-A)T^{1/2}+T^{1/2}(I-A)^2T^{1/2}+\dots,$$

$$G^{-1}=T+(T-TGT)+(T-2TGT+TGTGT)+\dots\;. \tag{31}$$

The shrinkage factor c is determined in such a way that the maximal module of the eigenvalues of B is minimized: $c=2/(\lambda_{max}+\lambda_{min})$. Here λ_{max} and λ_{min} are the maximal and the minimal eigenvalue of A_0. Then the arising series (31) converges for any positive definite G.

In practical applications the partial series can be used:

$$G^{(0)}=T$$

$$G^{(1)}=2T-TGT$$

$$G^{(2)}=3T-3TGT+TGTGT \tag{32}$$

$$\dots$$

They are also applicable in cases with a singular covariance matrix G. Cross-validation can be employed to decide which level of this hierarchy of models should be preferred.

Refernces

DasGupta, S. (1965): Optimum Classification Rules for Classification into Two Multivariate Normal Populations. Ann. Math. Statist. 36, 1174-1184

Sörbom, D. (1974): A general Method for Studying Differences in Factor Means and Factor Structure between Groups. Br. J. Math. Statist. Psychol., 27, 229-239

Jöreskog, K.G. and D. Sörbom (1984): LISREL VI - Analysis of Linear Structural Relationships by a Method of Maximum Likelihood. Mooresville. In: Scientific Software, Inc.

Läuter, J. (1986a): Discriminant Analysis in Special Models - Theoretical and Practical Results. Proc. Conf. DIANA 2, Liblice, ČSSR.

Läuter, J. (1986b): Discriminant Analysis for Special Parameter Structures. Bernoulli Proceedings, VNU Science Press, Utrecht, Netherlands.

Läuter, J. (1986c): Stable Discrimination Rules and Their Application. Proc. 7-th Internat. Summer School on Problems of Model Choice, Holzhau, GDR.

Faddejev, D.K. and W.N. Faddejeva (1963): Computing Methods in Linear Algebra (in Russian). Moscow-Leningrad.

ANALYSIS OF DATA WHEN CONSTRUCTING AN ADAPTIVE REGRESSION MODEL

Lukaschin, Y.P.
Academy of Sciences of the USSR
Institute of World Economy and
International Relations, Moscow

1. INTRODUCTION

Here we shall consider the discrete-time processes which evolve over time. The background of ordinary discrete-time regression analysis is a hypothesis that the behaviour of the underlying process may be approximated using a linear equation model with constant coefficients, which reflect the intensity of relation of the endogenous variable, y, and exogenous variables, x_i, i=1,2,...,p. The regression equation is

$$y_t = \sum_{i=1}^{p} a_i x_{it} + e_t \quad , \qquad (1)$$

where e_t is an error of the model, t is time, t=1,2,...,T, or in matrix notation

$$\bar{y} = \overline{Xa} + \bar{e} \quad , \qquad (2)$$

where $\bar{X}$ is a (Txp) matrix, $\bar{y}$ and $\bar{e}$ are (Tx1) vectors, $\bar{a}$ is a (px1) vector of coefficients to be estimated.

As it is well-known the estimate of the parameter vector under the least squares of the errors criterion is

$$\bar{a} = (\bar{X}'\bar{X})^{-1}\bar{X}'\bar{y} \ . \qquad (3)$$

However the intensity of interrelation of the variables is not constant often over time. Thus, the coefficient estimates obtained under the above hypothesis are only the average ones for a sampling period and it is doubtful that they could allow to make time analysis properly and to obtain good forecasts.

Besides the evolution of the underlying processes there are some other reasons to suspect that the parameters of many regression models are not stable over time. It is possible to note four of them, Sarris (1973). Many of regression equations are not correctly specified, i.e. they don't contain some important variables, which should be included. A nonlinear relationship, approximated with linear one, is also a source of parameter changes. The other sources are the substitution of a true variable with another one (due to an error or absence of statistical data) and the procedure of aggregation and using of the composite time-series which often leads to loosing of a homogeneity of time-series due to a revision of the methodology of its calculation.

Thus, the multiple regression (1) with constant coefficients is too rigid in many cases. And it is often quite desirable to incorporate a tool of adaptation of the coefficients in model (1) to correct their values as soon as a new observation of time-series become available. This would allow to outline the changes of the coefficients over time, to enlarge the economic interpretation of the results, to give an idea about tendency of movement of the process, to determine the perspective directions of model reconstruction.

The most known tool for this aim is the Kalman filter originally used in engineering. It was developed in Kalman (1960), Kalman and Bucy (1961), Mehra (1972). Then Cooley and Prescott (1973,1976) have proposed an adaptive regression model for economic applications under the hypothesis of Markoff motion of the coefficients. A survey of the papers on time-varying coefficient regression analysis may be found, for instance, in Raj and Ullah (1981). The common shortcoming of these approaches when they are applied to economic research is the necessity to have a priori some information which can't be obtained from anywhere, such as the knowledge of the covariance matrix of nonobservable random variables or coefficients; in other cases it may be a hypothesis about the transition matrix in Markoff scheme for the coefficients, etc. As a result the application of these approaches comes across the difficulties. In Lukaschin (1979) the attempt is made to overcome these difficulties by improving of the procedure of Wheelwright and Makridakis (1973), in which an antigradient direction is used for adaptation of the coefficients. One shortcoming of the gradient approach may be a weak convergence, the other one is a high correlation of the coefficient corrections, because all of them are proportional to forecast error and therefore have the same sign if the value of endogenous variables are positive.

In Lukaschin (1986) a method of adaptation of the regression coefficients is proposed using exponentially-weighted moving average (EWMA). This is the method which we are developing here in Section 2. Section 3 is devoted to analysis of data when the adaptive regression model is constructing using this method.

2. ADAPTIVE REGRESSION MODEL

2.1. General ideas

Let us consider a regression equation with time-varying coefficients, which is of the form

$$y_t = \sum_{i=1}^{p} a_{it} x_{it} + e_t \,. \tag{4}$$

Let us examine the estimates of the parameters given by least-squares method under the hypothesis of constancy of the coefficients. After a simple rearranging the estimate of the parameter vector $\bar{a}$ may be written in terms of the sample averages of the cross products of the observations of the endogenous and exogenous variables taken in pairs, i.e.

$$\bar{a} = (\bar{X}'\bar{X})^{-1}\bar{X}'\bar{y}$$

$$= [\frac{1}{T}(\bar{X}'\bar{X})]^{-1}[\frac{1}{T}(\bar{X}'\bar{y})]$$

$$= \begin{bmatrix} m_{11} & m_{12} & \cdots & m_{1p} \\ \cdot & \cdot & \cdot & \cdot \\ \cdot & \cdot & \cdot & \cdot \\ m_{p1} & m_{p2} & \cdots & m_{pp} \end{bmatrix}^{-1} \begin{bmatrix} m_{1,p+1} \\ \cdot\;\cdot\;\cdot \\ \cdot\;\cdot\;\cdot \\ m_{p,p+1} \end{bmatrix} , \tag{5}$$

where $m_{ij} = \frac{1}{T}\sum_{t=1}^{T} x_{it}x_{jt}$, $i=1,2,\ldots,p$, $j=1,2,\ldots,p+1$ and for generality of notation it is admitted that $y_t=x_{p+1,t}$.

In what follows the attention will be paid to behaviour of the m_{ij}. A key to the problem of practical development of an adaptive regression model with time-varying coefficients is apparently in finding of a good tool for updating of the estimates of time-varying averages m_{ij}.

It is proposed to substitute in (5) the whole period averages m_{ij} by $c_{ij,t}$, which should be the estimates of local (or current) averages of the cross products of the regression variables taken in pairs. There are many different ways to obtain $c_{ij,t}$. For example, in context of a moving regression analysis $c_{ij,t}$ are computed as moving averages. The weights in this case are taken equal to $1/n$, where n is the extent of the average. Actually unequal weights may be used in moving averages. Say, more recent points in the extent of the average can be taken with greater weights, and first points with less ones. Such approach is more appropriate for a forecasting problem. It is possible as well to seek for a presence of time trends in the cross products and to approximate them with known functions of time or any other models.

As it was already noted, in most approaches to an adaptive regression analysis the equation of the dynamic coefficients' motion and sometimes even the values of the parameters of this equation are to be postulated a priori. But it is hardly realistic to think such a choice valid, for the coefficients are themselves nonobservable. The approach outlined here is based only on examination of the dynamics of the average values of the cross products of paired observable variables. These products form time-series, which can be presented on graphs and analized visually or using some analytical means. All these graphs in common show the structure and dynamics of the process under study. They allow to localize the points of suspicious changes. Thus, at the stage of analysis a multidimensional problem is decomposed into $p(p+3)/2$ uni-dimensional ones. However, uni-dimensional analysis shouldn't be carried out in isolation from analogous parallel studies. All uni-dimensional problems must be agreed, submitted to one global aim, to one criterion. Any intermediate, particular or indirect criterion may lead away from the main aim. That is why such criteria play only an auxiliary role at the initial stage of the model construction.

2.2. Case 1: Variables haven't time trends

In previous paper, Lukaschin (1986), we have treated in details the simplest case, when all the variables of the regression equation (4) haven't any visible trend. In this case it was proposed to substitute the arithmetic means m_{ij} in formula (5) by the EWMA $S_{ij,t}$. The EWMA is widely used in the adaptive analysis and has become a base of many procedures. In that case $c_{ij,t}$ will be renovated at each moment t as follows

$$S_{ij,t} = \beta \cdot S_{ij,t-1} + \alpha \cdot (x_{it}x_{jt}) \quad , \tag{6}$$

$$c_{ij,t} = S_{ij,t} \quad , \tag{7}$$

where $i=1,2,\ldots,p$, $j=1,2,\ldots,p+1$, α is a smoothing constant, which is taken in general from the interval $0<\alpha<1$, $\beta=1-\alpha$.

The formula (5) with $c_{ij,t}$ substituted for m_{ij} gives the estimates of the model coefficients a_i at moment t. To start the calculations using the recurrent type expression (6) it is necessary to have some starting value

$S_{ij,o}$ at moment t. It was proposed to determine it as the arithmetic mean of the first r observations of time-series, i.e.

$$S_{ij,o} = \frac{1}{r}\sum_{k=1}^{r} x_{ik}x_{jk} \quad . \tag{8}$$

To simplify the procedure r and smoothing parameter α were assumed the same for all pairs of i and j. Their best values were seeking for by minimizing the mean squared error of the one-step ahead forecasts

$$Q(\alpha,r) = \frac{1}{T}\sum_{i=1}^{T} e_i^2 \quad , \tag{9}$$

where $e_{t+1} = y_{t+1} - \hat{y}_{t+1}$ is an error of the forecast,

$y_{t+1} = \bar{x}'_{t+1}\hat{a}_t$ is the one-step ahead forecast,

$\hat{a}_t$ is an estimate of the parameter vector at moment t.

An interesting result was obtained in Griese and Matt (1973), from which it follows an important property of the outlined procedure. It turns out that application of the EWMA for smoothing of the cross products gives at each moment t (when t is great enough to neglect the influence of the starting values) the estimates of the parameters $\hat{a}_i$, which minimize exponentially-weighted sum of squared residuals of the regression

$$R_t = \sum_{k=1}^{t} \left(y_k - \sum_{i=1}^{p} \hat{a}_{it}x_{ik}\right)^2 \beta^{t-k} \quad . \tag{10}$$

2.3. Case 2: Variables have time trends

If some regression variables have time trends then the cross products will have them too, and the EWMA may not catch the mean level of the product. An attempt may be made to transform the original equation to obtain one with variables without trends using, for example, chain indices, rates of growth, differences of the proper order etc. If such transformations are not desirable then it is necessary to find satisfactory way to take trends into account. In particular, when the cross products have approximately polynomial trends we propose to present their motion using adaptive polynomial models of R.G.Brown (1963), which are based on multiple exponential smoothing.

As it is well-known the EWMA of order p is obtained by exponential smoothing of the EWMA of order p-1, that is

$$S_t^{[p]} = S_{t-1}^{[p]} + S_t^{[p-1]} \quad , \tag{11}$$

where p=1,2,... , $S_t^{[o]}$ is the original time series.

Brown has developed a procedure of renovation of parameters of a polynomial of order q, in which these parameters are known linear functions of the EWMA of order 1,2,...,q+1 and vice versa.

Thus, one needs a subroutine, which if necessary would allow to calculate the EWMA, say, of order 1,2 and 3 to construct the adaptive polynomials of order Ø,1,2. In particular problem the adaptive regression model must be developed taking into account the dynamic properties of the cross products of the regression variables. To choose a proper set of orders of the adaptive polynomials it is necessary to carry out some special preliminary analysis of data.

3. ANALYSIS OF DATA

When a set of variables is chosen and a form of a regression equation is determined the analysis of data may be carried out in three stages.

At the first stage it is worth-while to begin with examination of the regression equation with constant parameters and testing the hypothesis of the parameters' stability. It may be realized by different ways. For example, the substitution of a coefficient a_i by (a_i+b_it) and testing of significancy of the parameters may confirm or reject the stability hypothesis. Then it is possible to divide a sample into two subsamples and to compare the estimates of the corresponding coefficients in both, to apply test of Chow (1960). It is useful to estimate the regression equation with constant coefficients iteratively, starting from the sample size p and consecutively increasing it by 1. It gives the graph of the estimate against the sample size, which may be informative. Testing the constancy of the regression relationships over time may be carried out by examination of the errors of one-step ahead forecasts using CUSUM- or CUSUM of squares techniques proposed in Brown, Durbin, Evans (1975). If these or other tests indicate that regression coefficients are apparently time-varying then the analysis of data may be continued.

At the second stage the attention must be paid to dynamic properties of the regression variables and their cross products. It is reasonable to test a homogeneity of movement of the time-series, suspicious change-points etc. An annotated bibliography on statistical analysis of structural change may be found in Hackl and Westlund (1985). If nothing prevents from application of multiple exponential smoothing the further aim of preliminary analysis of data is to establish the proper order of adaptive polynomials to approximate the movement of the cross products. It may be carried out separately for each time-series $(x_ix_j)_t$ by trying and comparing different orders.

At the third stage it is necessary to determine some good initial conditions to start the recurrent calculations. Our experiments show that the behaviour of the model and results it gives including the optimal value of the smoothing constant are sensitive to initial values of the renovating quantities, i.e. of the EWMA of order 1,2,3 for each cross product.

Having carried out the data analysis one may proceed to synthesis and joint estimation of the adaptive regression model, using any global criterion.

4. CONCLUSIONS

In this paper some general questions of the adaptive regression analysis are considered, an approach to construction of an adaptive linear regression model with time-varying coefficients is presented. Adaptation of the coefficients is proposed to be realized by means of the decomposition of a multidimensional problem into some uni-dimensional ones and the following synthesis of the partial results into united system of estimation. In particular, Brown's adaptive polynomial models are proposed to be used for analysis and treatment of data in uni-dimensional space.

Our experiments show that a treatment of the adaptive regression model is considerably simplified if its variables (endogenous and exogenous) haven't any significant time trends and ordinary EWMA is enough to take into account the dynamics of their cross products. That is why it is worth-while to do one's best to reformulate if necessary the model in such a way. In some other cases the application of Brown's models may be useful for investigation of the coefficients' movement.

It may be noted that multicollinearity may cause agreed motion of two or some parameters in different directions. It is necessary to keep such situations under the control. Serious danger of this type comes from log-transformation, after which the variables used to be linearly dependent and correlated. To avoid the influence of the multicollinearity it is reasonable to consider the adaptive regression model preferably with small numbers of exogenous variables. Sometimes the adaptive regression exposed here may be considered as a tool of a preliminary analysis of the interrelation of the data. Then the obtained results may be used for formulation of a more sophisticated hypothesis about coefficients' movement to take it into account directly by reconstruction of the model.

Finally, it may be noted that extraction of more and more information about movement of the process under study from the same data is not indefinite, of course. More deep knowledge demand creation of more sensitive model. But such model may be unstable and work worse. Therefore in every case a researcher must find the reasonable level of investigation of the coefficients' dynamics.

5. REFERENCES

Brown, R.G. (1963). Smoothing, Forecasting and Prediction of Discrete Time Series. Prentice-Hall, Englewood Cliffs, N.J.

Brown, R.L., Durbin, J., Evans, J.M. (1975). Techniques for testing the constancy of regression relationchips over time. J.R.S.S., ser. B, 37(2).

Chow, G.C. (1960). Tests of equality between sets of coefficients in two linear regressions. Econometrica, 28 (3).

Cooley, T.F. and Prescott, E.C. (1973). The adaptive regression model. International Economic Review, 14 : 364-371.

Cooley, T.F. and Prescott, E.C. (1976). Estimation in the presence of stochastic parameter variation. Econometrica, 44 : 167-184.

Griese, J. und Matt,G. (1973). Beschreibung des Verfahrens der adaptiven Einflußgroßenkombination. In Prognoserechnung, Herausgegeben von Peter Mertens, Physica-Verlag, Wurzburg-Wien. Sect. 9.2. (In German).

Hackl, P., Westlund, A. (1985). Statistical analysis of 'Structural Change'. An annotated bibliography. CP-85-31. IIASA, Laxenburg.

Kalman, R.E. (1960). A new approach to linear filtering and prediction problems. Trans. ASME, ser.D, Journal of Basic Engineering, 82 : 35-45.

Kalman, R.E. and Bucy, R.S. (1961). New results in linear filtering and prediction theory. Trans. ASME, ser.D, Journal of Basic Engineering, 83 : 95-108.

Lukaschin, Y.P. (1979). Adaptive methods of short-term forecasting. Statistica, Moscow. (In Russian).

Lukaschin, Y.P. (1986). Adaptive correction of a regression with the use of the EWMA. Report presented at the conference of IIASA in Lodze on 'Statistical Analysis and Forecasting of Economic Structural Change'.

Mehra, R.K. (1972). Approaches to adaptive filtering. IEEE Trans. Automatic Control, AC-17 : 693-698.

Raj, B. and Ullah, A. (1981). Econometrics, a varying coefficients' approach. Croom Helm, London.

Sarris, A.H. (1973). A bayesian approach to estimation of time-varying regression coefficients. Annals of Economic and Social Measurement, 2(4).

Wheelwright, S.C. and Makridakis, S. (1973). Forecasting with adaptive filtering. Revue Francaise d'Automatique, d'Informatique et de Recherche Operationelle, Paris, ser.V, 7(1).

DEVELOPMENT OF A COMPUTER SYSTEM FOR MODEL SELECTION

Y. Nakamori
Department of Applied Mathematics, Konan University,
8-9-1 Okamoto, Higashinada-ku, Kobe 658, Japan.

1. INTRODUCTION

Data fitting of the regression type often used in econometric modeling requires trial-and-error methods in selectiong a set of explanatory variables. The stepwise or all-subset techniques implemented on a computer reduce our burden to some extent. But the interpretation of the results is still a large task because of difficulties in checking the validity of the hypothesis testing and in giving meaning to regression coefficients. Rethinking of the obtained equations is not feasible when the number of equations is large and the cause-effect relationships between variables are not known exactly in advance. Moreover, statistical reliability does not necessarily ensure applicability. Model building in uncertain environment calls for carft skills that are the mixture of science and art.

This paper introduces a computer system called the Interactive Modeling Support System (IMSS) that helps model building for those systems which are methodologically undeveloped in the sense that neither analytical nor statistical methods are adequate for dealing with. It aims at reflecting the practical knowledge and experience of experts on the models, at the same time, developing their ideas and exercising thier judgment and intuition. The computer system consists of a combined modeling techniques of statistical and graph-theoretical approaches, and related multi-stage man-machine dialogues. One of the main advantages of using this system is the facility for the structuring of both mental and mathematical models, that facilitates the model understanding and confidence.

After a brief description of the modeling system, its application to the modeling and simulation of NOx concentration is presented.

2. MODELING METHODOLOGY

The modeling procedure of using IMSS requires the following three types of information:

(a) A set of variables $S=\{x_i\}$ to describe the system under study.

(b) The corresponding measurement data table $X=(x_{ij})$.

(c) A cause-effect relation B, on the product set $S \times S$, or equivalently, the adjacency matrix $A=(a_{ij})$ with $a_{ij}=1$ if and only if $(x_i,x_j) \varepsilon B$.

The objective of the modeling is to obtain a set of linear equations that describes the underlying system and is capable of predicting the behavior of the system.

The modeling process consists of three different but interdependent stages of dialogues. The first stage dialogue is required for preparation of the modeling, including input of measurement data and the initial version of cause-effect relation on the set of variables, transformation of variables, data screening, and refinement of the cause-effect relation by referring to the statistical information.

The second stage dialogue is devoted to finding a trade-off between the measurement data and the modeler's knowledge about dependencies between variables. Based on the measurement data and the initial version of the cause-effect relation, using the option of regression method, a linear model and the corresponding digraph model are found. The modeler can modify the new relation referring to these computer models and his or her knowledge. The process continues repeatedly until no change occurs or the modeler is satisfied with the modified relation.

The third stage dialogue is related to model simplification and elaboration. Model simplification is based on the use of equivalence relation, and model elaboration is an application of regression analysis including the hypothesis testing on estimated coefficients, and examination of the explanatory and predictive powers of the model.

The first craft required is the selection of descriptive variables. The variable set S can include nonlinear reexpression or time-delayed variables of the initial variables. Following the traditional usage, we use the term "linear model" to describe a set of equations whose structural parameters are embedded linearly. Reexpression and time-shifting enable us to analyze nonlinear relationships and multiple autoregressive processes.

At the second and third stages, the corresponding data set is required to be complete in the sense that it is screened enough to avoid the influence of outliers or the problem of multicollinearity. This does not imply that the data should be measured absolutely correctly. Soft obsevation is allowed to compensate for lacking or extraordinary data. Hereafter, we use the term "observation" instead of "measurement", meaning that observation can include data estimated or modified by the modeler.

Because both the complexity and ambiguity of an object depend on the interests and capabilities of the individual, the introduction of a cause-effect relation is also a craft work. But in-depth considerations are not required initially; the remaining ambiguities are resolved after some iterative modeling sessions. In applications, it is often difficult to make the clear-cut distinction between input variables, output variables and intermediate variables. The purpose of the modeling also has an influence on the model. The flexibility in determining the model structure is most emphasized. However, for a complex system, to determine the model structure is often a hard task. Therefore, the pairwise cause-effect relationships are required first and then the validity of the total model structure is examined. This process is the most important part to reflect human mental models on the computer model.

In the second stage, the regression methods are used to obtain linear models and graph-theoretical techniques are used for man-machine interactions. The required human input is knowledge of the structural image of the system. This stage includes part of the model verification, because the modeler should judge whether the model behaves as he intends. Even the experts can hardly tell whether the obtained model is appropriate or not because the coefficients of a linear model do not necessarily have practical meanings. Therefore, the structure of the model is extracted and shown in the form of digraphs to help the understanding and modification of the computer model.

The third stage is concerned with judgments about the validity of the model in terms of its explanatory and predictive powers. But data concerning the results of policies not implemented are generally not available, so scenario analysis is prepared. Here, both cumulative experience and deep insight into the system are required.

3. INTERACTIVE MODELING SUPPORT SYSTEM

The Interactive Modeling Support System (IMSS) is a highly user-friendly software providing for an interactive person-computer dialogue facilitated by the use of advanced techniques to communicate directly graphic information to the computer and receive graphic output. The total modeling process of using IMSS is shown in FIGURE 1. The following main advantages of its use are emphasized:

(a) The data-screening features provide a powerful tool for debugging the data-set.

(b) The structural modeling features are helpful for organizing one's thinking with respect to the system under study.

(c) It enables rapid access to the set of relationships comprising the statistical model.

(d) It makes possible rapid validation and easy refinement of the statistical model.

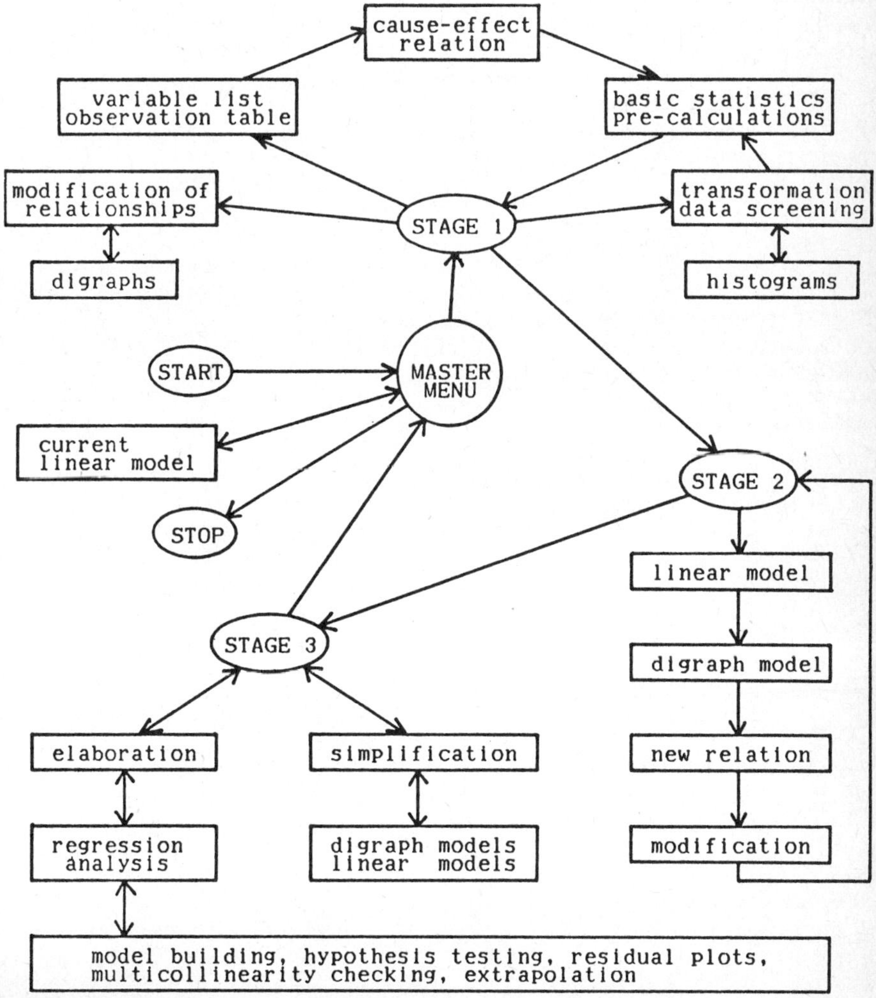

FIGURE 1 The total modeling process of using IMSS.

The modeling information (S,X,A) is put into the computer at the first step. IMSS has several facilities to read and preprocess the data set. The facility for data transformation makes it possible to analyze time-lag effects or functional relationships. Data transformation is also needed to make distributions of variables symmetric because, according to Hartwig and Dearing (1979), non-symmetric distributions and nonlinear relationships often exist together. If every distribution of variables is roughly symmetric, then we will have a high chance to obtain a linear model.

If at some step the modeler want to check distributions or outliers of the data for some variables, IMSS assists him by showing the list of candidates of outliers, histograms or scattergrams. The modeler can designate the case numbers which he does not want to use in the modeling. IMSS also checks and displays pairs of variables which have high correlation coefficients. To avoid the problem of multicollinearity and also to simplify the model, it is recommended that one of the pair is set aside when they are supposed to be linearly dependent. The modeler can be referred to the condensed basic statistics and scatter plots.

The manner of filling the adjacency matrix A should be negative. Here negative means that the modeler should enter the computer a part of his knowledge, putting 0's at the right places. The rest of entries will be filled with 1's by the computer. The underlying idea is that the modeler should inquire into strength of relationship between every pair of variables except those which are definitely irrelevant. An extension of binary relation is allowed in filling the matrix $A=(a_{ij})$:

$$a_{ij} = \begin{cases} 2 & \text{if } x_i \text{ certainly influences } x_j \\ 1 & \text{if } x_i \text{ might influence } x_j \\ 0 & \text{if } x_i \text{ never influences } x_j \end{cases} \qquad (1)$$

There is no difference between 1 and 2 in the structural modeling, but they are treated differently in the statistical modeling, i.e., the variables indicated by 2 are regarded as the core variables and those indicated by 1 the optional variables.

IMSS has another option of filling the matrix A. The relation considered is the cause and effect that is not necessarily transitive. But it may be quite feasible to employ the assumption of transitivity to develop a linear model. The modeler can choose the option of a transitive embedding method that is a modified version of that in Warfield (1976).

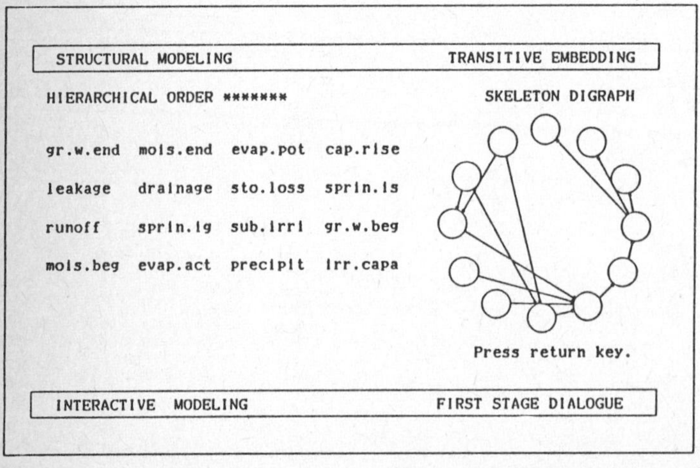

FIGURE 2 An example of developed digraph model.

The advantage of this method is that it can reduce the number of pairwise comparisons remarkably. One caution in using this method is that the modeler should consider indirect cause-effect relationships as well as direct ones. IMSS provides the digraph of hierarchy based on the adjacency matrix A, taking its transitive closure and extracting the skeleton. The interactive modification facility helps the refinement or rethinking of the relation. FIGURE 2 shows an example of developed digraph model.

After the first stage dialogue, the set of variables S and the data matrix X are fixed and will be used in the subsequent stages as they are. The adjacency matrix A is alone open for further modification. The purpose of the second stage is to elaborate the cause-effect relations which are summarized in A.

At the beginning of the second stage, the modeler must choose one of the options of regression methods with self-selection of explanatory variables. The options of these include:

(a) the forward selection procedure,
(b) the backward elimination procedure,
(c) the all possible selection procedure, and
(d) the group method of data handling.

The last one can be used when the number of data points is very small. It is a modified version of the original one (Ivakhnenko, 1968), i.e., the partial description is written in a linear form with respect to variables. FIGURE 3 shows the opening menu of the second stage dialogue.

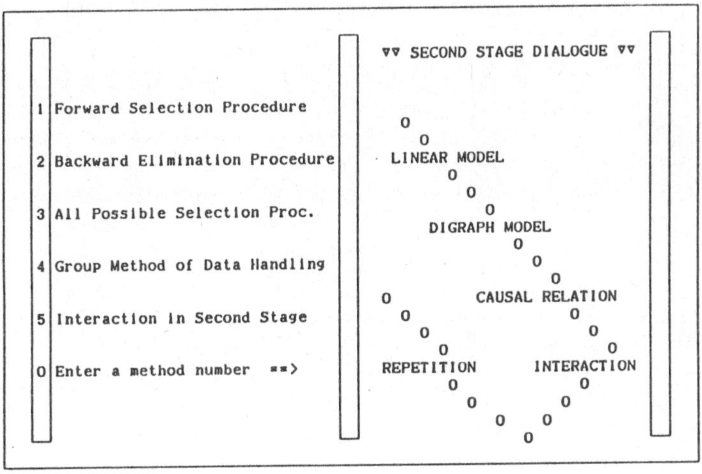

FIGURE 3 The opening menu of the second stage dialogue.

Let us denote by $\bar{C} = (c_0, C)$, where c_0 is an n-column vector and C an $n \times n$ matrix, the coefficient matrix of a set of linear equations which the computer will search from now on:

$$x = c_0 + Cx \quad \text{with} \quad c_{ii} = 0 \quad \text{for all } i, \tag{2}$$

where x denote the n-column vector whose components correspond to the names of variables $x_1, x_2, \cdots, x_n$.

By the selected automatic modeling method, the computer will estimate the row vectors of $\bar{C}$ one by one referring to the matrix A that can have been converted into a reachability matrix. Thus the computer finds a linear model:

$$M_C = (S, \bar{C}) \quad \text{or} \quad x = c_0 + Cx. \tag{3}$$

Then the adjacency matrix A and the corresponding relation B will be modified in an apparent manner.

Let us introduce a digraph D defined by

$$D = (S, B), \tag{4}$$

where the elements of S are identified as vertices and those of B arcs. The vertices are represented by points and there is a directed line heading from x_i to x_j if and only if (x_i, x_j) is in B.

Let $\bar{B}$ denote the transitive closure of B, and suppose the variable set S can be divided into m cycle sets $e_1, e_2, \cdots, e_m$; here e_p is defined by:

$$x_i,\ x_j \ \varepsilon\ e_p \text{ if } (x_i, x_j), (x_j, x_i) \ \varepsilon\ \bar{B}. \tag{5}$$

Then we can define new sets:

$$\bar{S} = \{ e_1, e_2, \cdots, e_m \} \tag{6}$$

$$B^* = \{ (e_p, e_q) \ ; \text{ some } (x_i, x_j) \ \varepsilon\ \bar{B},\ x_i \ \varepsilon\ e_p,\ x_j \ \varepsilon\ e_q \} \tag{7}$$

and the corresponding digraph $(\bar{S}, B^*)$ is called the condensation digraph. Finally we introduce the skeleton digraph $\bar{D}$ which is a minimum arc subdigraph of the condensation digraph, for which removal of any arc would destroy reachability present in the relation.

Actually the above process is carried out by some matrix operations in the computer. After all, the computer will have found the digraph model:

$$M_D = (\bar{S}, \bar{D}), \tag{8}$$

that is a visual version of the linear model M_C. If the modeler is satisfied with the model structure, the modeling process will proceed to the third stage. Otherwise, the second stage will be repeated again after amendments of the digraph model M_D. The modification facility of the digraph is one of the most fascinating parts of IMSS; but the detail description is omitted here. FIGURE 4 and FIGURE 5 show the dialogues in the second stage.

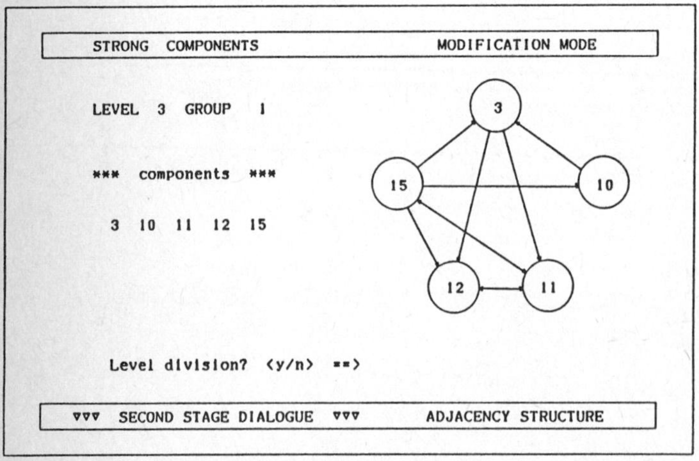

FIGURE 4 The modification module to the cycle sets.

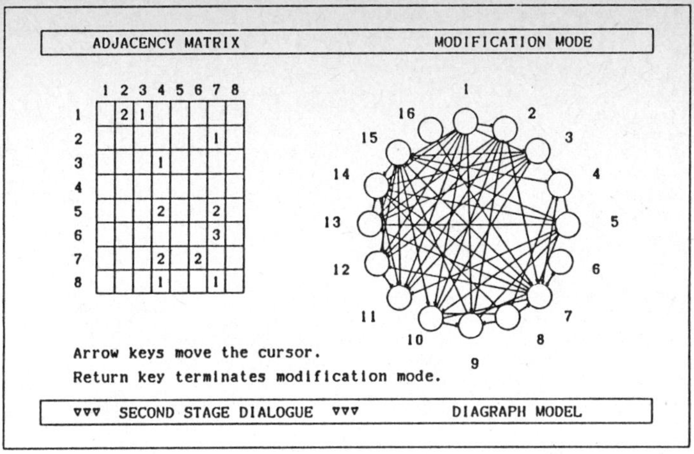

FIGURE 5 The modification module to the adjacency matrix.

Even an expert can hardly tell whether the obtained linear model is appropriate or not because of the difficulties of checking validity of the hypothesis testing and giving meanings to regression coefficients. The most emphasized point of using IMSS is that the refinement of the statistical model can be done by the modification of the structural model.

The third stage dialogue consists of two modes: model simplification and model elaboration. Model simplification is based on the use of equivalence relation and model elaboration is applications of regression analysis and scenario analysis. The simplification mode is prepared for reducing the obtained model into an optimization or simulation model. IMSS prepares most of the classical procedures in regression analysis including the hypothesis testing on the estimated coefficients, and the examination of explanatory and predictive powers of the model with the aid of graphic facilities of the computer. FIGURE 6 shows an example of regression result, and FIGURE 7 shows an example of obtained model equation.

RESULT 2	Regressand ==> variable X12		Ranking 1 / 1	
variable	coefficient	standard error	t-ratio	correlation
X1	-.2194D+01	0.8382D+00	-.2617D+01	0.5314
X2	-.2051D-01	0.6428D-02	-.3191D+01	-.4480
X3	-.1583D+01	0.6150D+00	-.2573D+01	0.4364
X7	0.1009D-01	0.4673D-02	0.2159D+01	0.3787
X11	0.3967D-01	0.5077D-02	0.7815D+01	0.6658
X15	-.6587D-01	0.1732D-01	-.3804D+01	0.4786
constant	0.8956D+01	[hit return]		
Degrees of Freedom = 21		Adjusted R-Square = 0.7893		
S.D. of Residual = 0.2444D+00			F-Ratio = 0.1785d+02	
T(21 , 0.05) = 2.0796		F(6 , 21 , 0.05) = 2.5727		

FIGURE 6 A result of linear modeling.

```
*** CURRENT LINEAR MODEL *** peel07 ***

--- equation for variable  mois.end ---

mois.end = 2.6751D+02  -1.2739D+02  gr.w.end  -1.4655-02  precipit

                        3.4723D-02  sprin.ig  -6.7754D-02 evap.pot

                        5.8402D-01  sub.irri

                                                 hit return
```

FIGURE 7 An example of obtained model equation.

The more detail description of IMSS and its application to the simplification of a comprehensive grounwater-crop production model are found in Nakamori et al. (1985) and Van Walsum et al. (1985), respectively.

4. APPLICATION TO AN ENVIRONMENTAL PROBLEM

As an example of using IMSS, let us build a simulation model to predict NOx concentration. The selected variables are shown in TABLE 1. For each variable, we have three years data (1977, 1980, 1983) from 22 cities in Japan; 66 data points in all.

TABLE 1 The list of selected variables.
(Every item represents the value in a defined area.)

Notations	Contents
NOx	yearly and spatially averaged NOx concentration
pop.tota	total population in the area
pop.dens	population density
pop.chen	changing rate of the population
pop.hous	average population in a family
farmland	percentage of the land use for agriculture
building	percentage of the land use for buildings
traffic	percentage of the land use for traffic
ind.tota	total amount of the shipment from the industries
ind.heav	shipment from the heavy industries per unit area
ind.ligh	shipment from the light industries per unit area
trade	amount of the wholesale and retail sales
temperat	annual mean temperature
wind.vel	annual mean wind velocity
dic.sea	distance between the area center and the seashore
dic.moun	distance between the area center and the mountains
altitude	altitude of the area
cities20	the number of cities within 20 km
cities40	the number of cities within 40 km
traf.car	traffic volume of cars
traf.bus	traffic volume of buses
traf.str	traffic volume of small trucks
traf.btr	traffic volume of trucks

An expert from the Japan National Institute for Environmental Studies introduced the initial version of cause-effect relation which is summarized in a digraph as shown in FIGURE 8.

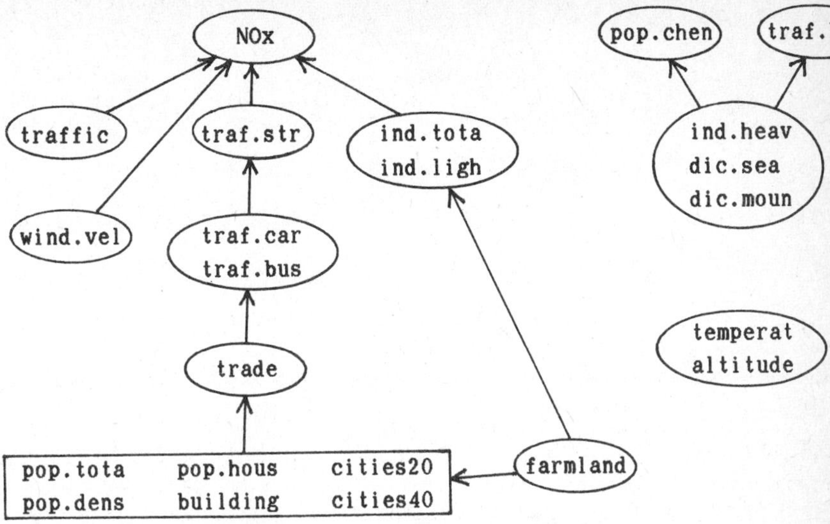

FIGURE 8 The initial version of cause-effect relation.

After the modeling sessions with the computer, we obtained the following set of equations and the corresponding model structure is shown in FIGURE 9.

NOx	=	2.5067e+01	-3.3672e-01	building	-1.2098e-07	ind.tota
			+3.2710e-05	ind.ligh	+2.3460e-01	cities40
			+2.0829e-03	traf.car	+2.8620e-04	traf.btr
pop.hous	=	3.3246e+00	-5.1593e-07	pop.tota	-5.5840e-05	pop.dens
			+7.0042e-03	building		
building	=	2.3243e+01	-3.9689e-05	pop.tota	+5.4968e-03	pop.dens
ind.ligh	=	2.0992e+04	+2.4290e-03	ind.tota		
trade	=	4.1107e+04	+6.1321e-03	pop.tota	-1.3588e+00	pop.dens
			-1.3967e+04	pop.hous	+9.2540e+01	farmland
			+2.3669e+02	building		
cities40	=	6.7757e-01	+3.2292e-03	pop.dens	+1.8973e+00	cities20
traf.bus	=	5.5582e+03	+1.2763e-03	pop.tota	-1.6272e+03	pop.hous
			+6.4841e+00	building	-1.3082e+01	cities20
			+1.2884e-01	traf.car		
traf.str	=	-1.1000e+03	+3.9610e-01	pop.dens	+1.4023e+01	building
			+2.4809e+01	cities40	+1.0873e+00	traf.car
traf.btr	=	4.1327e+03	+1.6459e+00	pop.dens	-1.5634e+02	building
			-1.4051e+02	traffic	+2.2359e-02	ind.heav
			+6.5000e-03	ind.ligh	+7.9807e-01	traf.str

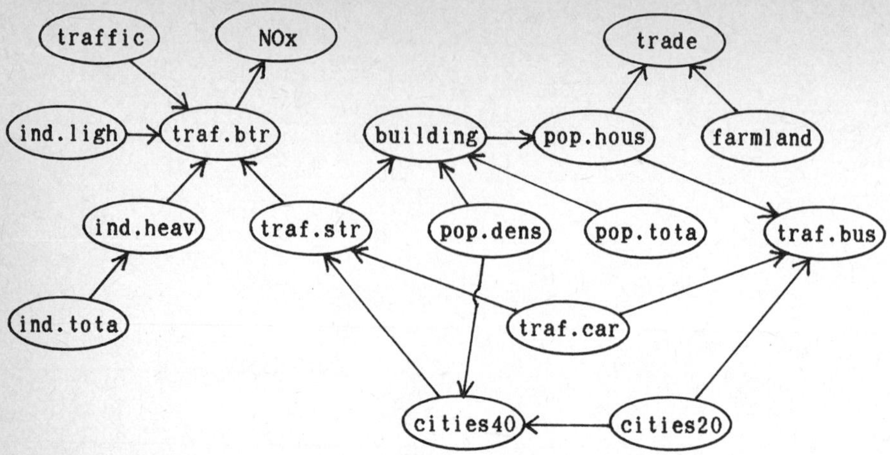

FIGURE 9 The model structure obtained after the modeling sessions.

5. CONCLUSION

The interactive modeling support system is a tool for enlightening both the modeler and the computer about the underlying system. The main point is how effectively extract reality from human mental models and also from measurement data with computer assistance. One of the fascinating application is to design a decision support system coupled with IMSS, because model building is the most important part in decision making. Moreover, we are developing an intelligent modeling system by adding a knowledge base system to IMSS.

ACKNOWLEDGMENT

The author is greatly indebted to Dr. S. Nishioka and Ms. M. Kainuma form the Japan National Institute for Environmental Studies for their helpful cooperation in gathering data and also in modeling and simulation.

REFERENCES

Hartwig, F., and Dearing, B.E. (1979). Exploratory Data Analysis, Sage, London.

Ivakhnenko, A.G. (1968). The group method of data handling, a rival of the method of stochastic approximation. Soviet Automatic Control, 13(3): 43-55.

Nakamori, Y., Ryobu, M., Fukawa, H. and Sawaragi, Y. (1985). An Interactive Modeling Support System. WP-85-77. International Institute for Applied Systems Analysis, Laxenburg, Austria.

Van Walsum, P.E.V., and Nakamori, Y. (1985). Simplification of a comprehensive hydrological model for scenario analysis. WP-85-92. International Institute for Applied Systems Analysis, Laxenburg, Austria.

Warfield, I.N. (1976). Societal Systems: Planning, Policy and Complexity. John Wiley, New York.

ON THE ESTIMATION OF PROBABILISTIC FUNCTIONS OF MARKOV CHAINS

E.E. Pickett and R.G. Whiting
Department of Industrial Engineering
University of Toronto
Toronto, Canada M5S 1A4

1. INTRODUCTION

The class of stochastic models to be examined here is representative of doubly stochastic processes. This latter term is used to denote processes which consist of an underlying process, in this case a Markov chain, which is not directly observed but which can be observed through another stochastic process. Models of this type are particularly appropriate for describing a seemingly very different problem: that is, the statistical problem of estimation from incomplete data (Dempster et al. 1977). In this latter case the output of the 'true' but concealed process is thought of as conditioning a second process which censores the input and produces the observed data. Both processes are considered to be parameterized and the problem is to determine the parameter set from the observations.

If the assumption is made that the underlying process is Markovian in the sense that its value at any time depends on only a finite interval of its immediate history then this restriction defines the partially observed Markov model. If the unobserved process is further restricted to be discrete it becomes a Markov chain and is the situation dealt with here.

For the class of ergodic partially observed Markov chain (POMC) models, the method of maximum likelihood (MLE), based on the likelihood of the observation sequence, is known to provide consistent parameter estimation (Baum and Petrie 1966). Baum's algorithm was originally proposed (Baum and Eagon 1967) as an iterative procedure for constrained maximization of homogeneous polynomials with positive coefficients. It has desirable numerical properties, including guaranteed local convergence with monotonic function improvement.

The algorithm has been generalized to a larger class of functions (Liporace 1982) and (Rabiner et al. 1985). It has been applied to parameter estimation problems involving polynomial likelihoods. Examples of this include estimation of linear learning models (Pruscha 1976), continuous key space approximations in cryptanalysis (Andelman and Reeds 1982), and in quality control (Whiting 1985). Statistically, Baum's algorithm is an example of the E-M (expectation-maximization) method for maximum likelihood estimation when sampling with incomplete information (Dempster et al. 1977). Numerically, it can be regarded as a form of fixed point iteration derivable from the necessary conditions for a local extremum (Whiting 1985).

Proof of convergence of the iterative method rests on the equivalence between the set of critical points of the likelihood function and the fixed points of the iteration. When the iteration is derived from the zeros of the gradient of the likelihood function under the parameter constraints, convergence to a local maximum will typically be linear (Whiting and Pickett 1984).

To improve this slow convergence rate, an extention of the secant method, known as Steffenson's method can be applied directly to the iterates provided by the Baum algorithm. This method typically exhibits superlinear convergence (Whiting 1985).

The subsequent organization of the paper is as follows: a description of Baum's algorithm is given in Section 2. for the case of the POMC with discrete observations; the relation between Baum's algorithm and the E-M method is shown in Section 3; the problem of model order estimation is addressed in Section 4 where the properties of a criterion due to Akaike (1974) are investigated; an experiment involving the 'sensitivity' of this model order estimation criterion is reported in Section 5; the results of an application of maximum likelihood estimation and model order estimation to quality monitoring in manufacturing are discussed in Section 6.

2. IMPLEMENTATION OF MLE WITH BAUM'S ALGORITHM

Let $X^T = (X(0), X(1), \ldots, X(T))$, $Y^T = (Y(1), \ldots, Y(T))$ denote the state (unobserved) and observation sequences from a POMC, respectively. Here $X(t) \in S_X$ and $Y(t) \in S_Y$ where $S_X = (1, \ldots, N)$ and $S_Y = (0, 1, \ldots, M-1)$ are discrete state and observation spaces. The process state is not observed directly: it serves to index the conditional distribution of the observation process Y(t).

The stochastic process X(t) is an ergodic Markov chain, with N x N transition matrix $P = (p_{ij})$ and state transition probabilities:

$$p_{ij} = Pr(X(t) = j \mid X(t+1) = i)\ , \qquad \text{where } i, j \in S_X$$

The initial state distribution vector $p = (p_i)$, is the probability that $X(t) = i$, $i \in S_X$ at some arbitrary time t=0.

Given the value of the process state X(t), the random variable Y(t) is independent of all other X(t'), Y(t'), t'≠t. The conditional distribution of Y(t) as a function of the unobserved state X(t) is given by $R = (r_{ik})$ where:

$$r_{ik} = Pr(Y(t) = k \mid X(t) = i)\ , \qquad \text{for } i \in S_X,\ k \in S_Y \text{ and all } t.$$

The POMC is fully specified through the N(N + M + 1) components of p, P, and R. Let $\theta \in \Lambda$ denote an N(N + M + 1), vector formed from these elements. There are N' = N(N + M -1)-1 independent parameters determined by the constraints:

$$\sum_{i=1}^{N} p_i - 1 = 0\ , \qquad \sum_{j=1}^{N} p_{ij} - 1 = 0\ , \qquad \sum_{k=0}^{M-1} r_{ik} - 1 = 0 \qquad i \in S_X\ . \tag{1}$$

Baum's algorithm is based on a state enumeration representation of the likelihood function. The likelihood, as a function of $\underline{\theta}$, is denoted $L(\underline{\theta}; Y^T) = Pr(Y^T; \underline{\theta})$. State enumeration yields $L(\underline{\theta}; Y^T) = \sum_{X^T} Pr(X^T, Y^T; \underline{\theta})$ where

$$Pr(X^T, Y^T; \underline{\theta}) = p_{X(0)} \prod_{t=1}^{T} p_{X(t-1)X(t)}\, r_{X(t)Y(t)}\ . \tag{2}$$

The polynomial form of $L(\underline{\theta}; Y^T)$ is revealed by expressing the above in an alternative fashion. Define the following:

$$U(X^T, i, j) = \sum_{t=1}^{T} \delta_{X(t-1), i}\, \delta_{X(t), j}$$

$$V(X^T, Y^T, k, j) = \sum_{t=1}^{T} \delta_{Y(t), k}\, \delta_{X(t), j} \tag{3}$$

where $i, j \in S_X$, $k \in S_Y$ and $\delta_{i,j}$ is the Kronecker delta. Summation over $i \in S_X$ or $k \in S_Y$ will be denoted by "$\bullet$".

U is the count of the number of transitions from state i to j appearing in X^T, and V is the number of times outcome k and state j occur together. Note that U and V constitute sufficient statistics for estimating $\underline{\theta}$ in the case of a completely observed system. Equation (2) can now be written:

$$\Pr\{X^T, Y^T; \underline{\theta}\} = p_{X(0)} \prod_{j=1}^{N} \Big(\prod_{k=0}^{M-1} r_{jk}^{\,V(X^T, Y^T, k, j)} \Big) \prod_{i=1}^{N} p_{ij}^{\,U(X^T, i, j)} \tag{4}$$

This is a polynomial of degree 2T + 1 in the elements of $\underline{\theta}$.

Baum's algorithm may be derived using an auxillary function approach (Baum et al. 1970). A more direct derivation is obtained by constructing the necessary conditions for a constrained extremum (using (1) and (4)), and deriving a fixed-point iteration from these conditions. Using this approach, the necessary conditions evaluated at the 'current' estimate $\underline{\theta}_n$ yield:

$$p_j = \frac{\sum_{X^T} \Pr\{X^T, Y^T; \underline{\theta}_n\}\, \delta_{X(0), j}}{\Pr\{Y^T; \underline{\theta}_n\}}$$

$$p_{ij} = \frac{\sum_{X^T} \Pr\{X^T, Y^T; \underline{\theta}_n\}\, U(X^T, i, j)}{\sum_{X^T} \Pr\{X^T, Y^T; \underline{\theta}_n\}\, U(X^T, i, \bullet)} \tag{5}$$

$$r_{jk} = \frac{\sum_{X^T} \Pr\{X^T, Y^T; \underline{\theta}_n\}\, V(X^T, Y^T, k, j)}{\sum_{X^T} \Pr\{X^T, Y^T; \underline{\theta}_n\}\, U(X^T, \bullet, j)}.$$

In a fixed-point iteration, the left side of (5) defines the n+1st estimate, $\underline{\theta}_{n+1}$. This iteration is Baum's algorithm for the POMC. Evaluating the right side is accomplished using the forward-backward algorithm, described in the following.

Baum and co-workers proposed a numerical procedure for evaluating successive iterates of the algorithm given by (5). The so-called forward-backward algorithm ((6) and (7) below) involves processing of observations in both the order observed ("forward" direction) and in reverse order ("backward" direction).

As originally proposed, the forward-backward algorithm requires both the "forward" probabilities:

$$\alpha_i(t) = \Pr\{Y^t \text{ and } X(t) = i \ ; \underline{\theta}_n\}, \qquad \text{for } i \in S_X ;$$

and the "backward" probabilities:

$$\beta_i(t) = \Pr\{Y(t+1), \ldots, Y(T) | X(t) = i \ ; \underline{\theta}_n\}, \quad \text{for } i \in S_X .$$

These are computed using the forward and backward recursions:

$$\alpha_j(t) = \sum_{i=1}^{N} \alpha_i(t-1) p_{ij} \, r_{jY(t)}, \qquad t=2, \ldots, T \ ; \ j \in S_X$$

and (6)

$$\beta_i(t) = \sum_{j=1}^{N} \alpha_j(t+1) p_{ij} \, r_{jY(t+1)}, \qquad t=T-1, \ldots, 1 \ ; \ i \in S_X .$$

If the above are evaluated at the current iterate from Baum's algorithm, $\underline{\theta}_n$, then the next iterate is given by:

$$p_i = \frac{\alpha_i(1)\,\beta_i(1)}{\Pr\{Y^T ; \underline{\theta}_n\}}$$

$$p_{ij} = \frac{\sum_{t=1}^{T-1} \alpha_i(t)\, p_{ij}\, r_{jY(t)}\, \beta_j(t+1)}{\sum_{t=1}^{T-1} \alpha_i(t)\, \beta_i(t)} \tag{7}$$

$$r_{jk} = \frac{\sum_{t=1}^{T} \alpha_j(t)\, \beta_j(t) \ \delta_{Y(t),k}}{\sum_{t=1}^{T-1} \alpha_j(t)\, \beta_j(t)} \qquad i, j \in S_X \ ; \ k \in S_Y .$$

where $Pr(Y^T;\underline{\theta}_n) = \sum_{i=1}^{N} \alpha_i(t) \ (=L(\underline{\theta}_n ; Y^T))$. Note that these expressions require storage of the β's, i.e. an Nx1 vector sequence of length T. As well, computation is delayed until all T observations become available. Implementation of Baum's algorithm with the forward-backward algorithm requires on the order of TN^2 and TN^2M flops for the parameters of P and R, respectively.

3. RELATION TO THE E-M ALGORITHM

The approach suggested by Baum and co-workers for the parameter estimation problem can be considered as a special case of the E-M algorithm applied to a doubly stochastic process. To show this relationship it is assumed, as before, that the observed data Y^T are a realization from S_Y and the corresponding $X \in S_X$ are observed only indirectly through Y. The process is completely specified by the parameter $\underline{\theta}$.

Each iteration of the E-M algorithm involves two steps, the expectation (E) step and the maximization (M) step. After k iterations of the algorithm, the E-step estimates the current value of the sufficient statistic t(x) as:

$$t^k = E(t(X) \mid Y^T, \underline{\theta}_k)$$

given the current value of the parameter $\underline{\theta}_k$. This is followed by the M-step in which a new value $\underline{\theta}_{k+1}$ is obtained as a solution to:

$$E(t(X) \mid \underline{\theta}_k) = t^k.$$

Further iterations of this two step procedure yields increasingly better estimates of $\underline{\theta}$.

For the partially observed Markov chain, sufficient statistics are counts of the frequency of occurrence of state-to-state transitions; as well as state and observation joint occurrences. These correspond directly to the sufficient statistics occurring with a fully observed Markov chain (Billingsley 1961).

Application of the E-M algorithm to the POMC first involves using the forward and backward recursions (6) to obtain the expected value of the sufficient statistics (the E-step) from the process $\{X(t), Y(t)\}$, $t \in 1, \ldots, T$. This requires the determination of the following values:

a_i - likelihood of the observation sequence Y^T given that the initial state is state i.

a - likelihood of the observation sequence Y^T.

b_{ij} - expected number of transitions from state i to state j, given Y^T.

b_i - expected number of transitions out of state i, given Y^T.

c_{jk} - expected number of occurrences of the outcome k while in state j, given Y^T.

c_j - expected number of occurrences of state j, given Y^T.

New estimates of p_i, p_{ij}, r_{jk} are obtained as follows (the M-step):

$$p_i = a_i/a, \quad p_{ij} = b_{ij}/b_i, \quad r_{jk} = c_{jk}/c_j.$$

These estimates have been shown by Baum et al. (1970) to increase the value of the likelihood function over the value achieved in the previous iteration. Furthermore these investigators have shown that repeated iterations will converge to a local maximum of the likelihood function.

4. MODEL ORDER ESTIMATION

The POMC model offers a flexible, dynamic representation of discrete state processes which are observed in the presence of noise. In practice, it is important to ascertain whether or not the basic model structure can be recovered from observation sequences. The most fundamental parameter of a POMC model in this regard is the dimension of the unobserved process state. Model order estimation criteria have been proposed which attempt to identify the number of independent model parameters, which is equivalent to the dimension of the process state in the absence of other restrictions.

Let k_j denote the model order (number of independent model parameters) of a POMC process with state dimension j. The value of k_j is given by: $k_j = j\,(j-1) + j\,(M-1)$, where the first term represents the number of independent parameters in the transition matrix P, and the second is the number required to specify the output distribution, i.e. the number of parameters in R. Missing from this expression is the number of parameters in the initial state distribution, which is not considered because of the assumption of stationarity which is made when examining consistency of estimation criteria.

The model order criterion investigated here is known as Akaike's information criterion, or AIC (Akaike 1974). The criterion can be simply stated: choose the model j which minimizes:

$$AIC\,(k_j) = -2 \log \Pr\,(Y^T; \hat{\underline{\theta}}_j) + 2k_j$$

where k_j is the number of independent parameters (defined above), and $\hat{\underline{\theta}}_j$ is the maximum likelihood estimate of the k_j model parameters. Note that calculation of AIC over a range of model orders, j, requires calculation of the MLE $\hat{\underline{\theta}}_j$ for each value of j. In practice, this represents a significant effort since it requires numerical optimization, e.g. using Baum's algorithm.

The AIC criterion has been shown not to be a consistent estimator of model order in many different settings (e.g. Katz (1981)). As outlined briefly below, the AIC criterion is also not consistent when applied to the POMC model. However, it has been demonstrated with observations from a simulated POMC process, that AIC performs better than other, consistent criteria for moderate length samples (Whiting 1985).

To show that AIC is not consistent, convergence of the likelihood ratio may be employed. This convergence is established in Baum and Petrie (1966), extending similar results for fully observed Markov chains, reported in Billingsley (1961).

The criterion $AIC(k_j)$ would be consistent if, in the large sample limit, its minimum value occurs for j=q, where q is the 'true' model order. Equivalently, the following must hold for j > q and j < q (Wax and Kailath 1985):

$$AIC\,(k_j) - AIC\,(k_q) > 0.$$

Consider the case j > q, so that $k_j > k_q$. The above can be written:

$$AIC\,(k_j) - AIC\,(k_q) = 2\,(k_j - k_q) - \chi(Y^T, k_j, k_q) \tag{8}$$

where:

$$\chi(Y^T, k_j, k_q) = 2\,\Big(\max_{\underline{\theta}\,\varepsilon\,\Lambda_{k_j}} \log \Pr(Y^T; \underline{\theta}) - \max_{\underline{\theta}\,\varepsilon\,\Lambda_{k_q}} \log \Pr\,(Y^T; \underline{\theta}\,)\Big)$$

and Λ_{k_j}, Λ_{k_q} are the sets of model parameters ($\underline{\theta}$) having k_j and k_q independent elements, respectively.

The latter term in equation (8) has an asymptotic $\chi^2_{k_j - k_q}$ distribution in the large sample limit. This is a statement of a result given in Baum and Petrie (1966). This result was established under the assumption that the models in the sets Λ_{k_j} and Λ_{k_q} possess an ergodic property. This property can be shown to hold when the unobserved Markov chain $X(t)$ is ergodic and the matrix R contains no zero elements.

As a consequence of this asymptotic convergence, the right-hand side of equation (8) is negative with non-zero probability, i.e. with the probability that $\chi^2_{k_j - k_q} > 2(k_j - k_q)$, in the large sample limit. The AIC criterion therefore has a non-zero probability of overestimating the true model order, so it is not a consistent criterion.

A number of criteria have been proposed which are similar to AIC, except for a weighting factor applied to the number of parameters that is an increasing function of T. Simulation evidence indicates that the tradeoff involved in using a consistent criterion is reduced sensitivity in the case of moderate sample lengths. In Section 6, a demonstration of the application of MLE to model identification from a sample of production data is provided, with AIC used in the estimation of model order.

5. AIC SENSITIVITY EXPERIMENT

Some evidence of the "sensitivity" of the AIC criterion for moderate length samples is provided by means of the following simulation study. Three 'true' models were simulated, with model orders 1, 2 and 3. The sample data length was 5000 samples, with the output distributions restricted to two values (i.e. binary observation, $Y(t) = 0$ or 1). Maximum likelihood estimates for models of order 1, 2 and 3 were obtained for each of the three 'true' models (model order 1 represents a single constant state, for which the MLE is the mean of the observations). The AIC was calculated for the nine resulting combinations. The entire experiment was replicated twice, and the results are summarized in Table 1.

TABLE 1: Model Order Estimation Using AIC

True Model Order	Replication	Order of Estimated Model: Order 1	Order 2	Order 3	AIC with true model
Order 1	1	1355.4	1358.3	1363.3	1355.8
	2	1407.0	1409.3	1414.3	1407.0
Order 2	1	1431.2	1426.6	1431.4	1428.5
	2	1450.3	1444.2	1448.1	1445.3
Order 3	1	1485.7	1473.2	1476.9	1478.8
	2	1481.1	1467.9	1472.3	1474.0

Note: a) Values tabulated are 1/2 AIC.
b) Underlined item indicates model order selected by AIC.
c) Run length = 5000 samples (binary observations).
d) Last column shows value of AIC with true model parameters.

The table indicates that model order estimation for moderate length samples is questionable. The order 1 and 2 models were correctly identified, but the order 3 model was mistakenly identified as order 2. This behaviour is not surprising in view of the sample size; the full information MLE (i.e. with the model states observed) showed significant errors. The "sensitivity" of the AIC is evident from the table. In the case of true model order 3, the AIC value for estimated order 3 was smaller than for order 1, i.e. although an error was made, the true model order was clearly the second choice in both replications.

6. MODEL IDENTIFICATION: AN APPLICATION

To illustrate the flexibility of the POMC model, and the use of MLE and the AIC model order estimation criterion on "real" data, the following application is described.

Observations were obtained from an incandescent lamp manufacturing process, which can be characterized as a high speed (roughly 3000 units per hour) transfer line. Two separate points were monitored in this line, with binary observations indicating acceptable or defective subassemblies. Results of the analysis of three separate one hour samples at each of the two monitoring points are reported here.

POMC models of order 1, 2 and 3 were estimated from each sample separately. Several starting values for P and R were considered to ensure a global maximum of the likelihood was found, using a variation of the Baum algorithm discussed earlier.

The results of the application of the AIC criterion, and machine performance statistics (proportion of acceptable items for each model state; and, duration of each state as obtained from the estimated transition matrix) are reported in Table 2. Generally, the model of order 1 (corresponding to a constant state, or "statistical control") was not indicated. The exception was the first sample from monitor 1, where the AIC was approximately equal for the order 1 and 2 cases. Note that the model of order 2 identified from this sample shows the second state as transient (state two was the indicated state in the initial distribution).

TABLE 2: Model Identification Results

Monitor Number	Sample Length	Observed Mean Performance	Model Order (AIC)	Performance Level By State			Mean Duration By State		
				1	2	3	1	2	3
1	2450	.91	2	.91	.81	---	∞	111	---
			or 1	.91	---	---	∞	---	---
	2650	.90	2	.91	0	---	500	5	---
	2600	.81	3	.98	.83	.58	19	125	12
2	2400	.89	2	.92	.83	---	333	167	---
	2950	.90	3	1.	.91	.87	37	125	500
			or 2	.95	.87	---	167	333	---
	2650	.88	2	.93	.82	---	125	111	---

Note: a) The first sample for monitor 1 and second for monitor 2 showed two AIC values which were approximately equal.

b) "Performance" implies proportion of good items produced in each state.

c) "Duration" is in units of machine cycles (items produced).

Several general conclusions can be made regarding this study: (1) significantly different performance levels can be discerned from production data using the POMC model; (2) temporary shifts in performance, representing both deterioration and improvement in product quality, are clearly evident, indicating the dynamic structure of the POMC model is of definite value in quality monitoring; (3) the structure of the Markov chain estimated from production data offers some insight into the nature of the "assignable causes" influencing performance (e.g. transient or recurrent, magnitude and duration of effect on product quality).

The use of a POMC model, and the maximum likelihood approach to model identification, can provide a flexible and sensitive measure of changing production states, but a source of extra information (such as more intensive sampling when degradation is indicated, or direct operator surveillance) is required to infer the cause of such change.

REFERENCES

Akaike, H. (1974). A new look at the statistical identification model, IEEE Trans. Auto. Control, 19: 716-723.

Andelman, D. and Reeds, J. (1982). On the cryptanalysis of rotor machines and substitution-permutation networks, IEEE Trans. on Infor. Theory, 28: 578-584.

Baum, L.E. and Eagon, J.A. (1967). An inequality with applications to statistical estimation for probabilistic functions of a Markov process and to a model for ecology, Bull. Amer. Math. Soc., 73: 360-363.

Baum, L.E. and Petrie, T. (1966). Statistical inference for probabilistic functions of finite state Markov chains, Ann. Math. Statist., 37: 1554-1563.

Baum, L.E., Petrie, T., Soules, G. and Weiss, N. (1970). A maximization technique occurring in the statistical analysis of probabilistic functions of Markov chains, Ann. Math. Statist., 41: 164-171.

Billingsley, P. (1961). Statistical Inference for Markov Processes, Univ. Chicago Press.

Dempster, A.P., Laird, N.M., and Rubin, D.B. (1977). Maximum likelihood from incomplete data via the EM algorithm (with discussion), J.R. Statist. Soc. B, 39: 1-38.

Katz, R.W. (1981). On some criteria for estimating the order of a Markov chain, Technometrics, 23: 243-249.

Liporace, L.A. (1982). Maximum likelihood estimation for multivariate observations of Markov sources, IEEE Trans. on Infor. Theory, 28: 729-734.

Pruscha, H. (1976). Maximum likelihood estimation in linear learning models, Biometrika, 63: 537-542.

Rabiner, L.R. Juang, B-H, Levinson, S.E., and Sondhi, M.M. (1985). Some properties of continuous hidden Markov model representations, AT & T Bell Lab. Tech. J., 64: 1251-1270.

Wax, M. and Kailath, T. (1985). Detection of signals by information theoretic criteria, IEEE Trans. on Acoustics, Speech, and Signal Proc., 33: 387-392.

Whiting, R.G. (1985). Quality monitoring in manufacturing systems: a partially observed Markov chain approach, Ph.D. dissertation, Dept. Indust. Eng., Univ. of Toronto.

Whiting, R.G., Pickett, E.E. ,. (1984). Linear convergence of a maximization technique occuring in the MLE of partially observed Markov chains, Working Paper 84-03, Dept. of Industrial Engineering, University of Toronto.

RANK VERSIONS OF MINIMAX CONTRASTS FOR TESTING AGAINST MULTIVARIATE TRENDS

Richard Pincus, Berlin (GDR)

1. INTRODUCTION

During a drug trial some blood constituents like erythrocytes, leukocytes, glucose etc. are measured in k groups of individuals which have been treated with different dosages $D_1 < D_2 < \ldots < D_k$, say. Denoting the group sizes by n_i, $i=1,\ldots,k$, we can write the observations

$$\begin{array}{l} y_{11}, \ldots, y_{1n_1} \\ \cdot \\ \cdot \\ \cdot \\ y_{k1}, \ldots, y_{kn_k} . \end{array}$$

Here y_{ij} stands for the p-dimensional vector of observed constituents of the j-th individuum in the i-th group. Interpreting the y_{ij}'s as realizations of random variables with distribution P_i, $i=1,\ldots,k$, we are interested in testing the

$$\text{Hypothesis: } P_1 = P_2 = \ldots = P_k , \tag{1}$$

against the

$$\text{Alternative: } P_1 < P_2 < \ldots < P_k \quad \text{or} \quad P_1 > P_2 > \ldots > P_k , \tag{2}$$

i.e. homogeneity against trend (or ordered) alternatives.

Here (2) means that for each of the p components separately there exists a stochastic (increasing or decreasing) ordering.

2. UNIVARIATE CONTRASTS

2.1. Normally distributed variables

If the number of observed components reduces to one, and additionally we assume the y_{ij} to be normally distributed with

$$E\, y_{ij} = \mu_i$$

and

$$\mathrm{Cov}\, y_{ij} = \sigma^2 \quad ,i=1,\ldots,k\ ;\ j=1,\ldots,n_i\ ,$$

then the hypothesis becomes

$$\mu_1 = \mu_2 = \ldots = \mu_k\ , \tag{3}$$

and the alternative

$$\mu_1 < \mu_2 < \ldots < \mu_k \ \text{ or } \ \mu_1 > \mu_2 > \ldots > \mu_k\ . \tag{4}$$

Abelson and Tukey (1963) considered the class of statistics

$$\sum_i c_i\, n_i (y_{i.} - y_{..})/s \tag{5}$$

or its square, respectively, the so called **linear contrasts**, and showed the existence of an optimal choice of $c_1, \ldots, c_k$ which maximizes the minimum power among all tests, based on linear contrasts. The $y_{i.}$, $y_{..}$ and s are defined by

$$y_{i.} = \sum_j y_{ij} \ /n_i\ ,$$

$$y_{..} = \sum_i \sum_j y_{ij}\ /n \quad , n=n_1 + \ldots + n_k\ ,$$

$$s = \sum_i \sum_j (y_{ij} - y_{i.})^2\ /(n-k).$$

Schaafsma (1966) gave an explicite expression for the optimal c's, namely

$$c_i = \left[-d_i^{1/2}\ (d_k - d_i)^{1/2} + d_{i-1}^{1/2}\ (d_k - d_{i-1})^{1/2} \right] /n_i \quad ,i=1,\ldots,k, \tag{6}$$

where $d_i = n_1 + \ldots + n_i$, $d_0 = 0$.

Actually Schaafsma used a test statistic equivalent to

$$\sum_i c_i\, n_i\ (y_{i.} - y_{..})/\sum_i \sum_j (y_{ij} - y_{..})^2 \tag{7}$$

or its square, respectively, which gives a **Most Stringent Somewhere Most Powerful Test.**

2.2. Rank versions

Now we drop the normality assumptions and denote by r_{ij} the rank of y_{ij} among all n observations. Consequently we denote

$$r_{i.} = \sum_j r_{ij} / n_i \quad , \quad i=1,\ldots,k,$$

and

$$r_{..} = (n+1)/2.$$

The rank analogon of the statistics (7) is given by

$$\sum_i c_i \; n_i \; (r_{i.} - r_{..}) \tag{8}$$

(Note that the denominator is a constant).

If the sample size n tends to infinity, $n \to \infty$, and n_i /n $\to \lambda_i$ >0, i=1,...,k, then the linear rank statistics (8) tends to a normal distribution. More exactly

$$\frac{\sum_i c_i \; n_i \; (r_{i.} - r_{..})}{n^{1/2} \; (\sum_i n_i \; c_i^2 \;)^{1/2} \quad ((n+1)/12)^{1/2}} \longrightarrow N(0,1).$$

This can be seen by writing (8) as a permutation statistic $\sum_i \sum_j c_i \; (r_{ij} - r_{..})$, see Puri and Sen (1971), ch. 3.4.

Considering **local alternatives**

$$\mu_{in} - \mu_i = \Delta_i / n^{1/2} \quad , \Delta_i > 0, \; i=2,\ldots,k, \tag{9}$$

then the $r_{i.}$ are asymptotically normally distributed and the choice of (6) has an interpretation as minimax solution among linear rank permutation statistics.

For non local alternatives such a justification is not available, a more natural choice of the weights c_i would be then

$$c_i = i \; , \; i=1,\ldots,k. \tag{10}$$

3. MULTIVARIATE CONTRASTS

3.1. Normally distributed variables

For normally distributed multivariate observations y_{ij} with

$$E\, y_{ij} = \mu_i$$

and

$$\mathrm{Cov}\, y = \Sigma, \quad \Sigma > 0, \; i=1,\ldots,k \; ; \; j=1,\ldots,n_i \; ,$$

one can construct linear combinations $a'y_{ij}$, say. Forming with these new univariate variables the linear contrast (5) gives

$$a' \textstyle\sum_i c_i n_i (y_{i.} - y_{..}) / (a'Sa) \quad , \tag{11}$$

where

$$y_{i.} = \textstyle\sum_j y_{ij} / n_i \; ,$$

$$y_{..} = \textstyle\sum_i \sum_j y_{ij} \; / n \; ,$$

$$S = \textstyle\sum_i \sum_j (y_{ij} - y_{i.})(y_{ij} - y_{i.})' / (n-k)$$

Hothorn and Pincus (1987) chose the linear combination a so, that (11) becomes as large as possible, i.e.they considered the statistic

$$T^2 = \max_a \frac{a'(\sum_i c_i n_i (y_{i.} - y_{..}))(\sum_i c_i n_i (y_{i.} - y_{..}))'a}{a' S a}$$

Under the hypothesis of homogeneity of the k groups, $\frac{1}{p} T^2 / (\sum_i c_i^2 n_i)$ has an $F_{p,n-k-p+1}$ -distribution. The same idea might be applied to Schaafsma's statistic (7) as well. This gives

$$B^2 = \max_a \frac{a'(\sum_i c_i n_i (y_{i.} - y_{..}))(\sum_i c_i n_i (y_{i.} - y_{..}))'a}{a'(\sum_i \sum_j (y_{ij} - y_{..})(y_{ij} - y_{..})')a} \; , \tag{12}$$

up to a constant $\sum_i c_i^2 n_i$ being $B_{(n-p)/2,\, p/2}$ -distributed.

3.2. Rank versions

Let now denote by $r_{ij}^{(l)}$, l=1,...,p, the rank of the l-th component of y_{ij} among all n l-th components, and by r_{ij} the vector $(r_{ij}^{(1)},...,r_{ij}^{(p)})'$. The nxp-matrix formed by the n row-vectors

$$(r_{ij}^{(1)}-(n+1)/2,...,r_{ij}^{(p)}-(n+1)/2),\ i=1,...,k,\ j=1,...,n_i\ ,$$

will be denoted by R. Finally we write c for the n-vector $(c_1/n_1^{1/2},...,c_1/n_1^{1/2},...,c_k/n_k^{1/2})'$.

The rank version of (12) with $y_{i.}$ and $y_{..}$ replaced by $r_{i.}$ and $r_{..}$ respectively, can be written as

$$c'R(R'R)^{-1}R'c. \qquad (13)$$

Applying the technique of Puri and Sen (1971), ch. 5.1, for multivariate permutation tests one can easily show, that if the n_i tend to infinity, the limit distribution of (13), normalized by $\sum_i c_i^2 n_i$, is a Chi-Square distribution with p degrees of freedom under the hypothesis. Especially for $c_i=i$, i=1,...,k this limit distribution holds for

$$(\textstyle\sum_i c_i n_i (r_{i.}-r_{..}))'(\sum_i\sum_j (r_{ij}-r_{..})(r_{ij}-r_{..})')^{-1}(\sum_i c_i n_i (r_{i.}-r_{..}))/\sum_i i^2 n_i$$

REFERENCES

Abelson, R.P. and Tukey, J.W. (1963). Efficient utilization of non numeric information in quantitative analysis. Ann Math. Statist. 34, 1374-1369.

Hothorn, L. and Pincus R. (1987). Use of minimax contrasts for multivariate tests for ordered alternatives with application in a toxicological problem. Submitted to Biom. J.

Puri, M.L. and Sen, P.K. (1971). Nonparametric Methods in Multivariate Analysis. Wiley, New York.

Schaafsma, W. (1966). Hypothesis Testing Problems with the Alternative Restricted by a Number of Inequalities. Univ. Groningen.

DATA ANALYSIS IN THE FREQUENCY DOMAIN: WIND- AND AIR-POLLUTION INTERACTION IN VIENNA

Wolfgang POLASEK, Institute for Statistics,
University of Vienna, A-1010 WIEN Universitatsstr. 5.

SUMMARY

The paper describes the interaction of SO_2 and windspeed at 5 different sites in Vienna for the year 1977. A multivariate time-series model is estimated for half-hourly data according to Akaikes's information criterion AIC. The estimates are used to derive the relative-power- contributions in a multivariate spectral analysis and to study the pollution interaction in the frequency domain. The interaction pattern between wind and SO_2 is summarized in a path diagram.

1. INTRODUCTION

Monitoring air pollution data has become increasingly important in recent years and many approaches for data analyses have been suggested. In order to study interaction over time and space, a large data base and multivariate models are needed. This paper uses a multivariate time-series framework and the so-called relative-power-contribution (PC) analysis developed by Akaike (1968) to describe SO_2-pollution and wind in Vienna.

Whilst univariate analyses of pollution data have sometimes stimulated the development of time-series techniques (e.g. Box and Tiao 1975), hardly any multivariate studies have been carried out. This is partly due to the difficult nature of pollution data (outliers, collinearity, and non-stationary influences) which makes any multivariate study highly sensitive to slight changes in the data. In order to model subtle interactions it is necessary to find a long and uninterrupted series of observations on air pollution and weather on several sites simultaneously. This study concentrates on SO_2 and wind interaction, since these variables only are recorded at sites in Vienna which allows a spatial interaction analysis. There is little choice of measurement sites: No distinction between roadside and background-pollution measurement sites can be found. It is surprising that, in a decade of increasing environmental interests, Vienna has no accurate and continous measurements of air pollution data. Hence I hope that this study will stimulate demand for a better air pollution data base in Vienna.

Section 2 describes the AIC estimation technique for vector autoregressive processes and then presents the relative power contribution analysis. Section 3 contains the major empirical results of this study based on path diagrams which summarizes the power contribution analysis. The final section lists some concluding remarks.

2. MULTIVARIATE TIME-SERIES MODELS

In what follows we briefly outline two methods for analysing the dynamic properties of a multivariate time-series model. First, we describe the so-called MAICE approach (minimum AIC estimate) for estimating a vector autoregressive (VAR) process, which is part of the TIMSAC-78 programs of Akaike et al. (1979). These estimates are the basis for power contribution (PC-) analysis, which can be viewed as a special type of causality analysis in the frequency domain.

A special class of multivariate time-series models, the vector AR models, are used frequently in econometrics and the technical sciences. The multivariate extension of the so-called Box-Jenkins (1970) method uses patterns within the autocorrelation function and cross-correlation function for identifying the orders of the time-series models (see e.g. Tiao and Tsay 1983). The development of information criteria (AIC, BIC, etc.) has encouraged the "automatic" approach ofmodel selection.

The vector AR(p) model for the K-dimensional time series $X(t) = (x_1(t),...,x_K(t))'$ has the form

$$X(t) - A_1X(t-1) - \dots - A_pX(t-p) = u(t) \ , \qquad (2.1)$$

where the A_i's are (K x K) parameter matrices, and u(t) is the multivariate white-noise error term which is assumed to have the following moments:

$$E[u(t)] = 0 \ , \ Var[u(t)] = \Sigma , \ \ t = 1,...,T, \qquad (2.2)$$

and Σ is positive definite. Also u(t) and u(s) are independent for $s \neq t$. Furthermore, we assume that the process (2.1) is stationary, which implies that the determinant of vector polynomial is nonzero inside the unit circle:

$$| I_K - A_1z - \dots - A_pz^p | = 0 \ \text{for} \ |z| \leq 1 . \qquad (2.3)$$

The estimation of the parameters A_i in (2.1) and Σ in (2.2) and the order p by the MAICE procedure requires us to pre-specify a maximum lag length p_{max}. Calculating the AIC (Akaike's (1973) Information Criterion) statistics defined by

$$AIC(p) = \ln | \Sigma_p | + 2K^2p/T , \qquad (2.4)$$

the minimum AIC-estimate of the order $\hat{p}$ is determined by

$$AIC(\hat{p}) = \min [AIC(1), \dots ,AIC(p_{max})] . \qquad (2.5)$$

This method can be viewed as extension of the maximum likelihood procedure for models with increasing numbers of parameters. The first term reflects the estimated log-likelihood of the process, which is a decreasing function of the rsidual variance. The second term in (2.4) is the so-called penalty function which is an increasing function of the number of parameters. In the case of AIC it is twice the number of parameters. The AIC overestimates the lag length p of the AR-process, whilst the BIC which uses ln(T) in the penalty term, and is defined by

$$BIC(p) = \ln | \Sigma_p | + K^2p \ln(T)/T , \qquad (2.6)$$

estimates p consistently. The reason for using AIC and not BIC is that BIC penalizes the order of multivariate models more than AIC and therefore produces AR-models with almost no interactions at all. In particular, Granger-type (1969) causality measures can be affected by this problem, since they compare residual variances of univariate and multivariate models.

2.1 Relative Power Contribution Analysis

Relative power contribution analysis is based on the estimation of a multivariate spectral matrix by a vector autoregressive process. We shall outline this approach only briefly. Further details can be found in Akaike (1968). A vector AR(p) process (2.1) whose order has been correctly determined by MAICE is capable of representing all the dynamics of a multivariate time series. Turning to the frequency domain, the information for the spectral matrix is contained in the vector AR-polynomial

$$A(s) = I_K - \sum_{m=1}^{p} A_m (s) . \qquad (2.7)$$

A spectral analysis of the process (2.1), which requires the Fourier- transform of the autocorrelation function, leads, after some algebra, to the following equation in the frequency domain:

$$A(f)\, P_x(f)\, A(f)^* = \Sigma . \qquad (2.8)$$

Here the *-superscript denotes conjugate transposed matrices, whilst A(f) is the z-transform of the AR-polynomial (2.7). Also

$$A(f) = I_K - \sum_{m=1}^{p} A(s) \exp(i2\pi fm), \qquad i = \sqrt{-1}, \qquad 0 \leq f \leq 1/2 ; \qquad (2.9)$$

and this has to be of full rank for any frequency f. Details of cross-spectral estimation can be found e.g. in Jenkins-Watts (1968). The spectral matrix $P_x(f)$ of the process (2.1) is now given by inverting the matrices A(f) from the left and from the right:

$$P_x(f) = A^{-1}(f)\, \Sigma\, A^{*\,-1}(f) . \qquad (2.10)$$

Since Σ is the diagonal covariance matrix of a white noise process (assumption 2.2), each univariate spectrum on the diagonal of the left-hand side is given as a sum of "power contributions" (PC) from variable i to variable j at frequency f, consisting of K elements given by

$$PC[\,i \to j\,](f) = |a^{ij}(f)|^2 s_{ii} , \qquad i,j = 1,\ldots,K, \qquad (2.11)$$

where a^{ij} denotes the (i,j)-th element of the inverse matrix A at frequency f and s_{ii} is the i-th diagonal element of Σ. The relative PC's are defined as the power contributions (2.12) divided by the estimated spectrum of variable i:

$$PC\%[\,i \to j\,](f) = PC[\,i \to j\,](f) \,/\, \hat{p}_i(f) , \qquad (2.12)$$

The estimated spectrum of the i-th variable should be the sum over all power contributions:

$$\hat{p}_i(f) = \Sigma_j\, PC[i \to j](f) . \qquad (2.13)$$

It is convenient to plot all the relative PC's for one variable in one box as is done in Figures 3.1 a-d. Note that the power contributions can be viewed as special types of causality measures in the frequency domain. A discussion on the relationship between this PC-approach and Geweke's (1982) feedback measures in the frequency domain can be found in Kunitomo (1984).

3. INTERACTION ANALYSIS

The results of the relative PC-analyses of Viennese air pollution are summarized in Figurs 3.1 to 3.5 by path diagrams based on different sets of variables. Fig 3.1.f describes the interaction of the SO_2-variables at 5 different places (HW: Hohe Warte, GG: Gerichtsgasse, St: St. Stephan, DT: Donauturm, and AP: Arthaberplatz) and summarizes the influence pattern in the form of a path diagram. Dotted lines represent "faint" influences and normal lines represent "average" influences. The magnitude of the influence corresponds to the area in a relative "PC-box". We can detect interactions between sites in the west of Vienna and unidirectional influences from the west-central to the east.

Fig. 3.2 contains the SO_2-interaction analysis for the same 5 places as in Fig. 3.1.f, but only for hourly data (192 observations). The results of our analysis may have been influenced by the length of the recording intervals. However the similarity of the path diagrams leads us to suspect that such influences are minor.

Fig. 3.3 contains the results of the PC-analysis for windspeed variables. Since windspeed and SO_2 are generally not recorded at the same sites, we have chosen the closest available sites for this purpose. The path diagram shows dominant interactions in the north-south direction along the Danube-valley.

Fig. 3.4 is the joint 10-dimensional analysis between the 5 SO_2 variables and the 5 windspeed variables on an hourly basis (windspeed is recorded only hourly). The path diagram shows influences of wind and SO_2 by differently marked arrows. Fig. 3.5 contains the same analysis, but only for 3 sites (St. Stephan and Gerichtsgasse are left out). The results of the 3-site and the 5-site analysis seems to be reasonably comparable. However, the spatial interaction is much richer for the 5-site analysis, while the wind/SO_2 interaction between HW and DT seems to dominate the 3-site analysis. Increasing the sites (and hence the dimensions) does not seem to be a way of validating lower dimensional findings. Interaction profiles tend to be richer with more dimensions. To what degrees these are artefacts created by multicollinearities or nonstationarities, is difficult to check with the present data. Cautious interpretation is advisable, since simple 2-dimensional models for the sites Gerichtsgassse/Strebersdorf does not indicate any interaction. However, the previous 10-dimensional analysis gave a faint indication of such influences.

The same phenomenon can be found for a 2-dimensional analysis between SO_2 and windspeed at the site St. Stephan. The "curse of dimensionality" seems to be at work also in a frequency domain data analysis. It is too soon to pass judgement on the usefulness of this approach, and further applications and simulations are needed to explore its applicability to pollution data.

4. CONCLUSIONS

As a major result, we see that high dimensional models exhibit more interactions between wind- and SO_2 -variables than low dimensional ones. This is true for purely SO_2 and wind models as well as for mixed models. Path diagrams help to summarize the results of the power contribution analysis.

The frequency-based exploration shows that most interactions between variables take place at low frequencies, without any regular cyclical influences. This contrasts a similar analysis in Tokyo (see Polasek and Kishino 1984), where a12 hour cycle had been observed because of the dominant daily land-sea wind cycle. Influence directions in Vienna are generally from the west to the east, or from the north-west to the south-east. This corresponds also with the dominating wind direction during the 5 winter-days of the observation period.

As a general result we find that a multivariate time-series analysis associated with a PC analysis is a useful tool to uncover the dynamic and spatial interaction of air pollution variables. The results are not always convincing because time-series estimates are generally very sensitive to any nonstationary disturbances which can be frequently found in air pollution data. Nevertheless, useful information can be provided by a frequency based path analysis, particular in addition to descriptive or exploratory studies which are usually carried out in the time domain.

REFERENCES

AKAIKE H. (1968). On the Use of A Linear Model for the Identification of Feedback Systems. Annals Inst. Statistical Mathematics.: 425-439.

AKAIKE H. (1973). Information Theory and An Extension of the Maximum Likelihood Principle. In B.N. Petrov and F. Czaki (eds.), 2nd Int. Symp. on Information Theory. Budapest, Academiai Kiado.

AKAIKE H., G. KITAGAWA, E. ARAHATA and F. TADA (1979). TIMSAC-78, Computer Science Monograph 11. The Inst. of Statistical Mathematics, Tokyo.

BOX G.E.P. and G. JENKINS (1970). Time Series Analysis, Forecasting and Control. Holden Day, San Francisco.

BOX G.E.P. and TIAO G.C. (1975). Intervention Analysis with Applications to Economic and Environmental Problems. JASA 70: 70-79.

GEWEKE J. (1982). Measurement of Linear Dependence and Feedback Between Multiple Time Series. JASA 77: 304-324.

GRANGER C.W.J. (1969). Investigating Causal Relations by Econometric Models and Cross Spectral Methods. Econometrica 37: 424-438.

JENKINS G. and D. WATTS (1968). Spectral Analysis of Time Series. Holden Day, San Francisco.

KUNITOMO N. (1984). Measures of Granger-Causality in Multivariate Auto- regressive Time Series Models. University of Tokyo, mimeo.

POLASEK W. and H. KISHINO (1984). A Multivariate Time Series Study of Tokyo Air Pollution Data. Inst. for Statistics, Vienna, mimeo.

TIAO G.C. and R.S. TSAY (1983). Multiple Time Series and Extended Sample Cross-Correlations. J. of Business & Economic Statistics 1: 43-56.

Fig 3.1 a: Site HOHE WARTE (HW)

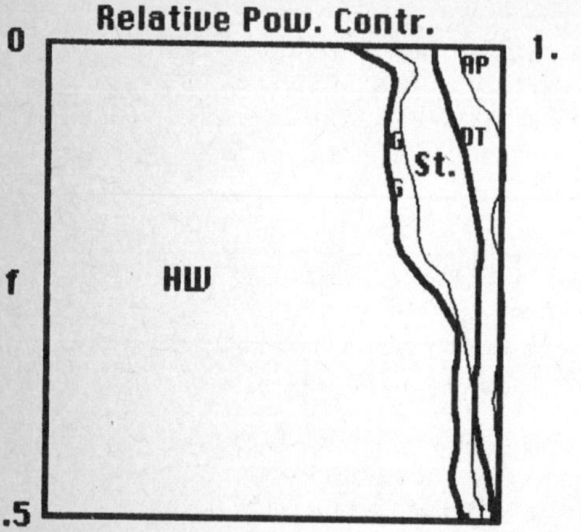

Fig 3.1.b: Site GERICHTSGASSE (GG)

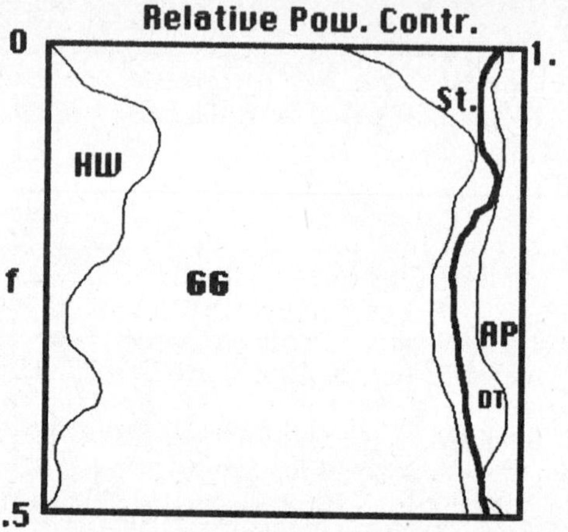

Fig. 3.1.c. Site St. STEPHAN (St.)

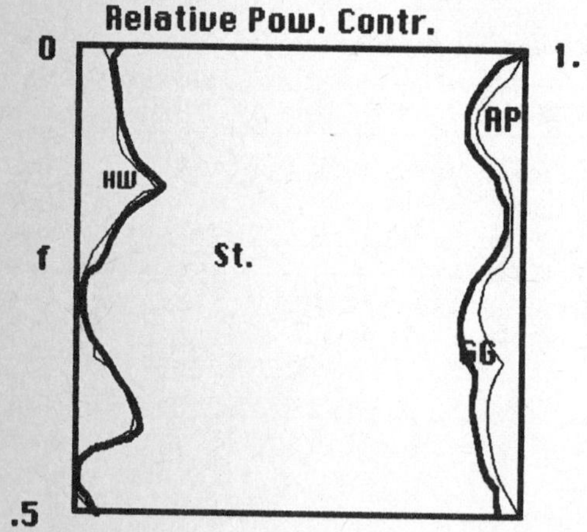

Fig. 3.1 d. Site DONAUTURM (DT)

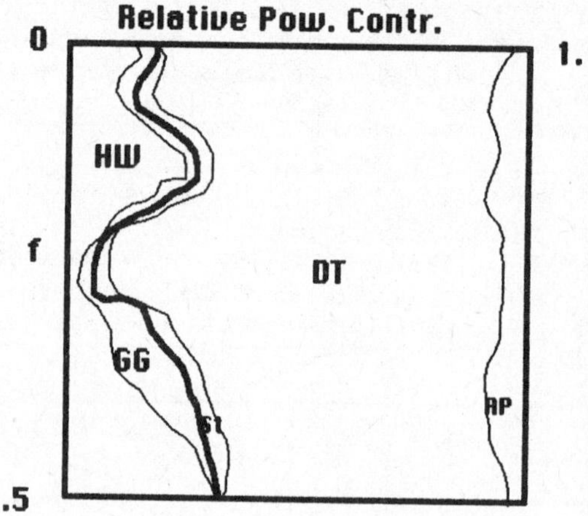

Fig. 3.1.e Site ARTHABERPLATZ (AP)

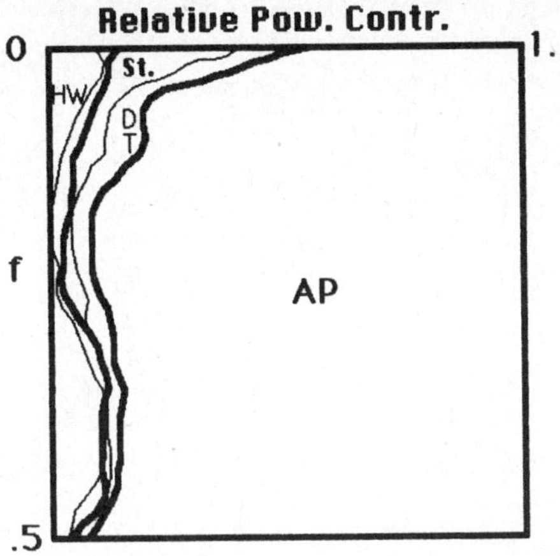

Fig. 3.1.f Path Diagram
SO2 -half hourly

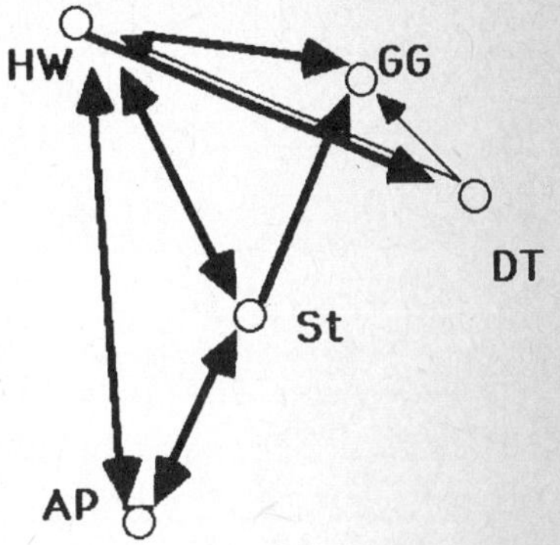

Fig. 3.2 Path Diagram
SO2 - hourly data

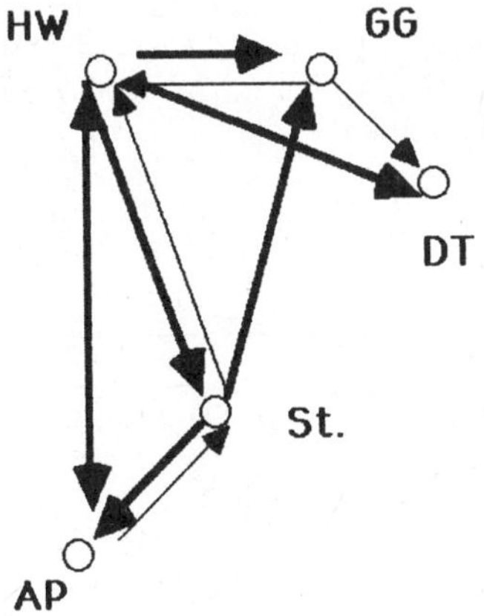

Fig 3.3 Path Diagram
Windspeed

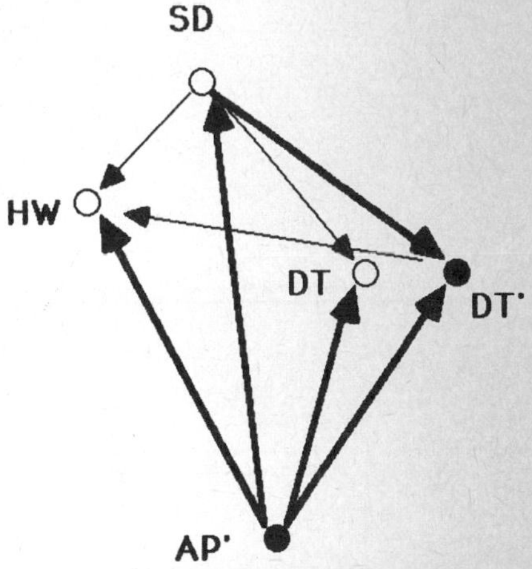

Fig 3.4 Path Diagram
5 Sites WS/SO2 - interaction

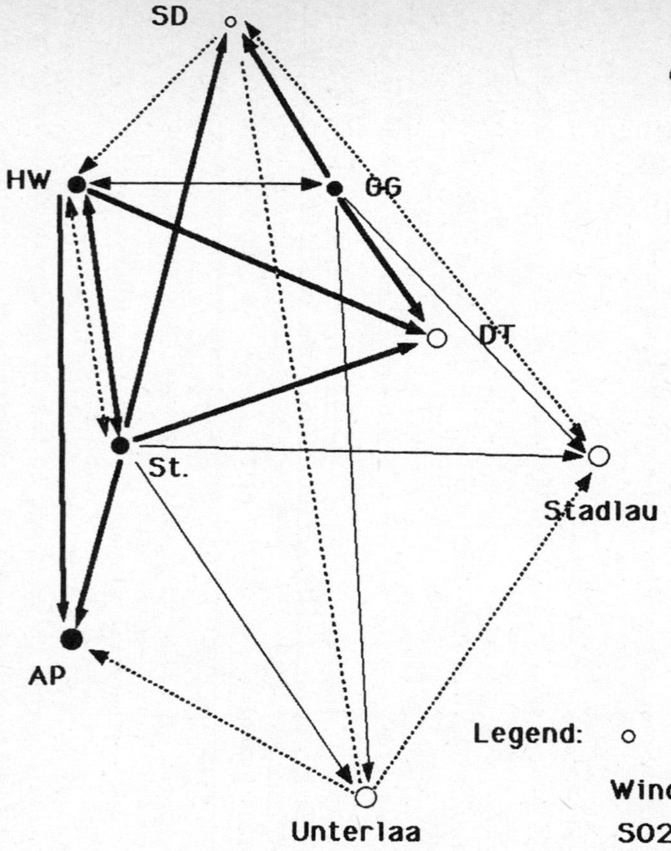

Fig 3.5 Path Diagram
3 sites WS/SO2 interaction

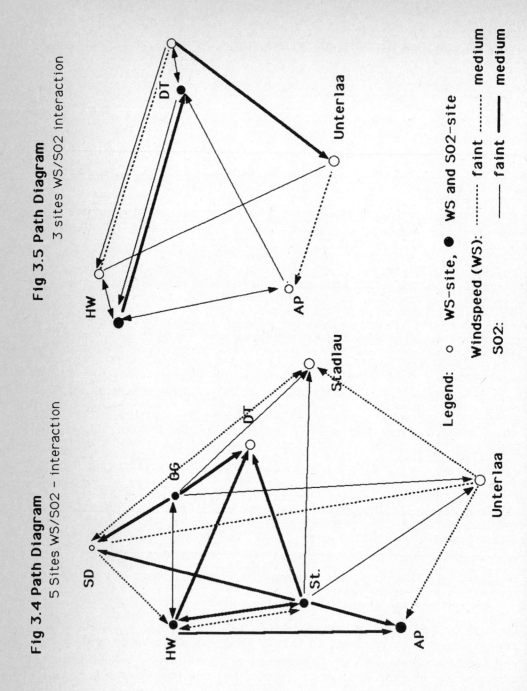

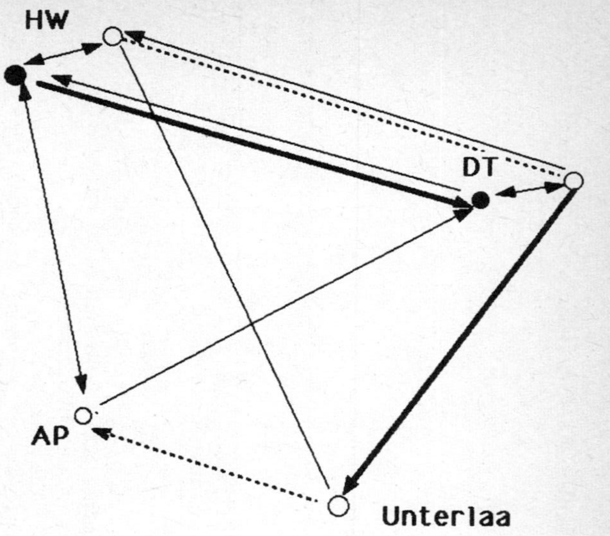

Legend: ○ WS-site, ● WS and SO2-site

Windspeed (WS): ········ faint ········ medium

SO2: —— faint ━━ medium

COMPARING CLASSICAL STATISTICAL CONTEXTS FOR GROUP MEMBERSHIP DISCUSSIONS

Willem Schaafsma
Department of Mathematics RUG, P.O.Box 800, Groningen, The Netherlands

1. INTRODUCTION

When consulted by a patient, the medical doctor will discuss the patient's group membership on the basis of his vector $z \in \mathbb{R}^p$ of signs and symptoms. Suppose that k mutually exclusive categories C(1),...,C(k) are of interest, e.g. k unordered diagnostic categories, or k ordered prognostic categories referring to remaining life length (degrees of malignancy). As there are many situations where a categorical diagnosis, prognosis, or gradation is doubtful, the medical doctor might prefer probabilistic terminology. The subjectivists have paid considerable attention to (1) the elicitation of personal probabilities, and (2) the performance of persons or systems generating such probabilities. The main reason for the use of subjective probabilities is that the form of much information is not suitable for a classical statistical approach while the model underlying such an approach is almost always questionable.

Though we accept the arguments in the preceding sentence, we do not accept subjectivism as the panacea. Instead of eliciting subjective opinions, we will try to elicit the underlying statistical information. If this is technically impossible, e.g. because an interpretation of literature is involved, then an elicited opinion may sometimes be replaced by equivalent artificial data. This is the basis of the procedures for incorporating expert opinions, implemented in the POSCON program to be discussed.

The present paper starts from the assumption, usual in discriminant analysis and pattern recognition, that the statistical data consist of : (1) the vector z of scores for the patient under investigation, (2) similar complete vectors of scores $x_{h1},\dots,x_{hn(h)} \in \mathbb{R}^p$ for an independent random sample of $n(h) = n_h$ elements from category $C_h(h=1,\dots,k)$. (The forthcoming POSCON book will consider some other forms as well, e.g. special forms of expert opinion.)

As indicated above, we adhere to the relative frequency definition of probability. Given the vector of scores z, the patient may be compared with other patients having approximately the same vector of scores. The probability that this patient if from C_h is a mathematical idealization of the relative frequency of category h in a reference population of hypothetical patients, with score vectors suitably chosen around z. This loose formulation shows that further specifications are needed if a mathematical definition is required of the vector $\rho(z) = (\rho_1(z),\dots,\rho_k(z))^T$ of the patient's "true" probabilities. Note that the meaning of $\rho(z)$ depends on the context chosen and on the patient's vector of scores z, rather than on the patient itself: the actual group membership of the patient is not determined by a probability vector but by a categorical statement.

As both the definition and the estimation of the vector $\rho(z)$ of the patient's probabilities depend on the mathematical context, the following questions appear: which is the most appropriate context, how many and which variables should be included in the analysis, etc. This is a sophisticated form of the problem of the reference class (Reichenbach, 1949).

In practice choosing the context is necessary if one wants to use one of the available programs for estimating $\rho(z)$, especially because some of these programs have many options for model specification. As the estimates depend on the context chosen, one will have to compare the performances of the underlying models. This comparison will have to be based on the data at hand, i.e. (x,z). The definition of adequate concepts of performance,however, may involve theoretical constructs like the 'actual'performance to be observed if, for fixed background information x, the model is used for making probability statements for many future individuals. This is where literature about subjective probability is useful (Section 2).

After having discussed some scoring functions, we shall show that life would be perfect if all population parameters were known (Section 3). We have already remarked that in practice we will have to rely on the data (x,z) at hand. The POSCON project is one of the attempts to develop adequate classical statistical methodology and corresponding computer programs (Section 4). The output of the POSCON program involves standard errors for the probability estimates. These standard errors can be used to discuss the performance of the POSCON context chosen. This enables the user to make a deliberate choice of context (Section 5). The paper provides a framework for discussing the effect of data reduction (Section 6).

2. BIAS AND ACCURACY OF PROBABILITY STATEMENTS

Suppose that a person or system has generated assessments $r_1,\dots,r_m$, on the basis of the vectors of scores $z_1,\dots,z_m$ of a large number (m) of individuals whose group membership labels $h_1,\dots,h_m$ are known to the researcher. Of course $r_i \in S_k = \{\rho \in \mathbb{R}^k;\ \rho_i \geq 0;\ \Sigma_i\rho_i = 1\}$, the unit simplex in k-dimensional space; $h_i \in \{1,\dots,k\}$, and $z_i \in \mathbb{R}^P (i=1,\dots,m)$.

Calibration. If one considers the individuals (i) with $r_{ih} > .90$, say, then (each of these individuals having an estimated C_h-membership probability of no less than 90%) the relative frequency

$$\#\{i\ ;\ r_{ih} > .90,\ h_i = h\}/\#\{i\ ;\ r_{ih} > .90\}$$

should not be (much) smaller than .90. Otherwise 'overconfidence' is displayed by the assessor.

Accuracy. Let $c : \{1,\dots,k\} \longrightarrow S_k$ be defined by $c(h)_j = \delta_{h,j} = 1(0)$ if $h = (\neq) j$. Note that one would like to have r_i close to $c_i = c(h_i)$. This suggests to use the Brier (1950) score

$$m^{-1}\Sigma_{i=1}^m \|r_i - c_i\|^2$$

to characterize the over-all lack of agreement between the true group membership c_i and the probability assessment $r_i (i=1,\ldots,n)$.

If the k categories display a certain ordering, e.g. because they correspond to the division of remaining life length into k successive intervals, then a slightly different scoring rule is indicated (Epstein, 1969).

For further reading, e.g. about other concepts of performance, we refer to Savage (1971), Staël von Holstein - Murphy (1978), the series of papers by Habbema et al. (1978, 1981), and Kahneman et al. (1984).

3. THE PERFORMANCE OF THE VECTOR P OF THE PATIENT'S TRUE PROBABILITIES

If the mathematical context would completely and correctly specify the joint distribution of H, or $I = c(H)$, and Z, then one would not be troubled by statistical uncertainties, errors due to misspecifications, etc. Thus, let us assume that the individuals to be considered are taken at random from some very large population for which all relative frequencies of interest are known. Let (H,Z) or (I,Z) describe category number and vector of scores for such an individual.

The population analogue of the Brier score,

$$E\|R - I\|^2 = E\, E(\|r(Z) - c(H)\|^2 | Z),$$

is minimal if the function $r : \mathbb{R}^p \rightarrow S_k$ is chosen such that the outcome r(z) of $R = r(Z)$ is equal to the vector

$$\rho(z) = E(c(H)|Z=z) = E(I|Z=z)$$

of the patient's true probabilities

$$\rho_h(z) = E(I_h|Z=z) = P(H=h|Z=z)$$

(h=1,...,k). This result displays that the Brier scoring function is proper in the sense that it encourages the assessor to use his actual opinion about the patient's probabilities. (In a decision-making context there are many situations where the scientific process of making inductive and predictive inferences can be corrupted, see Section 4.) The Epstein scoring function mentioned in Section 2 is also proper. In fact Staël von Holstein - Murphy (1978) shows that any quadratic scoring function is proper. In our notation the argument is as follows. Let Q be any positive-definite (symmetric) matrix and consider the minimization of

$$E(R-I)^T Q(R-I) = E(r(Z) - c(H))^T Q(r(Z) - c(H))$$

as a function of the procedure r. To show that $r = \rho$ is optimal, let P (capital rho) denote the vector $\rho(Z)$ of true posterior probabilities for a random patient and note that the form to be minimized is equal to

$$E(r(Z) - P + P - c(H))^T Q(r(Z) - P + P - c(H)) =$$
$$= E(r(Z) - P)^T Q(r(Z) - P) + E(P - c(H))^T (P - c(H))$$

because

$$E(r(Z) - P)^T Q(P - c(H)) = E(r(Z) - P)^T E(P - c(H)|Z) = 0.$$

As Q is positive-definite, the minimum is obtained by taking $r(Z) = P$.

Note that lack op calibration will not **appear** if one uses $P = \rho(z)$

for making probability assessments. In fact, calibration is also perfect if $r(z)$ is chosen by conditioning with respect to any other statistic $Y = f(Z)$. The underlying argument is as follows. Using the notation $P_f = E(I|Y)$, observe that, obviously,

$$E(I|P_f \in A) = E(P_f|P_f \in A)$$

for any $A \subset S_k$. This formula implies that calibration is perfect for $r(Z) = P_f$.

4. CLASSICAL STATISTICAL GROUP MEMBERSHIP DISCUSSIONS

Medical experts using their intuition for obtaining probabilities may display considerable lack of calibration, and poor interobserver reliability. Weather forecasters seem to perform better, probably because their forecasts are evaluated more easily and more frequently (see Kahneman et al., 1984).

We are interested in probabilistic reasoning as the basis of clinical decision making. How should the patient be informed before he is asked to consent to try out a certain treatment? What is the information content of the physician knowledge? Such questions require adequate discussion. The

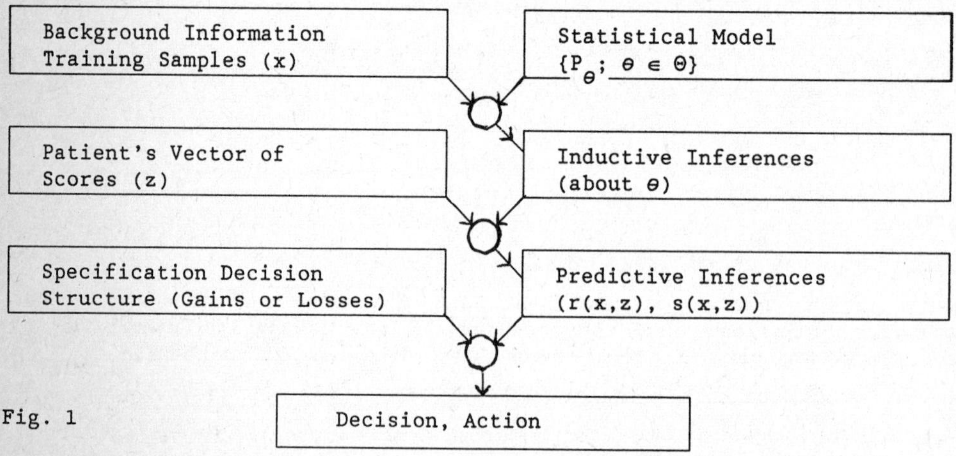

Fig. 1

structure of such scientific discussions is outlined in Fig. 1.

Note that actual clinical decision making in an ongoing process where data are collected depending on previous experiences, therapies are replaced by other ones, etc. Nevertheless, at certain crucial nodes, a discussion of the simple form presented in Fig. 1 is indicated.

The approach we follow belongs to classical mathematical statistics, the heritage form Fisher, Neyman, Wald, a.o. The background information x, the patient's true category number h, and its vector of scores z are regarded as outcomes of random variables X, H, and Z. Let P denote the 'true' joint distribution of (X,H,Z). This would be well-defined if the over-all population $C = V_h C_h$ and its partitioning into subclasses were specified. In practice, population definitions are somewhat hypothetical. The sampling assumptions behind the specification of P are also often questionable. We shall always assume, however, that X and (H,Z) are stochastically independent. This assumption is realistic in the discriminant-analysis situations we have in mind.

As the precise form of P is unknown in practice, we shall start from some statistical model. This means that a class $\{P_\theta ; \theta \in \Theta\}$ of probability distributions is defined and the assumption is made that $P \in \{P_\theta ; \theta \in \Theta\}$. Of course, any P_θ is such that X and (H,Z) are stochastically independent. In some situations we will discuss what happens if the assumption $P \in \{P_\theta ; \theta \in \Theta\}$ is not satisfied. Such robustness investigations are needed because models will always stretch reality to some extent.

Though inductive inference and decision making are interesting (see Fig. 1), we focus on the making of predictive inferences. As P is unknown, the patient's vector $\rho(z)$ of true probabilities is unknown. If we assume $P \in \{P_\theta ; \theta \in \Theta\}$ then there is some value of θ which is the true one. We are interested in the corresponding vector

$$\rho_\theta(z) = E_\theta(I|Z=z)$$

of probabilities. The background information x can be used for estimating θ (inductive inference) and $\rho_\theta(z)$ (predictive inference). Let r_z denote the estimator which assigns the estimate $r_z(x) = r(x,z)$ to the background information x. It is natural to study the bias

$$E_\theta(r_z(X)) - \rho_\theta(z) = b_\theta(z)$$

and the covariance matrix

$$E_\theta(r_z(X) - E_\theta r_z(X))(r_z(X) - E_\theta r_z(X))^T,$$

the diagonal elements (variances) in particular. The sum of these diagonal elements (the trace of the covariance matrix) will be denoted by $v_\theta(z)$. It will play some part later on. In practice the bias will be of order n^{-1} while the standard deviations of the estimates are of order $n^{-\frac{1}{2}}$. These standard deviations, the square roots of the diagonal elements of the covariance matrix of $r_z(X)$, can be expressed in mathematical form involving the unknown parameter θ. Thus it is natural to estimate these standard deviations. Let $s_z(x) = s(x,z) \in \mathbb{R}^k_+$ denote the resulting vector of so-called standard errors. Note that $\|s(x,z)\|^2$ is an estimate of $v_\theta(z)$.

The POSCON project (A.W. Ambergen, O.J.W.F. Kardaun, W. Schaafsma, D.M. Van Der Sluis, a.o.) is about the problems discussed in this section. Mathematical expressions for the covariance matrices were derived in Schaafsma (1976) (k=2), Ambergen - Schaafsma (1983,1985) (k>2), etc. Similar results were developed by Rigby (1982), Critchley - Ford (1985), etc. Early programs were written by Ambergen and applied to discuss group membership of the Border Cave skull (Ambergen - Schaafsma, 1983). After consulting with various colleagues from the medical profession, the POSCON program was written by Van Der Sluis. POSCON provides probability estimates r(x,z) and corresponding standard errors s(x,z) on the basis of data (x,z) and model $\{P_\theta ; \theta \in \Theta\}$. Many options have been made available to the user. The most important feature of the program is that the user is allowed to partition the vector of variables into a number of subvectors which subsequently are regarded as independent, conditionally given group membership. For each subvector a variety of options is available.

The choice of model $\{P_\theta ; \theta \in \Theta\}$, possibly after a reduction of the data, will have an effect upon the output $r(x,z)$,$s(x,z)$ of the program. The present paper attempts to give an adequate discussion of the choice of context.

Other features of the POSCON project are that expert opinions can be incorporated, variables can be discrete or continuous, covariance matrices can be equal or unequal, etc. A companion of POSCON is the program CONCERN by Kardaun (1986). The contexts implemented in POSCON are derived from discriminant analysis, those implemented in CONCERN belong to survival analysis (Cox's proportional hazards model). Programs like GLIM can also be used to generate probability estimates $r(x,z)$ equipped with standard errors $s(x,z)$. The contexts implemented in this program belong to (logistic) regression analysis.

5. THE PERFORMANCE OF A CLASSICAL STATISTICAL GROUP MEMBERSHIP DISCUSSION

If a large sample of future individuals with known group membership would be available, then one can study the actual performance of the classical statistical probability vector generating system $r_x : \mathbb{R}^p \rightarrow S_k$, for fixed background information x. The methods of Section 2 are applicable. Working along these lines, the theoretical pharmacists Hemel and Van Der Voet, and the mathematical statistician Tolboom found some lack of calibration of POSCON models in situations with small sample sizes $n_h \approx 10$ and large dimensionality $p \approx 15$. The standard errors presented by POSCON seemed unreliable if the corresponding estimates were close to 0 or 1. Note that the same thing happens if a probability is estimated by means of a relative frequency. If the relative frequency is 0 or 1 then the plug-in estimate of the standard deviation is 0 and this is not trustworthy.

Lack of calibration in the sense of overconfidence can be explained as follows. If one would use the true vector $\rho_\theta : \mathbb{R}^p \rightarrow S_k$ for generating probability vectors then calibration would be perfect (Section 3). The estimates $r_x(z)$ are scattered around the true values $\rho_\theta(z)$. If we replace an extreme event, e.g. $A_h = \{z ; (\rho_\theta(z))_h > .90\}$ by its sample-analogue, e.g. $B_h = \{z ; r_h(x,z) > .90\}$, then points with $(\rho_\theta(z))_h > .90$ disappear and points (from B_h) with $(\rho_\theta(z))_h < .90$ are included. This shows why strict unbiasedness of the estimators $r_z(X)$ can go together with lack of calibration and systematic overconfidence: sampling phenomena add to the tails of the relevant distributions.

Though much more experience is needed, we are confident that the classical statistical approach will perform well provided that one aims at low complexity and large sample sizes. An attempt to develop adequate theory is as follows.

In practice the data (x,z) is all we have. The probability vector $r(x,z)$ depends on the classical statistical context chosen: one has to specify the variables to be incorporated, the model $\{P_\theta ; \theta \in \Theta\}$, and the form of the estimator r_z of $\rho_\theta(z)$. If a large test set were available then we would compute the Brier score (see Section 2). Note that this would be done for fixed background information x. The Brier score is an unbiased estimate of the actual inaccuracy

$$E\|r_x(Z) - I\|^2 = E(\|R - I\|^2 | X = x),$$

a concept which is similar to the actual error rate (see Lachenbruch (1975), Mc Lachlan (1975), etc.) and the actual discriminatory value (see Schaafsma (1976, 1984), Khatri et al. (1987), etc.). The construction of a prediction interval $[\underline{d}(x),\bar{d}(x)]$ for this actual inaccuracy is a very relevant subject. Note that the procedure $[\underline{d},\bar{d}]$ would have to satisfy

$$E\, P((\underline{d}(X) \le E(\|R - I\|^2|X) \le \bar{d}(X)) \mid X) = 1 - \alpha.$$

It is easier to focus on the over-all inaccuracy $E\|R - I\|^2$. This quantity can be estimated almost unbiasedly by applying the leaving-one-out method.This holds in particular if the sample sizes $n_1,\ldots,n_k$ are related to the prior probabilities $\rho_1,\ldots,\rho_k$ in the sense that they constitute the outcome of a multinomial $M(n ; \rho_1,\ldots,\rho_k)$ distribution. If the relation is different then some precautions should be made.

From a theoretical point of view the following population analogue of Murphy's partition of the Brier score is of interest. We have

$$E\|R - I\|^2 = E\|R - P\|^2 + E\|P - I\|^2 = E\|R - P\|^2 - E\|P - \rho\|^2 + E\|\rho - I\|^2$$

because

$$E((R-P)^T(P-I)|Z=z) = E((r(X,z) - \rho(z))^T(\rho(z)-I)|Z=z) = 0$$

as X and $I = c(H)$ are independent conditionally given $Z = z$, while $E((\rho(z)-I)|Z=z) = 0$. Moreover, as $\rho = E(I) = EE(I|Z) = E\rho(Z) = EP$, we have

$$E((P-\rho)^T(\rho-I)|Z) = -E(\|P-\rho\|^2|Z)$$

(see Kahneman et al. (1984) p. 309).

The term $E\|R-P\|^2$ can nicely be studied by conditioning with respect to Z. We can always write

$$E\|r(X,z) - \rho(z)\|^2 = \text{trace Var }(r(X,z)) + \|Er(X,z) - \rho(z)\|^2$$

while for the special case $P \in \{P_\theta ; \theta \in \Theta\}$ we have

$$E_\theta\|r(X,z) - \rho(z)\|^2 = v_\theta(z) + \|b_\theta(z)\|^2$$

(see Section 4). If a parametric POSCON model is used, then the usual asymptotically efficient estimators $r_z(X)$ of $\rho_\theta(z)$ are such that $v_\theta(z)$ is of order n^{-1} just like $b_\theta(z)$. Hence $\|b_\theta(z)\|^2$ is of order n^{-2}. Thus we have

$$E_\theta\|R - P_\theta\|^2 = E_\theta v_\theta(Z) + 0(n^{-1})$$

where mathematical expressions for v_θ can be obtained from the theory underlying the POSCON program while numerical values can be read from the output. If $P = P_\theta$ then $E_\theta\|P_\theta - \rho\|^2$ can also be evaluated. These results are of some interest for theoretical work. The comparison of two models, however, is not very interesting if $P \in \{P_\theta ; \theta \in \Theta\}$ has to be assumed for both models: the smaller the model the better, provided that it is correct. From a practical point of view it is interesting to compare models without assuming that they are correct. The leaving-one-out method for estimating $E\|R - I\|^2$ gives a clue.

6. THE EFFECT OF A DATA REDUCTION

Starting from an original context with model $\{P_\theta \; ; \; \theta \in \Theta\}$, we consider the effect of a data reduction $f : \mathbb{R}^p \longrightarrow \mathbb{R}^q$, the intuitive background being that estimation errors will become smaller while accuracy may get lost. The induced model $\{P_\theta^f \; ; \; \theta \in \Theta\}$ will usually be such that θ is no longer identifiable. Suppose that reparametrization leads to the model $\{Q_\psi \; ; \; \psi \in \Psi\}$. Of course $P_\theta^f = Q_\psi$ for some $\psi = \bar{\theta} \in \Psi$. If the original model is suitable for POSCON evaluations then the reduced model is not necessarily of this form. Much depends on the model and the specification of f. If f is linear then normality and equality of covariance matrices is preserved, the independence of $X^{(1)}$ and $X^{(2)}$ is not invalidated, etc. To be practical, we assume that both models admit numerical evaluation by the computer resulting in output of the form $(r(x,z),s(x,z))$. Moreover we assume that $P \in \{P_\theta \; ; \; \theta \in \Theta\}$ with as a consequence that $P^f \in \{Q_\psi \; ; \; \psi \in \Psi\}$. Using Murphy's partition of the Brier score, we obtain

$$E\|R - I\|^2 - E\|R_f - I\|^2 = E\|R - P\|^2 - E\|R_f - P_f\|^2 - E\|P_f - P\|^2$$

because

$$E\|P - \rho\|^2 - E\|P_f - \rho\|^2 = E\|P - P_f + P_f - \rho\|^2 - E\|P_f - \rho\|^2$$

where

$$E((P-P_f)^T(P_f-\rho)|Y) = (E(P|Y) - P_f)^T(P_f-\rho) = 0.$$

The favourable effect of data reduction on estimation errors is expressed by

$$E\|R - P\|^2 - E\|R_f - P_f\|^2 \approx E_\theta(v_\theta(Z)) - E_\psi(v_{\psi,f}(Y))$$

where, of course, θ and $\psi = \bar{\theta}$ belong to the true distribution P. Note that the expressions in the r.h.s. can be estimated, either on the basis of output of the POSCON program or from the underlying formulas. In practice this favourable effect is of order n^{-1} whereas the unfavourable effect $E\|P_f - P\|^2$ is of order 1. An interesting application is as follows.

<u>The problem of the reference class</u>. We quote Reichenbach (1949): "If we are asked to find the probability holding for an individual future event, we must first incorporate the case in a suitable reference class. An individual thing or event may be incorporated in many reference classes, from which different probabilities will result. This ambiguity has been called *the problem of the reference class* ..... We then proceed by considering *the narrowest class for which reliable statistics can be compiled*".

Accordingly, let Z be a discrete variable with m + 1 possible outcomes or, equivalently, corresponding to a classification into one of the subsets $D_o, \ldots, D_m$ of the over-all reference population. We shall focus on the question whether the classes D_o and D_1 should be pooled. The notations of Fig. 2 are self explaining. The effect of the transformation

	$D_o \cdots D_m$	
C_1	$n_{10} \cdots n_{1m}$	n_{1+}
$\vdots$	$\vdots \quad \vdots$	$\vdots$
C_k	$n_{k0} \cdots n_{km}$	n_{k+}
	$n_{+0} \cdots n_{+m}$	n

$$N_{11},\ldots,N_{km}) \sim M\{n \; ; \; (\theta_{11},\ldots,\theta_{km})\}$$

$$\theta_{h+} = P_\theta(H=h) = \Sigma_{j=0}^{m} \theta_{hj} = \rho_h$$

$$\theta_{+j} = P_\theta(Z \in D_j) = \Sigma_{h=1}^{k} \theta_{hj}$$

$$\rho_h(j) = P_\theta(H=h | Z \in D_j) = \theta_{hj}/\theta_{+j}$$

Fig. 2

$f : \{0,\ldots,m) \longrightarrow \{1,\ldots,m\}$ with $f(z) = \max(z,1)$ is that on the one hand

$$E\|P - P_f\|^2 = \Sigma_{j=0}^{1}\theta_{+j}\Sigma_{h=1}^{k}\{\theta_{hj}/\theta_{+j} - (\theta_{ho}+\theta_{h1})/\theta_{+o} + \theta_{+1})\}^2$$

$$= \theta_{+o}\theta_{+1}(\theta_{+o} + \theta_{+1})^{-1}\Sigma_{h=1}^{k}\{\rho_h(0) - \rho_h(1)\}^2$$

expresses what one looses by pooling D_o and D_1 while on the other hand the reduction of variance $E_\theta v_\theta(Z) - E_\psi v_{\psi,f}(Y)$, expressing the gain, is approximately equal to

$$\Sigma_{j=o}^{1}P(Z\in D_j)\Sigma_{h=1}^{k}(n\theta_{+1})^{-1}\rho_h(j)(1-\rho_h(j)) - n^{-1}\Sigma_{h=1}^{k}\bar{\rho}_h(1-\bar{\rho}_h)$$

$$= n^{-1}(1-\Sigma_{j=o}^{1}\Sigma_{h=1}^{k}\rho_{hj}^2 + \Sigma_{h=1}^{k}\bar{\rho}_h^2) \approx n^{-1}(1-\Sigma_{h=1}^{k}\bar{\rho}_h^2)$$

where $\bar{\rho}_h = (\theta_{ho}+\theta_{h1})/(\theta_{+o}+\theta_{+1})$. Exact expressions can be obtained but are lengthy.

Conclusion. It is advantageous to pool D_o and D_1 if and only if

$$n^{-1}(1-\Sigma_{h=1}^{k}\bar{\rho}_h^2) > \theta_{+o}\theta_{+1}(\theta_{+o}+\theta_{+1})^{-1}\Sigma_{h=1}^{k}\{\rho_h(0) - \rho_h(1)\}^2.$$

ACKNOWLEDGEMENTS

Discussions with H. Van Der Voet, J. Hemel, and J. Tolboom were very stimulating. They studied the performance of the POSCON program by applying it to actual data using a part as design set and the other part as test set. They showed that the objectivistic background of the program is no guarantee for perfect calibration. Moreover they referred to relevant literature.

Cooperation with the physical anthropologist G.N. Van Vark and the author of the POSCON program D.M. Van Der Sluis is gratefully acknowledged. Without Van Der Sluis' inspiring activity, the project would not have been much more than a pipedream.

REFERENCES

Ambergen, A.W. and Schaafsma, W. (1983). Interval estimates for posterior probabilities, applications to Border Cave. In G.N. Van Vark and W.W. Howells (Ed.), Multivariate Statistical Methods. Reidel, Dordrecht.

Ambergen, A.W. and Schaafsma, W. (1985). Interval Estimates for Posterior Probabilities in a Multivariate Normal Classification Model. Journ. Mult. An. 16: 432-439.

Brier, G.W.(1950). Verification of Forecasts Expressed in Terms of Probability. Monthly Weather Reviews 78 : 1-3.

Critchley, F. and Ford, I. (1985). Interval estimation in discrimination: the multivariate normal equal covariance case. Biometrika 72: 109-116.

Epstein, E.S. (1969). A scoring system for probability forecasts of ranked categories. J. Appl. Meteor. 8: 985-987.

Habbema, J.D.F., Hilden, J., and Bjerregaard, B. (1978). The Measurement of Performance in Probabilistic Diagnosis I, II, III. Meth. Inform. Med. 17: 217-246.

Idem - IV, V (1981). Meth. Inform. Med. 20: 80-100.

Kahneman, D., Slovic, P. and Tversky, A. (1984). Judgement under uncertainty: Heuristics and biases. Cambridge U.P.

Kardaun, O.J.W.F. (1986). On Statistical Survival Analysis and its Applications in Medicine. Thesis. Dept. Math. Groningen University.

Khatri, C.G., Rao, C.R., Schaafsma, W., Steerneman, A.G.M., and Van Vark G.N. (1987). Inference about the performance of Fisher's linear discriminant function. TW-274 Dept. Math. Groningen University.

Lachenbruch, P.A. (1975). Discriminant Analysis. Hafner.

McLachlan, G.J. (1975). Confidence intervals for the conditional probabilities of misclassification in discriminant analysis. Biometrics 31: 161-167.

Reichenbach, H. (1949). The Theory of Probability. Un. Cal.Press, Berkeley and Los Angeles.

Rigby, R.A. (1982). A credibility interval for the probability that a new observation belongs to one of two multivariate normal populations. J. Roy. Statist. Soc. Ser. B 44: 212-220.

Savage, L.J. (1971). Elicitation of Personal Probabilities and Expectations. Journ. Am. Stat. Ass. 66: 783-801.

Schaafsma, W. (1976). The asymptotic distribution of some statistics from discriminant analysis. TW-176 Dept. Math. Groningen University.

Schaafsma, W. (1982). Selecting variables in discriminant analysis for improving upon classical procedures. Ch. 40 in P.R. Krishnaiah and L.H. Kanal (Eds.) Handbook of Statistics Vol. 2. North-Holland, Amsterdam.

Schaafsma, W. (1985). Standard errors of posterior probabilities and how to use them. In P.R. Krishnaiah (Ed.). Multivariate Analysis - VI: 527-548. Elsevier, Amsterdam.

Sluis, D.M. van der, Schaafsma, W., and Ambergen, A.W. (1986). POSCON, a decision support system in diagnosis and prognosis, user manual, Computer Center, P.O. Box 800, Groningen.

Staël von Holstein, C.A.S., and Murphy, A.H. (1978). The Family of Quadratic Scoring Rules. Monthly Weather Review 106: 917-924.

CONTRIBUTORS

S.A. Aivazyan, Central Institute for Economics and Mathematics, Ul. Krasikova 14, 117478 Moscow, USSR.

A.C. Atkinson, Imperial College of Science and Technology, Huxley Building, Queen's Gate, London SW7 2BZ, UK.

O. Bunke, Humboldt University, Department of Statistics, Unter den Linden 6, P.O. Box 1297, DDR-1000 Berlin, German Democratic Republic.

K. Chaloner, University of Minnesota, Department of Applied Statistics, School of Statistics, 352 Classroom-Office Building, 1994 Buford Avenue, St. Paul, MN 55108, USA.

N.R. Draper, Statistics Department, University of Wisconsin, 1210 W. Dayton Street, Madison, WI 53706, USA.

V.V. Fedorov, International Institute for Applied Systems Analysis (IIASA), A-2361 Laxenburg, Austria.

J. Fellman, Swedish School of Economics and Business Administration, Arkadiagatan 22, 00-100 Helsingfors 10, Finland.

S. Kounias, Department of Mathematics, Aristotle University of Thessaloniki, Thessaloniki, Greece.

J. Kunert, Department for Mathematics and Statistics, University of Trier, P.O. Box 3825, D-5500 Trier, Federal Republic of Germany.

V.G. Kurotschka, Free University of Berlin, Altenseinstrasse 40, D-1000 Berlin (West) 33.

H. Läuter, Karl Weierstrass Institute for Mathematics, Academy of Sciences of the GDR, Mohrenstrasse 39, DDR-1086 Berlin, German Democratic Republic.

J. Läuter, Karl Weierstrass Institute for Mathematics, Academy of Sciences of the GDR, Mohrenstrasse 39, DDR-1086 Berlin, German Democratic Republic.

Y.P. Lukaschin, Institute of World Economics and International Relations, Profsoyuznaya 23, 117342 Moscow, USSR.

M.B. Maljutov, Moscow State University, Leninskiy Gory, 119808 Moscow, USSR.

Y. Nakamori, Department of Applied Mathematics, Konan University, Higashinada, Kobe 658, Japan.

A. Pázman, Mathematical Institute, Slovak Academy of Sciences, vl. Obrancov mieru 49, CS-81473 Bratislava, Czechoslovakia.

E.E. Pickett, Department of Industrial Engineering, University of Toronto, Rosebrugh Building, 4 Taddle Creek Road, Toronto, Ontario M5S 1A4, Canada.

R. Pincus, Karl Weierstrass Institute for Mathematics, Academy of Sciences of the GDR, Mohrenstrasse 39, DDR-1086 Berlin, German Democratic Republic.

S. Pitovranov, Environmental Program, International Institute for Applied Systems Analysis (IIASA), A-2361 Laxenburg, Austria.

W. Polasek, Institute for Statistics, University of Vienna, Universitätsstrasse 5, A-1010 Vienna, Austria

L. Pronzato, Laboratoire des Signaux et Systèmes, Ecole Supérieure d'Electricité, Plateau du Moulon, F-91190 Gif sur Yvette, France.

F. Pukelsheim, Institute for Mathematics, University of Augsburg, Memminger Strasse 6, D-8900 Augsburg, Federal Republic of Germany.

W. Schaafsma, University of Groningen, Science Faculty, P.O. Box 800, NL-AV 9700 Groningen, Netherlands.

W.H. Schmidt, Humboldt University, Department of Mathematics, Unter den Linden 6, P.O. Box 1297, DDR-1000 Berlin, German Democratic Republic.

D.M. Titterington, University of Glasgow, Faculty of Science, Glasgow G12 8QW, UK.

I.N. Vuchkov, Department of Automation, Higher Institute of Chemical Technology, BG-1156 Sofia, Bulgaria.

P. Wynn, City University, Northampton Square, London EC1V 0HB, UK.

G.A. Young, Statistical Laboratory, Department of Pure Mathematics and Mathematical Statistics, University of Cambridge, 16 Mill Lane, Cambridge CB2 1SB, UK.

THE INTERNATIONAL INSTITUTE FOR APPLIED SYSTEMS ANALYSIS

is a nongovernmental research institution, bringing together scientists from around the world to work on problems of common concern. Situated in Laxenburg, Austria, IIASA was founded in October 1972 by the academies of science and equivalent organizations of twelve countries. Its founders gave IIASA a unique position outside national, disciplinary, and institutional boundaries so that it might take the broadest possible view in pursuing its objectives:

To promote international cooperation in solving problems arising from social, economic, technological, and environmental change

To create a network of institutions in the national member organization countries and elsewhere for joint scientific research

To develop and formalize systems analysis and the sciences contributing to it, and promote the use of analytical techniques needed to evaluate and address complex problems

To inform policy advisors and decision makers about the potential application of the Institute's work to such problems

The Institute now has national member organizations in the following countries:

Austria
The Austrian Academy of Sciences

Bulgaria
The National Committee for Applied Systems Analysis and Management

Canada
The Canadian Committee for IIASA

Czechoslovakia
The Committee for IIASA of the Czechoslovak Socialist Republic

Finland
The Finnish Committee for IIASA

France
The French Association for the Development of Systems Analysis

German Democratic Republic
The Academy of Sciences of the German Democratic Republic

Federal Republic of Germany
Association for the Advancement of IIASA

Hungary
The Hungarian Committee for Applied Systems Analysis

Italy
The National Research Council

Japan
The Japan Committee for IIASA

Netherlands
The Foundation IIASA–Netherlands

Poland
The Polish Academy of Sciences

Sweden
The Swedish Council for Planning and Coordination of Research

Union of Soviet Socialist Republics
The Academy of Sciences of the Union of Soviet Socialist Republics

United States of America
The American Academy of Arts and Sciences

Vol. 211: P. van den Heuvel, The Stability of a Macroeconomic System with Quantity Constraints. VII, 169 pages. 1983.

Vol. 212: R. Sato and T. Nôno, Invariance Principles and the Structure of Technology. V, 94 pages. 1983.

Vol. 213: Aspiration Levels in Bargaining and Economic Decision Making. Proceedings, 1982. Edited by R. Tietz. VIII, 406 pages. 1983.

Vol. 214: M. Faber, H. Niemes und G. Stephan, Entropie, Umweltschutz und Rohstoffverbrauch. IX, 181 Seiten. 1983.

Vol. 215: Semi-Infinite Programming and Applications. Proceedings, 1981. Edited by A.V. Fiacco and K.O. Kortanek. XI, 322 pages. 1983.

Vol. 216: H.H. Müller, Fiscal Policies in a General Equilibrium Model with Persistent Unemployment. VI, 92 pages. 1983.

Vol. 217: Ch. Grootaert, The Relation Between Final Demand and Income Distribution. XIV, 105 pages. 1983.

Vol. 218: P. van Loon, A Dynamic Theory of the Firm: Production, Finance and Investment. VII, 191 pages. 1983.

Vol. 219: E. van Damme, Refinements of the Nash Equilibrium Concept. VI, 151 pages. 1983.

Vol. 220: M. Aoki, Notes on Economic Time Series Analysis: System Theoretic Perspectives. IX, 249 pages. 1983.

Vol. 221: S. Nakamura, An Inter-Industry Translog Model of Prices and Technical Change for the West German Economy. XIV, 290 pages. 1984.

Vol. 222: P. Meier, Energy Systems Analysis for Developing Countries. VI, 344 pages. 1984.

Vol. 223: W. Trockel, Market Demand. VIII, 205 pages. 1984.

Vol. 224: M. Kiy, Ein disaggregiertes Prognosesystem für die Bundesrepublik Deutschland. XVIII, 276 Seiten. 1984.

Vol. 225: T.R. von Ungern-Sternberg, Zur Analyse von Märkten mit unvollständiger Nachfragerinformation. IX, 125 Seiten. 1984

Vol. 226: Selected Topics in Operations Research and Mathematical Economics. Proceedings, 1983. Edited by G. Hammer and D. Pallaschke. IX, 478 pages. 1984.

Vol. 227: Risk and Capital. Proceedings, 1983. Edited by G. Bamberg and K. Spremann. VII, 306 pages. 1984.

Vol. 228: Nonlinear Models of Fluctuating Growth. Proceedings, 1983. Edited by R.M. Goodwin, M. Krüger and A. Vercelli. XVII, 277 pages. 1984.

Vol. 229: Interactive Decision Analysis. Proceedings, 1983. Edited by M. Grauer and A.P. Wierzbicki. VIII, 269 pages. 1984.

Vol. 230: Macro-Economic Planning with Conflicting Goals. Proceedings, 1982. Edited by M. Despontin, P. Nijkamp and J. Spronk. VI, 297 pages. 1984.

Vol. 231: G.F. Newell, The M/M/∞ Service System with Ranked Servers in Heavy Traffic. XI, 126 pages. 1984.

Vol. 232: L. Bauwens, Bayesian Full Information Analysis of Simultaneous Equation Models Using Integration by Monte Carlo. VI, 114 pages. 1984.

Vol. 233: G. Wagenhals, The World Copper Market. XI, 190 pages. 1984.

Vol. 234: B.C. Eaves, A Course in Triangulations for Solving Equations with Deformations. III, 302 pages. 1984.

Vol. 235: Stochastic Models in Reliability Theory. Proceedings, 1984. Edited by S. Osaki and Y. Hatoyama. VII, 212 pages. 1984.

Vol. 236: G. Gandolfo, P.C. Padoan, A Disequilibrium Model of Real and Financial Accumulation in an Open Economy. VI, 172 pages. 1984.

Vol. 237: Misspecification Analysis. Proceedings, 1983. Edited by T.K. Dijkstra. V, 129 pages. 1984.

Vol. 238: W. Domschke, A. Drexl, Location and Layout Planning. IV, 134 pages. 1985.

Vol. 239: Microeconomic Models of Housing Markets. Edited by K. Stahl. VII, 197 pages. 1985.

Vol. 240: Contributions to Operations Research. Proceedings, 1984. Edited by K. Neumann and D. Pallaschke. V, 190 pages. 1985.

Vol. 241: U. Wittmann, Das Konzept rationaler Preiserwartungen. XI, 310 Seiten. 1985.

Vol. 242: Decision Making with Multiple Objectives. Proceedings, 1984. Edited by Y.Y. Haimes and V. Chankong. XI, 571 pages. 1985.

Vol. 243: Integer Programming and Related Areas. A Classified Bibliography 1981–1984. Edited by R. von Randow. XX, 386 pages. 1985.

Vol. 244: Advances in Equilibrium Theory. Proceedings, 1984. Edited by C.D. Aliprantis, O. Burkinshaw and N.J. Rothman. II, 235 pages. 1985.

Vol. 245: J.E.M. Wilhelm, Arbitrage Theory. VII, 114 pages. 1985.

Vol. 246: P.W. Otter, Dynamic Feature Space Modelling, Filtering and Self-Tuning Control of Stochastic Systems. XIV, 177 pages. 1985.

Vol. 247: Optimization and Discrete Choice in Urban Systems. Proceedings, 1983. Edited by B.G. Hutchinson, P. Nijkamp and M. Batty. VI, 371 pages. 1985.

Vol. 248: Plural Rationality and Interactive Decision Processes. Proceedings, 1984. Edited by M. Grauer, M. Thompson and A.P. Wierzbicki. VI, 354 pages. 1985.

Vol. 249: Spatial Price Equilibrium: Advances in Theory, Computation and Application. Proceedings, 1984. Edited by P. T. Harker. VII, 277 pages. 1985.

Vol. 250: M. Roubens, Ph. Vincke, Preference Modelling. VIII, 94 pages. 1985.

Vol. 251: Input-Output Modeling. Proceedings, 1984. Edited by A. Smyshlyaev. VI, 261 pages. 1985.

Vol. 252: A. Birolini, On the Use of Stochastic Processes in Modeling Reliability Problems. VI, 105 pages. 1985.

Vol. 253: C. Withagen, Economic Theory and International Trade in Natural Exhaustible Resources. VI, 172 pages. 1985.

Vol. 254: S. Müller, Arbitrage Pricing of Contingent Claims. VIII, 151 pages. 1985.

Vol. 255: Nondifferentiable Optimization: Motivations and Applications. Proceedings, 1984. Edited by V.F. Demyanov and D. Pallaschke. VI, 350 pages. 1985.

Vol. 256: Convexity and Duality in Optimization. Proceedings, 1984. Edited by J. Ponstein. V, 142 pages. 1985.

Vol. 257: Dynamics of Macrosystems. Proceedings, 1984. Edited by J.-P. Aubin, D. Saari and K. Sigmund. VI, 280 pages. 1985.

Vol. 258: H. Funke, Eine allgemeine Theorie der Polypol- und Oligopolpreisbildung. III, 237 pages. 1985.

Vol. 259: Infinite Programming. Proceedings, 1984. Edited by E.J. Anderson and A.B. Philpott. XIV, 244 pages. 1985.

Vol. 260: H.-J. Kruse, Degeneracy Graphs and the Neighbourhood Problem. VIII, 128 pages. 1986.

Vol. 261: Th.R. Gulledge, Jr., N.K. Womer, The Economics of Made-to-Order Production. VI, 134 pages. 1986.

Vol. 262: H.U. Buhl, A Neo-Classical Theory of Distribution and Wealth. V, 146 pages. 1986.

Vol. 263: M. Schäfer, Resource Extraction and Market Structure. XI, 154 pages. 1986.

Vol. 264: Models of Economic Dynamics. Proceedings, 1983. Edited by H.F. Sonnenschein. VII, 212 pages. 1986.

Vol. 265: Dynamic Games and Applications in Economics. Edited by T. Başar. IX, 288 pages. 1986.

Vol. 266: Multi-Stage Production Planning and Inventory Control. Edited by S. Axsäter, Ch. Schneeweiss and E. Silver. V, 264 pages. 1986.

Vol. 267: R. Bemelmans, The Capacity Aspect of Inventories. IX, 165 pages. 1986.

Vol. 268: V. Firchau, Information Evaluation in Capital Markets. VII, 103 pages. 1986.

Vol. 269: A. Borglin, H. Keiding, Optimality in Infinite Horizon Economies. VI, 180 pages. 1986.

Vol. 270: Technological Change, Employment and Spatial Dynamics. Proceedings 1985. Edited by P. Nijkamp. VII, 466 pages. 1986.

Vol. 271: C. Hildreth, The Cowles Commission in Chicago, 1939–1955. V, 176 pages. 1986.

Vol. 272: G. Clemenz, Credit Markets with Asymmetric Information. VIII, 212 pages. 1986.

Vol. 273: Large-Scale Modelling and Interactive Decision Analysis. Proceedings, 1985. Edited by G. Fandel, M. Grauer, A. Kurzhanski and A.P. Wierzbicki. VII, 363 pages. 1986.

Vol. 274: W.K. Klein Haneveld, Duality in Stochastic Linear and Dynamic Programming. VII, 295 pages. 1986.

Vol. 275: Competition, Instability, and Nonlinear Cycles. Proceedings, 1985. Edited by W. Semmler. XII, 340 pages. 1986.

Vol. 276: M.R. Baye, D.A. Black, Consumer Behavior, Cost of Living Measures, and the Income Tax. VII, 119 pages. 1986.

Vol. 277: Studies in Austrian Capital Theory, Investment and Time. Edited by M. Faber. VI, 317 pages. 1986.

Vol. 278: W.E. Diewert, The Measurement of the Economic Benefits of Infrastructure Services. V, 202 pages. 1986.

Vol. 279: H.-J. Büttler, G. Frei and B. Schips, Estimation of Disequilibrium Models. VI, 114 pages. 1986.

Vol. 280: H.T. Lau, Combinatorial Heuristic Algorithms with FORTRAN. VII, 126 pages. 1986.

Vol. 281: Ch.-L. Hwang, M.-J. Lin, Group Decision Making under Multiple Criteria. XI, 400 pages. 1987.

Vol. 282: K. Schittkowski, More Test Examples for Nonlinear Programming Codes. V, 261 pages. 1987.

Vol. 283: G. Gabisch, H.-W. Lorenz, Business Cycle Theory. VII, 229 pages. 1987.

Vol. 284: H. Lütkepohl, Forecasting Aggregated Vector ARMA Processes. X, 323 pages. 1987.

Vol. 285: Toward Interactive and Intelligent Decision Support Systems. Volume 1. Proceedings, 1986. Edited by Y. Sawaragi, K. Inoue and H. Nakayama. XII, 445 pages. 1987.

Vol. 286: Toward Interactive and Intelligent Decision Support Systems. Volume 2. Proceedings, 1986. Edited by Y. Sawaragi, K. Inoue and H. Nakayama. XII, 450 pages. 1987.

Vol. 287: Dynamical Systems. Proceedings, 1985. Edited by A.B. Kurzhanski and K. Sigmund. VI, 215 pages. 1987.

Vol. 288: G.D. Rudebusch, The Estimation of Macroeconomic Disequilibrium Models with Regime Classification Information. VII, 128 pages. 1987.

Vol. 289: B.R. Meijboom, Planning in Decentralized Firms. X, 168 pages. 1987.

Vol. 290: D.A. Carlson, A. Haurie, Infinite Horizon Optimal Control. XI, 254 pages. 1987.

Vol. 291: N. Takahashi, Design of Adaptive Organizations. VI, 140 pages. 1987.

Vol. 292: I. Tchijov, L. Tomaszewicz (Eds.), Input-Output Modeling. Proceedings, 1985. VI, 195 pages. 1987.

Vol. 293: D. Batten, J. Casti, B. Johansson (Eds.), Economic Evolution and Structural Adjustment. Proceedings, 1985. VI, 382 pages. 1987.

Vol. 294: J. Jahn, W. Krabs (Eds.), Recent Advances and Historical Development of Vector Optimization. VII, 405 pages. 1987.

Vol. 295: H. Meister, The Purification Problem for Constrained Games with Incomplete Information. X, 127 pages. 1987.

Vol. 296: A. Börsch-Supan, Econometric Analysis of Discrete Choice. VIII, 211 pages. 1987.

Vol. 297: V. Fedorov, H. Läuter (Eds.), Model-Oriented Data Analysis. Proceedings, 1987. VI, 239 pages. 1988.